A WORLD HISTORY OF RAILWAY CULTURES, 1830–1930

A WORLD HISTORY OF RAILWAY CULTURES, 1830–1930

Edited by
Matthew Esposito

Volume III
Continental Eurasia

LONDON AND NEW YORK

First published 2020
by Routledge
2 Park Square, Milton Park, Abingdon, Oxon OX14 4RN

and by Routledge
52 Vanderbilt Avenue, New York, NY 10017

Routledge is an imprint of the Taylor & Francis Group, an informa business

© 2020 selection and editorial matter, Matthew Esposito; individual owners retain copyright in their own material.

The right of Matthew Esposito to be identified as the author of the editorial material, and of the authors for their individual chapters, has been asserted in accordance with sections 77 and 78 of the Copyright, Designs and Patents Act 1988.

All rights reserved. No part of this book may be reprinted or reproduced or utilised in any form or by any electronic, mechanical, or other means, now known or hereafter invented, including photocopying and recording, or in any information storage or retrieval system, without permission in writing from the publishers.

Trademark notice: Product or corporate names may be trademarks or registered trademarks, and are used only for identification and explanation without intent to infringe.

British Library Cataloguing-in-Publication Data
A catalogue record for this book is available from the British Library

Library of Congress Cataloging-in-Publication Data
A catalog record for this book has been requested

ISBN: 978-0-8153-7722-1 (set)
eISBN: 978-1-351-21184-0 (set)
ISBN: 978-0-8153-7754-2 (Volume III)
eISBN: 978-1-351-21171-0 (Volume III)

Typeset in Times New Roman
by Apex CoVantage, LLC

Publisher's Note
References within each chapter are as they appear in the original complete work

CONTENTS

VOLUME III **Continental Eurasia**	**1**
The Godlike animator	3

PART 1
Mentalité **and the machine ensemble: France and colonies**   **43**

1   Paul Verlaine, 'The Scene behind the Carriage-Window Panes', in *Poems of Paul Verlaine*, Trans. Gertrude Hall (New York: Duffield, 1906), p. 22   45

2   William Makepeace Thackeray, *The Paris Sketchbook of Mr. M. A. Titmarsh; The Irish Sketch Book; & Notes of a Journey from Cornhill to Grand Cairo* (New York: Caxton, 1840), pp. 265–267   46

3   Michael J. Quin, *Steam Voyages on the Seine, the Moselle, & the Rhine, with Railroad Visits to the Principal Cities of Belgium*, 2 vols. (London: H. Colburn, 1843), II, pp. 71–75   48

4   George Musgrave, *The Parson, Pen, and Pencil: Or, Reminiscences and Illustrations of an Excursion to Paris, Tours, and Rouen in the Summer of 1847* (London: R. Bentley, 1848), I, pp. 124–135, II, pp. 251–252   50

5   George Musgrave, *By-roads and Battle-fields in Picardy*, 2 vols. (London: Bell and Daldy, 1861), I, pp. 12–13, 212–218   55

6   George Musgrave, *A Ramble into Brittany*, 2 vols. (London: Hurst and Blackett, 1870), I, pp. 91–94   61

CONTENTS

7 Thomas Adolphus Trollope, *Impressions of a Wanderer in Italy, Switzerland, France, and Spain* (London: H. Colburn, 1850), pp. 261–264   63

8 Andrew Dickinson, *My First Visit to Europe* (New York: G. P. Putnam, 1851), pp. 158–160   65

9 Frank B. Goodrich, *Tricolored Sketches in Paris during the Years 1851–2–3* (New York: Harper & Brothers, 1855), pp. 202–203, 205–206, 210, 216   67

10 Mark Twain, *The Innocents Abroad* (Hartford: American Publishing Company, 1875), pp. 106–112   70

11 Henry James, *A Little Tour in France* (Leipzig: B. Tauchnitz, 1885), pp. 258–261   74

12 Henry James, *Portraits of Places* (Boston: Houghton, Mifflin and Co., 1911), pp. 81–86   76

13 Émile Zola, *Germinal* (London: Chatto & Windus, 1914), pp. 1–10   79

14 Mary Raymond Williams, *July and August of 1914* (Cleveland: Press of the Brooks Company, 1915), pp. 78–103   87

15 Marcel Proust, *Swann's Way*, 2 vols. Trans. C. K. Moncrieff (New York: Holt, 1922), I, pp. 154–155 II, pp. 104–105, 232–234   100

16 Angus B. Reach, *Claret and Oliver, from the Garonne to the Rhone* (New York: G. P. Putnam, 1853), pp. 63–68   104

17 Charles Richard Weld, *The Pyrenees, West and East* (London: Longman, Brown, Green, Longmans, & Roberts, 1859), pp. 29–35, 45–46, 49   108

18 Gordon Casserly, *Algeria To-day* (New York: F. A. Stokes, n.d.), pp. 170–185   112

19 Lewis Gaston Leary, *Syria, the Land of Lebanon* (New York: McBride, Nast, 1913), pp. 72–78, 80–84, 86–87   121

CONTENTS

PART 2
Pathbreakers and stone breakers: Belgium, Holland, and colonies   **127**

20   E. H. Derby, *Two Months Abroad* (Boston: Redding & Co., 1844), pp. 36–38   129

21   W. C. Dana, *A Transatlantic Tour* (Philadelphia: Perkins & Purves, 1845), pp. 195–197, 216–219   132

22   Compagnie du Congo pour le commerce et l'industrie, Brussels, *The Congo Railway from Matadi to the Stanley-Pool* (Brussels: P. Weissenbruch, 1889), pp. 106–110   135

23   E. D. Morel, *Red Rubber: The Story of the Rubber Slave Trade Flourishing in the Congo in the Year of Grace 1906. With an Introduction by Sir Harry Johnston* (New York: The Nassau Print, 1906), pp. 91–103   138

24   Reverend J. H. Whitehead, 'Reports and Letter of Protest to the Governor-General', in E. D. Morel, *Recent Evidence from the Congo* (Liverpool: J. Richardson & Sons, 1907), pp. 14–17   147

PART 3
Incongruous *Eisenbahn*: railways in Austria, Switzerland, Germany, and colonies   **151**

25   J. G. Kohl, *Austria, Vienna, Hungary, Bohemia, and the Danube* (London: Chapman and Hall, 1843), pp. 156–158, 160   153

26   John W. Corson, *Loiterings in Europe* (New York: Harper & Brothers, 1848), pp. 222–227, 234–239, 263–266   157

27   Rachel Harriette Busk, *The Valleys of Tirol: Their Traditions and Customs, and How to Visit Them* (London: Longmans, Green, 1874), pp. 148–149, 168–170, 327   166

28   Robert L. Jefferson, *A New Ride to Khiva* (New York: New Amsterdam Book Co., 1900), pp. 32–43   169

29   E. H. Derby, *Two Months Abroad* (Boston: Redding & Co., 1844), pp. 20–32, 34–36   174

CONTENTS

30 Samuel Laing, *Notes of a Traveller, on the Social and Political State of France, Prussia, Switzerland, Italy, and Other Parts of Europe*, Second ed. (Philadelphia: Carey and Hart, 1846), pp. 165–169   178

31 Nathaniel Parker Willis, *Rural Letters and Other Records of Thought at Leisure* (New York: Baker and Scribner, 1849), pp. 288–289   182

32 Mark Twain, *A Tramp Abroad* (Hartford, Conn.: American Publishing Company, 1899), pp. 24, 103, 547–549   184

33 Peter Rosegger, *The Light Eternal* [The Eternal Light] (London: T. Fisher Unwin, 1907), pp. 246–248   186

34 Adolf Friedrich (Duke of Mecklenburg-Schwerin), *From the Congo to the Niger and the Nile*, 2 vols. (London: Duckworth & Co., 1913), I, pp. 3–10, II, pp. 196–198   188

35 A. D. C. Russell, 'The Bagdad Railway', *Quarterly Review* 235, 1921, 307–315   190

PART 4
Italia, España, Lusitania: railways in Italy, Spain, Portugal, and colonies   **197**

36 William J. L. Maxwell, *Letters of an Engineer while on Service in Syria in Connection with the Proposed Euphrates Valley Railway and the Beyrout Waterworks* (London: Marcus Ward & Co., 1886), pp. 5–10   199

37 Lina Duff Gordon (Lady Duff Gordon, Caroline Lucie Duff Gordon, Mrs. Aubrey Waterfield), *Home Life in Italy: Letters from the Apennines*, Second ed. (London: Metheun, 1909), pp. 12–14, 147–151, 174–175, 181–182   204

38 Edmondo de Amicis, *Spain and the Spaniards* (New York: Putnam, 1885), pp. 277–278   210

39 Henry N. Shore, *Three Pleasant Springs in Portugal* (London: S. Low, Marston & Company, 1899), pp. 307–314   212

40 James Johnston, *Reality versus Romance in South Central Africa* (New York: F. H. Revell Company, 1893), pp. 32–35   217

CONTENTS

PART 5
**Iron roads to the iron mountains of Scandinavia: railways
in Sweden, Norway, Finland, and Denmark**   **221**

41 Edwin Coolidge Kimball, *Midnight Sunbeams, or, Bits
of Travel through the Land of the Norseman* (Boston:
Cupples and Hurd, 1888), pp. 78–86   223

42 William Eleroy Curtis, *Denmark, Norway, and Sweden*
(Akron, Ohio: The Saalfield Publishing Co., 1903),
pp. 118–124, 127–128   227

43 Francis E. Clark and Sydney A. Clark, *The Charm of
Scandinavia* (Boston: Little, Brown, 1914), pp. 153–156   234

44 Théophile Gautier, *A Winter in Russia*, Trans. M. M.
Ripley (New York: H. Holt and Company, 1874), pp. 22–24   236

45 Finland Johnson Sherrick, *Letters of Travel* (N.p.: N.p.,
1905), pp. 79–82   238

PART 6
**Railways among the ruins: Greece, Ottoman Empire
(Turkey), Czechoslovakia, and Serbia**   **241**

46 Mark Twain, *The Innocents Abroad* (Hartford: American
Publishing Company, 1875), pp. 417–418   243

47 Mrs. Brassey, *Sunshine and Storm in the East, or Cruises
to Cyprus and Constantinople* (New York: H. Holt and
Company, 1880), pp. 354–357, 362–364   245

48 Olive Gilbreath, 'Men of Bohemia', *Harper's Magazine*
138, 1918–1919, 251–254   249

49 Mary Heaton Vorse, 'Milorad', *Harper's Magazine* 140,
1919–1920, 256–262   255

PART 7
Russian prologues, dialogues, travelogues   **265**

50 Théophile Gautier, *A Winter in Russia*, Trans. M. M. Ripley
(New York: H. Holt and Company, 1874), pp. 236–242   267

CONTENTS

51 Leo Tolstoy, *Anna Karenina*, Trans. Nathan Haskell Dole
(New York: Thomas Y. Crowell Company, 1886), pp. 721–725   272

52 The photography of Sergei Mikhailovich Prokudin-Gorskii
(1863–1944), Prokudin-Gorskii Collection. Library of
Congress Prints and Photographs Division. Washington D.C.   276

53 Maurice Baring, *Russian Essays and Stories*, Second Ed.
(London: Methuen, 1909), pp. 1–24, 52–55, 63–70   281

PART 8
Strategic Russian railways, resources, and representations   **293**

54 George Dobson, *Russia's Railway Advance into Central
Asia; Notes of a Journey from St. Petersburg to Samarkand*
(London: W. H. Allen & Co., 1890), pp. 71–73, 102–104,
109–113, 125–132, 139–144   295

55 C. E. Biddulph, *Four Months in Persia and a Visit to
Trans-Caspia* (London: Kegan Paul, Trench, Trübner &
Co., 1892), pp. 112–117   303

56 Sir Henry Norman, *All the Russias: Travels and Studies in
Contemporary Russia, Finland, Siberia, the Caucasus,
and Central Asia* (New York: Scribner's Sons, 1903),
pp. 231–235, 237   308

PART 9
Test of the Russian will: the Trans-Siberian Railway   **313**

57 Robert L. Jefferson, *Roughing it in Siberia* (London:
S. Low, Marston & Co., 1897), pp. 1–11   315

58 James Young Simpson, *Side-lights on Siberia; Some
Account of the Great Siberian Railroad, the Prisons and
Exile System* (Edinburgh and London: W. Blackwood and
Sons, 1898), pp. 147–149   319

59 Isabella L. Bird, *Korea and Her Neighbors: A Narrative
of Travel, with an Account of the Recent Vicissitudes and
Present Position of the Country* (New York: Fleming H.
Revell, 1898), pp. 239–244   321

CONTENTS

60 Annette M. B. Meakin, *A Ribbon of Iron* (Westminster:
A. Constable, 1901), pp. 21–25, 110–118, 156–159,
166–172, 273–277   325

61 Leo Deutsch, *Sixteen Years in Siberia* (New York: E. P.
Dutton, 1905), pp. 140–144, 324–327   335

62 Lindon Bates Jr., *The Russian Road to China* (Boston:
Houghton Mifflin Company, 1910), pp. 71–74   340

63 Richardson L. Wright and Bassett Digby, *Through Siberia:
An Empire in the Making* (New York: McBride, Nast &
Company, 1913), pp. 231–234   342

PART 10
The iron road meets the silk road: railways in Japan
and China   345

64 *Narrative of the Expedition of an American Squadron to
the China Seas and Japan, Performed in the Years 1852,
1853, and 1854, under the Command of Commodore M. C.
Perry*, Comp. Francis L. Hawks (New York: D. Appleton,
1856), pp. 414–418   347

65 Lilias Dunlop Finlay Swainson, *Letters from China &
Japan* (London: Henry S. King & Co., 1875), pp. 177–178,
181–183, 194–196   353

66 Isabella Bird, *Unbeaten Tracks in Japan. An Account of
Travels on Horseback in the Interior*, 2 vols. (New York:
G. P. Putnam's Sons, 1880), pp. 26–32   356

67 E. G. Holtham, *Eight Years in Japan, 1873–1881. Work,
Travel and Recreation* (London: Kegan Paul, Trench & Co.,
1883), pp. 6–11, 101–112, 122–131, 211–213, 216–217,
247–249, 253–254   360

68 W. S. Caine, *A Trip Round the World in 1887–8* (London:
G. Routledge & Sons, 1888), pp. 159–164   376

69 Lafcadio Hearn, *Out of the East: Reveries and Studies
in New Japan* (Boston: Houghton, Mifflin, 1899),
pp. 275–279   379

CONTENTS

70 Mrs. Hugh Fraser, *Letters from Japan* (New Edition. New York: Macmillan Co., 1904), pp. 43–45, 326–328, 331 — 381

71 Marie C. Stopes, *A Journal from Japan. A Daily Record of Life as Seen by a Scientist* (London: Blackie, 1910), pp. 46, 105–106 — 384

72 Baroness Albert d'Anethan (Eleanora Mary Anethan), *Fourteen Years of a Diplomatic Life in Japan* (London: S. Paul & Co., 1912), pp. 358–359 — 386

73 Frank E. Younghusband, *The Heart of a Continent* (New York: Scribner's Sons, 1896), pp. 50–52 — 388

74 John Foster Fraser, *The Real Siberia* (London: Cassell, 1902), pp. 220–230 — 391

75 R. Logan Jack, *The Back Blocks of China* (London: E. Arnold, 1904), pp. 89–93 — 397

76 Richardson L. Wright and Bassett Digby, *Through Siberia: An Empire in the Making* (New York: McBride, Nast & Company, 1913), pp. 203–208 — 400

77 Sir Alexander Hosie, *On the Trail of the Opium Poppy*, 2 vols. (London: G. Philip & Son, 1914), I, pp. 3–4, 165–167, 169–172, II, pp. 82–84 — 404

78 C. E. Bechhofer, *A Wanderer's Log* (London: Mills & Boon, 1922), pp. 91–93 — 408

Volume III

CONTINENTAL EURASIA

THE GODLIKE ANIMATOR

In the nineteenth century, philosophers, literary figures, travel writers, and artists of the Eurasian landmass presented the expansion of railways as an act of creation akin to God's formation of earth or the dawn of a new millennium. At the railway workshops of the Nord, George Musgrave described a scene of modern wizardry in France: "Every item and atom connected in the slightest way with railroads seemed to be in process of creation."[1] In the *Arcades Project*, Walter Benjamin analyzed the thought of French theorist Benjamin Gastineau, who once referred to the *chemin de fer* (railway) as a godlike animator.[2] To Gastineau, railways were a new natural phenomenon akin to a religious event, and he equated railway travel with Christ's resurrection:

> Before the creation of the railroads, nature did not yet pulsate. . . . The heavens themselves appeared immutable. The railroad animated everything. . . . The sky has become an active infinity, and nature a dynamic beauty. Christ is descended from his Cross; he has walked the earth, and he is leaving, far behind him on the dusty road, the old Ahasuerus.
>
> [Gastineau, La vie en chemin de fer, 50.]

In the same essay, Gastineau compared the exhilarating feeling of locomotive travel to the emotional excitement of revolutionary struggle and the achievement of liberty, equality, and fraternity. The railway journey symbolized France's momentous historical transition from the Old Regime and despotism to the Enlightenment and French Revolution. The train crosses the threatening archway and oppressive dark tunnel of the despotic past to the "exclamations of joy" and "light and liberty" that the present represents: "Hail to you, noble races of the future, scions of the railway!"[3] Mid-century romantic writers often used impassioned rhetoric charged with religio-historical imagery to appeal to citizens and subjects of incipient nation-states. Such propaganda from the Second Empire and French Third Republic played a huge role in the ongoing process of shifting loyalty from the Old Regime to the new and transferring sacrality from the Catholic Church to the nation. Gastineau's observations exemplified the mentality of an urban bourgeoisie that embraced steam-operated railways and, despite their initial construction under the July monarchy of Louis Philippe, a Bourbon monarch, were associated with republicanism after 1870.

Paul Verlaine's poem of that year "The Scene behind the Carriage-Window Panes" extols everything French train passengers viewed through their windows, including the countryside, plains, waters, crops, and trees. To Verlaine, even the telegraph wires paralleling the tracks appeared providential before the backdrop of the infinite sky. Several English translations of Verlaine's poem converge on the stanzas that present the duality of railways in the context of the poet's own triumphant and turbulent life. Verlaine's episodic career and troubled love life brought him into associations with the Parnassians, Communards, the Decadent movement which he helped found, and the Symbolists to whom he clearly belonged. He anguished over his secret love for a close cousin, a failed marriage, and a prolonged infatuation with poet Arthur Rimbaud that turned violent and landed Verlaine in prison for shooting his lover in the wrist. Although Verlaine self-identified as a *poète maudit* (cursed poet) and returned to the Catholic Church to atone for a life of alcoholism, drug abuse, and debauchery, his contemporaries honored his genius with the title "Prince of Poets," just before his death in 1896.

The English translations of Gertrude Hall, Ashmore Wingate, and Anne Green all confirm Verlaine's admiration of the railway.[4] The translations communicate his dramatic comparisons of the machine's infernal racket to the sound of a thousand chains, the howls of a thousand giants, and the drawn-out screech of an owl. There is no need to reproduce the translations here as the language and meanings range from similar to the same. Translations deviate, however, in the final stanza, where versions of Verlaine's valedictory imagery are as varied as the number of translations. Interpretations reflect the periods in which they were translated as well as the subjective interests of the translator. Gertrude Hall's minimalist, rhythmic, and unembellished translation appears in full as the first selection of this volume, the last stanza of which reads:

> What is it all to me? Since in mine eyes
> The vision lingers that beatifies,
> Since still the soft voice murmurs in mine ear,
> And since the Name, so sweet, so high, so dear,
> Pure pivot of this maddening whirl, prevails
> Above the brutal clangor of the rails?

Hall's un-gendered and rhyming version suggests that the grace of God ("Name") manifested as the beautiful vistas viewed through train windows mitigate the harsher realities of railways.

Wingate's translation of the same final stanza eschews rhyme and feminizes Nature as a lover in white form engaged in a tempest of sexual acts with the "fierce waggon's motion, pleasingly?"

> But why should this vex me, since in mine eyes
> Her white form glows who gladdens all my heart,
> Since her sweet voice still murmurs words for me,

And her fair Name, so noble and so rich,
Mixes itself, pure centre of the storm,
With the fierce waggon's motion, pleasingly?

Anne Green has taken the greatest liberty, not in translation but interpretation, revealing the poem's hidden meaning:

What does all that matter to me, since in my eyes I have
The white vision that lifts my heart,
Since the soft voice still murmurs for me,
Since the Name that is so beautiful, so noble and so resonant
Is mingled—a pure pivot for all this whirling—
With the rhythm of the brutal carriage, smoothly."

For Green, Verlaine's reference to "Name" is unknowable, unless it is the experience of the railway journey itself. Verlaine equates the railway journey to the act of writing, in which the white vision that lifted Verlaine's heart was a blank piece of paper about to be influenced by a "soft voice" that murmurs to the writer over the "pivot," "whirling," and "rhythm" of the "brutal carriage."[5] It is impossible for current-day readers to infer this from the turn-of-the-century translations of Hall and Wingate. To Green, the panorama of the French countryside that passes through the carriage window inspires the poetry of Verlaine. What all three translations confirm is that French men and women of letters and their interpreters thought deeply about the railway's meaning and registered countless unexpected delights and complaints about the sudden arrival of the machine ensemble. Opponents of the English railways such as Ruskin, Creevy, Wordsworth, and Thackeray all found kindred spirits in Flaubert and Baudelaire, but the French subjected the *chemin de fer* to critical structural analysis. For men and women of French letters, to create was to invite criticism, and the French physical construction of railways produced some of the world's most incisive deconstructions of their meaning.

To Belgium, the "godlike animator" metaphor had a special relevance. Belgium's birth as an independent nation-state and the Railway Age were simultaneous in 1830. In an early demonstration of unity, Belgium adopted a national railway policy before any other country in the world. Parliament and the Interior Ministry adopted a brilliant plan to unite north and south with a state-owned network. The Brussels to Malines line opened in May 1835 and another line formed from Mons to France. With Malines as the center point of an axis resembling a cross, construction crews linked Brussels with Antwerp (1836) and Malines with Termonde (1837). Ostend, Bruges, Ghent, Louvain, Liege, and the German border quickly followed. The system cost £5.37 million, but the state railways turned a 5 percent profit by 1853. The government also acquired most private ventures by 1870. More than half a million passengers traveled on the Brussels to Malines line in its inaugural year, exceeding the traffic carried on all English lines. The commercial gains were immediate and unprecedented. Between 1835 and 1845, imports increased 50 percent, coal production 100 percent, and exports of cast iron 800 percent.[6]

A major theme in German history is the near-universal acceptance of railways in all of the German states. This peculiar affinity for the newest steam technology contradicted the Germans' lukewarm reception of state road and canal construction projects, or even steam power. In large swaths of Germany, roads were built by private initiatives, and they were in a dismal state if they existed at all. In 1840, fewer than 615 steam engines powered factories and mines in Prussia. By comparison, France had 2,591 (1840) and Belgium 1,501 (1845).[7] Horses still drew canal barges, and widespread protests against construction of the *Mittelland-kanal* underlined the limits of the autocratic kingdoms.[8] It is, of course, a commonplace in German history to cite Helmuth von Moltke on railways. The vocal spokesman embodied a distinctly Prussian late-nineteenth-century militarism that emphasized the Prussian army's adept use of railways in the Wars of Unification. But this *post hoc ergo propter hoc* point of view coalesced late in Prussian history between 1866 and 1872. If anything, Prussia moved cautiously toward railways, reflecting Otto Michaelis's 1864 complaint that the government was a "lazy serf" of railway enterprise.[9] The great German historian Alfred von Treitschke provided a more accurate assessment for Greater Germany:

> It was the railways which first dragged the nation from its economic stagnation; they ended what the Zollverein only begun; with such power did they break in upon all the old habits of life, that already in the forties the aspect of Germany was completely changed.[10]

Abigail Green examined the symbiotic relationship between the Zollverein and the railways, as both helped integrate goods and financial markets.[11] Nineteenth-century railways in both the U.S. and Germany primarily served the interests of regional industrial capitalists. In many ways, Germany skipped the preindustrial phase of infrastructural development to attain modern forms of industrial transport. Germany's *deus ex-machina* was not the Prussian army's demigods but the railways' economic power. Its role in integrating German markets, industrializing the Rhineland and the Ruhr, and uniting east and west prevented the alternative of Balkanization.

Other European states with a long history of reliable but slow overland transport gravitated toward railways predominantly to overcome mountain ranges and frozen rivers. Holland, Italy, Switzerland, and Scandinavia all relied on massive bridge and tunnel projects like the St. Gotthard Tunnel or mountain railways through the Alps, the Apennines, or Throndhjem to shorten distances or access mines. Current research methodologies involving Global Information Systems, census information, and socioeconomic indicators reveal patterns of economic inequalities and uneven development in Spain and Portugal compared to France since 1870.[12] Mountainous regions with few navigable rivers were a serious challenge in Iberia. Geographers who specialize in orography have found that mountains, rather than oceans, have been the greatest impediment to human travel. Historically Spain and Portugal invested in maritime infrastructure, and both dynasties were in no hurry to expend scarce resources on tunneling, bridging, or gradient-related construction to overcome geographical barriers in the Alps and Pyrenees. In addition, Spain's minimally built system never met the nation's economic needs. Interconnectivity with towns and cities increased preexisting inequalities because whole regions like Galicia remained in complete isolation from any networks. Meanwhile, industrialization faltered. Spain's first significant Railway Law (1855) coincided with the founding of its first liberal democratic government.[13] Whereas France completed 18,600 miles of track by 1890, Spain had just under 5,000 and Portugal around 1,200. Railways in Portugal reached only 80 percent of its population by 1830.[14]

For Russia, the railway was a "godlike animator" because wherever it appeared in empty open spaces so did human productive activity, whether peasants, convicts, soldiers, and Chinese coolies liked it or not. But the animator erased as well. In summer 1896, James Young Simpson stepped off a train near the Barabinsky steppe at Krivoschekovo, a town on the Ob river bank. The old river town was more than 2,000 miles from Moscow and four *versts* (1 verst = .66 mile) from the nearest train station. The town had already begun to disappear as the new railway station of the same name drew the population of the old. Houses, barns, commercial establishments, and streets materialized within paces of the station, prompting Simpson to remark: "thus does the railway make and unmake places."[15] Simpson defined the train as a juggernaut that colonized empty space, while he depicted the *tarantass* that conveyed him to old Krivoschekovo as a "wicker basket" on wheels pulled by an unshod pony. The immigrant family from Periyaslav, the navvy dwellings made of sleepers, the military cantonments, and the convicts locked up behind spear-pointed palisades all appeared in a Siberian landscape created by the godlike animator.

Inception

Among the grievances of nineteenth-century train enthusiasts and critics in France were that railways took too long to complete. Post-Revolutionary French governments faced the painful truth that Napoleon and the *Corps des Ponts et Chaussées* had ushered in a century of infrastructural development that made France the envy of Europe. Indeed, unrivalled civil engineering of canals, bridges, and roads drew comparisons to imperial Rome. The combination of navigable waterways of the Seine, Rhône, Rhine, and Loire as well as reasonable overland transport costs on well-kept roads facilitated the passage of goods from the Atlantic to the Mediterranean coast. Yet, the first three phases of French railway development in 1835–1842, 1842–1857, and 1857–1879 were so pedestrian that historians have compensated for these fiascos by praising the Freycinet program (1879–1887) as a national triumph, when by world comparison the French simply began to meet universal standards. Civic leaders and entrepreneurs in Paris, Lyons, and

Marseilles certainly entertained grand visions to unite France and the continent with railways radiating from Paris, "the capital of Europe." Lines from Paris to St. Germain and Versailles were built quickly enough (1835–1837). The Paris to St. Germain line began operating on August 16, 1837. The lag between Great Britain and France was insignificant compared to the decadal surge of England's expansion.[16] In 1838, however, the French parliament defeated a one-billion-franc appropriations bill, inaugurating two more eras of indecision. In 1841, the Dufaure proposal was so expensive that the government voted itself far-reaching powers to expropriate property and grant concessions to private firms just to avoid the 274-million-franc price tag for a mere 500 track miles. The 1842 railway law empowered the government to survey lands, construct the road bed, and build viaducts, bridges, and tunnels, while private companies laid the track, built stations, acquired the rolling stock, and managed operations.[17] This "mixed system" of government and capitalist cooperation increased the number of contracts to forty private companies but did not generate enough track miles to be recognized as a milestone. In a country where urbanites looked down their noses at "la province" and most peasants never measured time in hours or minutes,[18] municipal governments refused to contribute two-thirds of all railway financing. Meanwhile, railway travel seemed patrician and inefficient. In 1847, the British travel writer George Musgrave marveled at Rouen Station, where he witnessed cranes lifting aristocratic carriages with their passengers still inside "suspended bodily" off the chassis, axles, and wheels of the coaches and onto a car platform for railway transport.[19] Subsequent legislatures passed laws to curb unbridled speculation and guarantee investor returns, but the Legrand Star out of Paris remained unbuilt. Nationalization of railways finally found its champion in Lamartine, but *laissez faire* economists defeated him. The popularity of early railways should have provided incentive for rapid growth. In 1850 alone, sixty-two million passengers per mile and sixty-two million tons of freight per mile traveled over the same meagre 2,200 miles of completed track.[20] In the same year, intercontinental visions waned; travel from Paris to Munich still took twenty-six hours, Paris to Milan sixty hours, and Vienna was not reachable by rail.[21] How did the nation with the greatest combined literary and artistic tradition and particular strengths in state bureaucracy and civil engineering lag so far behind in railway achievements?[22] In the gap between French letters and railway accomplishments lies the valid French national critique from 1830–1890.

Napoleon III finally implemented the "grans réseaux" plan. Four networks from Paris radiated in every direction like a star, supplemented by a fifth line from Cherbourg to Nantes and a sixth connecting Bordeaux and Toulouse.[23] Prior to 1857, however, France completed just 4,600 miles of line. The problem of iron shortages was resolved by the Anglo-French Treaty of Commerce (1860), which allowed for the import of duty-free bar-iron from England. This and other free trade policies forced the embittered ironmasters of France to compete with English iron by abandoning their mountain redoubts, modernizing their operations to smelt with coal, and improving their product. Liberal trade policies and declines in the price of iron revolutionized the French railway industry.[24] During the Second Empire (1852–1870), lines reached 9,200 miles, or about 500 miles per year, bringing railway communications to the German border, the Mediterranean, Italy, and Spain. By that time, it was possible for French writer Jules Verne to imagine a rocket to the moon and for historian Maxime du Camp to exclaim that the sparks from locomotive engines could illuminate the hereafter.[25] But fictional imagery quickly turns to delusion considering that the railway companies only averaged one or two track miles per day for nineteen years. This rate was acceptable for a single telescoping line but not for the expansion of the entire French national network, which radiated six trunk lines from Paris and established secondary spurs at the regional nodes of Bordeaux, Marseilles, Lyon, Tours, Nantes, and Lille. Falling prices for iron, cotton, wool, and wine—imported from Italy, Spain, and Algeria—proved that an integrated market emerged during the reign of Napoleon III. But the outcome of the Franco-Prussian War showed that a national railway system did not exist.

Popular frustration with slow rates of completion were compounded by quotidian impediments to reliable locomotive travel. The public faced packed trains, unbearably circuitous routes, long waits for reclaiming baggage, and dreadful conductor and porter services. Although private firms operated five of the seven main systems—the Est, Nord, Paris-Lyons-Méditerranée (PLM), Midi, and Paris-Orléans—the French people demanded railways to respond like a public utility because the government heavily subsidized private construction and regulated operations. "The people" actually demanded more as French alterations to the railway journey came in illicit forms as well. On a train from Paris to Boulogne in late 1850, an American traveler laughed when he read a vandalized sign that erased the words "not" from the following public service message: "Gentlemen are respectfully requested to smoke in the cars, and to put their feet on the cushions."[26] Public pressure on the government to improve the service was intense and seemed to produce results after amalgamation and privatization of the six lines. Service vastly improved even as rail density increased. Following the Great Exhibition of 1851, Paris hosted three universal expositions in 1878, 1889, and 1900. None of them would have been possible without railway transport. French railway companies hired women to control labor costs. In 1860, 1,500 of the 21,000 employees of the French railways were women. They served as cleaners, custodians, ticket sellers, and assistant gatekeepers and earned less than men, about 120 to 180 francs per year.[27] When comparing the railway services of France and the U.S. in the 1870s, Twain remarked that the former "zealously study your welfare and your interests instead of turning their talents to the invention of new methods of discommoding and snubbing you as is very often the main employment of that exceedingly self-satisfied monarch, the railroad conductor of America."[28] The only two government systems—the Alsace-Lorraine and Etat lines—together reached a respectable 7,400 miles. The star pattern gradually evolved into a series of triangles, with the apex at Paris and the bases on the frontiers. But every new political crisis and economic recession resulted in painful reorganizations and protracted litigation.[29] After the humiliating defeat in the Franco-Prussian War, the Ministry of Public Works and Chamber of Deputies spent another 25 years to complete the Freycinet plan and reach a period of respectability from 1887–1914. The war was a short-term setback; the indemnity of five billion francs surrendered to Germany represented over half the amount France spent on railways to 1871. France also lost Alsace and Lorraine, two provinces with over 500 miles of railway. But Minister of Public Works Charles Louis de Freycinet authorized a plan that doubled track mileage and brought the French system outside the richest regions to the exterior from 1879–1887.[30] The pace of construction remained unexceptional compared to those in Great Britain, Germany, India, the U.S., and Canada, in part because the plan coincided with the "long depression" when the Interior Ministry put citizens to work on canals, harbors, roads, and machinery. Whereas the French reached 21,000 miles by 1888 and 26,000 track miles by 1897, the U.S. had completed 156,000 and 220,000, respectively.[31] The French Third Republic spent 3.5 billion francs on railways to stimulate the economy and employ workers. Its leaders believed railways advanced the principles of political and social equality so long as they served the nation.

In rural France, the pulse of everyday life in peasant communities changed little with the arrival of the main trunk lines. Eugen Weber illustrates this in his microhistory *Peasants into Frenchmen*: "[i]ndeed, railways played no small part in the underdevelopment of the countryside."[32] France enjoyed the best canal, river, and road systems in continental Europe, and canal bargemen, stagecoach drivers, and horse breeders fought to preserve their businesses.[33] When the main lines arrived in France from 1860 to 1890, peasants paid little attention to trains that only served the interests of urban capital. If not for the pealing bells of churches and cathedrals, peasants paid no attention to the time of day. A woman in France remarked that her village was more isolated when trains bypassed it in 1865 than decades prior when stagecoaches delivered mail.[34] This had proved true also in England where the people of Water Newton saw 16 mail coaches pass through every day but only an occasional train.[35] Meanwhile, country folk willfully ignored the rails because traditional roads and trails led them to their local destinations. Commenting on peasant attitudes, one French railway inspector noted in the 1890s: "They close in on themselves to live off their own products instead of obeying the great law of exchange."[36] The self-reliance of peasant freeholders was the lament of capitalists everywhere.

France neglected railway development so long that most narrow-gauge branch lines remained unbuilt until the 1890s. Once secondary lines arrived railways transformed local communities. Two-thirds of the French population still lived in rural parishes in 1891 and two-thirds lived in towns with under 5,000 people in 1899. Regardless of the actual geographical distance from Paris, these towns and villages were remote vestiges of the past. Edmond de Goncourt described provincials and peasants as "natural history." A military officer in the mining country of the Nord compared his surroundings to a black village in Africa. Sedan chairs were still spotted in provincial France in the late 1880s because only nimble human carriers could negotiate the narrow winding streets.[37] Once built by 1900, no town in France with 10,000 or more people was untouched by the railway, and the percentage of urban residents connected to railways exceeded 96 percent.[38] Because of railways, English travelers who habitually crossed the Channel to attend the once-thriving market of Avranches in Normandy began to regret that all the French butter, eggs, fowls, salmon, and trout were shipped in baskets for Paris and London.[39] French towns with railway stations attracted the people from villages without them. Towns without stations along the Paris-Lyons-Méditerranée line lost one-quarter of their population from 1866–1936, while the populations around railheads surged.[40] The number of railroad employees increased from 222,800 in 1881 to 308,000 in 1907, as "the railway stations offered steady jobs for steady people—in the long run an influence more subversive of traditional institutions."[41] Trains also revolutionized agriculture by bringing fertilizer, diminishing the need to find manure on open roads where horses rode. Wherever they passed, economic activity increased and traditional occupations vanished. Carters no longer carried goods, bargemen went bankrupt, cottage producers succumbed to industrial producers. Those who fired charcoal-burning furnaces either adapted to coal or went under. Village youth turned to the modernizing economy for jobs. Railroads integrated the French countryside, national markets, and the modern world economy with generally positive effects on peasants but a negative impact on traditional lifestyles.[42]

The *fin de siècle* was good for railway expansion but the *belle époque* proved greater. France turned the corner of financial adversity. The country survived a massive general Railway Strike in 1910 and deployed railways to secure strategic advantages in WWI. The greatest evidence of this came in the weeks from August 1 to August 20, 1914, when the French Railways assisted the mobilization of 1.5 million soldiers, 400,000 horses, and 80,000 vehicles to stop the German army at the Marne.[43] After the war, France nationalized its railways in stages that culminated in 1921 and 1937. The evolution toward the state system benefited the French people over the *longue durée*. The history of French railways proved that state structures built to endure prevail. By 1935, French railways employed some 425,000 workers, conveyed 591 million passengers, and earned nearly 11 billion francs in revenue, despite expenses exceeding 14 billion.[44]

As Walter Benjamin noted, Marcel Proust portrayed the railway station as a tragic place in *Remembrance of Things Past*.[45] Marvelous in design and place-name, railway stations nonetheless unhappily evinced a longing for the familiar and represented a new form of spatial and temporal indeterminacy that resulted in dislocating experiences. Travelers set out for a remote destination fully expecting to discover miracles of the imagination by leaving the established comforts of home to "the pestiferous cavern through which we may have access to the mystery, into one of the vast, glass-roofed sheds, like that of Saint-Lazare into which I must go to find the train for Balbec." Proust's main character traded the panoramic view of Balbec from his bedroom window for

> the rent bowels of the city one of those bleak and boundless skies, heavy with an accumulation of dramatic menaces, like certain skies painted with an almost Parisian modernity by Mantegna or Veronese, beneath which could be accomplished only some solemn and tremendous act, such as a departure by train or the Elevation of the Cross.

In this passage, Proust associated "the solemn and tremendous act" of a train's departure not to the glory of the Christian symbol but to the dread of the crucifixion, as captured by the Baroque triptych altarpiece of Flemish painter Peter Paul Rubens (1610–1611). Proust expressed in elegant language and allegory his subjective emotional state at the train station as one of *departure*, fundamentally feeling the same sense of tragic loss at the time of someone's death: his own, a loved one's, or Christ's passing. In other contexts, railway scholars have referred to these detached states as "displacement," "dislocation," or "alienation," all products of industrial modernity, and Proust, pampered by doting parents but solitary for much of his life, designated the train station as a loci for spiritual departure. Earlier in the narrative, Proust revealed that his era was "infected with a mania for showing things only in the environment that properly belongs to them, thereby suppressing the essential thing, the act of the mind which isolated them from that environment."[46] Such references normalized the dislocating experience of modern life in Proust's fiction. He also theorized that the meaning of direct experiences eluded one until recollection clarified it.[47] Although Proust wrote much of *Remembrance of Things Past* prior to WWI, the metonym of a train station as gateway for the *departed* is particularly poignant in the context of the book's publication in the 1920s, when the French lived with the painful memories of sending so many young soldiers by train to die on the Western Front.

Reception

Unlike Belgium and France, Germany was not a united country when railways were first built in its territories, but in a very short time railways covered the thirty German states of central Europe. If the railway era began in England in 1830, with Belgium, France, and the United States following quickly in tow, the Central European states possessed little chance of keeping up. In 1836 only four miles of track existed in all Germany. The German states found an optimal formula to reach 340 miles of track by 1840 and a system of six trunk lines by 1860. Governments issued state bonds and offered loan guarantees to private investors, both subject to state regulation. The overnight success of German railways, especially the rate of expansion, reflected three economic advantages that had nothing to do with the Prussian military: 1) the availability of foreign and domestic capital, labor surpluses, and entrepreneurial commitments to build lines fast and cheap; 2) reverse engineering and replacement of British, Belgian, and American locomotive technology with German industrial products; and 3) astute state economic policies under Kaisers who happened to be train enthusiasts.[48] Early connecting lines to coal regions, iron mines, and steel factories played important roles in regional economic development as productive output of all three soared. The father of Prussian railways and the *Zollverein*, Friedrich List, studied the technology in England, America, and France before pursuing work on the Leipzig to Dresden line (April 1839).[49] Thereafter, Prussia followed his plan to construct six trunks exiting Berlin south to Leipzig and Dresden, southwest toward Köthen, Magdeburg, and Hanover, north to Stettin, east to Frankfurt-on-Oder and Posen, southeast to Upper Silesia, Teschen, and Cracow, and northeast to Danzig and East Prussia. The complementary Rhine-Weser and Thuringian lines linked river basins and old highways. The Prussian pace averaged about 850 miles every four years to reach 3,500 miles of tracks by 1860, a significant achievement, considering that parts of Pomerania had no publicly built cart roads at all. From his *eilwagen* on the road from Leipzig to Dresden, Edward Wilkey saw that an English engineer built the first railway connecting the two towns. He also observed the line under construction from Linz to Budweis in Bohemia, which later connected the salt mines of Salzkammergut to the Danube, Modau, and Elba river systems. Another British traveler learned that the railway line from Vienna to Raab relied on iron rails imported from England.[50] Together with Prussia and Saxony, the other German states of Hanover, Bavaria, Württemberg, Baden, and the city of Frankfurt combined for 7,000 miles by 1860. By this year, Austria had built an additional 2,800 miles.[51]

Literary scholar Paul A. Youngman's *Black Devil and Iron Angel* examined the dialectic of science and myth in the German people's receptivity of trains. While his focus on the realist literature of five German authors may appear narrow as an evidence base, his insightful conclusions are consistent with global trends. The first author, Berthold Auerbach, represented the transition to realism with an overwhelmingly positive view of railways consistent with the first half of the nineteenth century. In *The Nest on the Railway*, *On a Field Next to the Railway*, and *Convicts*, Auerbach set up negative connotations of the railway as foils for a new scientific narrative that exemplified three metonyms. The first, the railway as Messiah, asserted that railways used the new religion of science to break down traditional beliefs for "He who is employed by the railway, how can he be superstitious?"[52] Auerbach's characters dismissed peasant concerns that the railways did the devil's work. Instead, trains spread generalized happiness: "The railway made it possible to promote all of the creature comforts and beauty of the [German] culture in every single solitary spot on earth." A telegraph operator explained to a farmer that "man now paints with rays of sunshine, travels with steam, and speaks with lightning." Auerbach's second theme dealt with trains as purveyors of prosperity, opportunity, and luck. Main characters transgress in *Convicts*, but the trains contributed to their redemption through work. The arrival of a steam locomotive granted stature to the mundane life of Swabian peasants.

Trains brought good tidings and some characters insisted that bad news would never come to those who lived near railways. Military trains raced to and from the front, reporting only great events. Third, Auerbach rendered the train as a democratizing agent that enriched the lives of freer peoples by promoting notions of citizenship.[53]

Two other German realist authors found locomotives to reside on the spectrum closer to *schwarzerTeufel* (black devil) than *eiserner Engel* (iron angel). Peter Rosegger and Gerhart Hauptmann depicted characters that were frightfully aware of the fifteen-fold increase in railway expansion from 1846–1899. The Austrian Rosegger knew that the *Südbahn* (Southern railway) near his home represented the "nerve system of the common spirit," modernized farming, and advanced German literature. His works *The Village Train Station* and *The New Rail of Hochschwaben* examined particularism and technology as extensions of nature in the Styrian highlands of Austria. Rosegger's ambivalence stems from his belief that progress benefitted cultures on the rise but destroyed communities on the decline. The wise elders of villages distrusted railway entrepreneurs for cutting deals with Satan.[54] The character of the Postman in *The New Rail* considered the train a "monstrosity of the human mind," and Rosegger noted their "ironclad ability to crush anything that stood in their way." Youngman asserted that Rosegger portrayed the locomotive as a mythological beast that heralded spiritual chaos.[55] Gerhart Hauptmann's poem "In the Night Train" probed the leitmotif of trains as productive and destructive forces. The main character was a poor railway linesman, Franz Thiel, whose life begins to spiral downward with the *Ungetüm Glotzaugen* (monster with bloody goggle eyes, the train) in a tragic story that resulted in both killing the innocent.[56] In other German settings, the nobility feared that railways would lead to class equality. The same King Ernst August von Hannover who commissioned a statue of himself for placement at the railway station to promote himself scoffed at the idea that shoemakers and tailors should travel as quickly as he did.[57]

Youngman's important book begs the question of whether the principal cause of the German critique of railways was the particularism of its realist authors in the face of national unification. With the exception of Auerbach's works, perhaps the mythologies produced by the hegemonic scientific narratives of the realists were meant to undermine rather than exalt the modernizing state. The realists represented a specific German idyll that pulled with centrifugal force away from major German cities. Auerbach hailed from Nordstetten, Rosegger from the Austrian highlands, and Hauptmann from Lower Silesia. Fear of the devil was one thing, but fear of his urban legions and their "triumphal car[s] of industriousness" was quite another. The persistence of independent railways in the German states illustrated that Otto von Bismarck's vision of a united Germany came gradually to others as well. None of the pan-German political organizations, such as the Federal Diet of the German Confederation (Bund), the Zollverein, the Association of German Railway Administration (VDEV), or the Railway Leagues (Verbände) were strong enough to assert authority, set policy, and regulate railways.[58] The kingdoms of Saxony, Bavaria, and Württemberg, as well as the Grand Duchy of Baden all possessed their own short lines and trains, some with their respective royal coats of arms emblazoned on the doors of passenger compartments. These "fatherlands" used the railways as symbolic capital to associate the state with regional festivals such as Württemberg's *Cannstatter Volksfest*.[59] From 1850–1866, the railway workforces of the many German states rose nearly 800 percent from 26,000 to 205,000 from 1850–1866.[60] Prior to 1870, Saxony stood out for having the longest network outside of Belgium, and their employees organized and dressed like state functionaries and postal workers. King Ludwig I of Bavaria founded the first state network in Germany by nationalizing the Munich-Augsburg line, and Prussia anointed Bethel Henry Strousberg its railway king.

Moreover, as Allan Mitchell has argued, every southern German state except Baden oriented itself away from Prussia. Already in communication with Austria, Ludwig wanted to invest in a north-south axis. The mountainous and heavily wooded Württemberg felt the east-west crush of neighboring Bavaria and Baden and gazed south to Italy. The proximity of Baden to France left it with strategic railheads at Strasbourg and Mulhouse, but it prized the St. Gotthard Tunnel project to Switzerland.[61] While imperfect, the use of the *eisenbahn* in the Austro-Prussian War (1866) and Franco-Prussian War (1870–1871) prefaced a greater German union. Prussia's efficiently built network of state railways grew from five to twelve. Bismarck parlayed French war reparations into twenty-seven new railway concessions in newly annexed Schleswig-Holstein, Hanover, Hesse-Kessel, Nassau, and Frankfurt, all comprising the North German Confederation. Between unification in 1871 and 1910, the length of the German railways nearly doubled from 20,000 miles to 38,000 miles, representing the largest system in Europe until it was surpassed by Russia in 1930. The key year for Germany's consolidation of power was 1879, when the Prussian-Hessian State Railways formed from all of the private lines in adjoining states. That year one-fourth of all German investments were in railways.[62] Except for independent networks in the southern states of Württenberg and Bavaria, Germany had for the first time in history linked the industrial west of the Rhineland both to the ports at Rotterdam, Bremen, and Hamburg and to the agricultural breadbasket of East Prussia. Historians have emphasized the strategic implications of a Germany that could now fight a two-front war, but more importantly, it forged an economy capable of challenging England's in the Age of Empire and the Great War. In the Germany of Auerbach the railway transported the beauty and nobility of German culture; in the eyes of Rosegger and Hauptmann the train represented an all-too-real spiritual dissonance captured by Rudolf Eucken in 1897: "man paid for technological progress with his soul."[63]

Incursion

The disastrous French campaigns through North Africa cast a dark shadow over which railways expanded. After 1830, the westernmost reaches of the Muslim world succumbed to a brutal French invasion and occupation, with the exception of a small strip of territory that remained Spanish Morocco. French expeditionary forces under General Thomas Bugeaud deployed harsh tactics to defeat an equally atrocious Arab resistance led by Amir Abd al-Qadir. No amount of French "civilizing" justified the tragic deaths of three million Algerian Muslims as a result of war, drought, and famine in a deplorable chapter of European colonial history. French land policy displaced Muslim peasants from the best lands and gave them to French settlers, who then hired Algerians as day laborers.[64] General Léon de la Moricière wrote that the French army turned *madrasas* into barracks, confiscated goods from *mosques*, and otherwise "preached" to defiant Algerians with "rifle shots." Those who refused to convert to the Catholicism were met with anti-Islamic racism in the guise of Jacobin anti-clericalism. The French cult of science and reason was in this instance as fanatical as any religion.[65]

French-built railway networks in the Maghreb region of North Africa paralleled the Atlantic and Mediterranean coasts from Morocco, Algeria, and Tunisia to Libya. In the 1850s and 1860s, the French government granted private companies concessions to construct railways in Algeria. Trunk lines radiated from Algiers east to Constantine and west to Oran. Short branch lines extended out of population centers to bustling ports on the Mediterranean. Tunisia and Morocco followed this pattern, only later from Tunis and Tangier, while Libya ignored railway development until occupied by Italy in 1912. French imperial economic and military considerations governed most railway decisions in the Maghreb. Trains carried iron ore, lead, zinc, and phosphate to steelworks in Tunisia or to ports at Tunis, Sousse, and Sfax. Engineers overcame the Tellian Atlas—the fertile hills, plateaus, and mountains along the Algerian coast—that required curves and gradients more severe than the Swiss Alps. The plateaus of eastern Tunisia were easily negotiated by comparison. As late as 1912, passengers aboard the Algerian Eastern railway still took twelve hours to depart Algiers and reach Constantine, a distance of 288 miles. The grand vision was to connect French North Africa with the Niger and Congo, and to construct a trans-Saharan railway to French Equatorial Africa and the Sudan. WWI stalled both projects, but the French had completed a railway network between the Mediterranean and the Sahara.[66] When financing materialized for a railway in French equatorial territory, more than 20,000 forced laborers perished during construction.[67] A French company completed the first railway in the Middle East from Jaffa to Jerusalem (1892). On the day of its inauguration, three sheep with gilded horns were sacrificed before the Sultan and Turkish Cavalry. Westerners interpreted the Muslim offering as necessary to prevent evil genii from destroying the railway.[68] On the eve of WWI, the French competed directly with the meteoric rise of Germany, and the Berlin-Baghdad Railway was as convincing a prospect for Hohenzollern expansion and dominion as any example of railway imperialism.[69] In contrast stood French Indochina, where railways began the "painful disintegration of traditional social and economic bonds" because they were perceived as vehicles of coercive European colonial expansion as well as France's central public works project. Railways ultimately undermined positive Franco-Vietnamese relations.[70]

As historian Michael Adas explained, the presentation of European technology to Africans left the host cultures awestruck. What Europeans considered mundane in clocks, batteries, cameras, bottles, watches, rifles, pistols, compasses, telescopes, matches, buttons, mirrors, wheels, oil lamps, microscopes, and kaleidoscopes, Africans received with wonder. The overall effect of such material things, including trains, was that learned tribal elders believed that whites knew the secrets of immortality. As reported in Joseph Conrad's *Heart of Darkness*, the sound of the steamship whistle set Africans to flight.[71]

The vast distance from Paris to West Africa may as well have been an oceanic crossing. When Sir Harry Hamilton Johnston wrote his book on European colonization in Africa (1913), it still took nineteen days to travel from Paris to Timbuktu. Leaving Paris, a passenger reached any station in France in less than twenty-four hours. In contrast, the steamship from Bordeaux or Marseilles to Dakar, Senegal alone took eight days, and for the next ten days the traveler alternated with a slow train for two days and a slow steamer for the next three: Dakar to St. Louis; the Senegal River to Kayès; Kayès to Kulikoro on the Niger; and Kulikoro to Timbuktu. The Chemin de Fer Dakar-Niger through Senegal and Mali was the most significant railway in all of French West Africa, but engineers relied heavily on forced labor, low pay, and food rationing to complete it. Workers deserted, struck, and committed sabotage to escape their fate of probable death by disease, accident, or exhaustion.[72] Railways in French Dahomey and the Ivory Coast suffered the same shortfalls in the 1910s and 1920s as French railways did in the 1830s and 1840s.[73] Only a telegraph connected Timbuktu and Algeria. If the railway's attributes symbolically distinguished Europeans from Africans, no such distinction existed where railways never reached.

In the Belgian Congo, the rubber boom injected new life into the narrow-gauge railway between Matadi and Stanley Pool. The line involved 60,000 workers laying less than 250 miles of track. Estimates vary, but one report placed the number of deaths at 1,800 per year in 1892–1893, but unfortunately engineers were still clattering around with it for the next two decades. This made it one of the deadliest infrastructural projects in world history, comparable only to the Panama Railway and the Devil's Railway of Brazil. Most workers died of diseases such as malaria, beriberi, and dysentery, but the perilous construction of nearly 100 metal bridges over rapids made accidents a daily probability. The gravesites of Chinese, Barbadians, Congolese, and Europeans lined the tracks. Chinese railway workers who fled were later found 500 miles east of Leopoldville. Defectors from Barbados were shot as if they were soldiers. The contractor hired 200 men just to keep order.[74] Reluctant workers were chained and flogged; others died in dynamite explosions and derailments. Workers' quarters resembled prison camps. As in India, "the death a sleeper" metaphor circulated, although in the Congo whites died at a rate of one per telegraph pole. Author Adam Hochschild related the incident of 300 armed railway laborers who tried to commandeer a ship at Matadi and sail home to Sierra Leone. European officials later unveiled an appalling example of group statuary showing three exhausted life-sized porters with the following inscription: "The Railway Freed Them from Porterage."[75] Belgian King Leopold II diffused the "rubber terror" protests of missionaries like William Sheppard with carrot-and-stick offers of personal audiences and threats of taxation or expulsion.[76]

On the eve of WWI, German South-West Africa boasted the unlikely ratio of 11,000 Germans to less than 85,000 Bantu, Hottentot, Bushman, and half-castes. The construction of more than 1,000 track miles of railway meant that the fatherland had built one mile for every 11 Germans, and 85 Southwest Africans. Together with German East Africa and Tanyanika, the empire possessed more than one million square miles of African territory, with a population of 14.5 million Africans, and 30,700 whites, mainly Germans but also Dutch and English.[77]

Invasion

By 1914, there were 620,000 miles of track across the face of the planet. In 1882, Europeans constituted 72 percent of the two billion railway travelers throughout the world. Comparatively speaking, the next largest population of passengers, North Americans (U.S., Canada, and Mexico), represented just 20 percent. At the time, the 100,000 locomotive engines pulling 2.75 million carriages and wagons were mostly European.[78]

At a time when the nations of Europe basically doubled their track miles (between 1880 and 1913), some countries like Russia tripled their output. Foreign travelers in Russia remarked about how interesting it was for railways to transport them—backward in time. Life in the Caucuses, Caspians, and Siberias continued undisturbed by railways well into the twentieth century. Douglas Freshfield, the first mountain-climbing explorer of the Caucasus, described the region as "an ethnological museum where the invaders of Europe, as they travelled westward to be manufactured into nations, left behind samples of themselves in their raw condition."[79] Amateur paleontologist Basset Digby debunked the existence of live mammoths in Siberia, but he dug up some mastodon bones in Yakutsk nineteen days from the nearest railway and transported them by barge, sledge, and train to St. Petersburg, where they were displayed publically.[80] Early sojourners noted that every significant town on the Trans-Siberian Railway was three or more miles distant from the station as a concession to drosky-drivers and horse breeders, who still earned a good living.[81] Unfortunately, travelers could not help but notice outside their train windows that camel caravans, tarantass sledges, and a boy on a pony moved faster for short distances than Russian trains did, especially since railway stops kept passengers idle for hours.[82] Russians advised the Englishman Robert Jefferson to do a little sledging to relieve the monotony of three-hour stoppages on the Siberian Railway. The region was so vast that nomadic tribesmen such as the Bashkirs, Khirghiz, Tungus, Buriats, Votiaks, Kamchakdales, and Samoyedes could roam plains, steppes, and mountains without interacting with railways. They chose otherwise. Arriving by train to Tikhonitzka, Harry de Windt watched as shaggy ponies walked around the railway station grounds untethered like people. Cossacks "bristling with knives and silver cartridge belts, and wearing long, dark skirts and huge astrakan bonnets" descended from his railway carriage, gathered their loose ponies, and galloped away toward their homes.[83] In this way, the godlike animator encouraged nomadism over a much larger territory.

The English cyclist Robert Jefferson rode his bicycle along the railway tracks in Russia. Outside Samara toward the station of Marichevka, he and a local shipping magnate named Nicolai Demtrivitch Batushkoff bicycled their way between the Volga River and the railway tracks. Jefferson reported peasants wielding the crudest wooden spades amidst unproductive and "sickly" patches of wheat. After a long ride, he parted company with Batushkoff and followed the tracks to the railway station, where the lone hut of a signalman offered protection from a torrential downpour. The signalman looked puzzled for "although he has been used to the civilising influence of railway trains for some part of his life, the sight of a bicycle somewhat disconcerted him."[84] The cyclist spent the evening explaining to the signalman the workings of his bicycle and the purpose of his 6,000-mile journey from the UK to Uzbekistan. The next day, mud forced him to walk his bike along the tracks to Borskaia station, where he saw *moujiks* boarding fourth-class cattle wagons. On the way to Buzuluk, Jefferson waved at the driver of a passing luggage train, who ignored him but stared confusedly at the bicycle. For hundreds of versts, the sterile Khirghiz steppes nearly conquered Jefferson's spirit. At the depths of his despair, he came upon a small balding man with a pince-nez at the station outside Orenburg, who welcomed him on behalf of the Orenburg cyclists. A military band greeted Jefferson by playing "God Save the Queen."[85] To get to Khiva, Jefferson had only 1,400 miles to go due south.

Contrary to what western Europeans thought, Russians enjoyed their train rides. Passengers explained to apprehensive foreigners why trains stopped outside of every tunnel for twenty minutes. The completion of tunnels shortened journeys and altered timetables. Instead of changing the timetables, railway officers instructed locomotive engineers to stop before every new tunnel so they arrived at the next station according to the original timetables. The thought of changing train schedules occurred to officials, but the chaos that would ensue justified the delay of trains. Such habits prompted westerners to believe that Russians objected to time saving, which fueled claims of Russian "backwardness." But to Russians, halting at a tunnel compensated for the time gained by building it.[86] Sir Henry Norman related an adventure outside Odessa where snow blocked trains, stranding several thousand passengers for three days until a convoy of sleighs deployed by the military rescued them.[87] He reported that every train carried ladders, tools, and the electrical appliances needed to tap into telegraph wires to call for assistance in case of breakdowns.[88] To Russians, the minor inconveniences of delays were preferable to exposure to harsh climates and oppressive modern timetables.

What the godlike animator gave to Russians was also taken away. Foreign travelers reported that peasants feared sparks that flew from the large funnels of wood-burning locomotives because the resulting fires burned their pine cabins to the ground. They also expressed worry that railway employees would come for their log cabins since engines burned the same birch and pine logs.[89] In 1888, when Russia reached 17,700 track miles,[90] *Times* correspondent George Dobson accompanied members of the war ministry on the first trip of the Trans-Caspian Railway from St. Petersburg to Samarkand. Dobson noted that the only railway into Russia's own heartland was the Nicholas Railway from St. Petersburg to Moscow. All others had extended into lands that Russia annexed in previous centuries, including the Baltic provinces, Finland, and Poland. The Trans-Caspian Railway continued this trend south into Central Asia. The distance was more daunting: Moscow to the foot of the Caucuses measured 1,240 miles. The railway reduced the journey from St. Petersburg to Samarkand from two months to just under eleven hours. Dobson's excursion exceeded four days due to bridge and culvert failures. The reckless speed of its construction proved its original intent as a strategic military railway to the borders of Russian Turkistan, Persia (Iran), and British India. But millions of rubles of strategic resources poured into Russia from Trans-Caspia, including the two fuel sources that replaced wood on Russian locomotives: coal and petroleum. The Trans-Caucuses and Trans-Caspian lines both used petroleum in the 1890s.[91] Peasants no longer needed to worry about their cabins.

To explain Russia's dilatory railway expansion east, Jacques Barzun once quipped: "Russia's hinterland remained backward for lack of railroad builders with greedy intentions."[92] At five million square miles, Siberia lies east of the Urals and is about half the size of the U.S. Prior to the railway, a man on horseback took two to three years to reach Siberia from western Russia.[93] The Tsarevich, Nicholas II turned the first soil on May 19, 1891. Upon completion of the Trans-Siberian Railway, the journey from Moscow to Vladivostok was reduced to less than a month.[94] French capital financed the doubling of Russia's railway network between 1895 and 1905, including the trans-Siberian lines. Railway loans amounted to 975 million of the 8.5 billion rubles that France loaned Russia. In 1895, the trans-Siberian railway employed 66,057 men on the West, Middle, trans-Baikalian, and Ussuri divisions of the line: 36,629 navvies, 13,080 carters, 5,851 surfacemen, 4,310 carpenters, 4,096 stonemasons, and 2,091 riveters.[95] The pace of two *versts* per day (about 1 1/3 miles) ensured both rapid completion and costly maintenance of dangerous sections. Faulty construction of the track and breakdowns explain the difference between advertised durations of travel (twelve to thirteen days, and nine for express service) and the realities (four weeks). By 1914, Russia became Europe's largest debtor, with a liability of nine billion rubles. The 5,424-mile route cost $390 million, about $10 million less than the Panama Canal, but its returns were inestimable given that thousands of families settled new towns, and Siberia began to export meat, hides, wheat, furs, and eighty million pounds of butter annually. Siberia's population increased from 1.5 million to 10.5 million from 1891–1913.[96] Finance Minister Sergei Witte's relentless modernizing committed three-fourths of the imperial budget to railway development in the Urals and Siberia. As in India, the railways drove up grain prices, contributed to food scarcity, and exacerbated cycles of famine that killed tens of thousands of peasants, especially in 1891. The storied completion of the Trans-Siberian Railway, the world's longest railroad, belied the rural suffering and deaths of epidemic proportions. Nationalists accused Witte of selling out to foreign capitalists, but this argument was disingenuous and dangerous. Nationalists provoked the Russo-Japanese War, the outcome of which ended Witte's government as well as Russia's need for an Orient Express. In the aftermath of the war, a Russian artillery colonel between Rostov and Vladikavas told Harry de Windt: "I was shot in Manchuria and now I am asked to shoot my own countrymen!" Other soldiers aboard trains between Odessa and Austria reported the same.[97] The Trans-Siberian Railway has been described as a "great monument to Russia's culture of the nineteenth century."[98] Meant as a tribute, the phrase could easily have served as the inscription on the tombstone of nineteenth-century Russia.

Travelers on the Trans-Siberian Railway subjected themselves to Siberian experiences in microcosm. In 1896, Harry de Windt rode in the "crowded cattle pens" of intolerable third-class carriages that smelled of sheepskin.[99] A few years later, he felt a part of the desolate loneliness outside during his traveling incarceration, isolation, and exile from Moscow to Irkutsk. He described the visual monotony as unbearable:

> the eye rests vacantly upon a dreary white plain, alternating with green belts of woodland, while occasionally the train plunges into dense dark pine forest only to emerge again upon the same eternal 'plateau' of silence and snow . . . it is all very mournful and depressing.

He compared the train to a brook running forever, a silent ghost, and the cure for insomnia. He also claimed no one aboard knew the time of day and meals ran together—breakfasts, lunches, and dinners—at the oddest hours of the day. Then he arrived to Eastern Siberia and bemoaned "comfort will soon be a thing of the past."[100] Another wayfarer, Basset Digby, claimed that he counted just a half-dozen different types of scenery in the Siberian landscape: "Every additional glimpse is a repetition of one of the others." For emphasis, he listed the six repeating sights as birch trees, fir forests, village of log cabins, horse-drawn sledges, railway fences, and telegraph poles all covered in snow.[101]

Richardson Wright and Basset Digby proved observant on their Russian journeys. Trains ran on St. Petersburg time, and their inability to keep accurate time sharpened their attentiveness to spatial detail, especially at stops. Tcheliabinsk once served as a way station for political exiles but now provided temporary accommodations for up to 2,000 immigrants heading east along the railway or taking branch lines to Tiumen and Ekaterinburg. The train passed through the desolation of the Khirgis, Ishim, and Barbara steppes to reach Tobolsk, a wheat district, and Kurgan, a market town of 70,000. The names of Russian towns that ended with "-sk," like Petropavolask, meant they lay on a river. Tomsk was an educational capital of Russia and Omsk, where Dostoevsky spent time in jail, was the Chicago of Siberia with a population of 96,000. Both Siberian cities had log buildings but no street lighting, art galleries, or parks.[102]

Wright and Digby sweated through overheated trains to get to Siberia. They wrote of two ways to get there from Moscow: "by fast train which is slow; or by slow train, which was even slower." They traveled light compared to the Russian families who brought half their household with them, including bedding, kitchenware, and even the "scissors for cutting up sugar." Russians preserved high temperatures in their trains by closing vents, especially at night. The crude co-ed water closets and sleeping arrangements embarrassed the two. They slept an arm's-length away from grandma and the children, while a young woman rolling cigarettes in the bunk above spilled tobacco down on them. Their third-class locomotives were moved to sidings to make way for express trains and to wait for convict and immigrant cars to be attached. Conductors clipped their tickets thirty-one times before reaching Omsk five days later. Their fellow passengers openly fraternized with them. The westerners saw no evidence of spitting, drunkenness, squalor, filth, or vermin. Assistant conductors swept up cigarette butts and cedar nut shells every two hours. Women washed the linoleum floors of the cars every two days. Soldiers doubled as musicians and entertained folks in carriages with pipes and the mandolin-like *balalaika*. They slept comfortably in third-class sleeping shelves under camel-hair blankets. At stops, peasant women served and sold "good and cheap" rye bread, trout tarts, roasted goose quarters, and jam turnovers. Itinerant sellers also sold candles that could be affixed to five-kopeck coins and when set on a flat surface provided enough light to read or play cards.[103]

During the depression of the mid-1890s, U.S. railroad firms sought to invade British-dominated foreign markets, especially Japan.[104] Like the English and Americans, the Japanese have well-deserved pride and nostalgia for their national railroads. Although four main islands dominate the Japanese archipelago, 145,000 square miles in waters and over 6,500 islands makes Japan approximately as large as California (159,000 square miles). Prior to the arrival of railways and telegraphs, it took thirty days for a letter to reach the Kinshin Islands from Edo. Tokyo and Kyoto were only 300 miles apart, but road travel between the two largest cities took eight days. Since no point of any island was more than seventy-five miles from the coast, railways that could bore through mountains and bridge crevasses offered opportunities for national unification.[105]

In 1854, Commodore Matthew C. Perry presented the Tokugawa with a gift of a small locomotive (about one-fourth the normal size) and a short length of track. Between 1871 and 1911, Japan constructed more than 5,000 track miles throughout its empire and imported more than 1,023 trains from Great Britain, the U.S., and Germany. Earnings from the fares of passengers, who traveled in spring and autumnal fairs and pilgrimages to Shinto shrines and Buddhist temples, far exceeded private and public railway freight revenue.[106] Natural disasters, mountainous terrain, and the scarcity of capital delayed completion of Japan's railroads. Typhoons regularly stalled construction for months, but on October 28, 1891, a disastrous earthquake in the Mino-Owari region (Gifu prefecture) claimed 9,960 lives and destroyed the railroad. Far from wielding the large capital of *zaibatsu* business groups in major cities, most undercapitalized private rail lines relied on horse-pulled vehicles regulated by the interior ministry.[107] As a stopgap measure to deal with the lack of capital after the quake, Meiji authorities temporarily inaugurated human-drawn railroads (*jinshakido* or *jinsha-tetsudō*) in sections between Atami and Yoshihama, as well as in Taiwan in 1895.[108] Globetrotting travel writers such as the Anglo-Indian C. R. Sail found Japanese railway service detestable due to floods, broken bridges, and breached lines. Despite a high incidence of late trains in Kurihashi, Sail witnessed a carload of Japanese passengers praising their comfortable train ride while it poured rain outside.[109] On the twelve-hour journey from Yokohama to Nangoya, he observed passengers unpacking and eating their own food "kit" and beverages since none of the stations had restaurants or refreshment bars. Despite the "overpowering" politeness of the bowing Japanese, one portly priest occupied two-and-a-half seats in a compartment and yielded not an inch to a woman without a seat.[110] Japanese handbooks bitterly complained about the chronic lateness of trains in Yokohama in 1898: "The Railroad Department seems to be asleep! The whole railroad system is disorganised and upset. . . . We are now at our destination. We are three hours late."[111]

Even before workers laid the first tracks in Japan, the Tokugawa regime had brainstormed ways of using rail transport in its military operations. Under the Meiji, the military originally opposed railways because their prohibitive costs required foreign capital and their western engineering and construction endangered national sovereignty. Military commanders changed their opinions, however, when the state deployed railways to transport troops during the Satsuma Rebellion in 1877.[112] A decade later, military strategists published the book *On Railways* (*Tetsudōron*, 1888), which advised the Meiji government not to build railways near the coasts, where a hostile fleet could attack them from the sea. The authors instead recommended that railways traverse the central plateau and mountains of Honshu. Railways soon linked highland and coastal peoples, ended backwater rebellions, and supported Japan's motto: "prosperous country, strong military."[113] "One Railroad Family" (*Kokutetsu Ikka*) was another metaphor coined by railway leader Gotō Shimpei in 1908 to promote national identity among the railway staff.[114] The predominant metaphor for railways in Japan is still the iron bands of the *Tetsudō*, which further united the four main islands into the most powerful Asian country in the modern era and forged one of the most destructive variants of nationalism the world has ever seen.

No country opposed railways with greater vigor than China. The cost of Chinese hostility and obstruction was unrelenting victimization by Great Britain, Germany, France, Russia, and Japan, all of which exploited the enormous contradictions of the Celestial Empire. The most fervent opposition from China came from below. Chinese carters, boatmen, and peasants considered railways as threats to their livelihoods and disruptive of the natural harmony of agrarian life. Bureaucrats and army officers regarded them as a danger to China's political autonomy and economic independence because foreigners built them.[115] Railway construction also disrupted ancestral shrines and graves. C. F. Gordon Cumming claimed that the Chinese believed the mass defilement of gravesites would unleash disembodied spirits upon local villages. Such superstitions turned into tropes that allowed western writers to evoke, often in exaggerated terms, the cultural inertia that prohibited "progress and civilisation" under the Qing dynasty. Protestant missionary Arthur Smith condemned Chinese resistance to railways as futile backwardness, disregarding the interminable history of English protests against railways.[116] Gordon Cumming opined that the Chinese literati and sooth-sayers created the rules of "mystic adoration" and "feng-shui" just to inflame commoners in anti-foreign sentiment and arrest progress.[117] Peasants saw steam-boats, clipper ships, and junks on the waters of major rivers for decades. The Chinese also invented the clock but were disinterested in standardizing time-keeping even in treaty ports.[118] According to Daniel Headrick, some Chinese naval vessels even operated by steam power during the Opium Wars.[119] But when the unsightly aberrations of railways damaged farms and killed livestock, peasants concluded that overland mechanized transport jeopardized riverine and cart-road trade. In 1876, the first twelve-mile railway built by foreign merchants from Shanghai to Wusung was purchased by the provincial governor Shen Pao-chen just so that he could tear it up the following year. In a memorial to the emperor, the governor explained that he could not allow foreigners to control China's modernization. He shipped the rails to Taiwan, but the crew threw them overboard before arrival.[120] Railways in South China suffered long delays conquering riverine systems that had served the region for centuries.

Since great rivers flowed from west to east, the imperial dynasty had built mammoth canals that linked them. The earliest Chinese advocates of railways were naval commanders, who emphasized their roles in strategic military defense by uniting the north and south of China. Despite strong support from the Board of Admiralty after 1880, foreign railway interests in China still faced staunch popular opposition. In 1887, the memorials of statesmen and officers argued that railways facilitated the movement of troops, war material, and freight, as well as increased the trade and earnings of the merchant class. Although steam locomotives existed in Europe for sixty years, the Chinese government never considered passenger travel as desirable. The admiralty recommended construction of a line from Yenchuang to Lutai and Peitang, with another segment to the north shore of Taku and Tientsin. Such a line would overcome impassable coastal obstacles to communications and trade along the eastern seaboard.[121] A coal railway owned by the Kaiping Mining Company operated efficiently for decades. By 1897, China laid just 370 miles of track, mostly to transport coal. In contrast, the U.S. had completed 182,000, Great Britain 21,000, and France 25,000. When the Boxer Rebellion broke out, rebels killed foreign missionaries, railway engineers, and employees. Boxer propaganda accused Chinese Christians of vilifying their gods and sages and conspiring with foreigners to defile temples and graveyards, angering Heaven.[122] The Boxers ripped up tracks, burned railway stations, and cut telegraph lines. The European powers in China utilized the surviving railways to put down the uprising and forced the complicit Qing Dynasty to pay an indemnity of 450 million *taels*. Forced loans underwrote railway reconstruction and expansion.

European powers built the Chinese railways without regard for the Chinese. Outraged nationalists held rallies, started a rights-recovery movement, and stopped paying taxes. In 1911–1912, the army staged a railway protest to accuse the Qing government of selling out to foreigners. One army officer cut off his finger in protest; another wrote a letter to the Qing railway company in blood. Historian Jonathan Spence summarizes Chinese nationalist sentiment:

> In Sichuan itself, when a Qing general ordered those of his troops who were members of the antigovernment Railway League to step forward so they could be identified, and expelled from the ranks, all the troops stepped forward in a show of solidarity, and the general had to rescind his order.[123]

In 1928, a married couple—the celebrated Japanese feminist poet Yosano Akiko and her husband, the romantic poet Yosano Tekkan—boarded a train on the South Manchurian Railway (SMR) at Dalian and toured Japanese-occupied Northeastern China and Mongolia. The Osaka-born Yosano Akiko enjoyed a forty-year career that spanned the Meiji (1868–1912), Taishō (1912–1926), and Shōwa (1926–1989) periods, during which she produced twenty-one collections of poems.[124] In many ways her excursion, which the SMR sponsored as a celebrity tour to promote the railway, amounted to a typical imperial visit to the colonies. The touring party visited the battlefields of the Sino-Japanese and Russo-Japanese Wars, paid their respects to Buddhist and Daoist temples and shrines, and spent leisure hours at hot springs and regional banquets. While on the trains, the Yosanos wrote poems that expressed their appreciation for the natural beauty of Manchuria and Mongolia and later interlaced them throughout a travel narrative they published. Yosano Akiko identified flora and fauna in the tradition of Humboldt and many Japanese travel writers. Transferring from the SMR to the Chinese Eastern Railway, the couple took narrow-gauge mining and colliery lines to return hastily to main depots. Sino-Japanese political tensions threatened to erupt into violence while they toured China, and the traveling party took the precautions of cancelling the journey to Beijing and staying close to the railway, which remained protected by the military. Yosano's travel narrative differs from sources generated by westerners. The Japanese feminist disapproved of the vulgarity of Japanese troops she observed at the Liaodong Hotel: "Imperialism and the smell of liquor ripled [sic] through, and the atmosphere of this inn became thoroughly incompatible with our desire to write poems about the gentle White Pagoda and the willow catkins."[125] While she was influenced by the structure and style of western travel narratives and wrote of China in a way that was consistent with Victorian worldviews, she alluded to the train's alterity in Manchuria through the perhaps unconscious but constant references to opium dens, brothels, and other forms of vice that took place in liminal spaces distant from the railways. Japanese railways in Manchuria had normalized state surveillance of heterotopias.

When travel writers from Europe and Japan described the familiar in China, they essentially illustrated the degree to which European cultural imperialism pervaded and embedded itself in foreign lands. Upon describing Manchuria, Yosano Akiko interwove powerful poetic imagery about China's natural beauty with the mundane descriptions of Japanese railway employees, innkeepers, businessmen, and their wives, who had settled in Northeastern China but insulated themselves from the Chinese.[126] Bound by the national, these writers recorded impressions of European and Japanese enclaves in China through a lens colored by the perceived prospective receptions of their reading audiences. There was no market in 1920s Japan for descriptions of the hard life of Chinese coolies, but Yosano Akiko proved conscientious and insightful, witnessing incidents that involved them along the South Manchurian Railway.

Part 1: mentalité and the machine ensemble: France and colonies

France offers a rich history of experimentation with the railway as symbols of national unification. Paul Verlaine's poem "The Scene behind the Carriage-Window Panes" initiated a conversation about the railway as window or portal into French countrysides that millions abandoned with ambivalence in search of urban industrial employment in the long nineteenth century. The rural to urban migration of landless peasants to cities predated the completion of a national network, and the railways that extended from Paris to the French frontiers offered the bourgeoisie and industrial proletariat a means to retrace their steps or reverse the journeys of their parents to pastoral birthplaces. Once built, railways continued the process of depopulating rural villages. Verlaine, the quintessential fin-de-siècle French Symbolist, evoked simple pleasures through a combination of plain language and veiled lyrics. Other nineteenth-century observers such as Andrew Dickinson took in the breathtaking scenery of a country endowed with natural beauty. Selections from the writings of George Musgrave reveal the emergence of modern railway activities, experiences, and cultures during the reigns of Louis Philippe (1847) and Napoleon III (1860s): signs inside trains posted passenger rules and prohibitions; sellers hawked newspapers at Rouen station; cranes lifted occupied carriages onto railcars; passengers fell fast asleep on a ramble to Brittany; and porters loaded sixty-two articles for a family of eight, causing the train's delay at Ardres station near Calais. Significantly, Musgrave observed the mass entry of women into the public workforce, including the presence of uniformed women as railway station attendants and signalwomen.

The picturesque French countryside transformed upon entry into a Paris that was widely considered to be the capital of Europe. Michael Quin departed the station of St. Germain-en-Laye and arrived at Paris to the sound of trumpets. In stark contrast to positive experiences were the remarks from the reliable contrarians William Makepeace Thackeray, who missed the old uncomfortable *coucous* in the journey from Paris to Versailles ("the age of horseflesh is gone"), and Mark Twain, who avowed the universality of railway "discrepancies" and "Old

Travelers," despite his claims that French trains ran like clockwork and never made mistakes ("It is hard to make railroading pleasant, in any country"). Thomas Adolphus Trollope faulted the "iron-trod intruder" for defiling a well-known French cemetery in Arles. Henry James wondered why railway travel engendered so many discomforts in the country of amenities. He abhorred the surveillance of the armed military-like railway administration and referred to the cramped enclosures of French railway carriages as human sheep-pens. The novels of Émile Zola—*Germinal* and *The Human Beast*—provided unrivaled imagery of the runaway effects of industrialism in France. The selections from Marcel Proust's *Swann's Way*, later incorporated into *Remembrance of Things Past*, explored the ways the passage of time affected childhood memories and the formation of French *mentalité*, sentimentality, and identity. All of these writers explored the heights and depths of modern industrialized transport.

Several of the selections illustrate the inseparability of French railways from the political life of the country. Frank B. Goodrich traveled through Paris during the fateful years of 1851 and 1852, which brought Louis Napoleon to power. Instead of lining the streets, adoring citizens gathered at the railway stations and along the tracks in hopes of catching a glimpse of the royal passage to cry "*Vive l'Empereur!*" Henry James succumbed to excessive Anglo-American pride when advancing the theme of France's arrested development in railways. Mary Raymond Williams offered timely observations of French railways on the eve of WWI. The section includes vignettes from Angus B. Reach and Charles Weld from the French Landes. Gordon Casserly and Lewis Gaston Leary reported on French Algeria and Syria, respectively.

Part 2: pathbreakers and stone breakers:
Belgium, Holland, and colonies

Belgium inaugurated the railway age by embracing a national railway policy and state-built lines at the time of its political formation. E. H. Derby traveled between Verviers and Liege, where a stationary engine pulled his train up an inclined plane and then shifted to locomotive power on its way to Louvain, Malines, and Antwerp. Derby traveled at a time when the railway buildings were still incomplete, but he predicted stations to be of substantial character. At that time in the early 1840s, first-class carriages stood five feet high on four wheels and passengers stooped to get in. Compartment seats sat nine passengers facing one another. The second-class carriages had curtains instead of windows. Up to forty passengers rode in the third-class. Interestingly, multilingual Belgians referred to railways in the French *chemin de fer*, the local Latinate term for tramway *via ferrem*, and the German *isebar*. Toward the end of the extract, Derby provided an early description of the central station of Malines. W. C. Dana took the "fiery-footed iron steed" into the Netherlands and Belgium. He noted the difference in speed between canal transport in Holland and the new twenty-mile-per-hour overland transport, wondering how the Dutch learned to tolerate it. He rode in the regions between Amsterdam and Leyden on the Rhine, and Haarlem and Amsterdam, mostly atop dikes and embankments that granted such panoramic views that Dana felt like he moved across the surface of the sea. After several hours' travel, he found himself in Liege, Belgium, where he violated the sensibilities of children he mistook for "impudent beggars." He joined the crowds on the double-decked omnibus and the train station to Verviers. Dana felt some anti-British sentiment one generation removed from events at Waterloo, but when he corrected Belgians with assertions that he was American, they warmed to him.

The last entries move to the Belgian Congo to examine the promotional literature for railways and critiques of railway imperialism by E. D. Morel and Reverend J. H. Whitehead. Both France and Belgium struggled to form more perfect unions and empires, one track mile at a time, but the Belgium experiment in Africa was an unredeemable disaster. In the brochure *The Congo Railway from Matadi to the Stanley-Pool*, railway promoters in Brussels turned into propagandists by categorizing and commodifying African laborers to increase investor confidence in King Leopold's latest venture. The Brussels-based railway company hoped to keep wages in Africa by hiring local workers to construct the Matadi to Stanley Pool line. Unfortunately, they only understood Africa as an endless labor pool at a time when slavery had just ended in the last holdouts of the western hemisphere: Spanish Cuba and Brazil. Theoretically, wage laborers such as the *Krooboys*, *Why*, and *Haoussas* were to build Congo railways at the competitive salaries published in the pamphlet. But when the company upheld as exemplary the contract labor systems the Portuguese used at Sao Thomé Island (St. Thomas), questions arise between theory and reality, as virtually every other facet of railway construction dehumanized the wage laborers and trickled away their earnings. Evident in the brochure was the different costs of transporting workers from distant regions, which affected pay rates. The Congolese referred to white administrators such as Henry Morton Stanley as "Bula Matadi," or stone breakers, but the metaphor emerged from African work gangs who participated in the demolition of rock during railway construction. E. D. Morel's *Red Rubber* (1906) famously exposed the unfree labor system in the Belgian Congo, and Reverend J. H. Whitehead discussed his mission to end forced labor regimes and unjustifiable taxation in "Reports and Letter of Protest to the Governor-General," an essay later published in Morel's *Recent Evidence from the Congo* (1907). Morel asked administrators to look past the artifice of progress in river steamers, railways, ocean steamers, stations, posts, and factories into the very jungle squalor where half-starved Congolese peoples lived in complete subjugation and humiliation. Rubber was the instrument of their pacification and enslavement.

Part 3: incongruous *eisenbahn*: railways in Austria, Switzerland, Germany, and colonies

Foreigners who traveled through Central Europe for the first time wrote extensively about the incongruity between the abysmal roads and highways of greater Germany on the one hand and the impressive railways on the other. In 1846,

Samuel Laing doubted that railways improved commerce and free movement so long as feeder roads were in such disrepair or nonexistent: "The Germans wish to begin building their house from the top downwards, instead of from the foundation upwards." Laing believed Germany lacked capital, "the productive industry of people," and the light manufacturing firms that lead to new jobs, products, businesses, communications, roads, and outlets for goods. He stated clearly Germany's many impediments to industrial growth and the free circulation of domestic goods in its home market. Laing cautioned also against reliance on the profitability of passenger trains. He thought railways would remain an idle fancy, until twenty-six million Germans moved beyond their "abject social state" of producing what they consume, without buying anything.

Central Europeans from major cities embraced railway transport, because the poor state of their roads was immediately visible at the outskirts. "One lives to live," a common Viennese expression from mid-century, informed the progressive urban bourgeoisie, which sought to complement their high culture in literature, music, and dance with the amenities of modern life. The Austrian *Norbahn* dates from 1837, after which European writers such as J. G. Kohl began recording the explosion of cultural activities that Viennese consumers took part in during excursions outside of the city. John W. Corson's aptly named travel diary *Loiterings in Europe* followed the occasionally rude American to Austrian cities such as Gratz and Olmutz. He recognized the American locomotive engine that pulled the Austrian train, emphasized the "stately magnificence" of Vienna as an ethnically diverse capital of the empire, and fawned over Prague, where he toured the university and Jewish quarter. Corson was among the first to ride the train from Berlin to the mouth of the Elba River, describing austere Mecklenburg-Schwerin and the colorful material culture of Hamburg. The avid transcontinental cyclist Robert L. Jefferson left his impressions of road and travel conditions in an Austria encased with muddy streets but equipped with a fully operational night train. Other authors focused on what they saw and experienced instead of succumbing to the common complaint about different timetables in each country. E. H. Derby and Nathaniel Parker Willis rode German trains around 1850. Mark Twain crossed Germany and Denmark, while Rachel Harriette Busk ventured into the Tyrol to learn about the train's use for Catholic pilgrimages to shrines. Austrian writer Peter Rosegger explored the sudden onset of the railway monster in his novel *The Light Eternal* (The Eternal Light, 1907). German cartels helped build railways throughout the world. The Duke of Mecklenburg-Schwerin, M. Longworth Dames, and A. D. C. Russell discussed German railways in Southeast Africa and the Middle East.

Part 4: Italia, España, Lusitania: railways in Italy, Spain, Portugal, and colonies

Railways in the Iberian Peninsula and Italy reflected the need for nation-states to justify the costs of overcoming tremendous geographical obstacles without having completed their industrialization processes. Engineer William J. L. Maxwell was complimentary of the Italian railways to Brindisi, which he touts as an engineering marvel save for their lack of punctuality. In 1870, he toured the mountain railway of Cenis, the fertile valley of Susa, and the grand railway station of Turin. The railway ran past the Alps, the Apennines, Ancona, and Fumini. From Brindisi, on the blue waters of the Adriatic, Maxwell took an Austrian steamer for his destination of Syria. Lina Duff Gordon embedded herself in the Italian community of Brunella in the Apennines. Her writings illuminated the important social roles of trains in courtship rituals, elopement, and emigration in 1905. A vignette authored by Edmondo de Amicis sheds light on railway cultures in Spain. Likewise, Henry N. Shore spent three springs acquainting himself with the Portuguese railway system, while also honing his skills in sarcasm. He noted the slow pace of the steam engines, large number of stops, and the great courtesy with which well-meaning railway officials masked their "badge of servitude" while having to partake of these interminable journeys themselves. Timetables that showed fourteen hours of travel time from Lisbon to Oporto (215 miles) suggested to him an average rate of fourteen miles per hour plus stops in the late 1890s. He wonders why the express with twelve fewer stops still took eleven hours, which made it impossible for travelers to conduct round-trip excursions in a single day. He suspected an overnight stay along the line was obligatory by design. The relaxed pace of transport in the land of *amanha* (tomorrow) nevertheless allowed him to view the country's natural beauty, criticize the "incubus of officialdom" that strolled leisurely at every halt, and report on Portuguese women selling *agua fresca*, working in fields, and engaging in railway construction. His train broke down within view of its destination. The many works of James Johnston exposed the painful realities of colonial life and labor in Africa. In this selection, Johnston called attention to women railway gangs and excoriates the Portuguese for enslaving native "contract workers" in Benguela (Angola) in the early 1890s.

Part 5: iron roads to the iron mountain of Scandinavia: railways in Sweden, Norway, Finland, and Denmark

For centuries, Norwegians prioritized mastery of the winding fjords that ringed their country and considered overland transport as a secondary concern. Norwegian steamship lines had achieved such a high level of safety and first-class comfort by the late nineteenth century that travelers preferred them to any form of locomotive travel. The government invested only a small share of its annual budgets on very costly railways, most of which radiated out of Christiania to towns no further than sixty miles away. Robert Stephenson actually planned the first forty-mile line to Myosen Lake, which earned him honors conferred by the King of Norway and Sweden. Horse-carts called *stolkjaerre* and *carriole* (also *kariol*)—wooden boxes that seated passengers and a driver, and pulled by celebrated breeds of Norwegian ponies—served population centers. The longest rail line in the country extended hundreds of miles to Throndhjem, a mountainous region laden with iron deposits. The Norwegians called the railway *jernbane*, iron paths that carved their way through iron mountains. By the 1880s, steamers navigated the fjords so well that Scandinavian companies began to offer huge ferries that loaded and carried entire trains leaving Denmark for Christiania and Copenhagen. While plying the waters of the North Sea, travelers often reported the picturesque scene of tugboats that serviced the steam ferry lines. Edwin Coolidge Kimball related his railway experiences traveling almost 500 miles west from Upsala, Storvik, and Ostersund stations in Sweden to Storlien, where he switched to a Norwegian train in which a railway guard announced, "Gentlemen, this is Hell; we stop for five minutes." Kimball was impressed with the quiet comfort of Swedish smorgasbords and compared the landscapes to regions in his American homeland such as New England and the Rockies. At Throndhjem on Norway's west coast, he arrived at the northernmost station in the world on a parallel line with the southern coast of Iceland. American journalist William Eleroy Curtis toured Denmark and Sweden, but his writings on Norway explained the engineering difficulties of building railways in such harsh mountainous environments. He called attention to a conversation with a customs official about his typewriter in a Norwegian sleeping car called a *slopwagen*. The "skyds-stationer" were the 1,000 inns or farmhouses that met the needs of travelers. Almost all of them near train stations rented out horses for anyone in need of local transportation. The owners used the familiar line "Be good to the horse," before entrusting any pony to guests. While the lack of railway miles limited passenger traffic, Scandinavian governments settled on the appropriate mix of transportation methods to fit their unique topographies. The letters of Francis E. and Sydney A. Clark indicated that railway travel in Finland charmed them. They traveled to and from Tammerfors in the great lake region. The authors learned that the state-owned rail system could not compete with the comfort of steamers but did provide service on the Gulf of Bothnia and ran a respectable express to St. Petersburg. The area north to Haparanda on the Swedish border reminded the Americans of New Hampshire and the Dakotas. Directions and regulations were translated in six languages, and there was never any need to rush to and from the simple wooden station buildings. Fins of the humble class suffered through the hard wooden seating of third class and relied on the foods sold by women sellers not affiliated with the railway station. Trains in Finland departed without auditory signal, so their quiet departure left behind any dilatory stragglers. Ever the dramatist, French travel writer Théophile Gautier launched his grand Russian tour with a few days in Denmark. In between his forced references to Hamlet, Balzac, and the Tower of Babel, Gautier noted losing his hat and the train stopping in the middle of a field, where passengers boarded an omnibus to take them to Schleswig. Finland Johnson Sherrick's letters of travel in Denmark addressed the topics of Danish farming and the Tivoli grounds of Copenhagen. Danish railways crossed highways on grade, and gates with women guards and a booth to shelter them in bad weather prevented highway traffic from crossing the tracks at the wrong time. Sherrick regretted that the same system did not exist in the U.S.

Part 6: railways among the ruins: Greece, the Ottoman Empire (Turkey), Czechoslovakia, and Serbia

When new railways ran among the ruins of once-great civilizations, they empha-sized not their restoration but their continued decay in the modern world. Mark Twain traveled extensively throughout Eurasia and believed that Smyrna on the Aegean coast of Anatolia (Turkey) was the gateway to Asia. In *The Innocents Abroad* (1875), the American author referred to the city of Ephesus, the ancient Greek home of the Temple of Artemis and one of the seven wonders of the ancient world. Twain also linked the region to early Christian history. He felt odd that trains ran through such hallowed grounds, surrounded by ruins from the classical world. There was something profane about a failing railway that carried a mere eight hundred pounds of figs a year through the birthplace of the gods. Twain's traveling party included sixty donkeys for travel beyond the end of the railway. Annie Brassey's *Sunshine and Storm in the East*—published just after the Russo-Turkish War (1878)—pursued the theme of declining empires with despondent poetry and complaints about bad weather, food scarcity and filth at Tchorlou sta-tion, and the French company that botched the railway line. Her arrival at Lilli Bourgas, controlled by the Russians, hardly improved travel conditions to Adri-anople (a Russian soldier tried to steal Brassey's luggage but was foiled by her servant). Brassey reported on heart-wrenching scenes. Starving Turkish refugees lined up for miles at railway stations hoping for free passage on steps and buf-fers, even though paying customers made this unlikely by filling the carriages of departing trains. Carts brought food to those in line and left with corpses, espe-cially after overnight frosts that took the lives of children. Olive Gilbreath's *Men of Bohemia* (1918) traced the *hegira* of Czech regiments from Bohemia, who fought in WWI alongside their Slavic brethren in Russia, seized Kiev, but fled to Siberia when Germany recaptured the city. War-torn Europe was also the setting for "Milorad," the name of a Serbian orphan in Mary Heaton Vorse's short story from *Harper's Magazine* (1919).

Part 7: Russian prologues, dialogues, and travelogues

Russian travelogues are rich resources of information because travel writers always had plenty of time on their hands to furnish thick descriptions of what they saw and experienced. At railway stations, they endured the longest waiting times in the world. The distances they traveled were among the longest in the world. At rates of fifteen miles per hour in the 1890s, the time it took to cover those distances were the longest in the world. And as we shall see, Russian trains did not have to break down for conductors to slow to a deliberate crawl. The Russian section begins in St. Petersburg in the 1870s, where the routine delay detained Theóphile Gautier long enough to witness a unique custom. Russians bade fare-well to their friends and loved ones by boarding the train with them, riding for a stop or two, then returning to the original station of departure after the prolonged goodbye. Standing idly on freezing railway platforms was sheer folly. Rather than expose themselves to the bluster of winter, families made the most of situations in the perfect comfort of warm, oversized Russian railway carriages. Decked in "pelisse of marten, cap of beaver, furred boots," Gautier observed a railway culture fully acclimated to temperatures of −30 and −40 degrees Fahrenheit. In Moscow, passengers found no outdoor tables for *samovars* (urns) of tea or hot water, which quickly froze. They entered railway carriages by balustrade and ante-room and warmed their hands at wood stoves in each railcar. Felt weather-stripping sealed windows from cold drafts. And spring-seated armchairs that resembled living room furniture gave the impression of riding in a "house on wheels." Gautier concluded that one might actually feel colder on the Spanish train from Burgos to Valladolid.

To say nothing of the Trans-Siberian Railway, the severe climate and desolate landscape along the tracks from St. Petersburg to Moscow resembled the surface of the moon. Snow concealed roads until the galloping horses that pulled the troika, sledge, or tarantass uncovered them. Gautier spied the occasional green-lighted bulbs or copper cupulas that topped church steeples but only saw human activity when trains halted in the middle of magnificent railway stations. Once passengers from every direction disembarked, they reconstituted the Tower of Babel at every railway junction. To most Russians the railways represented shelter from the storm, but to others they offered no protection of any kind. Tolstoy, more than any other celebrated Russian author, despised the railway and all that it represented. To Russian political dissidents, railways symbolized imprisonment, exile, and their status as pariahs in isolated Siberia. To Russian convicts, railways signified years of hard labor as punishment for their crimes. A common scene in Tsarist Russia was the prison train pulling mobile jail cells full of prisoners on their way to Siberia. None of Tolstoy's utterings demonized the iron monster quite like the denouement of his protagonist in the novel *Anna Karenina*.

The family of Russian photographer Sergei Mikhailovich Prokudin-Gorskii kindly bestowed the treasure of his life's work to the U.S. Library of Congress. The images serve as an unmatched prologue to three sections on Russian railways. Prokudin-Gorskii traveled extensively by train and handcar throughout the Russian Empire from 1905–1915, on a mission supported by Tsar Nicholas II to document with visual images the incredible ethnic diversity of its peoples. To conduct this variant of internal colonialism, the Ministry of Transportation provided him with a passenger car that doubled as his living area and photo-developing laboratory. Prokudin-Gorskii toured the Russian northwest city of Petrozavodska (Karelia). He later stopped at villages close to the rails in the Volga-Baltic waterway, the Caucuses and Black Sea regions of Georgia, Artvin (Turkey), Dagestan (along the Caspian Sea), Samarkand (in Azerbaijan), and the Bakal and Ekhia areas of the Urals. Less interested in photographing the "Kompaund" steam engine with its Schmidt super-heater that pulled his carriage, the photographer focused instead on the ethnographic themes of quotidian life and material culture: what women and men wore daily and on special occasions, how their log homes and yurts reflected domestic adaptation to their environmental surroundings, and how village traditions influenced their lifestyles. Since the settings and contexts of the photographs are known, as well as chosen, the subjects of Prokudin-Gorskii's photography are in fact modern. The customary dresses of women might be traditional, but they wear them for still portraits composed by a professional photographer. The rugs, log cabins, and park surroundings similarly support participating in the ethnographic present. The writings of Maurice Baring provide literary narratives for the visual images left by Russia's photographer. As the travel writer for the *Morning Post*, Baring was among the most influential and accomplished travel writers of his times.

Part 8: strategic Russian railways, resources, and representations

British Correspondent Charles Dobson covered the opening of Russia's Trans-Caspian Railway for the *Times* (London) in spring 1888. Two years later he published a revised and expanded version of those writings in his book *Russia's Railway Advance into Central Asia: Notes of a Journey from St. Petersburg to Samarkand* (1890). The Russian War Ministry invited him and several journalists from Reuters on the maiden journey of the completed line. Dobson's adventure suggested everything but a completed line, but he successfully explained the difficulties the Russian empire faced carving a path through mountains, deserts, oases, and flood-plains inhabited by trans-Caspian peoples from centuries of religious and cultural traditions. At 10,000 square miles, the trans-Caspian region is larger than France. The astute observations culled from Dobson's journey rendered the region understandable. C. E. Biddulph traveled the trans-Caspian line two years later, praising modifications, comparing the region to the Sind and Punjab in British India (modern Pakistan), and identifying its commercial potential as an exporter of agriculture. In *Four Months in Persia and a Visit to Trans-Caspia* (1892), Biddulph was less interested in Russian military objectives so much as the magical "civilizing" influence of the railway on the "troublesome races." These themes were further explored in Sir Henry Norman's writings in *All the Russias* (1903), which chronicled his 20,000-mile journey through European and Asiatic Russia. Railway construction through the Caucuses and Caspian regions in the 1870s and 1880s served as precedents for railway expansion into Siberia in the 1890s.

Part 9: test of the Russian will: the Trans-Siberian Railway

At five million square miles, Siberia is twenty-five times the size of Germany. The Trans-Siberian Railway, built from 1891–1898, was a colossal undertaking that tested Russia's will to consolidate its empire and confront the modern world on its own terms, even if underprepared. Russia built the railway by commencing construction simultaneously from both ends. Although sections of it were shoddily built, the railway survived the Russo-Japanese War, WWI, and the Romanov Dynasty that completed it. Before it achieved its reputation as a great feat in railway engineering, Russia's lifeline to East Asia fell under intense scrutiny from the first wave of westerners who breeched Siberia in Russian trains. One such critic, Robert L. Jefferson, shared his opinions before the rail's completion and seemed not to understand what "roughing it" meant until his travels to Omsk, Tomsk, and Krasnoyarsk. Jefferson's incisive and often humorous critique of the early days of the Siberian line was a cautionary tale not of the railway's positive influence on Siberia but of Siberia's notoriety in the minds of western readers. James Young Simpson, a contributor to *Blackwood's Magazine*, added to this negative impression when he toured Siberian prisons, studied the exile system, and witnessed first-hand the mass migration of peasants to Siberia in summer 1896. At many points in his narrative, Simpson sympathizes with and apologizes for Russian officials, against convicts and political prisoners, but he deplored fourth-class travel conditions for emigrants on their week-long journeys aboard railways. He detailed Russian convict labor policy and explained the hardships felt by settlers at Atchinsk, where his train derailed for three hours; another fourth-class carriage he rode decoupled, and four days passed covering a section that normally took thirty-six hours. Travel conditions for foreigners, however, far surpassed the hard rabble life of Siberians. Without a mill in sight, each sleeper, supporting pile, and piece of lattice-girder bridge was hand-sawed by workers who earned 1 ½ rubles daily. Listening to hungry peasants sing folk songs, Simpson wondered: "Why had they left Poltava to die on the Siberian steppe?" Although he did not criticize the government railways, his detailed narrative led readers to condemn the Ministry of Transportation for not using its railway network to alleviate the suffering of abandoned underclasses. The same may not be said about Isabella L. Bird's complimentary description of the Ussuri Railway out of Vladivostok west to Khabarovsk on the eastern section of the Trans-Siberian Railway. Bird's comments on railway development in the Amur and Ussuri provinces of Eastern Siberia date from 1894, two years before the painful ordeals of Jefferson and Simpson. Russia resolved many shortcomings on its Siberian lines by the time second-wave rider Annette M. B. Meakin experienced the railway cultures of Siberia. In stark contrast to earlier accounts, Meakin labelled the "Train de Luxe" Siberian Express her "Liberty Hall," for the coveted privacy and relaxed speeds it offered her and her mother in May 1900. Carriage compartments were fitted with electric lights, and the dining car featured a Bechstein piano, a bookcase full of Russian novels, and portraits of the emperor and empress. During the long journey, Meakin learned about Russian superstitions, sighted the landmark Alexander Bridge over the Volga, witnessed a railway employee attend to a typhus victim, visited the Church Railway Carriage, rode the ice-breaker on Lake Baikal, and discovered the utter meaningless of time and distance in Siberia. Travel conditions worsened the farther east she traveled, until she faced the prospect of joining the very emigrants she described as "lying in heaps" at stations and in fourth-class carriages.

A fascinating shift toward systematic persecution and revolutionary violence took place in Russia, according to the observations of third-wave travelers in Russia after 1890. Leo Deutsch, the Bolshevik revolutionary Lev Grigorievich Deutsch, recalled his own arrest, exile to the Kara region of Siberia, and escape in 1900. Lindon Bates, Jr. related the stories of political prisoners he interviewed in *The Russian Road to China*. Even the light fare of Richardson L. Wright, Basset Digby, and their intrepid fox-terrier Jack intensified during the fifty-hour train ride from Irkutsk to Stretrensk.

Part 10: the iron road meets the silk road: railways in Japan and China

Two years after Commodore Matthew C. Perry sailed to Japan, Francis L. Hawks compiled and published his *Narrative of the Expedition of an American Squadron to the China Seas and Japan*. The account reported that the Japanese remained apprehensive about the motives of the American mission and listed the inventory of "presents" that Perry gave to Japanese authorities. It also delineated roles played by Captains Adams and Abbott, telegraphic experts Draper and Williams, and railway engineers Gay and Danby. The letters of L. D. F. Swainson described the Mikado and the modernizing policies of Japan in 1872, when he inaugurated the Edo to Yokohama line. Isabella Bird subjected Japan to her eternal scrutiny in a diary she published as *Unbeaten Tracks in Japan: An Account of Travels on Horseback in the Interior*. She wondered why the railroad stations were not carpeted to accommodate the resonant clogs of Japanese women. Although she rode in English-built railway cars, she noted a few differences in their seating arrangement and appointments. She disliked the adoption of English fashion, but the *daimyo yashikis* or nobility's mansions elicited her attention. E. G. Holtham spent eight years in Japan (1873–1881) as a railway contractor involved in the construction of its earliest lines. He commented on the difficulties of waiting for authorization and complimented Japanese railway employees. W. S. Caine's *Trip Round the World* brought him to several cities in 1887–1888, including Edo, Yokohama, Nikko, and Utsunomiya. By that time Japan had 150 miles of track laid and another 450 projected. He and other travelers still rode "rickshaws," a corruption of the Japanese word *jinrickisha* for single-seat vehicles pulled by a man. Locals seemed fascinated with Caine's foreign appearance, especially his red beard. Lafcadio Hearn's shocking short story "Red Bridal" appeared in a collection entitled *Out of the East: Reveries and Studies in New Japan*. Mrs. Hugh Fraser's *Letters from Japan* center on the demoralizing effects of the railways out of Yokukawa. Marie C. Stopes was a scientist in Japan whose journal included sections on her railway experiences. Baroness Albert d'Anethan (Eleanora Mary Anethan) highlighted her long stay in Tokyo with a record of Japan's initial reactions to news about the war in *Fourteen Years of a Diplomatic Life in Japan*.

The section on China begins with Frank E. Younghusband's *The Heart of a Continent*. Younghusband wrote about the deaths of Chinese settlers in Manchuria and conversations he overheard among British Navvies at Kaiping. John Foster Fraser reminded the world that Chinese Harbin (also Kharbin) in Manchuria was a Russian town with a Chinese workforce. R. Logan Jack was stuck in Chengtu on the Tsientsin Railway during the Boxer uprising. Wright's and Digby's best joint publication, *Through Siberia: An Empire in the Making*, narrated their experiences in Russian Kharbin as well as the Chinese village called Tsitsitcar. *On the Trail of the Opium Poppy* was Sir Alexander Hosie's travel narrative through Peking to the Yellow River. A glimpse of Canton by C. E. Bechhofer closes the section on Eurasia.

Notes

1 George Musgrave, *The Parson, Pen, and Pencil: Or, Reminiscences and Illustrations of an Excursion to Paris, Tours, and Rouen in the Summer of 1847*, 2 vols. (London: R. Bentley, 1848), I: 129–130.

2 Benjamin Gastineau, *La vie en chemin de fer* (Paris: E. Dentu, 1861), 50. Cited in Walter Benjamin, *The Arcades Project* (Cambridge: Belknap Press of Harvard University), 588.

3 *Ibid.*

4 Paul Verlaine, *Poems of Paul Verlaine*, Trans. Gertrude Hall (New York: Duffield, 1906), 22; Paul Verlaine, *Poems*, Trans. Ashmore Wingate (London: The Walter Scott Pub. Co., 1904), 77; Anne Green, *Changing France: Literature and Material Culture in the Second Empire* (London: Anthem, 2011), 62–64.

5 Green, 62–63.

6 J. H. Clapham, *The Economic Development of France and Germany*, Fourth ed. (Cambridge: Cambridge University Press, 1968), 140–143.

7 Michael G. Mulhall, *The Dictionary of Statistics* (London: George Routledge and Sons, 1892), 545–547.

8 Dietrich Orlow, *A History of Modern Germany, 1871 to Present* (Englewood Cliffs, N.J.: Prentice Hall, 1987), 89.

9 Michaelis was editor of the *National-Zeitung*. See James M. Brophy, *Capitalism, Politics, and Railroads in Prussia, 1830–1870* (Columbus: The Ohio State University Press, 1998), 22–23, 165.

10 Clapham, 150.

11 Green, *Fatherlands: State-Building and Nationhood in Nineteenth-Century Germany* (Cambridge: Cambridge University Press, 2011), 223–266.

12 Laia Mojica and Jordi Martí-Henneberg, "Railways and Population Distribution: France, Spain, and Portugal, 1870–2000," *Journal of Interdisciplinary History* XLII: 1 (Summer 2011), 18.

13 Mojica and Martí-Henneberg, 23–26.

14 *Ibid.*, 23, Figure 3.

15 James Young Simpson, *Side-lights on Siberia; Some Account of the Great Siberian Railroad, the Prisons and Exile System* (Edinburgh and London: W. Blackwood and Sons, 1898), 39–45, quote on 40.

16 Mojica and Martí-Henneberg, 19.

17 Clapham, 145.

18 Eugen Weber, *France: Fin de Siècle* (Cambridge: Belknap Press of Harvard University, 1986), 52, 68.

19 Musgrave, I: 129–130.

20 Kimon A. Doukas, *The French Railroads and the State* (New York: Columbia University Press, 1945), Table 1, p. 24. Converted from the km.

21 Allan Mitchell, *The Great Train Race: Railways and the Franco-German Rivalry, 1815–1914* (New York: Berghahn Books, 2000), 9.

22 Mitchell, 1–4.

23 Doukas, 22–23, 29–30.

24 Arthur Louis Dunham, *The Anglo-French Treaty of Commerce of 1860 and the Progress of the Industrial Revolution in France* (Ann Arbor: University of Michigan Press, 1930; reprint ed., New York: Octagon Books, 1971), 14, 20, 141, 168, 177.

25 Verne, *From the Earth to the Moon*, Trans. Eleanor E. King (New York: Scribner, Armstrong, 1874); Maxime du Camp cited in Green, 36 and 36fn5.

26 A. T. J. Bullard, *Sights and Scenes in Europe: A Series of Letters from England, France, Germany, Switzerland, and Italy, in 1850* (St. Louis: Chambers & Knapp, 1852), 216.

27 Mitchell, 24.

28 Mark Twain, *The Innocents Abroad* (Hartford: American Publishing Company, 1875), 108.

29 Pierre Lévy, "The Railroads in France," Trans. E. Douglass Burdick, *The Annals of the American Academy of Political Science* 187: 1 (Sept. 1936), 184; Clapham, 147; Doukas, 12–15.

30 Lévy, 184–192; Doukas, 11–48.

31 Mulhall, (1892), 546; (1899), 496; Augustus D. Webb, *A New Dictionary of Statistics* (London: George Routledge & Sons, 1911), 511, 518.

32 Eugen Weber, *Peasants into Frenchmen: The Modernization of Rural France, 1870–1914* (Stanford: Stanford University Press, 1976), 197.

33 Doukas, 24.

34 Weber, *Peasants into Frenchmen*, 197; Weber, *France: Fin de Siècle*, 68.

35 James John Hissey, *Over Fen and Wold* (London: Macmillan and Co., 1898), 127.

36 Weber, *Peasants into Frenchmen*, 197, 205. Quote on 205.

37 Weber, *France: Fin de Siècle*, 51–53.

38 Mojica and Martí-Henneberg, 23 (Figure 3), 26.

39 Henry Blackburn, *Artistic Travel* (London: S. Low, Marston, 1892), 38.

40 Weber, 203–206. From 1882 to 1910, the multi-billion-franc Freycinet Plan extended the length of rail in France from 26,327 km to 64,898 km.

41 Weber, *Peasants into Frenchmen*, 210.

42 *Ibid.*, 206–220.

43 Doukas, 92.

44 Lévy, 184.

45 Marcel Proust, *Remembrance of Things Past*, Trans. C. K. Scott Moncrief, 2 vols. (New York: Random House, 1934), I: 490. For Benjamin's reference see *The Arcades Project*, 561.

46 *Ibid.*

47 C. K. Moncrieff, "Introduction," in *Ibid.*, vii.

48 Orlow, 10, 22.

49 Clapham, 150–151; Green, 223.

50 Edward Wilkey, *Wanderings in Germany*, 2 vols. (London: Ball, Arnold, 1839), 64, 209; Peter Swan Turnbull, *Austria*, 2 vols. (London: J. Murray, 1840), II: 362.

51 Mulhall (1892), 495; Clapham, 152–153.

52 Quoted in Youngman, 21, 50.

53 *Ibid.*, 10, 31, 41, 46–48. Quotes on pp. 10 and 31.

54 *Ibid.*, 55–56, 64–67.

55 *Ibid.*, 67, 70–71, 153.

56 Youngman, 118, 126. The other two authors Youngman analyzes are Theodor Fontane and Max Eyth. Fontane is less deliberate about using railways as an integral literary device. Since Eyth began his writing career at age 60, and his work is less known.

57 Green, 240; Youngman, 6–7.

58 Mitchell, 38–42.

59 Green, 256–259.

60 Youngman, 6.

61 Mitchell, 43–46, 50.

62 *Ibid.*, 52; Youngman, 5–6.

63 Youngman, 19.

64 Edmund Burke II, "The Terror and Religion: Brittany and Algeria," in Gregory Blue, Martin Bunton, and Ralph Croizier, eds., *Colonialism and the Modern World: Selected Studies* (New York: M. E. Sharpe, 2002), 40–50.

65 *Ibid.*, 49–50.

66 E. D. Brant, *Railways of North Africa* (Newton Abbot: David & Charles, 1971), 11–16, 20, 25, 32–33; Benjamin E. Thomas, "The Railways of French North Africa," *Economic Geography* 29: 2 (April 1953), 95–106.

67 Adam Hochschild, *King Leopold's Ghost* (New York: Houghton Mifflin, 1998), 281.

68 John Pendleton, *Our Railways: Their Origin, Development, Incident and Romance*, 2 vols. (London: Cassell and Company, 1894), II: 101.

69 See Sean McMeekin, *The Berlin-Baghdad Express: The Ottoman Empire and Germany's Bid for World Power* (Cambridge: Belknap Press of Harvard University Press, 2010).

70 David Wilson Del Testa, "Paint the Trains Red: Labor, Nationalism, and the Railroads in French Colonial Indochina, 1898–1945," (Ph.D. dissertation, University of California, Davis, 2001), 2, 33.

71 Michael Adas, *Machines as the Measure of Men: Science, Technology, and the Ideologies of Western Dominance* (Ithaca: Cornell University Press, 1989), 159–163.

72 James A. Jones, *Industrial Labor in the Colonial World: Workers of the Chemin de Fer Dakar-Niger, 1881–1963* (Portsmouth, N.H.: Heinemann, 2002).

73 Sir Harry Hamilton Johnston, *A History of the Colonization of Africa* (London: Cambridge University Press, 1913), 210–211.

74 Hochschild, 170–171.

75 *Ibid.*, 171.

76 *Ibid.*, 173. Cited in Hochschild; Sigbert Axelson, *Culture Confrontation in the Lower Congo: From the Old Congo Kingdom to the Congo Independent State with Special Reference to the Swedish Missionaries in the 1880s and 1890s* (Falkoping, Sweden: Gummessons, 1970), 204.

77 Johnston, 420, 422.

78 Eric J. Hobsbawm, *The Age of Empire, 1875–1914* (London: Weidenfeld and Nicolson, 1987), 27, 52, 62.

79 Cited in Sir Henry Norman, *All the Russias: Travels and Studies in Contemporary Russia, Finland, Siberia, the Caucasus, and Central Asia* (New York: Scribner's Sons, 1903), 172.

80 *The Mammoth and Mammoth-Hunting in North-East Siberia* (New York: D. Appleton and Company, 1926), 96.

81 Robert L. Jefferson, *Roughing it in Siberia* (London: S. Low, Marston & Co., 1897), 21.

82 Jefferson, 2–4, 14; Simpson, 39.

83 Harry de Windt, *Through Savage Europe* (London: T. F. Unwin, 1907), 282.

84 Robert L. Jefferson, *A New Ride to Khiva* (New York: New Amsterdam Book Co., 1900), 161.

85 *Ibid.*, 163–165.

86 de Windt, *Through Savage Europe*, 280.

87 Sir Henry Norman, 43.

88 *Ibid.*

89 Théophile Gautier, *A Winter in Russia*, Trans. M. M. Ripley (New York: H. Holt and Company, 1874), 238. See also Wirt Gerrare (William Oliver Greener), *Greater Russia: The Continental Empire of the Old World* (New York: Macmillan, 1904).

90 Mulhall (1892), 495.

91 *Russia's Railway Advance into Central Asia: Notes of a Journey from St. Petersburg to Samarkand* (London: W. H. Allen, 1890), 29.

92 *From Dawn to Decadence: 500 Years of Western Cultural Life, 1500 to the Present* (New York: HarperCollins, 2000), 542.

93 Christian Wolmar, *Engines of War: How Wars Were Won and Lost on the Railways* (New York: Public Affairs, 2010), 111.

94 Anthony Heywood, *Modernizing Lenin's Russia: Economic Reconstruction, Foreign Trade, and the Railways* (Cambridge: Cambridge University Press, 1999), 14–15; Wolmar, *Engines of War*, 111.

95 Simpson, 25.

96 Wright and Digby, *Through Siberia: An Empire in the Making* (New York: McBride, Nash, 1913), 14–16.

97 de Windt, *Through Savage Europe*, 280.

98 Simpson, 60.

99 Harry de Windt, *The New Siberia* (London: Chapman and Hall, 1896), 147. For an introduction to travel along the Siberian Railway, see Deborah Manley, *The Trans-Siberian Railway: A Traveller's Anthology* (Oxford: Signal Books, 2009).

100 Harry de Windt, *From Paris to New York by Land* (New York: F. Warne & Company, 1904), 11–12.

101 Digby, *Unknown Siberia*, 15.

102 *Ibid.*, 7–11.

103 Wright and Digby, *Through Siberia*, 2–11, Quotes on 2–3.

104 Steven J. Ericson, "Taming the Iron Horse: Western Locomotive Makers and Technology Transfer in Japan, 1870–1914," in Gail Lee Bernstein, Andrew Gordon, and Kate Wildman Nakai, eds., *Public Spheres, Private Lives in Modern Japan, 1600–1950: Essays in Honor of Albert M. Craig* (Cambridge: Harvard University Asia Center, 2005), 191.

105 Bentaro Kamiyama, "Railway Transportation in Japan," (Unpublished Ph.D. dissertation, University of Wisconsin, 1905), 1–2.

106 *Ibid.*, 71.

107 Eiichi Aoki "Railway Construction as Viewed from Local Society," unpublished manuscript, The United Nations University, 1980, 19.

108 Tom Richards and Charles Rudd, *Japanese Railways in the Meiji Period, 1868–1912* (Uxbridge: Brunel University, 1991), 1, 12, 14.

109 *Farthest East, and South and West: Notes of a Journey through Japan, Australasia, and America by an Anglo-Indian Globetrotter* (London: W.H. Allen & Co., 1892), 73–74, 81, 116–117.

110 *Ibid.*, 107–108

111 Sir Hugh Cortazzi, "Introduction," in Richards and Rudd, *Japanese Railways in the Meiji Period*, 1.

112 Kamiyama, 7–8.

113 Aoki, 12; Ericson, 18.

114 Paul H. Noguchi, *Delayed Departures, Overdue Arrivals: Industrial Familialism and the Japanese National Railways* (Honolulu: University of Hawai'i Press, 1990), 22, 82.

115 John King Fairbank, *China: A New History* (Cambridge: The Belknap Press of Harvard University Press, 1992), 219.

116 Adas, 160.

117 C. F. Gordon Cumming, *Wanderings in China* (Edinburgh: W. Blackwood & Sons, 1888), 234–235.

118 Adas, 249.

119 The *Tools of Empire: Technology and European Imperialism in the Nineteenth Century* (New York: Oxford University Press, 1981), Chapters 1 and 2.

120 John King Fairbank, *The Great Chinese Revolution, 1800–1985* (New York: Harper and Row, 1987), 4, 99, 118; Adas, *Machines as the Measure of Men*, 232; Clarence B. Davis, "Railway Imperialism in China, 1895–1939," in Clarence B. Davis and Kenneth E. Wilburn, Jr., eds. with Ronald Robinson, *Railway Imperialism* (New York: Greenwood Press, 1991), 159.

121 "Railways" and "Prospectus of the First Chinese Railway," in R. S. Gundry, *China: Present and Past* (London: Chapman and Hall, 1895), Appendices C and D, 394–400.

122 Fairbank, 137.

123 Jonathan Spence, *The Search for Modern China* (New York: W.W. Norton, 1990), 228–254. Quote appears on p. 254. See also Bruce Elleman and Steven Kotkin, eds., *Manchurian Railways and the Opening of China: An International History* (New York: M.E. Sharpe, 2010).

124 Janine Beichman, *Embracing the Firebird: Yosano Akiko and the Birth of the Female Voice in Modern Japanese Poetry* (Honolulu: University of Hawai'i Press, 2002), 1–2.

125 Yosano Akiko, *Travels in Manchuria and Mongolia: A Feminist Poet from Japan Encounters Prewar China* (New York: Columbia University Press, 2001), 43.

126 Joshua A. Fogel, "Yosano Akiko and Her China Travelogue," in Yosano Akiko, *Travels in Manchuria and Mongolia*, 6.

Part 1

MENTALITÉ AND THE MACHINE ENSEMBLE
France and colonies

1

PAUL VERLAINE, 'THE SCENE BEHIND THE CARRIAGE-WINDOW PANES', IN *POEMS OF PAUL VERLAINE*, TRANS. GERTRUDE HALL (NEW YORK: DUFFIELD, 1906), P. 22

THE scene behind the carriage window-panes
Goes flitting past in furious flight; whole plains
With streams and harvest-fields and trees and blue
Are swallowed by the whirlpool, whereinto
The telegraph's slim pillars topple o'er,
Whose wires look strangely like a music-score.

A smell of smoke and steam, a horrid din
As of a thousand clanking chains that pin
A thousand giants that are whipped and howl,—
And, suddenly, long hoots as of an owl.

What is it all to me? Since in mine eyes
The vision lingers that beatifies,
Since still the soft voice murmurs in mine ear,
And since the Name, so sweet, so high, so dear,
Pure pivot of this madding whirl, prevails
Above the brutal clangor of the rails?

2

WILLIAM MAKEPEACE THACKERAY, *THE PARIS SKETCHBOOK OF MR. M. A. TITMARSH; THE IRISH SKETCH BOOK; & NOTES OF A JOURNEY FROM CORNHILL TO GRAND CAIRO* (NEW YORK: CAXTON, 1840), PP. 265–267

Meditations at Versailles

THE palace of Versailles has been turned into a bric-a-brac shop of late years, and its time-honored walls have been covered with many thousand yards of the worst pictures that eye ever looked on. I don't know how many leagues of battles and sieges the unhappy visitor is now obliged to march through, amidst a crowd of chattering Paris cockneys, who are never tired of looking at the glories of the Grenadier Français; to the chronicling of whose deeds this old palace of the old kings is now altogether devoted. A whizzing, screaming steam-engine rushes hither from Paris, bringing shoals of *badauds* in its wake. The old *coucous* are all gone, and their place knows them no longer. Smooth asphaltum terraces, tawdry lamps, and great hideous Egyptian obelisks, have frightened them away from the pleasant station they used to occupy under the trees of the Champs Elysées; and though the old *coucous* were just the most uncomfortable vehicles that human ingenuity ever constructed, one can't help looking back to the days of their existence with a tender regret; for there was pleasure then in the little trip of three leagues: and who ever had pleasure in a railroad journey? Does any reader of this venture to say that, on such a voyage, he ever dared to be pleasant? Do the most hardened stokers joke with one another? I don't believe it. Look into every single car of the train, and you will see that every single face is solemn. They take their seats gravely, and are silent, for the most part, during the journey; they dare not look out of window, for fear of being blinded by the smoke that comes whizzing by, or of losing their heads in one of the windows of the down train; they ride for miles in utter damp and darkness: through awful pipes of brick, that have been run pitilessly through the bowels of gentle mother earth, the cast-iron Frankenstein of an engine gallops on, puffing and screaming. Does any man pretend to say that he *enjoys* the journey?—he might as well say that he enjoyed having his hair cut; he bears it, but that is all: he will not allow the world to laugh at him, for any exhibition of slavish fear; and pretends, therefore, to be at his ease; but he *is* afraid: nay, ought to be, under the circumstances. I am sure Hannibal or Napoleon would, were they locked suddenly into a car; there kept close prisoners for a certain number of hours, and whirled along at this dizzy pace. You can't stop, if you would:—you may die, but you can't stop; the engine may explode upon the road, and up you go along with it; or, may be a bolter, and take a fancy to go down a hill, or into a river: all this you must bear, for the privilege of travelling twenty miles an hour.

This little journey, then, from Paris to Versailles, that used to be so merry of old, has lost its pleasures since the disappearance of the *coucous;* and I would as lief have for companions the statues that lately took a coach from the bridge opposite the Chamber of Deputies, and stepped out in the court of Versailles, as the most part of the people who now travel on the railroad. The stone figures are not a whit more cold and silent than these persons, who used to be, in the old *coucous,* so talkative and merry. The prattling grisette and her swain from the Ecole de Droit; the huge Alsacian carabinier, grimly smiling under his sandy mustaches and glittering brass helmet; the jolly nurse, in red calico, who had been to Paris to show mamma her darling Lolo, or Auguste;—what merry companions used one to find squeezed into the crazy old vehicles that formerly performed the journey! But the age of horseflesh is gone—that of engineers, economists, and calculators has succeeded; and the pleasure of *coucoudom* is extinguished forever. Why not mourn over it, as Mr. Burke did over his cheap defence of nations and unbought grace of life; that age of chivalry, which he lamented, àpropos of a trip to Versailles, some half a century back?

Without stopping to discuss (as might be done, in rather a neat and successful manner) whether the age of chivalry was cheap or dear, and whether, in the time of the unbought grace of life, there was not more bribery, robbery, villany, tyranny, and corruption, than exists even in our own happy days,—let us make a few moral and historical remarks upon the town of Versailles; where, between railroad and *coucou,* we are surely arrived by this time.

The town is, certainly, the most moral of towns. You pass from the railroad station through a long, lonely suburb, with dusty rows of stunted trees on either side, and some few miserable beggars, idle boys, and ragged old women under them. Behind the trees are gaunt, mouldy houses; palaces once, where (in the days of the unbought grace of life) the cheap defence of nations gambled, ogled, swindled, intrigued; whence high-born duchesses used to issue, in old times, to act as chambermaids to lovely Du Barri; and mighty princes rolled away, in gilt caroches, hot for the honor of lighting his Majesty to bed, or of presenting his stockings when he rose, or of holding his napkin when he dined. Tailors, chandlers, tinmen, wretched hucksters, and greengrocers, are now established in the mansions of the old peers; small children are yelling at the doors, with mouths besmeared with bread and treacle; damp rags are hanging out of every one of the windows, steaming in the sun; oyster-shells, cabbage stalks, broken crockery, old papers, lie basking in the same cheerful light. A solitary water-cart goes jingling down the wide pavement, and spirts a feeble refreshment over the dusty, thirsty stones.

3

MICHAEL J. QUIN, *STEAM VOYAGES ON THE SEINE, THE MOSELLE, & THE RHINE, WITH RAILROAD VISITS TO THE PRINCIPAL CITIES OF BELGIUM, 2 VOLS. (LONDON: H. COLBURN, 1843), II, PP. 71–75*

The extensive park belonging to this splendid domain has been lately divided into a considerable number of allotments, for the erection of villas and cottages in the old English style, such as we see in the Regent's Park village. But the ancient trees have not been all cut down, as they infallibly would have been by an English builder in the first instance. The old avenues and plantations are preserved as much as the advantageous disposal of the ground will permit, and with a view to the embellishment of the cottages constructed amongst them. More than a hundred of these charming country habitations have been already finished and occupied. Being situated upon rising ground, they command ample prospects of the territory all round; and as the journey from them to Paris, especially since the railway to St. Germain-en-Laye has come into operation, is reduced to a few sous in expense, and to less than an hour in point of time, they have been much sought after by the prosperous citizens.

We arrived at St. Germain-en-Laye at a quarter past seven o'clock; landed, walked to the railway station-house in eight or ten minutes, and obtained there tickets in return for checks, which were put into our hands as we quitted the steamer. The charge for these tickets, which I believe is half a franc, was included in our fare; so, of course, we had nothing to pay. The station-house is a magnificent building, and the arrangements for the accommodation of passengers appeared to me in every respect unobjectionable. There were a great many applicants for places: but no rude contentions—no pushing about—no disorder of any kind.

We entered the carriage indicated by our tickets, a roomy and well-constructed vehicle, without much show about it, and set off to the sound of a trumpet, slowly at first; the speed then was gradually increased until it attained a velocity, at no time, I think, exceeding fifteen miles an hour. The trumpeter kept on sounding the whole way—a precaution that might be introduced into our railway arrangements with the most useful effect. The warning would be heard to a considerable distance; and if it had been in use here these last two years, it would have undoubtedly prevented many accidents of a most disastrous nature. The vibration of the train of carriages was somewhat more than I had been accustomed to in England.

We traversed the distance from the point of our departure to Paris in twenty-seven minutes. At the terminus, omnibuses were in waiting for passengers to all parts of the capital. We entered one, which conveyed us to the Rue de Rivoli for six sous: stopping at the gate of Meurice's hotel, we descended, and found ourselves in the *salon* of that most comfortable establishment, precisely at half-past eight o'clock.

In all my travels I never performed a journey more delightful than this was in every way. We quitted London at ten o'clock on the Wednesday morning—reached Havre in eighteen hours, that is, at four o'clock on Thursday morning—stopped there until seven—embarked on board the "Normandie"—arrived at Rouen about one the same day—left Rouen on Friday morning at half-past four—and sat down in Meurice's hotel at half-past eight the same evening. Thus the possibility of fatigue was, I may say, excluded. We slept, ate, drank, walked about, nearly as we should have done if we had been at home; passed through a long succession of the most beautiful and diversified scenery in France, took a short survey of one of its most thriving ports, saw the "lions" in one of its most ancient and interesting towns, breathing all the way the fresh air of heaven, and the fragrance of myriads of wild-flowers, and feasting upon the records and traditions of former ages, of which we were reminded by old castles and monasteries, palaces, churches, ruins, mountains, full of the memories of robbers, warriors, holy men, statesmen, court intriguers, princes, kings, and dynasties now no more. The whole, when I look back upon it as I now write, seems to have been a pageant of the middle ages, suddenly come, suddenly passed away, in the midst of the toils of a busy London life.

4

GEORGE MUSGRAVE,
THE PARSON, PEN, AND PENCIL: OR, REMINISCENCES AND ILLUSTRATIONS OF AN EXCURSION TO PARIS, TOURS, AND ROUEN IN THE SUMMER OF 1847 (LONDON: R. BENTLEY, 1848), I, PP. 124–135, II, PP. 251–252

We had been conveyed in a sort of omnibus from the Hôtel de France, at a charge of fivepence each, to this station, where we paid nine shillings and threepence each for tickets in a second-class carriage to Paris; and a very commodious and pleasant carriage it was. The padding and stuffing of the cushions, back, and sides, were so full, and yet so elastic, as to remind one of Mackintosh's inflated pillows: the glass in the door measured two feet by fourteen inches; the smaller windows, eleven inches by ten. There were curtains drawing right across to keep out the glare of sunshine. The furniture or cover of the cushions and sides, was of blue and white stripe, with a lace edging of red and black; reminding us of a gentleman's carriage lined for the sea-side season. Two lighted lamps were in the carriage, and shone brilliantly in the tunnels; and the height of the carriage itself was a source of much comfort, considering the intense heat of the weather. From the boards under our feet to the roof, was a space of six feet. We espied two cards nailed up above our heads, exhibiting printed regulations, which forbade—1. Opening the door during the journey. 2. Leaning over the door. 3. Getting out before the train should be perfectly still. 4. Bringing a dog into the carriage. 5. Getting in without a ticket. 6. Entering a carriage of higher class than the ticket indicated. 7. Smoking either in the carriage, or on the platform, or precincts of the station, or in the waiting-room. 8. Also directing passengers to keep their tickets secure until the journey should be terminated. 9. To show the ticket when required. 10. In case of any cause of complaint, to write into a book kept open for that purpose at each station, any representation of misconduct or grievance; which particulars the *sous inspecteur-chef de train* would be sure to record in his daily reports. This is a very rational plan for maintaining order and comfort in the journey. The pace at which the trains run on these newly-constructed lines is tardy in comparison with railway-speed in our country; but there is no loitering or needless hinderance. We performed the distance of ninety-one miles in four hours and twenty minutes; starting from Amiens at twenty-five minutes to eleven, and reaching the capital at fifty minutes past two.

Being once again on a French railroad, I may as well record a few particulars descriptive of this comparatively new order of things across the channel.

It is hardly necessary to apprise the reader that the expression denoting railway, is *chemin de fer*, road, or way, of iron. They adopt our term "station." That part of the station which is under cover is called the *gare*. The waiting-room is called the *salle d'attente;* the refreshment-room is *le buffet*. Our word "baggage," is adopted with the omission of one g: *bagages* being the French term. Goods are denominated *marchandises*. A train is called *convoi*, though the word "train" is also in common use. "Le service des facteurs dans l'intérieur des gares est entière-ment gratuit. Il leur est interdit de recevoir aucun pourboire." *i. e.* The services performed by the porters within the precincts of the stations are, in all cases, to be without fee or reward; they are forbidden to accept of any gratuity—literally, any money given to buy drink.

Slow trains for luggage are *transports de marchandises à petite vitesse*. Express trains are *trains à grande vitesse:* special ditto, *trains specials à grande vitesse*. Extra trains are *departs supplementaires*.

There are also *voitures salons*—carriages fitted up for pleasure excursions, like little sitting-rooms; and the charge for these is regulated according to the num-ber of *places de luxe* (literally, places for a luxurious scale of accommodation) required by the party applying.

If you go to the terminus for the purpose of setting off on a journey, it is (to you) the *embarcadère*. When, having completed your journey, you quit the termi-nus, it is, as regards your *voyage accompli*, the *débarcadère*,—terms analogous to embarkation and debarkation with reference to ships.

When the clock hand arrives at five minutes before the hour of the train's depar-ture, the ticket-vendor closes his *bureau de distribution de billets*. No more *billets* (tickets) can be purchased; and if the unlucky traveller chance to lose his ticket, supposing him to be even a third-class passenger, he is compelled to pay down, at the first station where he reveals his loss, the price of a first-class ticket, calcu-lated from the remotest point of the distance he may have travelled. This is sharp practice.

All the baggage must be brought in at least a quarter of an hour before the train starts, and every parcel or package (*colis*) must bear its address in very legible writing.

They apply the term *marchant* oddly enough: the up-train to Paris is *le train marchant vers Paris*.

All their head stations are on a magnificent scale: that of the Great North-ern in Paris is of immense extent. Imagine a vast tract of land under process of clearance by a tribe of active, intelligent, persevering settlers. On all sides were huge buildings, some nearly as large as the glazed pents at Chatham under which the shipwrights work; store-houses, forges, timber-yards, iron-foundries, brass-fitting *dépôts*, mechanical apparatus, reservoirs, tanks, saw-pits, timber-stacks, wheelers'-yards, pipes and boilers, *à choix*, and mountain heaps of coal and coke. Every item and atom connected in the slightest way with railroads seemed to be in process of creation there, from the sleepers and trains to the patent reverberators and plate-glass windows, silk curtains, and leather or silk cushions.

The passengers' waiting-room at the Great Northern is simple in its design, yet grand and startling in general effect. The chairs were of handsome pattern, highly gilt, and having green plush seats. The ingredients of *comfort* have found entry through the instrumentality of our countrymen, the Lancashire contractors and directors, whose plans and purses have befriended the French project of establishing railways of first-rate character—an undertaking which has, beyond doubt, been achieved in the most creditable manner, placing ten hours only between St. Martin's le Grand and Rue J. J. Rousseau.

The waiting-room at the terminus where parties procure tickets to go to Versailles, on the right bank of the Seine, is a beautiful apartment, nearly eighteen feet high and a hundred in length, looking on to garden-ground most invitingly laid out. In some of these rooms (at the Rouen station in Paris, for instance,) there are folding-doors leading on to the *gare*, or platform parallel with the train; and at about three or four minutes previous to the departure of the train, a bell is rung, at the sound of which all the passengers in waiting gather together at these folding-doors. Presently, each door being drawn back *into* the wall, the parties make with all speed for the carriages, some, of course, wishing to sit with their back "to the horses," as we may hear people sometimes say; others with their face looking, like Chilo, to the point of destination and the end of their career.

As Horace and I preferred sitting *vis-à-vis* at a window (*portière* is the term employed for the railway carriage-door), we were among the most sedulous in thus hurrying to the carriages.

When we arrived with our luggage, on these occasions of commencing a journey, we were requested to state the farthest point to which we purposed going. The name of that place, or of the station nearest to it (if out of the line) was then affixed, in print, with a number, to our portmanteau; and a counter-mark of the number was handed over to us, without the production of which, when claiming our luggage, nothing would be given up to us. The said ticket announced a piece of intelligence, not altogether very palatable, to this effect: that if, by any accident, the portmanteau should be lost, the company would award one pound thirteen shillings and fourpence in satisfaction thereof. The collar, back, and sleeves of only one of our coats were worth all the money!

As in London, the newspaper vendors are all on the *qui vive* at the stations, selling the daily journals, railway guides, &c. "Siècle! Siècle!" "Debats!" "Presse!" "l'Illustration!" "Journal Universel!" The "Illustration" is an admirable paper, with twenty or thirty woodcuts, illustrating the line of railway.

Many diligences also arrive at these stations, as the stage-coaches do in our country, but are treated in a way peculiarly French. They are detached from their carriages (I speak in the coach-makers' terms), that is, they are parted from their wheels and axles, and craned up from a windlass on high, into the air, where, *with all their passengers*, they are suspended bodily, till a locomotive framework on wheels, adapted for working in the train, is run underneath; and then the carriage and cargo descend, and are rivetted on to the apparatus which is to go with them *en train* to the end of their journey. I saw this done very often, and could not help smiling at the very peculiar expression of the countenances of the seventeen or twenty passengers in a state of suspense, who seemed to be meditating on the possibility of a link of chain giving way, and letting them down ("facilis descensus Averni!") to mother earth, and to the dislocation of every joint and tooth in their several bodies.

Gentlemen's carriages, however, are disposed of as in our country.

I may now quit this topic, which I should hardly have introduced but for the supposition, on my part, that every one in England, who has not been to France since the railway-travelling has been established there, must be as little acquainted as I was with these little details, which, after all, insignificant as they are, supply many a question when parties on this side of the channel fall into gossip, as they are whirled along our lines, and wonder how they manage these things in France. My countrymen may be assured, that whoever comes home from that country will bear cheerful testimony to the excellence of the arrangements already in force for rendering even the longest journeys as compatible with an Englishman's notions of comfort and convenience as they are here. Indeed, I go further than this: the second-class carriages are, as I have already said, hardly inferior to our first;—in point of arm and leg comforts they are altogether equal, and in the matter of height, superior. As to the fares, the discrepancy is great indeed.

The South-Eastern Railway time-bill states, that from

LONDON TO DOVER } is a distance, by railway, of 88 miles.
The second-class fare is 12*s.*

The Paris and Amiens Railway bill states, that from

AMIENS TO PARIS } is a distance of 91 miles.
The second-class fare is 9*s.* 2*d.*

The mail-train performs the journey from London to Dover in three hours and a half.

The corresponding train in France leaves Paris at eight in the morning, and reaches Amiens in three hours and twenty-five minutes.

This indicates a greater speed in the French train, and a difference in the fare of nearly three shillings; which, without the slightest exaggeration, are well worth all the four shillings and sixpence of difference between the South-Eastern Company's first and second class fares, on the above-mentioned distance.

The country beyond Amboise reminded me of the Edenbridge and Marden districts in Kent. Here were some fine hay crops yielding nearly two tons the acre. And at about a mile and a half distance from the road were tens of thousands of poplar trees. We saw one field of fifty acres of rye within ten miles of Tours. At Vouvray, seven miles from that city, the meadow-hay was being "bottled" in enormous quantities. As we drew near to Tours the crops were exclusively of wheat, rye, and potatoes.

We entered this venerable town at half-past three, in one of the hottest days of July. I never encountered more intense heat during a summer in the Mediterranean.

The station is noble. The oak-panelling and the doors are on a superb scale, and the ventilation is perfect. It was absolutely refreshing to linger a while in the waiting-room and shake off a little of the dust we had brought as samples of the various soils through fifty leagues of the province. In this waiting-room was a notice to the public denouncing,—1st, The penalty of death to any individual detected in throwing any substance on to the railway which should occasion an accident causing death. 2. Imprisonment and hard labour for a certain period of time, when such act has been committed without fatal consequences, but with injury to the person. 3. Close custody for a period, where the act has been committed without any individual having been killed or hurt.

Tours is a decidedly handsome and agreeable city, improving hourly on acquaintance; and testifying its worth as the traveller's knowledge of its merits increases. Its long streets, white houses, clean pavements and causeways, convenient and showy shops, and a generally cheerful aspect, commend it at a moment's glance to whoever enters it for the first time; and its public buildings, cathedral, bridge, and government-houses, stamp its importance.

5

GEORGE MUSGRAVE, *BY-ROADS AND BATTLE-FIELDS IN PICARDY*, 2 VOLS. (LONDON: BELL AND DALDY, 1861), I, PP. 12–13, 212–218

As soon as WIMEREUX disappears, the road towards AMBLETEUSE traverses a dreary breadth of sand hills, dotted with tufts of uneatable herbage and rank weeds, hardly less wild than the Val Demona of Sicily, though wanting its charcoal blackness. This repulsive feature prevailed till we crossed the little river Slack, which comes hurrying down between two high banks till it reaches a sluice constructed six years ago by the engineers of the camp already spoken of as having been stationed in this locality; and hence it trickles along as a mere rivulet to the beach. Healthy vegetation and careful tillage follow close, in breadths of barley, rye, beans, and potatoes, upon absolute barrenness. One of the most conspicuous results of railway traffic is the improvement in French farm homesteads. The change is startling. The old mud walls, and tottering sheds, and rotten thatch roofs, and unglazed windows, are everywhere disappearing, and in their stead we behold large substantial buildings of eighteen and fourteen-inch brickwork, tastefully decorated with stone coigns, copings and labellings, and roofed with slate. Instead of the tall old wooden porches leading into the yards, containing five loads of timber and looking like gigantic Lichgates, we see handsome stone-built arches, almost fit to be park entries; and close upon these stylish farm-yards lie the rich productive orchards, surrounded by stonemasonry substantial enough to enclose a barrack-yard. The stone material is raised from quarries at no great distance from the spot, as we see on the Cumberland estates; and the bricks and slates are brought from the nearest kilns and dépôts by railway, at a reduction of five shillings per thousand on the prices current before the line was laid down; besides a vast saving of horses' and men's labour with small carts to and from the remote brickfields. No one that remembers France fifty, or even twenty-five years ago, can fail to remark the pleasing contrast presented by the present appearance of things in this category of social progress. The old "wattle and dab" frontages have been superseded by substantial and well-pointed courses of brick: whole streets have been rebuilt, and lamps erected, and road-side laystalls and dung-mixens removed out of sight: and many important sanitary regulations have purified the kennels and watercourses. Much of this, certainly, proceeds from the wide circulation of money—a sure precursor of civilization and refining improvements. The proprietorships in the district of which I am especially speaking are large; and the farming is good in proportion. The hoe and the one-horse plough are duly employed, and the fairest plots in the garden of England could not display more careful husbandry. Wheat, barley, oats, beans, and clover, were growing in luxuriant abundance; and the manure lay in enormous heaps on the ploughed lands; but not a field of turnips, not a flock of sheep, was to be seen.

At length, after a sand-drift right in our teeth, we reached Ambleteuse, ten miles distant from Boulogne. It proved to be as desolate, dull, and melancholy a spot as Wimereux, where the inhabitants, occupying some sixty dwellings, a feeble folk like the conies around them (who are equally fond of stony rocks and sand hills), half-starved in appearance, and spiritless as convicts, eke out a scanty subsistence by fishing. And yet time was when here stood a town flanked by walls and towers.

Having alluded in a preceding page to the circumstances of competency enjoyed by our English labourers in the rural districts, where, if there be no staple trade or local manufacture such as lace-making, gloving, or straw-plaiting, the women take work (and work well too,) in the fields,—I may here advert to the great exertions now made in the Departments of France, generally, on behalf of the Female population. Upon the strength of this movement in an excellent direction, this class begins to surmount many of the difficulties, I may say—the wrongs—of their hitherto overlooked position in the social scale. They have from time immemorial laboured on the farm lands; but the influence of such hard toil has been brutalizing; and the introduction of young girls into promiscuous occupations on the homesteads has been considered most prejudicial to the cause of morality and social progress. Women meet the eye now where they never appeared before, but where they would always have served to advantage. They stand at the Railway side waving the signal flag:—they sell the Railway tickets—They are check takers in Theatres, Museums, and many similar institutions: they set the work, and watch the machinery, in Factories, and, with young children, fill the percussion caps for gunsmiths:—Indeed, I might place on record a long list of the tasks to which Common Sense has directed their dexterity and faithfulness.

The Committees appointed for the carrying out of this new project—one which cannot be too highly commended; for in handiwork they often greatly excel us—have, in Picardy as in numerous other Provinces of France, specified many sources of maintenance to which female intellect and energy may be addressed with decisive advantage both to the employer and employed. On the Coast stations,—the elderly women, in particular—old crones who long before attaining the age of sixty used to fall upon their parishes—have for some time been elected as privileged workers; and well do they discharge their functions. Whoever has seen the women of Dieppe conveying the cargoes of Salt from the vessels in port to the warehouses,—a privilege enjoyed by their sisterhood from the days of Louis XIII.—must have borne witness to the marvellous agility and dispatch with which these fetchers and carriers, saline as anchovies and active as sand eels, accomplish all they have to do. It is a perfect illustration of females labouring truly to get their own living, and to do their duty in that state of life unto which it has pleased God to call them. Between that port and St. Vallery a large detachment of women, half of them being Normans, half Picards, were drafted out from the communes to throw up earth-works. The bureau d'administration, or local Board of Works, supplied to each of them a wheelbarrow of lighter construction than those used by men, with which they ran along rapidly, up and down plank and bank;—and if here and there one of the large wheelbarrows were at hand, two addressed themselves to the load, and trundled it along with ease. These females received each ninepence halfpenny a day, for six months. All along the coast of the Department of the Somme the shrimp, cockle, and winkle, fishery is restricted to the females. It is not so, exactly, on the River Exe in South Devon;—but there, too, the women bending down in the mud and sand are in the proportion of eight to two of the other sex. I may add that many of them wear tight black pantaloons; and at a distance resemble 'shabby genteel' beaux in the evening dress of forty years ago, groping at low water for lost treasure. In the Cantonniers' districts, also, (the Road Contractors') the women and children alone are employed to pick up stones from the fields for the repair of the highways. A similar preference and privilege has been accorded to the women living in villages bordering on the peat fields which abound towards the Western extremity of the Somme. They have the exclusive right to wheel away the cubes of turf from the field to the barges which lie alongside to fetch away this extensively used fuel. In many towns they have been appointed the sole Water Carriers. As for those tough, wiry, 'old girls' so familiar to the eyes of our Countrymen landing at Boulogne, it is needless to describe their power of muscle and locomotion. There, too, they are the sole privileged and patent porters: and wonderful loads they carry—[I remember the days when they used to carry *men* from ship to shore] with a nimbleness of step and willingness to work which it is impossible to behold without pleasure as well as surprise. Two portmanteaux, a carpet bag, a gun-case, a hat-case, Cinq pièces? Voilà! One of these sexagenarian locomotives takes up and scuds along with the whole lot, and deposits it at the Hotel du Nord for a "nimble nine-pence." The spirit of these preferential appointments aims very wisely at the more equal and profitable distribution of labour. It directs male labour to waste and fallow land, to large breadths of soil which, for want of care and cultivation, either produces only half of what it otherwise would, or nothing but weeds. It sends the strong able-bodied men to the mines, the machinery and great engines of the country; to the Railway embankments and tunnels, or to well-sinking, drainage, and brick-making. They are the force to be employed on the ocean and its productions; they are to occupy their business in the great waters, in trading vessels and general navigation; not to mention the numberless occupations for the thews and sinews of masculine strength held out in all the departments subservient to the Military and Naval services; in Dockyards and Laboratories, Wharves and Stores of the munitions of War. The leaders of this movement repudiate the notion of a distaff being held in the hands of those who might with benefit to themselves and their country be wielding an axe or making a furrow. Their aim is to enable Woman, where she can be spared from the claims of maternal and domestic duty, to take her position in the ranks of the manufacturing industry of France. There is a wide field, also, ever open to her sex in cultivated breadths of Land, where man's toil would be thrown away:—in Weeding. This indispensable work, never oppressively severe, should be exclusively confined to the female portion of a village. The Committee are far from discouraging aged men from applying for work; but they urge the desirableness and duty of supplying vacancies out of the female population, whenever a man vacates. The system in vogue immediately after the Great Revolution, when women were liberated from this department of service, as being unworthy of Sœurs citoyennes, inflicted great evils on the rural population. The enactments which thus paralysed the arms of an able-bodied Woman called upon the Man to redouble his efforts: for it was self-evident that if she was not to work at all, he must work for her. Men had to serve their country in arms; men were also of necessity wanted to work as carpenters, masons, tilers, miners, and engineers; and Woman was condemned to inactivity and idleness while the hardier sex was compelled to make good the deficit arising from the withdrawal of female exertion when this standstill in national industry was created. It is self-evident that all employment found for the woman must be conducive towards the maintenance of her husband and of all other members of the family. If I give one of my cottagers a mangle, I am empowering the female portion of the residents in that home to earn not only the full amount of the Rent, but a considerable proportion of the cost of soap, candle, and clothing. But the view taken by the promoters of an enlarged sphere of female employment directs its attention as carefully to the *towns* as to the villages. In my opinion this is a more serious care than the latter seems to call for. A woman who has neither father nor husband, and can betake herself to no steady occupation, is, in a town, supported by public charity; I mean by a poor-rate dole. The funds affording that relief being drawn from every taxable householder are thus made accessory to female indolence. If the relief be withheld, petty theft, purloining, mendicancy, or vicious living in all its deplorable phases of degradation, is the alternative. The tendency, therefore, of a measure which would thus gather women into the hive of industry, discourages the number of those men who crowd into the towns intent upon being employed in the Cotton mills, wool-spinning factories, and such like establishments, instead of taking agricultural employment. The hundreds of places thus pre-occupied and monopolized by strong, sturdy men whose every task within the walls of the Manufactories would be in all particulars as well executed, if not, indeed, better, by females, constitute a wrong: and that wrong is at length become so flagrant, and, now that the manufactories have increased so widely is creating so great distress and dissatisfaction among the women, that the general expectation anticipates some Governmental enactment on the subject which will, at least, divide the labour. The municipalities have testified, in all the Departments, to the deteriorated condition of the wives of the working men. Provisions have long been dear, compared with former years: potatoes and fruit have frequently failed—and yet wages have not been augmented in proportion. The women, mothers of children especially, are not sufficiently nourished: Badly clothed, badly lodged, they become emaciated at an early period of life; and, after bringing into existence a puny and consumptive family, collapse, as it were, into helplessness, and sink rapidly into premature decay. How rarely do women of fifty years of age, in French villages or in the narrow, unwholesome, streets of the towns, appear to be less than sixty-five years old! The origin of the evil is to be traced to that idleness which results from the impossibility of the woman's procuring work, or from the very inadequate remuneration awarded to her when she has obtained it and done justice to her employer. Of these two predicaments the first is occasioned in a great degree, in France as in England, by the extensive use of Machinery; but more decidedly by the vast influx of men into the towns, who, preferring the stir and excitement of the streets to the insipidity and dulness of the villages, (a partiality with which many of the wisest and best among us sympathise!) usurp the places which ought to be reserved for females; and take up stations in work-rooms, galleries, and shops where all they have to do might be as well and as expeditiously done by the tenderer sex. If an exception be reserved, it should be with regard to large Drapers' Shops and fashionable depôts of elegance, the exclusive resort of ladies. I asked a London draper's foreman, some few months since, if he did not believe that twenty intelligent, active, young, women would not in every respect be as serviceable behind the counter as twenty men. He said the business of the largest and most popular Firm would rapidly fail and become extinct if such a substitution were attempted. The men, he said, demeaned themselves with a deferential courtesy and with an earnest effort and desire to please, (not to say, to humour,) the lady customers, which one of those customers' sex would not exhibit. Women would take umbrage at remarks and at manners which shopmen patiently regard with indifference,—only aiming at the eventful satisfaction of the customer: But were a woman compelled, as the men are, to bring this and bring that bulky roll of silk, and then remove it as a rejected sample; and spread twenty gown pieces, or a dozen shawls or mantles on the counter, or across a frame, and, after all, see the lady leave the shop without purchasing a shred of all that had been offered, she, the female shop assistant, would in her countenance and manner indicate her weariness and disgust; and this would speedily hurt the connexion, and prove a cause of irremediable loss. It has been said, moreover, that few women could stand from ten till six or seven o'clock; or sustain the fatigue of the routine attendance from 7 A.M. till 10 P.M. (on Stock-taking nights, 12, perhaps)—in relief of which the early closing movement is, even now, restricted to Saturdays.

The French Employers, like many other on *our* side of the straits, cherish the absurd prejudice that a woman must, as a matter of course, be less dexterous in her work than a man is; and that, therefore, she ought to receive much smaller remuneration. But here the friends of the woman interpose with a plain common sense view of such objection. There is no intention of indiscreetly taxing woman's strength, or of causing her to compromise the interests of her employers by her failures: She should be installed in that department of labour which is consistent with her sex and capacities. The long-enduring patience and toiling perseverance of even young girls in Factory work, and at the Lyonnais looms, are notorious. In this particular I could, as an eye-witness, affirm that they are transcendently superior to our sex, though toiling under harder conditions. Where common integrity has its perfect work the remuneration would be proportionate to the amount of labour, and the excellence, or otherwise, of the work executed: and by these two considerations alone the wages of the day should be regulated. This principle, it is urged, might be acted upon in the villages. The cottage itself might become sub-auxiliary to the support of the family through work easily capable of being executed by the females after the domestic duties have been duly attended to. As in England, such task includes needlework and straw-plaiting;—but in both countries there are manifold operations in Book-binding which are particularly in women's province, and admitting of being completed at home; as well as toy manufacturing, basket-weaving, bonnet-making, and such like easy labour: not an indication of which is to be found in any of the cottages at present, but which would contribute through the channels of public encouragement to the maintenance of thousands who, being excluded from the hive of industry in the towns, live the inglorious life of drones where, under wise regulation, each thrifty mother and daughter might divert the hours of leisure by helping to support the house. The increase of population and the evils inseparably associated with an inadequately employed multitude of females in every town press this subject on the Legislative mind; and we must acknowledge the present agitation in so excellent a cause as the interest of the labouring classes to be the most commendable, if not among the most vital, of all the projects soliciting the attention and care of France.

6

GEORGE MUSGRAVE, *A RAMBLE INTO BRITTANY*, 2 VOLS. (LONDON: HURST AND BLACKETT, 1870), I, PP. 91–94

12th.—Left Douai for Paris. A barrier of considerable strength had been thrown up at the railway station to prevent dangerous pressure and confusion arising from many hundreds departing and arriving. Their numbers were pretty evenly balanced. Those who were on their way into the town came mostly after the fashion of "the children of Ephraim, armed and carrying bows," to win fresh honours in the Archery Field, where a target was to be shot for, and Douai's Toxophilite Association were ready to contend with all comers. After a punch in the ribs from a trombone, which the owner had not space nor leisure to disjoint and pack up for the journey, and a shove or two from the double drum which was on its way to Ghent, I was once more on wheels, and heard the steam getting up with all alacrity for Creil and Paris.

Often as I have travelled along this line of country I should always admire the high cultivation which characterizes both sides of the road up to Arras. Wheat, flax, beet-root, buckwheat, poppy (for oil), and hemp, chequer the soil with white and green crops of luxuriant growth, fenced in with quickset hedges of beautiful compactness and regularity, among surrounding farm-premises, and cottages of substantial structure, well slated and glazed, which, being interspersed in all directions, indicate that distribution of labour so essential to success in agriculture.

Beyond Arras, whose principal steeple soars in air, reminding every Londoner of St. Bride's in Fleet Street, the land is cut up on all sides by the *Parcellement* system; and all the detriments accruing to even the most prolific soil from petty proprietorship are manifest at a glance. I made this survey in silent, solitary complacency; for, as is almost invariably the case, travel through what country we may,—be it as ugly as the *Landes* of the South, or beautiful as the valleys of Brittany,—the Frenchmen compose themselves, after ten minutes' riding, to sleep, from which they only wake when the train stops at any station. The indifference of these men to the face of Nature, and their seeming incapability of plunging into thought and salutary reflection, have irritated my feelings through thousands of miles: much more in first-class carriages than in second: as, "in the old coaching times" of England, it was the common report of gentlemen travellers that they invariably found outside places infinitely more agreeable, in respect of sociability, than the inside, where there was so much 'nodding' and stupid sleepiness.

After leaving at some distance behind us the turf fields of AMIENS and those vast breadths of vegetable produce which are cultivated exclusively for the markets of Paris and London—(artichokes, cauliflowers, onions, carrots, and lettuces in profuse abundance),—my stupified fellow-travellers, interdicted from smoking, betook themselves to snoring; two of them having placed their dusty, uncleaned boots on the new, fine, light drab-coloured cloth of the seats before them. These first-class passengers use the carriages shamefully. I should say that the majority of those with whom I travelled in the course of six weeks and over nearly fifteen hundred miles, would have been more consistently placed in the third-class carriages. They loll and lie along, with their feet doubled up on the cushions, and their unkempt greasy heads and gloveless, dirty, hands soiling the padding and lace wherever they come in contact with either; and there they recline ['procumbit humi bos' fashion] like cattle. I sometimes imputed this degrading condition of body and mind to the excessive use of absinthe, vermuth, and frequent resort to brandy, rum, and compounds to which the male portion of the population are now more than ever addicted; for it certainly was not thus that we were mated in our land journeys thirty years ago. After a month's experience of it, I fell in with a very intelligent gentleman (not in a railway carriage), whose sensible remarks and power of observation led into long and interesting discourse, and it occurred to me to ask if he could in any general way account for the wide discrepancy between firstclass travellers in his own country and the same denomination in ours. His reply went a great way towards solving my problem. "Monsieur, the majority of men you meet journeying through France are by many degrees below the rank of what you in your country designate as 'gentlefolk.' . . . These emissaries are not only in receipt of the large salaries I have told you of, but are furnished with a printed pass, at sight of which the railway officials and hotel keepers regard them as privileged first-class travellers; and thus they travel in the best compartments of the train, are lodged in elegant rooms, and dine luxuriously where their betters sit next to them at table. They are not what we should term an uneducated class. Many of them understand, though they do not let the fact transpire, four European languages: and, while looking all unconsciousness, lay up in memory any fact they may wish to remember and record, when two Germans or Dutchmen or Spaniards have maintained a long and confidential conversation, believing themselves to have talked in a tongue not understood by the strangers!

7

THOMAS ADOLPHUS TROLLOPE, *IMPRESSIONS OF A WANDERER IN ITALY, SWITZERLAND, FRANCE, AND SPAIN* (LONDON: H. COLBURN, 1850), PP. 261–264

A railway in its onward course is, as we have often seen, as little a respecter of places as Death is of persons. The iron-shod intruder has accordingly been found in many strange positions and incongruous companionships:—but never did he thrust his disturbing presence anywhere with more audacious disregard for propriety, and for the venerable sanctities of time-honoured antiquity, than when he bored his way through the centre of the ancient cemetery of Arles, known as Les Aliscamps. This name is a corruption of *Elysii Campi;* and the vast Necropolis, which it designates, is—or rather was—one of the most interesting specimens extant of an undisturbed burial field of the Romans and of the early Christians. Both Pagans and primitive Christians had buried here over a very large space of ground; and the latter had hallowed the spot by the erection of several larger and smaller oratories and chapels. One good-sized church, Sainte Marie-des-Graces, still remains, an exceedingly picturesque ruin. A very pretty fragment of a smaller building, known as St. Crucifix, is yet standing at no great distance from the former. Around these two have been gathered all the very considerable number of sarcophagi and stone tombs which the works for the railway routed out from their resting-places. This disturbance and ousting of the ancient tenants has been the more extensive from the circumstance that, not only has the railway passed through the cemetery, but the unfortunate spot has been selected for the purpose of erecting large workshops, engine-houses, and all those extraordinarily-shaped and especially hideous edifices that railroads always erect at their places of predilection.

The result of this wholesale disturbance of a spot held sacred during so many centuries has produced one of the strangest scenes imaginable. The entire distance between the two ruined buildings above mentioned has assumed the appearance of a complete street of tombs. The sarcophagi are ranged on either side as thickly as they can stand; many retain their huge ark-shaped stone covers, but more perhaps are without them. Here and there a bone or two still remain at the bottom of their rifled resting-place. The majority are quite empty. Around the larger ruin of Notre Dame des Graces the whole ground is strewn with a vast quantity of them, mostly covered, and grouped in every possible variety of confusion. Locked within a part of the ruined church still capable of affording some shelter and protection, there are to be seen three or four metal coffins, whose tenants have for some chance reason been treated with more respect. Of these one contains the tolerably perfect skeleton of a Pagan maiden whose brief history was found inscribed on her grave-stone. She died at the age of seventeen, on the day of her marriage! The cause of her death is not stated. Her immediate neighbours now, as they lie side by side on the pavement of the ruined chancel, are two of the ancient Archbishops of Arles! She has one on each side of her. Their skeletons also are nearly perfect. Misfortune—which in life, as the proverb teaches us, has the effect of bringing us into strange companionship—sometimes produces, it should seem, similar effects even after death. Poor Pagan maiden!—one of the comely girls of Arelas, whose "madonna" was Venus! She would hardly have found her way into such reverend company without the assistance of the great leveller; nor even by his alone, without the additional aid of that other modern leveller, the Railway, with his pickaxe and shovel!

8

ANDREW DICKINSON, *MY FIRST VISIT TO EUROPE* (NEW YORK: G. P. PUTNAM, 1851), PP. 158–160

While waiting for the railway, I strolled about the rural suburbs, the pleasant groves and farms, but saw no bright villas—nothing but a few farm-cottages of the poor. At nine I took the railway for Lille, where I arrived in the afternoon. The day was beautiful, with occasional light showers, after which the sun would look joyously down from the blue serene on the hills and vales of France, covered with green and yellow harvests. The country is not so bold as England, though very picturesque. Men, women and children dressed in blue blouse, were out in the fields harvesting. The country was under high culture, without a foot of neglected land. Square and oblong plots and strips of grain and herbage of different colours, spread over the vales and undulating hills, almost treeless, look like patchwork; and such, indeed, it is—a very pleasing novelty. I saw the same operation of cutting turf as in Ireland. It is cut in oblong pieces, the size of a large brick, and piled in pyramidal stacks to dry, and makes the best of fuel. The northern, or grape-growing part of France, is not so fertile as the south. I looked in vain for the luxuriant, nicely-plashed hawthorn hedges and spacious parks, with their herds of deer, to be seen all over England. The fields have no fences, except a kind of paling by the roadside; yet along the railways are many hawthorn hedges newly planted. The French diligence is a clumsy but comfortable mode of travelling. Of these I saw but few. Good railways now communicate with all parts of France. When a diligence meets a drove of sheep, it is curious to see the dextrous sagacity of the dogs, which are trained to drive them all on one side of the road till the vehicle passes!

At every town I saw plenty of monks, monks, monks, with jolly round faces, dressed in black surtouts reaching down to the heels, and buttoned up to the chin, with broad-rimmed hats. They always have a book under the arm to awe the credulous vulgar. Whoever has anxieties they have none. These ecclesiastics are getting into great favour with the government of republican France, and republican Italy. I had the company of a monk in the railway, and a very pleasant fellow he was. The reader would have laughed to see me taking my second lesson in French. He knew enough English to learn of me that I was at the beginning of pupilage; and though I did not bid fair to become a promising scholar, yet seeing the schoolmaster was abroad, without business, I gladly encouraged his works of charity. Near Lille I counted in two miles over a hundred windmills; yet in the same space might be seen as many of the ecclesiastical windmills aforesaid. I always managed to get a seat at the window, and had fine sights all the way to Paris.

In pleasant construction of railway carriages, the French are as much behind the English, as the British are behind the Americans. You enter the French carriage by a side door to a compartment completely closed front and rear! In England it is similar, except the nonsensical partition. The English and French take the lead in systematic management, a cheap and uniform scale of prices, solid permanence of the roads, and the astonishing magnitude, massive strength, and beauty of their railway stations, especially the English. Yet our long, convenient, republican cars, will always go ahead. At any rate, we can give unrivalled despatch to the greatest number of passengers! Of this we have too many striking examples. The French ought to have credit for one capital improvement, unknown in England—lighting up the cars on passing a tunnel.

Lille is a dark and uninviting old town, resembling Dunkerque. Refreshments at the hotels and stations are high. Here I was to take the railway for Belgium; but illness and my experience at Dunkerque damped my courage a little, and I thought best not to try an incursion into the Dutch country and language. I had even intended a visit to Prussia and the banks of the Rhine; and though English is spoken at the best hotels, these plans are set down as foregone resolutions.

Arras is the next town of note, and a few leagues more brings us to Amiens, where the treaty of peace was signed. The numerous pretty villages of the way recede from the mind as they do from sight, for thoughts of absorbing wonder.

"That's Paris!" said an English gentleman. It was now ten o'clock; and the sight of the long line of gas lamps reaching for miles on both sides of the railway, was glorious to behold! On passing out of the railway station, an officer shouted, "Passe-porte!" I responded with a Frenchified enunciation, "Dunkerque!" and passed on. It was not his fault that he took me for a Frenchman. "Pretty well!" thought I, "for the third lesson in French!"

9

FRANK B. GOODRICH, *TRICOLORED SKETCHES IN PARIS DURING THE YEARS 1851–2–3* (NEW YORK: HARPER & BROTHERS, 1855), PP. 202–203, 205–206, 210, 216

September 10th, 1852.

There was a large crowd of spectators in the vicinity of the Paris station, and it seems positive that the cry of *Vive l'Empereur* was freely mingled with that of *Vive Napoléon.* The President will have the pleasure of seeing upon his route all the *matériel* of the *fêtes* of Paris, down to the lemonade glasses filled with green and yellow oil, that have so often done the honours of the Boulevards and the Champs Elysées. You may make up your mind that this triumphal progress is nothing else than a prelude to the Empire; and that, if no untoward and unlooked for circumstance should occur in the interval, the Senate will be convoked to make the necessary hole in the constitution. Petitions for the Empire are now circulating in Paris, the text by a member of the society of the 10th December, approved by Persigny; and the people are crying "Hurrah for the Emperor!" along the zigzag line of railroad from here to the Mediterranean. I leave you to transfer as many of these hurrahs, and as much of this artificial enthusiasm, to your columns as you may think proper; you will probably find enough of it in the English journals, which have sent special correspondents with the imperial cortege.

We have news of the royal progress from station to station; nothing extraordinary has yet occurred, unless it be that the Cardinal of Bourges addressed the President as "Your Imperial Highness," and that the *Moniteur* is unusually careful to note the prevalence of cries of *Vive l'Empereur*, and to insist upon the spontaneity of the manifestation. The Parisians seem to consider the Empire as a *fait accompli*, or, at any rate, one to be accomplished before the close of the year.

September 18th, 1852.

Every floral inscription upon the railroad stations of "Vive l'Empereur," may therefore be considered as having been formally approved at Paris; every sentiment wrought in evergreen, expressing imperial yearnings, every crown of laurels tossed into his carriage, every speech aimed at him, every address and petition of which the Empire is the burden, must be viewed as so many successive links of the chain forged beforehand. The prefect dresses the station in holiday attire, and his wife twines the myrtle and the silver fir into the mystic letters agreed upon for the motto along the cornice; the prefect prints the badges to be worn around the peasants' hats, draws up the speeches, couches the petitions in appropriate language, and presides at the whole passage of the cortege through the limits of his department; and this prefect is in close relations with the Minister of the Interior, who, in his turn, is the President's right-hand man, and an ardent promoter of imperial enthusiasm.

The prefects obey with alacrity and subserviency; for they know that if, on any point of the route, the welcome is cold, the attendance thin, the delirium feeble, they will be held responsible. The government well knows that the peasants can be wielded at will by any one placed in authority over them, and removal and disgrace is the portion of him whose lukewarmness has failed to kindle the slumbering energies of the dwellers within his borders. The ribbon of the Legion of Honor, on the other hand, rewards the zeal of him who does willing and effective service. The Empire has been determined upon, and the necessary step of causing the initiative to appear to come from the people is in a fair way of successful realization.

September 28th, 1852.

WESTWARD the star of empire makes its way! North, South, and Eastward too, the poet might have added, had he been speaking, prophetically, of France; for the movement in behalf of the restoration has now become general throughout the country. Every possible means of propagation is resorted to. In the South, the principal engine is the evergreen inscription upon railway stations, the badge upon the hat, the imperial emblem done in fire, and the imperial shout uttered by the lips. In the East, the circulation of petitions, and the collection of signatures, are the absorbing occupations of the prefects just now. The zeal evinced by these functionaries, and the utter unscrupulousness with which they pursue their object, is described as something very remarkable. Since the commencement of the President's tour, the *Moniteur* has been profusely posted upon the walls of Paris, that the lower classes may read and be convinced. In the country towns, immense editions of the Lyons speech, printed at Paris, have been placarded or distributed among the inhabitants. The prefect of the Seine and the Municipal Council of Paris are busy at present in preparing a programme of welcome, to be extended to the President upon his return. I have no doubt that the official reception will be so handily managed that it will seem really to come from the unconverted population of this city. This government is clever enough to make the attempt and succeed. I should not be astonished to find myself cheering lustily and waving handkerchiefs innumerable, having been previously possessed by a Government Devil, and converted into an Imperial Automaton, for the purposes of the hour.

We have an infernal machine in earnest at last. No gas-pipes sewed up in tarred duck, but a monster engine of 254 gun barrels, and of 1,500 bullet power. I am not prepared to say that the conspirators deserve the guillotine for this intended attempt upon the life of the President; but they certainly do deserve it for their imbecile management. It is impossible to believe that they hoped to escape detection. They hired two apartments upon the principal street of Marseilles, in one of which they erected their absurd contrivance—composed of four cannons and 250 musket bores. Two rifles, with an unerring eye behind each, would have been as sure of success as their clumsy invention was certain of miscarriage. The conspirators are said to have been captured, and may reckon upon a speedy and ignominious exit from this world of care, trespasses when thou art sure we have repented. Lead us not into the temptation of office seeking, but deliver us from the evils of secret societies, newspapers, and elections of all sorts. Amen!"

October 14th, 1852.

I STRING together a few of the inscriptions done in evergreen, upon arches of triumph and railroad stations, along the Prince's route. Generally they bear ample testimony to the zeal of the mayor that composed them, though some few are decidedly too prosaic and matter-of-fact for this delirious period of French history:—

> "What a happy day for France the 2nd of December was!"
> "Vive le coup-d'état!"
> "Hurrah for NAPOLEON I!"
> "Hurrah for NAPOLEON II!"
> "Hurrah for NAPOLEON III!"
> "The City of Nevers desires the restoration of the Empire."
> "May Heaven watch over you!"
> "God bless you!"
> "The City of St. Nicaise prays for you."
> "Vox Populi, Vox Dei, 7,500,000."
> "Domine, Salvum fac Ludovicum Napoleonem."
> "The children of the old soldiers salute the nephew of the Emperor."
> "Aquilas turribus insidere juvat."
> "Render unto Cæsar the things that are Cæsar's."
> "To the friend of the workman, the Savior of France."
> "Vive la joie!"
> "A tous les Bonapartes!"
> "To Louis Napoleon, his faithful Angoulême!"
> "Hurrah for our side!"

10

MARK TWAIN, *THE INNOCENTS ABROAD* (HARTFORD: AMERICAN PUBLISHING COMPANY, 1875), PP. 106–112

We are not infatuated with these French railway cars, though. We took first class passage, not because we wished to attract attention by doing a thing which is uncommon in Europe, but because we could make our journey quicker by so doing. It is hard to make railroading pleasant, in any country. It is too tedious. Stage-coaching is infinitely more delightful. Once I crossed the plains and deserts and mountains of the West, in a stage-coach, from the Missouri line to California, and since then all my pleasure trips must be measured to that rare holiday frolic. Two thousand miles of ceaseless rush and rattle and clatter, by night and by day, and never a weary moment, never a lapse of interest! The first seven hundred miles a level continent, its grassy carpet greener and softer and smoother than any sea, and figured with designs fitted to its magnitude—the shadows of the clouds. Here were no scenes but summer scenes, and no disposition inspired by them but to lie at full length on the mail sacks, in the grateful breeze and dreamily smoke the pipe of peace—what other, where all was repose and contentment? In cool mornings, before the sun was fairly up, it was worth a lifetime of city toiling and moiling, to perch in the foretop with the driver and see the six mustangs scamper under the sharp snapping of a whip that never touched them; to scan the blue distances of a world that knew no lords but us; to cleave the wind with uncovered head and feel the sluggish pulses rousing to the spirit of a speed that pretended to the resistless rush of a typhoon! Then thirteen hundred miles of desert solitudes; of limitless panoramas of bewildering perspective; of mimic cities, of pinnacled cathedrals, of massive fortresses, counterfeited in the eternal rocks and splendid with the crimson and gold of the setting sun; of dizzy altitudes among fog-wreathed peaks and never-melting snows, where thunders and lightnings and tempests warred magnificently at our feet and the storm-clouds above swung their shredded banners in our very faces!

But I forgot. I am in elegant France, now, and not skurrying through the great South Pass and the Wind River Mountains, among antelopes and buffaloes, and painted Indians on the war path. It is not meet that I should make too disparaging comparisons between hum-drum travel on a railway and that royal summer flight across a continent in a stage-coach. I meant in the beginning, to say that railway journeying is tedious and tiresome, and so it is—though at the time, I was thinking particularly of a dismal fifty-hour pilgrimage between New York and St. Louis. Of course our trip through France was not really tedious, because all its scenes and experiences were new and strange; but as Dan says, it had its "discrepancies."

The cars are built in compartments that hold eight persons each. Each compartment is partially subdivided, and so there are two tolerably distinct parties of four in it. Four face the other four. The seats and backs are thickly padded and cushioned and are very comfortable; you can smoke, if you wish; there are no bothersome peddlers; you are saved the infliction of a multitude of disagreeable fellow-passengers. So far, so well. But then the conductor locks you in when the train starts; there is no water to drink, in the car; there is no heating apparatus for night travel; if a drunken rowdy should get in, you could not remove a matter of twenty seats from him, or enter another car; but above all, if you are worn out and must sleep, you must sit up and do it in naps, with cramped legs and in a torturing misery that leaves you withered and lifeless the next day—for behold they have not that culmination of all charity and human kindness, a sleeping car, in all France. I prefer the American system. It has not so many grievous "discrepancies."

In France, all is clockwork, all is order. They make no mistakes. Every third man wears a uniform, and whether he be a Marshal of the Empire or a brakeman, he is ready and perfectly willing to answer all your questions with tireless politeness, ready to tell you which car to take, yea, and ready to go and put you into it to make sure that you shall not go astray. You can not pass into the waiting-room of the depot till you have secured your ticket, and you can not pass from its only exit till the train is at its threshold to receive you. Once on board, the train will not start till your ticket has been examined—till every passenger's ticket has been inspected. This is chiefly for your own good. If by any possibility you have managed to take the wrong train, you will be handed over to a polite official who will take you whither you belong, and bestow you with many an affable bow. Your ticket will be inspected every now and then along the route, and when it is time to change cars you will know it. You are in the hands of officials who zealously study your welfare and your interest, instead of turning their talents to the invention of new methods of discommoding and snubbing you, as is very often the main employment of that exceedingly self-satisfied monarch, the railroad conductor of America.

But the happiest regulation in French railway government, is—thirty minutes to dinner! No five-minute boltings of flabby rolls, muddy coffee, questionable eggs, gutta-percha beef, and pies whose conception and execution are a dark and bloody mystery to all save the cook that created them! No; we sat calmly down—it was in old Dijon, which is so easy to spell and so impossible to pronounce, except when you civilize it and call it Demijohn—and poured out rich Burgundian wines and munched calmly through a long table d'hote bill of fare, snail-patties, delicious fruits and all, then paid the trifle it cost and stepped happily aboard the train again, without once cursing the railroad company. A rare experience, and one to be treasured forever.

They say they do not have accidents on these French roads, and I think it must be true. If I remember rightly, we passed high above wagon roads, or through tunnels under them, but never crossed them on their own level. About every quarter of a mile, it seemed to me, a man came out and held up a club till the train went by, to signify that every thing was safe ahead. Switches were changed a mile in advance, by pulling a wire rope that passed along the ground by the rail, from station to station. Signals for the day and signals for the night gave constant and timely notice of the position of switches.

No, they have no railroad accidents to speak of in France. But why? Because when one occurs, *somebody* has to hang for it! Not hang, may be, but be punished at least with such vigor of emphasis as to make negligence a thing to be shuddered at by railroad officials for many a day thereafter. "No blame attached to the officers"—that lying and disaster-breeding verdict so common to our soft-hearted juries, is seldom rendered in France. If the trouble occurred in the conductor's department, that officer must suffer if his subordinate can not be proven guilty; if in the engineer's department, and the case be similar, the engineer must answer.

The Old Travelers—those delightful parrots who have "been here before," and know more about the country than Louis Napoleon knows now or ever will know,—tell us these things, and we believe them because they are pleasant things to believe, and because they are plausible and savor of the rigid subjection to law and order which we behold about us every where.

But we love the Old Travelers. We love to hear them prate, and drivel and lie. We can tell them the moment we see them. They always throw out a few feelers; they never cast themselves adrift till they have sounded every individual and know that he has not traveled. Then they open their throttle-valves, and how they do brag, and sneer, and swell, and soar, and blaspheme the sacred name of Truth! Their central idea, their grand aim, is to subjugate you, keep you down, make you feel insignificant and humble in the blaze of their cosmopolitan glory! They will not let you know any thing. They sneer at your most inoffensive suggestions; they laugh unfeelingly at your treasured dreams of foreign lands; they brand the statements of your traveled aunts and uncles as the stupidest absurdities; they deride your most trusted authors and demolish the fair images they have set up for your willing worship with the pitiless ferocity of the fanatic iconoclast! But still I love the Old Travelers. I love them for their witless platitudes; for their supernatural ability to bore; for their delightful asinine vanity; for their luxuriant fertility of imagination; for their startling, their brilliant, their overwhelming mendacity!

By Lyons and the Saone (where we saw the lady of Lyons and thought little of her comeliness;) by Villa Franca, Tonnere, venerable Sens, Melun, Fontainebleau, and scores of other beautiful cities, we swept, always noting the absence of hog-wallows, broken fences, cowlots, unpainted houses and mud, and always noting, as well, the presence of cleanliness, grace, taste in adorning and beautifying, even to the disposition of a tree or the turning of a hedge, the marvel of roads in perfect repair, void of ruts and guiltless of even an inequality of surface—we bowled along, hour after hour, that brilliant summer day, and as nightfall approached we entered a wilderness of odorous flowers and shrubbery, sped through it, and then, excited, delighted, and half persuaded that we were only the sport of a beautiful dream, lo, we stood in magnificent Paris!

What excellent order they kept about that vast depot! There was no frantic crowding and jostling, no shouting and swearing, and no swaggering intrusion of services by rowdy hackmen. These latter gentry stood outside—stood quietly by their long line of vehicles and said never a word. A kind of hackman-general seemed to have the whole matter of transportation in his hands. He politely received the passengers and ushered them to the kind of conveyance they wanted, and told the driver where to deliver them. There was no "talking back," no dissatisfaction about overcharging, no grumbling about any thing. In a little while we were speeding through the streets of Paris, and delightfully recognizing certain names and places with which books had long ago made us familiar. It was like meeting an old friend when we read *"Rue de Rivoli"* on the street corner; we knew the genuine vast palace of the Louvre as well as we knew its picture; when we passed by the Column of July we needed no one to tell us what it was, or to remind us that on its site once stood the grim Bastile, that grave of human hopes and happiness, that dismal prison-house within whose dungeons so many young faces put on the wrinkles of age, so many proud spirits grew humble, so many brave hearts broke.

11

HENRY JAMES, *A LITTLE TOUR IN FRANCE* (LEIPZIG: B. TAUCHNITZ, 1885), PP. 258–261

I HAVE been trying to remember whether I fasted all the way to Macon, which I reached at an advanced hour of the evening, and think I must have done so except for the purchase of a box of nougat at Montélimart (the place is famous for the manufacture of this confection, which, at the station, is hawked at the windows of the train) and for a bouillon, very much later, at Lyons. The journey beside the Rhone—past Valence, past Tournon, past Vienne—would have been charming, on that luminous Sunday, but for two disagreeable accidents. The express from Marseilles, which I took at Orange, was full to overflowing; and the only refuge I could find was an inside angle in a carriage laden with Germans, who had command of the windows, which they occupied as strongly as they have been known to occupy other strategical positions. I scarcely know, however, why I linger on this particular discomfort, for it was but a single item in a considerable list of grievances,—grievances dispersed through six weeks of constant railway travel in France. I have not touched upon them at an earlier stage of this chronicle, but my reserve is not owing to any sweetness of association. This form of locomotion, in the country of the amenities, is attended with a dozen discomforts; almost all the conditions of the business are detestable. They force the sentimental tourist again and again to ask himself whether, in consideration of such mortal annoyances, the game is worth the candle. Fortunately, a railway journey is a good deal like a sea voyage; its miseries fade from the mind as soon as you arrive. That is why I completed, to my great satisfaction, my little tour in France. Let this small effusion of ill-nature be my first and last tribute to the whole despotic *gare:* the deadly *salle d'attente*, the insufferable delays over one's luggage, the porterless platform, the overcrowded and illiberal train. How many a time did I permit myself the secret reflection that it is in perfidious Albion that they order this matter best! How many a time did the eager British mercenary, clad in velveteen and clinging to the door of the carriage as it glides into the station, revisit my invidious dreams! The paternal porter and the responsive hansom are among the best gifts of the English genius to the world. I hasten to add, faithful to my habit (so insufferable to some of my friends) of ever and again readjusting the balance after I have given it an honest tip, that the bouillon at Lyons, which I spoke of above, was, though by no means an ideal bouillon, much better than any I could have obtained at an English railway station. After I had imbibed it, I sat in the train (which waited a long time at Lyons) and, by the light of one of the big lamps on the platform, read all sorts of disagreeable things in certain radical newspapers which I had bought at the book-stall. I gathered from these sheets that Lyons was in extreme commotion. The Rhone and the Saone, which form a girdle for the splendid town, were almost in the streets, as I could easily believe from what I had seen of the country after leaving Orange. The Rhone, all the way to Lyons, had been in all sorts of places where it had no business to be, and matters were naturally not improved by its confluence with the charming and copious stream which, at Macon, is said once to have given such a happy opportunity to the egotism of the capital. A visitor from Paris (the anecdote is very old), being asked on the quay of that city whether he didn't admire the Saone, replied good-naturedly that it was very pretty, but that in Paris they spelled it with the *ei*. This moment of general alarm at Lyons had been chosen by certain ingenious persons (I credit them, perhaps, with too sure a prevision of the rise of the rivers) for practising further upon the apprehensions of the public. A bombshell filled with dynamite had been thrown into a café, and various votaries of the comparatively innocuous *petit verre* had been wounded (I am not sure whether any one had been killed) by the irruption. Of course there had been arrests and incarcerations, and the "Intransigeant" and the "Rappel" were filled with the echoes of the explosion. The tone of these organs is rarely edifying, and it had never been less so than on this occasion. I wondered, as I looked through them, whether I was losing all my radicalism; and then I wondered whether, after all, I had any to lose. Even in so long a wait as that tiresome delay at Lyons I failed to settle the question, any more than I made up my mind as to the probable future of the militant democracy, or the ultimate form of a civilization which should have blown up everything else. A few days later, the waters went down at Lyons; but the democracy has not gone down.

I remember vividly the remainder of that evening which I spent at Macon,—remember it with a chattering of the teeth. I know not what had got into the place; the temperature, for the last day of October, was eccentric and incredible.

12

HENRY JAMES, *PORTRAITS OF PLACES* (BOSTON: HOUGHTON, MIFFLIN AND CO., 1911), PP. 81–86

I said just now that no two things could well be more unlike than England and France; and though the remark is not original, I uttered it with the spontaneity that it must have on the lips of a traveller who, having left either country, has just disembarked in the other. It is of course by this time a very trite observation, but it will continue to be made so long as Boulogne remains the same lively antithesis of Folkestone. An American, conscious of the family-likeness diffused over his own huge continent, never quite unlearns his surprise at finding that so little of either of these two almost contiguous towns has rubbed off upon the other. He is surprised at certain English people feeling so far away from France, and at all French people feeling so far away from England. I travelled from Boulogne the other day in the same railway-carriage with a couple of amiable and ingenuous young Britons, who had come over to spend ten days in Paris. It was their first landing in France; they had never yet quitted their native island; and in the course of a little conversation that I had with them I was struck with the scantiness of their information in regard to French manners and customs. They were very intelligent lads; they were apparently fresh from a university; but in respect to the interesting country they were about to enter, their minds were almost a blank. If the conductor, appearing at the carriage door to ask for our tickets, had had the leg of a frog sticking out of his pocket, I think their only very definite preconception would have been confirmed. I parted with them at the Paris station, and I have no doubt that they very soon began to make precious discoveries; and I have alluded to them not in the least to throw ridicule upon their "insularity"—which indeed, being accompanied with great modesty, I thought a very pretty spectacle—but because having become, since my last visit to France, a little insular myself, I was more conscious of the emotions that attend on an arrival.

The brightness always seems to begin while you are still out in the channel, when you fairly begin to see the French coast. You pass into a region of intenser light—a zone of clearness and colour. These properties brighten and deepen as you approach the land, and when you fairly stand upon that good Boulognese quay, among the blue and red douaniers and soldiers, the small ugly men in cerulean blouses, the charming fishwives, with their folded kerchiefs and their crisp cap-frills, their short striped petticoats, their tightly-drawn stockings, and their little clicking sabots—when you look about you at the smokeless air, at the pink and yellow houses, at the white-fronted café, close at hand, with its bright blue letters, its mirrors and marble-topped tables, its white-aproned, alert, undignified waiter, grasping a huge coffee-pot by a long handle—when you perceive all these things you feel the additional savour that foreignness gives to the picturesque; or feel rather, I should say, that simple foreignness may itself make the picturesque; for certainly the elements in the picture I have just sketched are not especially exquisite. No matter; you are amused, and your amusement continues—being sensibly stimulated by a visit to the buffet at the railway-station, which is better than the refreshment-room at Folkestone. It is a pleasure to have people offering you soup again, of their own movement; it is a pleasure to find a little pint of Bordeaux standing naturally before your plate; it is a pleasure to have a napkin; it is a pleasure, above all, to take up one of the good long sticks of French bread—as bread is called the staff of life, the French bake it literally in the shape of staves—and break off a loose, crisp, crusty morsel.

There are impressions, certainly, that imperil your good-humour. No honest Anglo-Saxon can like a French railway-station; and I was on the point of adding that no honest Anglo-Saxon can like a French railway-official. But I will not go so far as that; for after all I cannot remember any great harm that such a functionary has ever done me—except in locking me up as a malefactor. It is necessary to say, however, that the honest Anglo-Saxon, in a French railway-station, is in a state of chronic irritation—an irritation arising from his sense of the injurious effect upon the genial French nature of the possession of an administrative uniform. I believe that the consciousness of brass buttons on his coat and stripes on his trousers has spoiled many a modest and amiable Frenchman, and the sight of these aggressive insignia always stirs within me a moral protest. I repeat that my aversion to them is partly theoretic, for I have found, as a general thing, that an inquiry civilly made extracts a civil answer from even the most official-looking personage. But I have also found that such a personage's measure of the civility due to him is inordinately large; if he places himself in any degree at your service, it is apparently from the sense that true greatness can afford to unbend. You are constantly reminded that you must not presume. In England these intimations never proceed from one's "inferiors." In France the "administration" is the first thing that touches you; in a little while you get used to it, but you feel somehow that, in the process, you have lost the flower of your self-respect. Of course you are under some obligation to it. It has taken you off the steamer at Folkestone; made you tell your name to a gentleman with a sword, stationed at the farther end of the plank—not a drawn sword, it is true, but still, at the best, a very nasty weapon; marshalled you into the railway-station; assigned you to a carriage—I was going to say to a seat; transported you to Paris, marshalled you again out of the train, and under a sort of military surveillance, into an enclosure containing a number of human sheep-pens, in one of which it has imprisoned you for some half-hour. I am always on the point, in these places, of asking one of my gaolers if I may not be allowed to walk about on parole. The administration at any rate has finally taken you out of your pen, and, through the medium of a functionary who "inscribes" you in a little book, transferred you to a cab selected by a logic of its own. In doing all this it has certainly done a great deal for you; but somehow its good offices have made you feel sombre and resentful. The other day, on arriving from London, while I was waiting for my luggage, I saw several of the porters who convey travellers' impedimenta to the cab come up and deliver over the coin they had just received for this service to a functionary posted *ad hoc* in a corner, and armed with a little book in which he noted down these remittances. The *pourboires* are apparently thrown into a common fund and divided among the guild of porters. The system is doubtless an excellent one, excellently carried out; but the sight of the poor round-shouldered man of burdens dropping his coin into the hand of the official arithmetician was to my fancy but another reminder that the individual, as an individual, loses by all that the administration assumes.

After living a while in England you observe the individual in Paris with quickened attention; and I think it must be said that at first he makes an indifferent figure. You are struck with the race being physically and personally a poorer one than that great family of largely-modelled, fresh-coloured people you have left upon the other side of the channel. I remember that in going to England a year ago and disembarking of a dismal, sleety Sunday evening at Folkestone, the first thing that struck me was the good looks of the railway porters—their broad shoulders, their big brown beards, their well-cut features. In like manner, landing lately at Boulogne of a brilliant Sunday morning, it was impossible not to think the little men in numbered caps who were gesticulating and chattering in one's path, rather ugly fellows. In arriving from other countries one is struck with a certain want of dignity in the French face. I do not know, however, whether this is anything worse than the fact that the French face is expressive; for it may be said that, in a certain sense, to express anything is to compromise with one's dignity, which likes to be understood without taking trouble. As regards the lower classes, at any rate, the impression I speak of always passes away; you perceive that the good looks of the French working-people are to be found in their look of intelligence. These people, in Paris, strike me afresh as the cleverest, the most perceptive, and, intellectually speaking, the most human of their kind. The Paris *ouvrier*, with his democratic blouse, his expressive, demonstrative, agreeable eye, his meagre limbs, his irregular, pointed features, his sallow complexion, his face at once fatigued and animated, his light, nervous organisation, is a figure that I always encounter again with pleasure. In some cases he looks depraved and perverted, but at his worst he looks refined; he is full of vivacity of perception, of something that one can appeal to.

13

ÉMILE ZOLA, *GERMINAL* (LONDON: CHATTO & WINDUS, 1914), PP. 1–10

Germinal

UNDER the starless sky of a night of dense inky blackness, a man was following, all alone, the highroad from Marchiennes by Montsou, some six miles and more of pavement cutting straight across the low-lying plain between the beetroot fields. He could not even see the black ground in front of him, and was only conscious of the vast level horizon through feeling the March wind, which blew in broad gusts like those of the open sea and was icy from contact with miles and miles of marsh and woodless land. Not the faintest shadow of a tree loomed against the sky; the pavement spread out straight ahead like a jetty amidst the blinding, misty gloom.

The man had left Marchiennes a little before two o'clock. He was walking with a quick step and shivering beneath his well-worn cotton jacket and corduroy trousers. A small bundle tied in a chequered handkerchief seemed to inconvenience him very much. He hugged it to his sides first with one, then with the other elbow, in order that he might slip both his benumbed hands into his pockets, for the cutting blast made them bleed. But one idea occupied the brain of this workman without work and without shelter—the hope that the cold would abate with daybreak. And he tramped along in this way for about an hour, when, on his left, at a mile or so from Montsou, he suddenly perceived some reddish lights—three braziers burning in the open air, in which they seemed to be suspended. At first the man hesitated, a nameless fear taking possession of him; but he could not resist his painful craving to warm his hands, if only for an instant.

A steep hollow suddenly opened before him and everything then disappeared from his view. On his right was a hoarding of coarse deal boards, an enclosure to some railway siding probably; and on his left rose a grassy embankment, atop of which appeared a confused mass of gables, the low regular roofs of village houses. The man advanced another two hundred steps. Suddenly, at a bend of the road, the fires reappeared close to him, though he could not understand any more than before how it was that they burned so high in the lifeless sky like incandescent moons. Down below, however, another sight made him pause. There was a heavy mass, a thick-set pile of irregular buildings, from amidst which rose the silhouette of a factory chimney. Infrequent flashes of light came through the grimy windows, and five or six lanterns, burning low, hung outside from blackened woodwork, which vaguely suggested gigantic trestles. And from this phantom-like place, steeped in darkness and smoke, there arose but one sound—the deep prolonged panting of a steam-engine which could not be seen.

Then the man knew that he was near a coal-pit, and his false shame again got the better of him. What was the good of asking? There would surely be no work. Instead of going towards the building, he at last ventured to climb a huge mound of shale on the top of which the three coal fires were burning in iron braziers to give light and warmth to those who were still toiling. The quarrymen had no doubt worked till late, for shale was still being taken out of the pit. The new-comer could hear the banksmen pushing the trains on to the huge settle-board, and could distinguish shadowy forms tilting the trucks near each fire.

'Good morning,' he said, approaching one of the braziers.

With his back to the fire stood a waggoner, a diminutive old man, wearing a violet-coloured woollen jersey and a rabbit-skin cap. His horse, a big yellowish animal, stood by stock-still, waiting for the six trucks which he had drawn up the incline to be emptied. The man working the tilter—a tall, lean, reddish fellow— was apparently in no hurry; he handled his lever in a heavy sleepy way. And above it all the wind was careering madly; it was an icy blast, whose broad gusts swept by like the strokes of a scythe.

'Good morning,' answered the old carter.

Then both became silent. The new-comer, who felt himself eyed suspiciously, gave his name.

'My name is Étienne Lantier,' said he; 'I am an engine-man. Any chance of getting a job here?'

The flames of the fire in the brazier lit up his handsome, dark features. He might be about one-and-twenty, and looked strong, in spite of his small limbs. The waggoner, no longer distrustful, shook his head.

'A job for an engine-man? I'm sure there isn't. Two called here yesterday. They went away as they came.'

A gust of wind cut short his speech. Then Étienne, pointing to the sombre mass of buildings at the foot of the mound, asked, 'It's a coal-pit, isn't it?'

This time the old man could not answer at all. A violent fit of coughing almost choked him. At last he expectorated, and his saliva left a black stain on the purplish ground.

'Yes, it's a pit—the Voreux pit. Look, the miners' village is quite close.'

And with outstretched arm he indicated the village, whose roofs the young man had vaguely perceived in the darkness. But the six trucks were empty by this time; so the waggoner, his legs stiff with rheumatism, went on behind them without so much as cracking his whip; while the yellowish horse started of his own accord, lazily trudging between the rails to the accompaniment of a fresh blast which made the hair of his coat stand on end.

The Voreux pit began to look less fantastic to Étienne, as he lingered before the fire, warming his poor, bleeding hands. He recognised each part of the mechanism whereby the pit was worked—the large coal staiths, their walls coated with tar, the top of the shaft, the vast engine-room and the square tower of the pumping machine. This mine, with its stunted brick buildings lying in a hollow, and its chimney rising like a threatening horn, assumed in his eyes the evil aspect of some voracious wild beast crouching there to devour everybody. While examining each detail, he began to think of the vagabond life he had been leading for the last week, vainly looking for a new situation. He again saw himself in his shed at the railway works slapping his overseer's face; driven away from Lille; getting the cold shoulder everywhere. On the Saturday he had got as far as Marchiennes, where folks had said there was a job to be had at the ironworks; but there was neither a job at the ironworks nor even at Sonneville's place. His Sunday had been spent in a wheelwright's timber-yard, whence the watchman had expelled him at two in the morning. He hadn't a penny in the world, nor a crust of bread to eat, so what was to become of him, wandering across the country without any definite aim, without any shelter from the bitter blast? Yes, this was a pit right enough; the lanterns lighted the enclosure around the shaft, and the sudden opening of a door enabled him to catch a glimpse of the red-hot furnaces of the boiler-room. He even explained to himself the noise of the pumping engine, that deep incessant panting which was like the monster's husky breath.

The fellow at the tilting crane had not yet taken the least notice of Étienne's presence, and the latter was just about to pick up his little bundle, which had fallen to the ground, when the sound of coughing apprised him of the waggoner's return. He saw the old man slowly emerge from the darkness, followed by the yellowish horse, which was pulling six newly-filled trucks.

'Are there any factories at Montsou?' Étienne inquired.

The old chap spat again, and answered amidst the whistling of the wind. 'There's factories enough as far as that goes. You should have been here three or four years ago! Everything was brisk then; there weren't hands enough; wages had never been better. But now we've got to play pinch-belly again. It's real misery throughout the region; the masters are sending away their hands; all the factories are shutting up one after another. May be it's not the Emperor's fault, but why does he want to go fighting in America? Without reckoning that the animals are dying of the cholera as well as human folk.'

Then both men went on complaining—their short phrases cut shorter still every now and then by the wind. Étienne spoke of his useless peregrinations during the last week. Was he to die of hunger, then? The highroads would soon be swarming with beggars. To which the old waggoner replied that it would end by something dreadful happening, for it was not right that so many Christians should be thrown on to the streets.

'One hasn't meat every day.'

'Ah! if one only had bread!'

Their voices died away—gusts of wind carried off certain words in a melancholy howl.

'Look!' shouted the waggoner, as he turned towards the south; 'Montsou is over yonder.'

And with outstretched hand he indicated certain spots invisible in the darkness, naming them as he did so. Over at Montsou Fauvelle's sugar works were still going, but the Hoton refinery had dismissed half its hands. The only establishments that seemed able to bear up were Dutilleul's flour-mills and Bleuze's rope-yard, where they manufactured mine cables. Then, with a sweeping motion of his hand, embracing half of the northern horizon, he went on: Sonneville's building yards had not got a third of their usual orders; at the Marchiennes smelting works only two furnaces out of three were alight; and a strike had been threatening at the Gagebois glassworks because the masters wanted to lower the wages.

'I know—I know,' the young man repeated at each fresh indication. 'I've been there.'

'As for ourselves,' continued the waggoner, 'we're still kept going, though all the pits have lowered their output. And look over yonder at the Victory blasting works; they've only two fires alight there.'

Then once more he started off behind his sleepy horse and empty trucks.

From the spot where Étienne stood he could overlook the whole of the country. The darkness was as dense as ever, but the old chap's waving hand seemed to have filled it with a crushing, hopeless misery, which the young man felt to be everywhere around him in that boundless expanse. Was it not a wail of hunger that the March wind sent howling over the bleak, bare country? The squalls seemed to be lashing themselves into a fury—to be sounding the death-knell of all labour—to be bringing a famine that would lay low thousands of men. And Étienne's glances, wandering hither and thither, tried to pierce the gloom—eager and yet afraid to see what there might be there. But everything was chaotic in that abyss of darkness. All he could see in the distance was the flames of coke ovens and smelting furnaces. The former, with their batteries of a hundred chimneys, displayed lines of ruddy flames, while the two towers more to the left sent a bluish glow skywards like gigantic torches. There was all the melancholy of a threatening conflagration about the scene. No other stars arose on the horizon save those nocturnal fires of the land of coal and iron.

'You belong to Belgium, perhaps?' suddenly resumed the old waggoner, who had come back and was standing behind Étienne.

He had only brought three trucks this time. They might as well be emptied while an accident that had happened to the cage was being repaired. A bolt that had given way would prevent further work for at least a quarter of an hour. Down below everything had become silent; the banksmen were standing still; the rumbling of the trucks over the platform had ceased. Only the distant sound of a smith's hammer beating iron fell upon the ear.

'No, I come from the south,' answered the young man.

Then the red-haired fellow who worked the tilter, having emptied the trucks, came to sit down on the mound, well pleased with the accident. He kept obstinately silent, only raising his big, dull eyes to look at the old carter as if overwhelmed by so many words. In fact, the carter was, as a rule, by no means talkative. But the stranger's face evidently pleased him, and he was taken with some itching of the tongue, some desire to unburthen himself, such as sometimes causes old folks to talk aloud to themselves.

'I,' said he, 'belong to Montsou; my name is Jollycorpse.'

'A nickname, surely?' asked Étienne, in surprise.

The old man sniggered contentedly, and pointed to the Voreux pit. 'That's it. Three times have they taken me out of there in pieces: the first time with every hair of my body singed; the second time with my carcase choke-full of earth; the third time with my stomach full of water, like a frog's. Then, as they saw that I wouldn't kick the bucket, they named me Jollycorpse just for fun. But my real name's Vincent Maheu.'

His gaiety increased, his laugh sounding like the creaking of a badly greased wheel and ending in a violent fit of coughing. The fire was shining full upon his huge head, with white and scanty hair, and a flat face of a livid pallor speckled with bluish spots. He was very short, with an apoplectical neck, misshapen legs, and long arms whose square hands descended to his knees. Like his horse, too, which remained motionless without sign of being inconvenienced by the wind, he seemed to be made of stone— as if he neither felt the biting cold nor heard the squalls whistling past his ears. When he had done coughing he spat, and invariably brought up coal-dust.

'You have been at work for a good many years at the mine, I suppose?' said Étienne, who noticed this.

Jollycorpse opened his long arms. 'For a good many years?' he repeated. 'I should think so. I was barely eight when I first went down into the Voreux here, and now I am fifty-eight; so reckon it out for yourself. I've been everything down there—from trammer, as soon as I had the strength to push the trucks, to hewer, when I could ply a pick; eighteen years of the last job. Then, on account of my wretched legs, they set me to quarrying, cogging, and looking after the props, until they had to take me out because the doctor said I was likely to leave my bones there. Five years ago I became waggoner. So I've had fifty years of it in all—forty-five of them down below. That's a pretty record, isn't it?'

While he was talking some pieces of flaming coal that fell from the brazier cast a sanguineous glow upon his livid face.

'They tell me to take some rest,' he went on, 'but I don't mean to. I'm not such a flat as they think me. I'm right enough for another two years, until I'm sixty, and then I shall have my pension of a hundred and eighty francs. If I were to say good-bye now they'd ship me off with one of a hundred and fifty. They're sharp as needles, the masters are. Besides, if it weren't for my legs I should be strong enough; but it's that confounded water that's got into me; I used to get so soaked in the cuttings. There are days when I can't stir without pain.'

MENTALITÉ AND THE MACHINE ENSEMBLE

Another fit of coughing made him pause.

'And it makes you cough also?' said Étienne.

But he shook his head violently, and, when he was at length able to speak, replied: 'No, no; but I caught cold a month ago. I never had a cough before, and now I can't get rid of it. It's odd, too, but I keep on spitting and spitting—'

Again he had to stop for fully a minute.

'Is it blood you bring up?' asked Étienne.

Jollycorpse slowly wiped his lips with the back of his hand. 'No, it's coal. I've got enough of it inside me to keep me warm for the rest of my days. And still, it's five years since I set foot below. It seems I had it in stock without being aware of it. Never mind! Coal preserves one, you know!'

Silence fell once more. The strokes of the smith's hammer ascended rhythmically from the shaft below. The wind howled by like a wail of hunger and weariness from the depths of the night. Standing there before the flickering flames, the old miner went on, recalling the past. It wasn't since yesterday that he and his had been plying the pick down below. The family had worked for the Montson Mining Company ever since it started—a matter of a hundred and six years already. His grandfather, Guillaume Maheu, when but a stripling of fifteen, had been the first to find caking coal in the old Réquillart pit, the first that the company had worked, over yonder, near the Fauvelle sugar refinery. This was known all over the country, for the seam had been called the Guillaume seam, after his grandfather's Christian name. He, Jollycorpse, had never known his grandfather, but, from what he had been told, he must have been very strong and tall, though he died at sixty of old age. Then his father, Nicolas Maheu, called the Red, had been killed, when barely forty, down in that very Voreux pit, which was being sunk at the time. There was a slip, and he was found flat as a pancake, both blood and bones being crushed out of him by the masses of fallen rock. Two of Jollycorpse's uncles and his three brothers had also left their skins below. He himself, who had come out of it fairly perfect, with only his legs damaged, was considered a clever fellow. Oh, there were risks. But what could a man do? He had to work at something, so as well work at this trade as at any other. His son, Toussaint Maheu, and his grandsons, and all his family, who were living opposite in the miners' village, risked their lives down below every day. Over a hundred years of coal-mining, the young ones after the elders, and all for the same 'guv'nor.' Ah! there were a good many trader folks who couldn't tell their family history so well.

'After all, as long as one gets food, what's the odds?' observed Étienne.

'That's what I say. As long as one gets bread to eat one can manage to live.' Then Jollycorpse lapsed into silence, and turned towards the miners' village, where a few lights began to twinkle behind the windows. The clock of Montsou struck four. The cold was becoming keener.

'Is your company very rich?' resumed Étienne.

The old man shrugged his shoulders, then dropped them as if overwhelmed by a weight of money.

'Rich? I should think so, indeed. Perhaps not so rich as its neighbour, the Anzin Company; but there are untold millions, for all that. Nineteen pits in all: thirteen for working—the Voreux, the Victory, Crèvecœur, Mirou, Saint-Thomas, Madeleine, Feutry-Cantel, and others besides—and six for pumping or ventilation, like Réquillart. Then there are ten thousand workmen, and rights spreading over sixty-seven communes, an output of five thousand tons a day, a railway connecting all the pits, and all sorts of workshops and factories. Yes, yes, there is plenty of brass in it all!'

The rumbling of some trucks on the settle-board made the yellowish horse prick its ears. The cage must have been repaired by this time, for the banksmen had resumed work. While putting his four-footed companion to the trucks, the waggoner added in a low voice, addressing himself to the animal, 'Shouldn't get in the habit of jabbering like that, you idle brute. If Monsieur Hennebeau only knew that you were wasting your time like this!'

At this, Étienne, who wrapped in thought had been looking up at the sky, inquired, 'Then the mine belongs to Monsieur Hennebeau?'

'No,' explained the old man, 'Monsieur Hennebeau is only the general manager. He is paid, like the rest of us.'

Thereupon the young fellow pointed to the vast expanse which he divined, as it were, behind the darkness. 'To whom does all that belong, then?'

But Jollycorpse could not answer immediately. He was seized with another fit of coughing, so violent, indeed, that it took him some minutes to recover his breath.

'All that? We don't know. To somebody or other,' he said at last, and with his forefinger he pointed to some distant undefined spot, peopled by the folk for whom the Maheus had been working for over a century. His voice had assumed a tone of religious awe: it was as if he alluded to some inaccessible tabernacle, where crouched the insatiable power to which they sacrificed their flesh and blood, without ever beholding it face to face.

'If one at least had sufficient bread to eat,' resumed Étienne, reverting to his original train of thought, without any apparent transition.

'Yes, as you say, if one always had bread to eat; but that would be too much of a good thing!' retorted Jollycorpse.

His horse had started off, and he in his turn disappeared with the dragging step of an invalid. Meantime the red-haired fellow attending to the tilting crane had not stirred. Gathered up almost in a ball, with his chin betwixt his knees, he stared vacantly before him with his big, dim eyes.

Étienne still lingered there, though he had taken up his bundle. He felt his back chilled by the bitter blast, while his chest roasted before the fierce fire. He would, perhaps, after all, do well to inquire at the pit: the old man might not know. Besides, he would take any job. What was to become of him? Where was he to go in that region, starving for want of work? Was he to die like a dog behind some wall? Yet he hesitated. He felt a nameless fear of that Voreux pit, in the midst of that bleak country, steeped in the densest obscurity. At each squall the wind seemed to increase in violence, as though it blew from an ever extending horizon. Not a gleam of dawn whitened the lifeless heavens. Only the coke ovens and smelting furnaces threw up a lurid glow, imparting a blood-like tinge to the darkness without illumining its unknown depths. And the Voreux pit down in the hollow, where it crouched like some evil beast, panted yet more noisily, as if it experienced growing difficulty and pain in its digestion of human flesh and blood.

14

MARY RAYMOND WILLIAMS, *JULY AND AUGUST OF 1914* (CLEVELAND: PRESS OF THE BROOKS COMPANY, 1915), PP. 78–103

Saturday, August 1st

The morning was beautiful, but as the sun grew brighter the afternoon became really hot while the atmosphere of uneasiness about Zürich increased in the same proportion.

First of all the hotel would not accept our paper money for breakfast, so that meal was charged for the time being. Ed hardly waited to finish his breakfast in his anxiety to get to the bank, and Hilda, quite on the alert for more excitement, went too. Every bank was closed, but Cook's, equal to the emergency, gave us a hundred francs in gold and silver.

By noon our hotel had settled down systematically and without any panicky signs to a necessarily new set of regulations. Twenty German waiters had already left for their country, the elevator boys were expecting to leave at any time. Service in every respect had to be curtailed, so we were asked to be as considerate as possible in the use of towels and linen. The elevator would run only through the busiest hours and we were all asked to come to our meals at the same time.

Next to me at the long luncheon table was a lady who told me the worst, but what we had expected since last evening's news, that Germany—reckless, aggressive, head of the Teutons, had declared war upon Russia. This American had been planning with her friend to stay in Switzerland until November, but now although carrying a large letter of credit, she could only procure four pounds in Zürich this morning, so she was giving up all thought of her attractive rooms engaged at a pension in Lucerne and was planning to take the first train this afternoon for that city, expecting to look for rooms at eight francs a day, then go to Geneva as soon as possible in hopes of catching a steamer for America. Poor woman! I should like to have offered to help them along somehow with our Hotchkiss, but Ed reminded me we could not count with any certainty on again using that French car with its Swiss driver.

After luncheon we walked to the office of the American Consul, not feeling we should afford the luxury of a taxi nor even a *sous* for the "extras" which were being called at every corner. It seemed a month since yesterday morning when I was spending my francs with such keen pleasure over the linens of Lucerne and now felt no certainty at all of covering the many miles of railroad to Paris.

Every store with the exception of the smallest shops had pulled its shutters tight and the banks all appeared to be closed as if for a long holiday. The office of our Consul was overflowing with Americans, asking many questions, all leading to the same problem, "What shall we do?" to which the poor, harrassed representative of our country had but one reply which seemed to safely cover a multitude of perplexities. "If you have a passport you can travel without trouble; if not, go to Berne and apply for one and do it at once," for he had heard that in all likelihood, for the next few days, there would be no trains out of Switzerland.

At the station we found crowds, nobody being allowed to enter without a ticket to show. We had none, but every kind person who was lucky enough to be blest with a pass of any sort was ready to help his neighbor, and so it happened that an American who had a Cook's pass, took Ed in with him while Hilda and I waited outside, a part of scores of Americans, each telling their situation to one another and wondering if their paper money would be honored.

The result of Ed's railroad expedition was that a train was due to leave the city for Paris at nine-forty this evening, and that we might be able to buy sleeping apartments later, but in order to do so, Ed would have to go back again at four o'clock and stand in line. We found Charlet in the garage still working on the broken spring; one of the workmen who had been helping him had been called to join his army and had actually had to drop his tools and run. Charlet had heard that the petrol in Switzerland had been called into requisition for the army, so even were his machine in good shape now, he could not run it far without the petrol. Also, he was Swiss born and would probably not find it easy to leave the country in its present state, so, hard as it was, and to me it seemed like actually deserting the guide who had given us such comfort and pleasure, there was no question about it, we had to part, leaving Charlet to go to Berne for his passport, while we risked the trip without one.

Returning to the hotel for a moment, Ed met a man who had gone to America from Switzerland fifteen years ago but had not taken out naturalization papers. He was visiting here with his automobile and both he and his machine had been pressed into service.

Hilda and I spent the remainder of the afternoon in packing, while Ed returned to the station. Fortunately he found a man from Cook's who was our good angel, and it was due to his untiring persistency that finally our tickets and sleeping accommodations were bought and paid for. Cook's had refused in the morning to give us any more money but they were willing to sell us the tickets and charge the value of them on our letter of credit. We checked our automobile trunk to London. Ed called the train a "perhaps" train. Perhaps there would be a train through from Austria, perhaps there would be a sleeper on it, perhaps this sleeper would not join it until it reached Basle and perhaps we could get something on it. It was a hard decision to make because there was no way of knowing until we saw the thing through, whether we were wise in leaving the hotel where we were comfortable and trying to get out of the city.

For dinner more travelers had arrived, among them the C.'s who had come from Munich, looking for safety and quiet and were appalled to find the state of things that existed in Zurich. In spite of the unfavorable conditions the hotel people show their patriotism this evening. On the long dining tables were large ships made of some candied pastry with the Swiss flag flying, labeled August first. We were told this was in celebration of the five hundredth anniversary of the Swiss Republic. We thought it very plucky of these people, doing their best to commemorate the occasion, though short of hands, and with the prospect of a scarcity of provisions, as Switzerland is quite dependent upon other countries for a large part of her food supplies.

The hotel motor took us to the station, Charlet going along to see us off, and the Cook man met us with our tickets. The crowd was tremendous, soldiers everywhere, and after much pushing and shoving by ourselves and the crowd, we reached our train and were off at nine-forty. Shortly after eleven we reached Basle and left the train, wondering whether we would find the other train for Paris and whether our sleeping car would be on it. Sure enough at eleven-thirty the other train was ready to go and had a sleeper, but, alas, it was not ours. Then there was more of the "perhaps." Perhaps another section would go and perhaps the sleeper would be on it. This station, too, was full of people and soldiers. Basle is a border town and we understood the station was only two or three blocks away from the German line.

About one-thirty another train had pulled in and we found our two compartments ready for us. We boarded it and went to bed, looking forward to arrival in Paris some time during the morning, and London tomorrow evening or the next morning.

Sunday, August 2nd

At three-thirty I awoke to find we were standing still at the border town of Delle, and crowds of people were walking back and forth on the station platform. I watched the daylight come and at six-thirty dressed and, informed by the porter that there was something to eat at the buffet station, started forth, leaving Hilda and Ed still sound asleep. Hundreds of people must have already been there, and though I saw pieces of bread and bottles of wine on the counter, there was so much of *café au lait* and wine running from the bare tables to the floors, where, in the rush it had been spilled, it was all in such a smelly state of mess and dirt that my appetite grew small as I looked about. I saw soldiers walking back into the town and followed. The first café they turned into did not look prepossessing, but at the next, full of soldiers, I found the hostess interested in my wants, as apparently, I was the only woman who had tried her restaurant. I went into the kitchen where her children stood about, their big eyes full of wonder at the crowds of hungry people and, I suppose, anxious lest the soldiers would leave nothing for them. The mother cut me four slices of dark bread, a piece of cheese and sold me a cake of chocolate and a bottle of Vichy. I asked for meat, not feeling any certainty of a dining car, but the woman showed me her only meat—one small piece of ham, and in pathetic French explained that with the bordering countries at war, their chance of provisions, aside from dairy products, was very small. Armed with my purchases, I went back to the train and found Hilda dressed, the weary Ed still sleeping. We washed at the station pump as the others were doing and I showed Hilda the station restaurant, one sight of which was enough for her.

Soon Ed awoke and we all ate our breakfast in the car, then walked up and down and watched the crowds. The poor Italians! I felt so sorry for them, they could not go across the French frontier on our train so they had to get out and with their baggage on their backs, many women and children had to foot it to some place nearer the Italian frontier where they could cross into their native land.

Just before we finally pulled out of the station, I heard a Frenchman, excitedly asking a Frenchwoman if she could explain, in English, to an American lady who, it seems had lost her friend, that the Mayor of the town wished to bury the body rather than have it carried away. I could see the poor woman looking most distressed and was wondering what I could do for her when the signal for leaving was given; we had to hurry to our seats and at nine o'clock were actually on our way, leaving this distressed American woman behind. It was sad to be compelled to desert her. It was distressing, too, to see the women with small babies in the third class compartments; they had no place upon which to lay their heads all night and might have to go through part of another night in the same uncomfortable way; but most tragic of all was the sight of the swarms of soldiers everywhere, young men, the flower of the country, who were leaving their families and all, perhaps, never to return.

The best part of our day was the hour in the dining car where we had a real luncheon of three courses, served to the entire car full of people by two waiters, one of whom spilled a little of everything en route, but in spite of this loss, we had a great plenty, which was fortunate as our dinner consisted of a hard boiled egg apiece and one meat pastry pie between us. This food was snatched up from a station where we stopped five minutes and I only hope that others fared as well as we did, though I am afraid the woman at the buffet stand did not, for we were told that men fairly grabbed food from her counters and ran back to the train without stopping to pay. Always as soon as we stopped for any length of time, both men and women ran with bottles to the nearest station pump to put in a water supply.

At Belfort, among crowds of French soldiers, we saw about a dozen carried upon litters and others limping and leaning upon the shoulders of their comrades, evidently the first of the wounded in a skirmish with the Germans. Amidst the rush and excitement at this station, an Englishman, calm and unperturbed, tried to negotiate with the conductor for passage on our car. The conductor gesticulated violently and made it quite plain that there was not an extra seat to be had, but the Englishman, nothing daunted, remarked in a mixture of his own language and a French drawl that the English had made themselves the best friends of the French, and without more ado he boarded our car. Ed came to the rescue and offered his room and berth to the new passenger, for which the Englishman thanked him and remarked with great complacency, "I say, you've not had a shave this morning, have you?" He proved a quite enlivening addition to our car as he was full of conversation—too much so for the fatigued porter, who grew gradually indifferent to his *"Que pensez vous de la Guerre?"* and *"Pour quoi arrêtons nous ici?"* and gave up all attempts at answering what Hilda called "foolish questions."

I asked the porter at about eleven o'clock if he did not think it a good idea to make up our berths, but apparently he was short of bed linen, for he gave me the most decided answer he had yet given any of us, and that was quite negative. All day long, poor man, he had been asked in French, German and English, when we would reach Paris. He had been on duty for over twenty-four hours, with no chance for relief nor one square meal. As far as I could see, his only food was the scraps of our sumptuous fare which we shared with him. His only answer to all our questions was *"Mobilization."* Three times the train seemed to have crashed into something and every head went out of the window, our first natural thought being dynamited by the Germans. At the first crash I needed more of an assuring answer than that oft repeated *"Mobilization."* Hilda was asleep in one chair and Ed in another, so I turned to a Frenchman who explained the situation to me so satisfactorily that when another shock came and the tumblers on our table broke and added to the noise, and Hilda and Ed, of course, awoke, I was quite ready to assure them that, due to our very heavy train of sixteen compartment cars, when we turned a curve, the cars in the rear in catching up with the forward ones moved with such jerks that a clumsy bumping was the result.

Our friend the Englishman was sleeping the sleep of the unconcerned in Ed's berth when this last jar awoke him, whereupon he complained to two men outside that their conversation disturbed his slumber.

Monday, August 3rd

Warm and sunny. At four o'clock I watched dawn appear, thankful the weary night was over. It was a still, calm morning which shed its early light over the meadows full of golden wheat, much of it uncut for lack of labourers who have had to drop the scythe and arm themselves with the sword. I do hope reapers may be found, for this year's harvest has the appearance of a plentiful one and France will need it for her army.

The little towns seemed asleep as if war had not yet entered into their homes. At one small station where we stopped for a few moments, I saw a French dragoon, looking really gorgeous in his fine uniform and high hat with horsehair plume. He stopped at a house, knocked quietly and waited until a night-capped woman appeared at the upper window; he evidently asked for a bed in which to rest, and his answer must have been, there was not a vacant one, for I saw him, just as our train started, knocking at the next house, and I could only hope he had better luck.

It was rather amusing after hearing the discussions of our fellow passengers as to what Paris hotel would consider us as occupants at the hour of two or three in the morning, to arrive at the quite respectable hour of eight o'clock. It was rather a joke, too, on the Englishman who had suggested to us to have our luggage ready at a window through which the *"facteur"* would seize it, for him to find no *"facteur"* waiting. But such a Paris! It seemed inconceivable that so great a change could have taken place in our two weeks' absence. The city is fairly turned up side down. We had arrived at the Gare de l'Est and not one porter to relieve us of our four bags. We had crossed the street before we saw any signs of a porter and then one wholly unenthusiastic man did consent to handle our bags and volunteered the information that the near-by Gare du Nord, to which we were bound, was being used only for military purposes and we would have to take our train from the Gare St. Lazare, way across the city; but how were we to get there? We did not know the way and the porter's efforts to find us a cab were quite futile. Every taxi was rushed about at a break-neck speed full of soldiers or officials having to do with the army, and instead of the customary horse cabs waiting anxiously for a passenger, they were so apparently engaged for the day that they did not even stop to turn back their *"libre"* signs. There was no tram running today so we gave a fee to our man for having done nothing but hold our bags for five minutes, and started on foot, having little idea as to the direction of our station. It proved a circuitous route so we stopped often to inquire the way. The simple question as to our course brought forth a half dozen responses from as many people who excitedly collected about us, eager to help but with such a volley of French I had to ask them to speak more slowly. Our destination almost reached and our arms tired with the weight of bags, we met an empty horse cab and rode the remaining distance.

At the station we had to show our London tickets to be allowed to enter—and such a crowd! We found one empty corner near a buffet where we had a breakfast of chocolate and rolls. Ed left us here, telling us to make the most of the luxury of a chair while he went to inquire about trains for London. There was so much uncertainty apparent in the crowds which thronged the station that while waiting for him, I walked about looking for a telephone booth, thinking to call up our former Hotel de Meurice and see if they could take care of us if it should turn out to be necessary for us to remain in Paris over night. While doing this, I noticed a passageway with the sign "Terminal Hotel." This proved to be of the greatest good fortune as I walked through into the hotel resolved to take any accommodations that were available. The proprietor seemed anxious to be accommodating and although he had only one double room vacant, said he could easily put in an extra cot, so immediately I engaged the room, and a comfort it indeed proved to be! I went back to the station where I had left Hilda and found Ed had returned. He had learned that a train was to be sent to Havre at three-thirty the next morning to take passengers to the steamer La France which had postponed its sailing from the previous Saturday. His instructions were that ticket window number four would be opened at twelve o'clock and that he had better get in line for that. He first went with us to look at the room I engaged and approved of what had been done. Leaving us there, Hilda and I were soon asleep, but no such luck for Ed. He took only a sandwich and then went to the ticket line. At eleven o'clock the would-be travellers were all told to come and line up along the street outside the door. This they did, and Ed stood there for about five hours. It proved merely to be a ruse on the part of the station officials to get the crowd out of the station, and at six o'clock in the evening, the people were notified that the window was not to be opened at all and that they should all disperse.

In the meantime Ed had met Dr. Graham Taylor of Chicago, who introduced to him Bishop Hamilton of Boston and two or three other clergymen who together formed part of the American delegation to the International Church Peace Conference which was to have opened this week in Constance.

About four o'clock Ed gave up the idea of standing in the line longer and decided to go to the American Embassy to see what he could learn there. While Ed did not wish to obtrude our own affairs upon Ambassador Herrick, when he must be so busy and when there must be so many cases that were much more distressing, he nevertheless wrote on one of his cards that he was staying at the Grand Terminal Hotel with his wife and daughter and might have to ask him for assistance later. Upon arriving at the Embassy, he learned that it was necessary for all Americans to provide themselves with passports and that the French Government had extended, for two or three days, the time in which they might procure them. He was given a numbered card indicating his turn to go through the office formalities and was told that he should come back with the card about eleven o'clock the next day. Ambassador Herrick passed where he was standing and he had opportunity merely to say "How-do-you-do" and to ask him to look at the card when he had leisure to do so.

The evening News says that the Germans are crossing into Luxembourg, having violated the neutrality of Belgium. They gave that country twenty-four hours in which to decide if she would allow them to use her territory for their troops, and upon her indignant refusal, their army has started an attack upon her frontier. Great excitement in this city! The French are frantic at this outrage and all this evening the streets are full of *"La Guerre à Berlin"* and *"Vive la France!"* It seems that today France made upon Germany her actual declaration of war. England is plainly attempting to avoid the necessity of declaring war, but announces that she will protect the French sea ports from attack.

Tired as I was, there was so much excitement on the streets that I could hardly keep away from the window. In the afternoon we had seen a mob attack a taxi driver and push his cab down the street out of sight. In the evening I had no sooner gone to bed than I heard the angry murmur of a crowd and from the window saw the same occurrence again and watched the crowd until they were out of sight. Undoubtedly the drivers were Germans. Poor creatures, they will not have a comfortable time in the Paris of today.

Finally I went to sleep with the strains of the Marseillaise in my ears and dreamed I had gone with the French to the relief of the Belgians.

Tuesday, August 4th

We awoke to the sound of the French National Airs and from our window saw hundreds of men marching along the streets, reservists who had not yet received their uniforms, with wives and children trudging by their sides and helping to carry their queer shaped bags so quickly improvised from necessity. The sight of those responsible and determined looking men who showed no sign of sadness but a steadfast purpose to win for their country, moved me as no full dress parade could. There seems to be such a certainty as to the justice of their cause, no sane person could doubt it.

With breakfast came the news which France has been waiting for; the waiter who served us was jubilant over its announcement and I don't wonder. Today England declares war against the Teutonic Alliance and definitely binds herself to the support of France and Belgium.

Hilda and I spent the morning in our room which we turned into a laundry and washed clothes, feeling the want of the extra clean linen which we had not carried in our bags, thinking when we left Switzerland, that we would be in London Sunday, and back to the things in our trunks.

Ed started forth again and made an attempt to get berths, second or third class, or anything possible on the La France sailing tomorrow, but there was not a berth left. He met a fortunate Clevelander who had been able to get a reservation on the La France and then stood in line for three hours in order to buy his train ticket. At Cook's Ed was given forty dollars in gold, paying a premium of five dollars to get it. Morgan Harjes, although most obliging and helpful in every way, could only spare us paper money. Every other bank is closed, even the large Crédit Lyonnais. The first use our gold was put to was the payment of a cable to our family in Gloucester. We had waited, on account of the necessity of change, for no paper money was accepted for messages, nor were codes allowed. The cost was eight francs.

At eleven, Ed went to the Embassy as instructed the day before. He met on the sidewalk outside, Mr. D., a Cleveland friend who had been living in Paris and who agreed to wait for him until he could get his passport and instructions. Mr. Herrick saw him in the crowd and invited him into his office. He was greatly impressed with the stupendous job on the shoulders of the Ambassador and his staff. In addition to the crowds of Americans who needed to be cared for, there was the regular and extra business of the Embassy, and on top of all this, the Austrian and German Governments had, on the withdrawal of their own ambassadors, placed their interests in care of the representative of the American Government.

Mr. Herrick thought that the wisest thing to do for those who had no important engagements or early sailing dates was to stay quietly for a while in Paris. His officials had told Ed that it would be necessary to go to the Police Commissaire in the *Arrondissement* in which we were staying and get from him a *Permit de Sejour*, if we were going to stay in Paris, or, a *Laisser d'Aller* if we wanted to leave the city. This, Mr. Herrick advised promptly doing. He said he had been communicating with the American Government to see if they could not send a naval vessel or army transport over to help get the Americans home. One of his great problems was to furnish funds to those who needed them, including all of us. The school teacher or stenographer, who had come over with moderate funds and spent them all in the expectation that their vacation was over and they were to sail, were no worse off than the people who carried large letters of credit. No one could get funds for a few days.

Mr. Herrick asked Ed if he would like to work on the Committee which was being formed, which Ed said he would gladly do after his family were settled with some security, unless in the meantime he was able to get across to London. Meanwhile he referred him to Mr. D., who was awaiting him outside, and who proved to be just the man for Embassy work.

While waiting in the office before his conversation with Mr. Herrick, Ed found the crowd very interesting. He saw one young woman of not more than thirty, who had been escorting a party of young American girls of about sixteen to eighteen years of age on a European trip. They had got back as far as Paris, had their return tickets, expecting to sail from Cherbourg on a German boat next Saturday and now did not know when they could get away; without funds, without means of cabling home, without any knowledge of the immediate future, the distress of the young woman responsible for all of these girls may well be imagined.

We all lunched as economically as possible at the hotel, then started for the office of the Police. The crowd before its doors was as great as ever, and Hilda and I deciding we were not helping Ed nor the crowd by adding our presence, walked about the neighborhood. On the Rue de Clichy we saw the remnants of two stores of German proprietorship; there were only a few fragments of broken glass to show where the windows had been left by the enraged French. At a street corner there was another controversy between a cab driver and the occupant of the taxi, and a crowd was already collecting. The driver was apparently trying to make the most of the scarcity of cab service and asking an exorbitant rate, but the crowd took the part of the passenger and the driver made a hasty retreat.

Finding Ed still before the Police office, Hilda and I were anxious to have another glimpse of the Tuileries and our familiar haunts, so we walked towards the river, passing through street after street of closed shops. Upon many were the words *"Pour cause de mobilization."* At the meat and grocery stores, signs announced that their doors would be opened at three o'clock, and women with their market baskets, their children and dogs, stood patiently in line waiting to buy.

At the Place Vendôme we found the Hotels du Rhin and Ritz closed. The former is the French name for the Rhine. Evidently, fearing a mob attack, the white letters of the name had been painted out. We could see very faintly where they were. The Rue de Rivoli did not at all look its part. Instead of finding the smiling shop keepers standing at the door step, always alert and ready for our trade, most of the doors were closed and the shutters drawn; while in the few that were open, the owners looked as if they had before them a more serious business than that of feeding and dressing the tourists in this general reorganization of life and its industries.

We found at our attractive Hotel Meurice only one of the attendants whom we had known. The hotel was closing and this porter was superintending the last moving van. He told us that one hundred and twenty-six of the kitchen workers had gone to the front and he, himself, was off the next day and he spoke as if he were going off on a holiday, with the same calm cheerfulness that impressed me so in the Swiss. One hears much of the pity of losing the best of one's country, the educated and cultured, who must go forth and fight at the call to arms, but my heart aches for the waiter, the efficient, faithful man who has given his years to the drudgery and service of the hotel guests, knowing few of the comforts of life. He has spent his efforts tirelessly in waiting upon the wants of others, and with anything but the training needed for the army, marches and camp, he drops his apron and joins the ranks.

At the Rue de Rivoli entrance of the Meurice, the glass had been knocked out from the doors. The Meurice manager was a German, which accounted for that demonstration. A German on the Rue de Castiglione was killed last evening, but the Government had dealt with the mobs promptly and we saw the white paper announcements upon the walls of the Tuileries gardens which show that we are living under martial law. Cafés and restaurants must close at nine o'clock, mob demonstration will be severely punished, there must be no singing in the streets, and cab drivers charging more than ordinary tariff rate will be subject to imprisonment.

We sat in the gardens and watched the few families who had come to their usual place of recreation. There was such a marked lack of activity among the mothers and nurses whose fingers are ordinarily so busy with the mending basket. The children's play did not seem to have its usual spontaneity and even the sparrows were almost forgotten; I saw only one little girl feeding them this afternoon.

We rested where we had a good view of the Rue de Rivoli and watched the horses that had been requisitioned being led away; the splendid drays, then the cab horses, hundreds of them, until only the most dilapidated were left for city use and so forlorn looking were they that I could not have had the heart to ride behind one, if I had had the fare, but lack of money keeps cab rides at a safe distance just now.

I could afford a copy of "La Patrie" which the women sell every evening, so we were glad to read of three successful repulses the Servians had given the Austrians. On the other hand the Germans, this afternoon, were able to overpower of the Russians at the little town of Czenstochow near Lublin. There was a beautiful tribute to Jaures, the much loved socialist, who was assassinated last Saturday. Crowds of his admiring friends attended his funeral at which words of appreciation and praise were spoken by Viviani.

Ed did not stay in front of the Police station all day. There was a crowd of three or four hundred there, Germans and Austrians were being given the preference. He timed the rate at which they were being taken in and found that only about five went in each hour. He felt, therefore, that if he looked around at the end of each day and found they were still taking people, he could not get into trouble, as he felt that the time allowed for securing the necessary papers would necessarily have to be extended from day to day until all were taken care of.

Wednesday, August 5th

The day began with a shower and we were thankful that we had been able to obtain a little money from Cook's, even though at a premium, because one of the things it enabled us to do was to purchase an umbrella.

Ed made his usual pilgrimage to the Police and Hilda and I went to the Galeries Lafayette where we luxuriated in thirty-five dollars worth of clothes, which gave us a dress apiece and changes of underclothing, so that now we feel we are prepared to stay in Paris for weeks if necessary. It was enlightening to see how the employers of this leading store are conducting their large organization. In order to keep their men and women employed, they were busy cutting and rolling bandages, and making gray shirts for their soldiers. There was hardly a clerk I talked with who did not have a relative or friend who had gone to the front. They all spoke with appreciation of their employers who would not let them suffer in this hour of need. The hours, of course, were shortened, the store opening only in the afternoon, but they were given their usual luncheon, and while we were still there, the telephone rang and gave a bulletin of the latest news from the front. As to customers, there were only half a dozen of us during the hour we spent at shopping.

Our next step was to register at the New York Herald office. These rooms and those of Morgan Harjes are veritable headquarters for Americans. They come in streams from early morning until the doors are closed. Everybody seems to be looking for friends and acquaintances or wishing to have friends and acquaintances find them. It is assumed that almost everybody touring through this country will necessarily drift back to Paris and that all who are traveling in Switzerland and Germany will attempt to reach this City or London. Hence, everybody is registering at the office of the New York Herald, the American Express Company and Morgan Harjes. Although our sailings for home are booked for the Laconia from Liverpool, September first, and our trunks are in London, the feeling of uncertainty in the future is so great that we, like everybody else, would take any sailings that were offered us, chancing a refund on our other tickets and the ultimate return of our baggage.

Accordingly we joined the throng at the office of the Companie Transatlantique to see if there was a new sailing to be had, or, if by a slim chance some passenger booked for the Chicago had given up his passage, but the chance was too slim, the Chicago was full to overflowing.

We three then lunched at Duval's, near our hotel, for ninety-two cents. Our meals today have reached our maximum of economy—five dollars, tips and all.

The Figaro says the Germans are trying to break in upon the Belgian frontier.

Sir Edward Gray has announced to the House of Commons the purport of Germany's note asking Belgium to allow the Germans to march through her land, also the response of that brave little country. This communication was greeted with great applause. Japan did not ally herself to Austria, but will side with the Triple Entente in loyal adherence to the obligations of her treaty with England.

The Herald speaks enthusiastically of the work of the American Ambassador and his wife. In fact, it is seldom that one man in a difficult position receives such unanimous praise from all sources. American travelers, Americans resident in Paris, the French, all commend the fine work Mr. Herrick is doing. A committee is being formed to take up the work of providing for those of our countrymen who are in need; to help find accommodation, for all a passage home as soon as possible, to assist in locating and bringing together families and friends and the multifarious other things that are necessary to be done until things become adjusted to the conditions imposed by the war. This committee is under the chairmanship of Judge Gary.

While many people are suffering every mental concern as to how they will fare, the courage and mutual helpfulness of every one is noticeable to a degree and makes us proud of our countrymen. Occasionally someone will strike a little different note. For example, Ed heard today of a prominent United States Senator who had arrived without any baggage, had ruined the clothes he was wearing, was in a suit which he had borrowed from Judge Gary and could not quite understand why all war preparations could not be temporarily deferred until the Senator from ———— could get a suit of clothes.

This evening Ed introduced himself to a gentleman who, with his wife and two children, were in the hotel dining-room. He proved to be a former United States cabinet member, Mr. B., whom he found attractive, as were also the ladies and his son, who had just graduated from Princeton.

Hilda and I have quite decided, if we are to be here another day, to walk over to the American Church, which has been made a temporary shelter for refugees and to offer our services in whatever way we can.

Thursday, August 6th

In the morning Ed made his same unoriginal trip to the Police.

Mr. B. of New York showed Ed a Herald in which the Packard Company, in a notice tucked away in a corner, advertised trips to French ports. This seemed a God-send to the many tourists who had not been able to board a train, if only they were able to pay the fare for touring and could be one of the comparative few who could be accommodated this way. Ed and Mr. B., without waiting to tell us about this, immediately went to the Packard office and secured a car apiece at a charge of one hundred and fifty dollars to be paid if they succeeded in delivering us at Havre. Ed had not been able to secure any money adequate to take care of this charge or even to pay his hotel bill, but nevertheless arranged to have it call for us at the earliest time they could start us away, which they said would be three o'clock.

It was then necessary for him to provide himself with funds. Mr. B. offered to introduce him to Mr. Harjes, who was acting as Treasurer for the American committee. He told Mr. Harjes that he had engaged the car, that he had a hotel bill to pay, that he wanted enough French money to take care of us and get us back to Paris should we fail to get through to the coast, and enough English money— preferably gold, to keep him two or three days until he could make his connections in London, should we succeed in getting through. He had been told that one or two similar requests had been made the day before and that when five hundred dollars had been mentioned as the sum desired, those who had solicited the money had been able to get only three hundred. Ed, accordingly, asked for five hundred dollars and much to his surprise, due undoubtedly to Mr. B.'s introduction, he was told that the amount asked was entirely reasonable, and got it.

So far he had not been able to reach the Commissaire of Police to get his passport stamped with the *Laisser d'Aller* or permission to go. Fortunately he met Dr. Graham Taylor again, who told him there was a special *Commissaire* in the

Gare St. Lazare, authorized to issue these permits. Through Dr. Taylor's influence, he was able to reach this official, and got the necessary authority stamped upon our passports.

It was noon before he was able to get back to the hotel and notify us to get our things in order for the start for Havre. It seemed to us like a momentous decision. In Paris we at least had shelter and a place to rest our heads at night. We could not be sure that we could get through to Havre. It seemed entirely possible that if we did reach there, we would find no boats crossing the Channel. Furthermore, it was almost certain that if there were no boats, we would find thousands of Americans and English who had gone to the coast for the same purpose, who would have more than filled all the hotels. If such should prove to be the case when we reached Havre, what were we going to be able to do? Nevertheless the decision was made and the cars came for us about three o'clock. The condition of the times was brought close home to us during the morning when a porter removed the cot from our room, saying that the two top floors of the hotel were being converted into a hospital and that they would require the cot for there.

We said good-bye to our host of the Terminal who had treated us with such thought and courtesy in spite of his much curtailed force of domestics. Our bill for the three nights in his comfortable hotel was only thirty-six dollars and eighty-five cents, when he had a chance to charge us any amount and we could not have complained. His hotel has been full of Americans who have crossed the water to spend money and idle away their hours, meanwhile his peaceful country has become a battlefield, his men are being called away daily, his supply of provisions has run short and yet he has catered to these foreign guests of his without the slightest sign of impatience or annoyance.

We drove first to the Packard office to arrange the payment for the car. Ed told them that he could only pay them fifty dollars in money and would give them a check for the other hundred payable at his bank in Cleveland. To his surprise and delight they were perfectly willing to accept this arrangement. While this was just another instance of the way in which everybody helped during these trying days, we felt very appreciative of the whole treatment we had received from the Paris representative of the Packard Company.

At three-thirty, it seemed almost a miracle, we passed through the Porte de Champerret and were soon making our way along the outskirts of St. Germain. A break-neck speed was necessary to reach our destination before night-fall so we lurched from one side of the road to the other in anything but comfort. According to a new regulation which was enforced today for the first time, and of which the Packard people had not been advised before we started, no automobiles were allowed to travel on the high roads after six o'clock. The roads were lined with soldiers, troops and farm horses and wagons full of provisions, whole regiments of them being led to the concentration camps, and at every smallest town or station we were thoroughly looked over and required to show our permit.

15

MARCEL PROUST, *SWANN'S WAY*, 2 VOLS. TRANS. C. K. MONCRIEFF (NEW YORK: HOLT, 1922), I, PP. 154–155 II, PP. 104–105, 232–234

Sometimes we would go as far as the viaduct, which began to stride on its long legs of stone at the railway station, and to me typified all the wretchedness of exile beyond the last outposts of civilisation, because every year, as we came down from Paris, we would be warned to take special care, when we got to Combray, not to miss the station, to be ready before the train stopped, since it would start again in two minutes and proceed across the viaduct, out of the lands of Christendom, of which Combray, to me, represented the farthest limit. We would return by the Boulevard de la Gare, which contained the most attractive villas in the town. In each of their gardens the moonlight, copying the art of Hubert Robert, had scattered its broken staircases of white marble, its fountains of water and gates temptingly ajar. Its beams had swept away the telegraph office. All that was left of it was a column, half shattered, but preserving the beauty of a ruin which endures for all time. I would by now be dragging my weary limbs, and ready to drop with sleep; the balmy scent of the lime-trees seemed a consolation which I could obtain only at the price of great suffering and exhaustion, and not worthy of the effort. From gates far apart the watchdogs, awakened by our steps in the silence, would set up an antiphonal barking, as I still hear them bark, at times, in the evenings, and it is in their custody (when the public gardens of Combray were constructed on its site) that the Boulevard de la Gare must have taken refuge, for wherever I may be, as soon as they begin their alternate challenge and acceptance, I can see it again with all its lime-trees, and its pavement glistening beneath the moon.

Suddenly my father would bring us to a standstill and ask my mother—"Where are we?" Utterly worn out by the walk but still proud of her husband, she would lovingly confess that she had not the least idea. He would shrug his shoulders and laugh. And then, as though it had slipped, with his latchkey, from his waistcoat pocket, he would point out to us, where it stood before our eyes, the back-gate of our own garden, which had come, hand-in-hand with the familiar corner of the Rue du Saint-Esprit, to await us, to greet us at the end of our wanderings over paths unknown. My mother would murmur admiringly "You really are wonderful!" And from that instant I had not to take another step; the ground moved forward under my feet in that garden where, for so long, my actions had ceased to require any control, or even attention, from my will. Custom came to take me in her arms, carried me all the way up to my bed, and laid me down there like a little child.

But when she had set off for Dreux or Pierrefonds—alas, without allowing him to appear there, as though by accident, at her side, for, as she said, that would "create a dreadful impression,"—he would plunge into the most intoxicating romance in the lover's library, the railway time-table, from which he learned the ways of joining her there in the afternoon, in the evening, even in the morning. The ways? More than that, the authority, the right to join her. For, after all, the time-table, and the trains themselves, were not meant for dogs. If the public were carefully informed, by means of printed advertisements, that at eight o'clock in the morning a train started for Pierrefonds which arrived there at ten, that could only be because going to Pierrefonds was a lawful act, for which permission from Odette would be superfluous; an act, moreover, which might be performed from a motive altogether different from the desire to see Odette, since persons who had never even heard of her performed it daily, and in such numbers as justified the labour and expense of stoking the engines.

So it came to this; that she could not prevent him from going to Pierrefonds if he chose to do so. Now that was precisely what he found that he did choose to do, and would at that moment be doing were he, like the travelling public, not acquainted with Odette. For a long time past he had wanted to form a more definite impression of Viollet-le-Duc's work as a restorer. And the weather being what it was, he felt an overwhelming desire to spend the day roaming in the forest of Compiègne.

It was, indeed, a piece of bad luck that she had forbidden him access to the one spot that tempted him to-day. To-day! Why, if he went down there, in defiance of her prohibition, he would be able to see her that very day! But then, whereas, if she had met, at Pierrefonds, some one who did not matter, she would have hailed him with obvious pleasure: "What, you here?" and would have invited him to come and see her at the hotel where she was staying with the Verdurins, if, on the other hand, it was himself, Swann, that she encountered there, she would be annoyed, would complain that she was being followed, would love him less in consequence, might even turn away in anger when she caught sight of him "So, then, I am not to be allowed to go away for a day anywhere!" she would reproach him on her return, whereas in fact it was he himself who was not allowed to go.

I should have liked to take, the very next day, the good, the generous train at one twenty-two, of which never without a palpitating heart could I read, in the railway company's bills or in advertisements of circular tours, the hour of departure: it seemed to me to cut, at a precise point in every afternoon, a most fascinating groove, a mysterious mark, from which the diverted hours still led one on, of course, towards evening, towards to-morrow morning, but to an evening and morning which one would behold, not in Paris but in one of those towns through which the train passed and among which it allowed one to choose; for it stopped at Bayeux, at Coutances, at Vitré, at Questambert, at Pontorson, at Balbec, at Lannion, at Lamballe, at Benodet, at Pont-Aven, at Quimperlé, and progressed magnificently surcharged with names which it offered me, so that, among them all, I did not know which to choose, so impossible was it to sacrifice any. But even without waiting for the train next day, I could, by rising and dressing myself with all speed, leave Paris that very evening, should my parents permit, and arrive at Balbec as dawn spread westward over the raging sea, from whose driven foam I would seek shelter in that church in the Persian manner. But at the approach of the Easter holidays, when my parents had promised to let me spend them, for once, in the North of Italy, lo! in place of those dreams of tempests, by which I had been entirely possessed, not wishing to see anything but waves dashing in from all sides, mounting always higher, upon the wildest of coasts, beside churches as rugged and precipitous as cliffs, in whose towers the sea-birds would be wailing; suddenly, effacing them, taking away all their charm, excluding them because they were its opposite and could only have weakened its effect, was substituted in me the converse dream of the most variegated of springs, not the spring of Combray, still pricking with all the needle-points of the winter's frost, but that which already covered with lilies and anemones the meadows of Fiesole, and gave Florence a dazzling golden background, like those in Fra Angelico's pictures. From that moment, only sunlight, perfumes, colours, seemed to me to have any value; for this alternation of images had effected a change of front in my desire, and—as abrupt as those that occur sometimes in music,—a complete change of tone in my sensibility. Thus it came about that a mere atmospheric variation would be sufficient to provoke in me that modulation, without there being any need for me to await the return of a season. For often we find a day, in one, that has strayed from another season, and makes us live in that other, summons at once into our presence and makes us long for its peculiar pleasures, and interrupts the dreams that we were in process of weaving, by inserting, out of its turn, too early or too late, this leaf, torn from another chapter, in the interpolated calendar of Happiness. But soon it happened that, like those natural phenomena from which our comfort or our health can derive but an accidental and all too modest benefit, until the day when science takes control of them, and, producing them at will, places in our hands the power to order their appearance, withdrawn from the tutelage and independent of the consent of chance; similarly the production of these dreams of the Atlantic and of Italy ceased to depend entirely upon the changes of the seasons and of the weather. I need only, to make them reappear, pronounce the names: Balbec, Venice, Florence, within whose syllables had gradually accumulated all the longing inspired in me by the places for which they stood. Even in spring, to come in a book upon the name of Balbec sufficed to awaken in me the desire for storms at sea and for the Norman gothic; even on a stormy day the name of Florence or of Venice would awaken the desire for sunshine, for lilies, for the Palace of the Doges and for Santa Maria del Fiore.

But if their names thus permanently absorbed the image that I had formed of these towns, it was only by transforming that image, by subordinating its reappearance in me to their own special laws; and in consequence of this they made it more beautiful, but at the same time more different from anything that the towns of Normandy or Tuscany could in reality be, and, by increasing the arbitrary delights of my imagination, aggravated the disenchantment that was in store for me when I set out upon my travels. They magnified the idea that I formed of certain points on the earth's surface, making them more special, and in consequence more real.

16

ANGUS B. REACH, *CLARET AND OLIVER, FROM THE GARONNE TO THE RHONE* (NEW YORK: G. P. PUTNAM, 1853), PP. 63–68

At length the tedious hour and a half wore away, and I entered the terminus—a roughly built wooden shed. The train consisted of a first, second, and third-class carriage; but there were no first-class passengers, only one solitary second-class, and about a dozen third-classes, with whom I cast my lot. Miserable as the freight was, the locomotive whistled as loud and panted as vehemently as if it were yoked to a Great Western Express; and off we went through the broad belt of nursery gardens, which encircles every French town, and where the very best examples of the working of the small proprietary system are to be seen. A rapid run through the once greatly famed and still esteemed vineyards of Hautbrion, and we found ourselves skirring along over a negative sort of country—here a bit of heath, there a bit of vineyard—now a bald spot of sand, anon a plot of irregularly-cut stubble; while a black horizon of pine-wood rose gradually on the right and left. On flew the train, and drearier grew the landscape; the heath was bleaker—the pines began to appear in clumps—the sand-stretches grew wider—every thing green, and fertile, and *riant* disappeared. He, indeed, who enters the Landes, appears to have crossed a French frontier, and left the merry land behind. No more bright vineyards—no more rich fields of waving corn—no more clustered villages—no more chateau-turrets—no more tapering spires. You look up to heaven to see whether the sky is not changed, as well as the land. No; all there is blue and serene as before, and the keen, hot sun glares intensely down upon undulating wastes of marsh, fir, and sand, among which you may travel for leagues without seeing a man, hearing a dog bark, or a bird sing. At last we were fairly among the woods, shooting down what seemed an eternal straight tunnel, cleft by lightning through the pines. The trees stood up stark and stiff, like cast-iron; the fir is at once a solemn and a rigid tree—the Puritan of the forest; and down the side of each Puritan I noticed a straight, yellowish gash, running perpendicularly from the spread of the branches almost to the earth, and turned for explanation to an intelligent-looking man, evidently a citizen of Bordeaux, opposite me.

"Ah!" he said, "you are new to our Landes."

I admitted it.

"And these gashes down the trees—these, monsieur, give us the harvest of the Landes."

"The harvest! What harvest?"

"What harvest? Resin, to be sure."

"Ay, resin," said an old fellow with a blouse and a quick eye; "resin, monsieur; the only harvest that man can grow in sand."

"*Tenez*," said my first interlocutor; "the peasants cut that gash in the tree; and at the root they scoop a little hollow in the ground. The resin perspires out of the wood, flows slowly and glutinously down the gash, and in a month or so, according to the heat of the weather, the hole is full, and the man who rents the trees takes up the sticky stuff, like soup, with a ladle."

"That's a very good description," said the old bloused gentleman. "And then, sir" (addressing me), "we barrel our crop of the Landes. Yes, indeed, we barrel it, as well as they do the crop of the Medoc."

"Only you wouldn't like to drink it so well," said the Bordeaux man.

Presently we pulled up at a station—a mere shed, with a clearing around it, as there might have been in Texas or Maine. I observed the name—Tohua-Cohoa, and remarked that it did not look like a French one.

"French one!" said he of Bordeaux; "you don't expect to find French in this chaos? No, no; it is some of the gibberish the savages hereabout speak."

"No such gibberish, and no such savages either," said the little keen-eyed man. "*Moi, je suis de Landes;* and the Landes language is a far finer language than French. French! phoo, phoo!"

And he took a pinch of snuff indignantly and triumphantly. The Bordeaux gentleman winked blandly at me, as if the keen-eyed man was a character to be humoured, and then looked doubtful and unconvinced.

"Tohua-Cohoa," he said; "it has a *sacré tonnerre* of a barbarous sound; has it any meaning?"

"Meaning!" exclaimed the man of the Landes; "I should think so. Tohua-Cohoa means, in French, *Allez doucement;* and the place was so called because there was there a dangerous swamp, in which many a donkey coming up from Teste with fish to you of Bordeaux was smothered; and so it got to be quite proverbial among the drivers of the donkeys, and they used to shout to each other, 'Tohua-Cohoa!' whenever they came near the slough; meaning to look out, and go gently, and take care of the soft places."

The man with the blouse, who was clearly the champion of the Landes, then turned indignantly from the Bordeaux man and addressed himself to me. "The language which the poor people here speak, monsieur, is a fine and expressive language, and liker the Spanish than the French. The people are poor, and very ignorant. They believe, monsieur, in ghosts, and witches, and sorceries, just as all France did two or three hundred years ago. Very few of them can read, monsieur, and they have bad food and no wine. But nevertheless, monsieur, they are *bons enfants—braves, gens*, monsieur. They love their pine-woods and their sands as much as other people do their corn-fields and their vines, monsieur. They would

MENTALITÉ AND THE MACHINE ENSEMBLE

die, monsieur, if you took them away from the sand and the trees. They are not like the Auvergnats, who go in troops to Paris to carry water from the fountains, and who are *betes—betes—bien betes!* They stay at home, monsieur. They wear their sheep-skins and walk upon their stilts, like their forefathers before them, monsieur; and if you are coming here to see the Landes, and if you lose yourself in the woods, and see a light glimmering through the trees, and rap at the cottage door, monsieur, you will be welcomed, monsieur, and have the best they can offer to eat, and the softest they can offer to sleep on. *Tenez, tenez; nous sommes pauvres et ignorants mais nous sommes, loyals et bons!"*

The tears fairly stood in the keen black eyes of the Landes man as he concluded his harangue, of which I have only reported the main points; for, truth to tell, the poor fellow's vehemence was so great, and his utterance so rapid, that I lost nearly as much as I caught. The Bordeaux gentleman hammered the floor with his umbrella in satirical approbation, the rest of the passengers looked curiously on, and, the engine whistling, we pulled up again at a station similar to the first—a shed—a clearing, and black pine all around. There were just three persons on the rough platform—the station-master in a blouse, and two yellow-breeched *gens-d'armes.* What could they find to occupy them among these drear pine-woods? What thief, who had not made a vow of voluntary starvation, or who had not a morbid taste for living upon resin, would ever have ventured among them? But the authorities! Catch a bit of France without an "authority!" As they certainly are omnipotent, and profess to be omniscient, it is only to be supposed that they should be omnipresent. One man left the train at the station in question—a slouching, stupid, swarthy peasant, the authorities pounced upon him, evidently in prodigious glee at catching somebody to be *autoritised* over, and we left them, spelling and squabbling over the greasy-looking "papers" presented by the profoundly respectful Jacques or Pierre.

And now, before proceeding further, I may be allowed to describe, with some minuteness, the landscape which will greet the traveller in the Landes. Its mere surface-aspect I have already sketched; but general terms go but a small way towards indicating the dreary grandeurs of that solemn wilderness. Over all its gloom and barrenness—over all its "blasted heaths" and monotonous pine-woods, and sodden morasses, and glaring heaps of shifting sand—there is a strong and pervading sense of loneliness, a grandeur and intensity of desolation, which, as it were, clothes the land with a sad, solemn poetry peculiar to itself. Emerging from black forests of fir, the wanderer may find himself upon a plain, flat as a billiard-table, and apparently boundless as the ocean, clad in one unvaried, unbroken robe of dusky heath. Sometimes stripes and ridges, or great ragged patches of sand, glisten in the fervid sunshine; sometimes belts of scraggy young fir-trees appear rising from the horizon on the left, and fading into the horizon on the right. Occasionally a brighter shade of green, with jungles of willows and coarse water-weeds, giant rushes, and marish-mosses, and tangled msases of dank vegetation, will tell of the unfathomable swamp beneath. Dark veins of muddy water will traverse the flat oozy land, sometimes, perhaps, losing themselves in broad shallow lakes, bordered again by the endless sand-banks and stretches of shadowy pine. The dwellings which dot this dreary, yet, in its way, solemnly poetic landscape, are generally mere isolated huts, separated sometimes by many miles, often by many leagues. Round them the wanderer will descry a miserable field or two, planted with a stunted crop of rye, millet, or maize. The cottages are mouldering heaps of sod and unhewn and unmortared stones, clustered round with ragged sheds composed of masses of tangled bushes, pine stakes, and broad-leaved reeds, beneath which cluster, when not seeking their miserable forage in the woods, two or three cows, mere skin and bone, and a score or two of the most abject-looking sheep which ever browsed.

Proceeding through the Landes towards the coast, a long chain of lakes and water-courses, running parallel to the ocean, breaks their uniformity. The country becomes a waste of shallow pools, and of land which is parched in summer and submerged in winter. Running in devious arms and windings through moss and moor and pine, these "lakes of the dismal swamp" form labyrinths of gulfs and morasses which only the most experienced shepherds can safely thread. Here and there a village, or rather bourg, will be seen upon their banks, half hidden in the pine-woods; and a roughly-built fishing-punt or two will be observed floating like the canoe of a savage in the woodland lakes. Sometimes, as in the case of the basin of Arcachon, which will be presently described, these waters are arms of the sea; and the retreating tide leaves scores of square miles of putrid swamp. Sometimes they are mere collections of surface-drainage, accumulating without any means of escape to the ocean, and perilous in the extreme to the dwellers on their shores.

17

CHARLES RICHARD WELD, *THE PYRENEES, WEST AND EAST* (LONDON: LONGMAN, BROWN, GREEN, LONGMANS, & ROBERTS, 1859), PP. 29–35, 45–46, 49

Having heard much at Bordeaux in praise of Arcachon, a small and peculiar bathing place, forty miles south of that city, I determined on spending a quiet week there before commencing my Pyrenean rambles. Accordingly I left Bordeaux early in the morning by the Bayonne railway. The construction of this railway is a great triumph of English engineering, for the work was attended with most formidable difficulties. A few miles from Bordeaux you enter the Landes, across which the line is carried to Bayonne.

Nothing more dreary than these apparently interminable wastes. Your passage across them suggests ideas of the ocean, with this great difference however, that whereas the latter is rarely at rest, the vast tract of the Landes, comprising 600,000 hectares, equal to 1,482,600 acres, except when swept by hurricanes, presents a still and monotonous surface. The soil is sand—endless sand—vertically as well as superficially. Artesian wells have been sunk to the depth of nearly 1000 feet, and then a scanty supply of wretched yellow water has been the only result. As may be supposed, the lives of the inhabitants of this unpromising region are short, feverish, and sickly. The Landais have a proverb,

> "Tant que Lande sera Lande
> La pellagre te demande;"

said pellagre being a fatal disease occasioned by malaria and bad water. Amidst these wastes, lying to the east of the pine forests which fringe the sea coast, the Landais, who are, with few exceptions, shepherds, spend the long summer days with their flocks of sheep, each animal being as well known to them as their dogs. The Landais shepherd is a primitive being, fond of solitude, rarely venturing near the railway; when he does, he gazes wonderingly at the rushing train—so to see him you must penetrate into his wilderness. There, amidst the great wastes, clothed in sheep skins and wearing the Navarre cap, you will find him mounted on tall stilts, become, from long habit, like a second pair of legs, for he has been accustomed to them from childhood; probably knitting while his flock crop the scanty herbage. There he stands, resting against his pole, a strange tripod-looking figure—stranger still when he strides across the Landes in hot haste after a wandering sheep. He has a small hut, sometimes a wife, who aids him in cultivating a small patch of ground, from which he obtains a little corn and a few vegetables. A miserable existence is this, but the dawn of brighter days has, we may hope, appeared for the poor Landais. After innumerable futile attempts to reclaim and fertilise portions of this desert, two joint-stock companies (Compagnie des Landes and Compagnie d'Arcachon) have succeeded in reclaiming a considerable tract of the Plaine de Cazaux. Sheltered from the prevailing west winds by the great maritime pine forest, of which we shall have something to say presently, the Plaine de Cazaux, situated to the east or leeward, as may be said of that forest, is not so liable to the destructive effects of the great sand storms as other parts of the Landes. Rice, tobacco, and the *topinambour*, or Jerusalem artichoke, for which the soil is admirably adapted, are the chief crops. The improvements are, in a great measure, due to a M. Pierre, an agricultural genius, who, having studied agriculture, and particularly drainage under scientific teachers, devised a system of reclaiming and husbandry which has been very successful.

Prosperity is rapidly following these improvements, and, what is better, malaria no longer poisons the reclaimed districts. The peasantry enjoy better health, and M. Pierre firmly believes that the terrible pellagre will be soon unknown in the Landes. His system has been approved by the Emperor, who has lately extended his patronage to M. Pierre by purchasing a large tract of the Landes, which is to be cultivated according to his method. The imperial estate lies to the east of Labouheyre station, and the Landais have marked their sense of his Majesty's advent among them as a landowner by erecting a pillar, surmounted by a gilt eagle, on the spot where the Emperor first entered the Landes.

An hour and a half's whirl through clouds of sand, and we came to a stand still at Lamothe, the junction station of the Bayonne and Teste Railway. Here we changed carriages, and continued our journey on a single line of rails to Arcachon. Soon we caught glimpses of the Atlantic, fringed by tawny *dunes*, and of the Bassin d'Arcachon. Teste de Buch, a small fishing town, is situated at the head of the lagune, on the site of the ancient Testa Baïrum, founded 300 B.C. Traces of the Roman road between Teste and Bordeaux are still visible. A short distance beyond Teste, the railway plunges into the pine forest, through which it is carried by a deep cutting to Arcachon, or rather to a station in the middle of the forest. Here the scene is curious. Wild nature around, reminding one of an American backwood railway station; but, instead of sturdy emigrants, you see Bordeaux *élégantes*, with a sprinkling of Parisian fashionables.

Gaily painted omnibuses were waiting to convey us to Arcachon. Climbing to the roof of one, bearing the name of Hôtel des Empereurs, we drove along a sandy road, lined with pines, and came presently to the skirts of this new and peculiar watering-place.

Look at a map of France, and you will see the coast between Bordeaux and Bayonne indented with creeks, some expanding into large lagunes of fanciful shapes, the result of their shifting boundaries of sand. By far the largest of these *étangs*, as they are called, is the Bassin d'Arcachon, sixty-eight miles in circumference. Up to 1856, the shores of this inland sea were occupied merely by a few fishermen's huts. In that year some Bordeaux merchants, who were staying at La Teste, appreciated the advantages of Arcachon, sheltered from the east by the pine forest, and possessing a strand admirably adapted for walking or riding. The bathing too is excellent, the water being sufficiently land-locked to permit the most timid or weak person to enjoy a bath, when it would be impossible to face the great sea breakers on the coast. Small villas were erected on the margin of the bay, and the example having been rapidly followed, Arcachon soon emerged from obscurity, and now promises to become a formidable rival to Biarritz. Fantastic as Chinese suburban residences are these little villas, which would most assuredly be demolished by the frequent storms, were they not sheltered by the pine forest. The Bordeaux merchants seem, indeed, to have vied with each other in building comical little boxes, in utter defiance of all architectural principles. Nevertheless, there is a great charm in these many-peaked and gabled gaily painted summer nests, set in gardens radiant with flowers and luxuriant exotic shrubs, happily ignorant of topiary art.

Having driven for half a mile on a road lined by these villas, the omnibus turned down an avenue, at the end of which was the Hôtel des Empereurs. The fact was announced by a scarlet flag suspended from adjacent trees, and some such information is necessary, for the house has no appearance of belonging to the hotel genus.

THE most direct railway route to the Pyrenees is by the Bordeaux and Bayonne line as far as Dax, from whence diligences run to Pau. But as Bayonne is only thirty-one miles beyond Dax, and Biaritz, the pet watering-place of the fair Empress Eugénie, is but a short distance from Bayonne, I resolved on visiting these places before going among the mountains.

So I left Arcachon at eight in the morning, and, after a rapid transit across the Landes, had the satisfaction of seeing the purple Pyrenees stretching far to the west. The change from the arid sterility of the Landes to the prolific vegetation of the country round Bayonne is extremely striking. But the beauty of the landscape is much marred by groves of cork-trees, whose blasted-like boles are sadly unpicturesque: venerable trees, for the most part, and therefore frequently barked, for it is a curious property of the cork-tree, that it flourishes all the better for being periodically stripped of its coat. The operation is performed every eight or ten years, and continued until the tree is about two centuries old, when signs of decay appear.

Presently semi-Spanish Bayonne was in sight, and in a few minutes more we came to a halt under the fortress walls in the suburb of St. Esprit. Here two omnibuses of vast capacity were waiting to convey passengers to Biaritz; not, however, too large for their requirements, as twenty-four persons were stowed inside each vehicle, and the same number clambered on the roof, perching themselves as they best could amidst a mountain of luggage, consisting principally of huge boxes.

Charming is the drive to Biaritz—only six miles. Even on an omnibus you wish it were more. Southern vegetation drapes the walls of the villas near Bayonne. Beyond, there are undulating fields chequered with rich corn crops and various fruit trees, and to the south the Pyrenean range appears so near that you see the many-folded mountains, and can peer into their purple glens.

But soon the scene changes. For when you ascend a hill midway between Bayonne and Biaritz, the mighty Atlantic is full before you, and the rich vegetation becomes suddenly dwarfed. You would think that some magic influence were at work to effect so great and sudden a change. 'Tis the strong and stern west wind that sweeps unbroken across the Biscayan bay, before which vegetation cannot make head. Down, and up, and then the houses of Biaritz appear nestling in the wrinkles of the cliffs, where they have been wisely built, for the fragile cockney-ish boxes would have but a poor chance of existence on unsheltered eminences.

18

GORDON CASSERLY, *ALGERIA TO-DAY* (NEW YORK: F. A. STOKES, N.D.), PP. 170–185

From Biskra to Tougourt

PASS on from Biskra, for the true Sahara lies beyond! The railway that runs another hundred and thirty miles to the south has not yet vulgarised the sand wastes, the great palm groves and the vast dried salt lakes over which the Fairies of the Mirage dance. And the little desert town of Tougourt at its end is still unspoilt.

Those who would savour the real life of the Sahara may yet travel to this outpost of civilisation by camel and caravan and spend half a dozen days in doing so. But the wise who do not disdain the advantages of modern transport take the one train, white-painted against the heat, comfortable and up-to-date, that pulls out from Biskra every second day and reaches Tougourt in eight hours, returning on the morrow. In winter it goes by daylight; but in the dread summer months it steals over the desert in the night hours to escape man's enemy there, the sun.

A motley and interesting crowd of travellers it carries. A stately, olive-faced Arab in flowing white burnous, a *hlafa* or thin cloth covering the high felt cap on his head bound round by many turns of a brown string of camel-hair cord and falling to his waist, stalks to a third-class carriage followed by what might be two automatic upright white bolsters were it not for the fair foreheads and the beautiful black eyes appearing above the *adjar*, or veil which covers the rest of the face, and the bare ankles and the little feet thrust into heel-less slippers. They are his wives carefully shrouded against profane male gaze. Behind them come a couple of men who, but for their red checchias and semi-Arab dress might be Scotsmen by their blue eyes, fair skins and sandy moustaches. They are Kabyles, in whose veins runs the mixed blood of aborigine, Roman and Vandal. Two Tirailleurs Indigènes, smart, dark-complexioned soldiers in their turquoise blue Zouave jackets and baggy trousers, salute a handsome subaltern officer of the French aviation service in dark blue tunic and breeches and black gaiters. On his breast are the Legion of Honour and the Croix de Guerre, the latter with two metal palm branches across its ribbon to show that it was won thrice. And over his left shoulder the aiguillette cord of the *fourragère* tells that he has belonged to a corps whose standard has been decorated for bravery. A fair-skinned, black-bearded Mozabite in Arab dress, one of the small but industrious race from the towns and oases in the Sahara below Laghouat scowled at as heretics by devout Moslems, climbs up into a second-class compartment behind a stout Frenchwoman on her way to rejoin her stationmaster husband half-way down the line.

Energetic hotel-guides conducting parties of American and European travellers push aside bewildered groups of desert-dwelling women with unveiled faces, mere bundles of odd garments. A horn squeaks, and the train slides quietly out into the desert. First it passes high, mud-walled houses, tall palm trees, a loop-holed stone tower on a hillock facing out towards the wild and the aviation hangars from which the military aeroplanes fly out to keep watch over the waste. Then Biskra and its environs and its oases are left behind, and the true Sahara appears.

But where are the glaring plains of drifting sand, the golden dunes heaped up, the dread bareness of lifeless desert that the untravelled—aye, and the man who has seen Egypt and the dead shores of the Gulf of Suez and the Red Sea—expect? For here and almost everywhere along the way to Tougourt the ground is heaped in tiny hummocks crowned with foot-high bright green bushes, clumps of grass eighteen inches long or drier stuff that resembles *alfa*. Although close to the train one can see the sand between the bunches of vegetation, yet gazing farther away towards the horizon the eyes seem to be ranging over a dark stretch of gorse-bushes and in the distance the tops of the trees in a pinewood.

Lifeless? Dotted among the hummocks are camels grazing, camels brown or black, in ones, in twos, in dozens, sometimes in charge of a small Arab child, oftener alone. The universal donkey, too, in groups, and herds of lop-eared goats are busy; and it is evident that in this part of the desert at least there is good feeding for hardy animals. Here and there dunes do crop up, and farther along the railway are lines of bare sandhills. But as a rule the undulating ground is dotted with little clumps of green plants, and the surface of the sand is hard. Between the bushes it is strewn with loose stones glistening like mica, which mineral is found plentifully between Tougourt and Ghardaia. But the sand, ridged as on a seashore, shows that when a strong wind blows over the desert it can rise in suffocating clouds.

So far from being absolutely dry little streams and narrow pools and here and there bigger ponds are visible from the train. But the ground is covered in very many places with snow-white patches of magnesia or mineral salts, which show that the earth is everywhere impregnated with them, so that the surface water is brackish and undrinkable. The oases of date-palms that dot the desert owe their existence to the artesian wells sunk deep, sometimes many hundreds of feet below the surface.

The month is March and the sun shines brilliantly in the clear blue sky, yet the heat is not great. In fact, with the windows of the carriages open even the European travellers in the train wear furs and overcoats up to noon. The nomad Arabs who wander far south in the winter months to return northward when the scorching sun of summer drives them back, are still absent, though occasionally low tents of striped cloth guarded by fierce dogs dot the desert here and there; beside tethered camels lazy, white-burnoused men lie on the ground and gaze indifferently at the passing train. But the women of the *douar* are too busy to raise their eyes towards it, for they are doing all the hard work of the encampment.

The Aurès Mountains are not yet lost to sight. They thrust forward on either flank and seem to hem the railway in. At their feet are frequent great palm-groves, oases nourished by the water flowing down from the hills, and though lost to sight underground only waiting to be tapped by wells. But at last the mountains sink beneath the horizon and sandy hillocks blot them from sight.

The train runs past a well-built European house beside the line, the dwelling of some French platelayer, and his wife stands on the verandah to watch us go by. Near the door is a pump, and by it is tethered a great horned sheep. Farther on a well-peopled oasis lies close to the railway. Above the flat roofs of the blank, mud-walled huts the tall palms rustle their fronds in the light breeze. From the village an Arab on a thin brown mare, closely followed by a foal, ambles down the sunk road white with magnesia that leads between earthen banks to the line.

And then the train slides in alongside a building that, owing to its whitewashed walls and its dome surmounted by a gilt crescent, looks like a mosque or a holy marabout's tomb, but it is only the first station out from Biskra, Oumache. The blue-uniformed railway officials in it look sadly out of keeping with its Oriental appearance. One feels that they should garb themselves in burnous and *hlafa* like the expectant travellers on the platform. But then, to look the part also, the train would have to disguise itself as a camel. It certainly behaves like one in the station; for it stops with as much noise and grumbling and shows as little indecent haste to move on again as the long-necked, bad-tempered animal that it is replacing in the desert.

And when at last it departs from Oumache and sees before it a river, like the camel it swerves out of the straight line to seek the narrowest place to cross. An iron three-span bridge stretches over the wide, almost empty river-bed which, however, often fills so suddenly by a spate from the hills that it drowns unwary travellers and women washing clothes in it. And this is the Sahara that one pictures as a waterless waste!

Now comes Chegga station, another cement building with dome and golden crescent, where on one side of the line a garden of flowers and vegetables, of tamarinds and young palms, blooms to show what water can make of the desert soil. The European passengers crowd to stare over its wall into a mud-brick house sheltering a Sahara gazelle, a pretty, slim-legged creature with short, curved horns.

Beyond Chegga there are more streams, pools and ponds; but the water in them must be brackish, for everywhere between the tiny bushes the ground is white with magnesia or mineral salts. The desert is still the same, undulating, covered with low vegetation, or at intervals dotted with the clustering palms of oases.

Traditional pictures are not wanting. A herd of camels stalk by, shepherded by a couple of Arabs on horseback and a third man afoot with gun slung on his back. They pass a string of the same supercilious, long-legged beasts heavily laden, a caravan on its way south with flour from Biskra; for though the railway runs today the Arabs use the transport that their forefathers did centuries ago. And the desert takes its toll of man and animals as of yore. Not a hundred yards from the iron road lies the complete skeleton of a camel with the big white skull still adhering in some way to the cervical vertebræ. And half a mile farther on is another, fallen to pieces this one. And though the troopers of France patrol the Sahara raiders still swoop down on caravans in the south and men's life-blood stains the hot sand.

More oases, more stations. Some of the latter vary in architecture from the first ones, though still presenting the Eastern touch.

And now far away to the left of the railway lies a large lake, a truly magnificent sheet of water bordered by sandy cliffs, dotted with islets; cliffs and islets reflected clearly in the shining water. Farther on the far shore runs out of sight and horizon and water blend. Here and there are large fishing-boats. The tourists crowd the windows of the train corridor to gaze in wonder and admiration at the beautiful expanse of water. It stretches for miles parallel to the railway; and our surprise is great that so vast a lake lies so far inside the Sahara. Guide-book maps are consulted. Yes, here it is in all of them, marked by a wash of blue, one of a chain of similar coloured patches extending to the Gulf of Gabes in Tunisia. The guide-books term them Chotts and call them salt-lakes. Small inland seas they must be. This one is the Chott El Melghir, 170 miles long.

Astonishment, unbelief, are evinced by the tourists when fellow travellers who reside in Tougourt or elsewhere along the line declare that there is practically no water, fresh or salt, in this beautiful lake, that its shining expanse with its faithful reflections of islets, cliffs and boats is all delusion. It is a mirage. What we see is the bed of a dried-up lake covered white with magnesia. We cannot believe it until the railway line passes over a portion of it—here, they say, sixteen metres below sea level. It is over these Chotts that the Mediterranean Sea is to be brought into the heart of the Sahara when the scheme is ripe—some day, perhaps.

This mirage is beyond belief. I have seen many in India, but I stared long at this Chott before I could realise the truth.

Water, real, fresh water, comes, and strange to say comes unwelcome to the desert. Only the day before a storm had swept over the district, torrents of rain fell, river beds filled to the brim, and for several kilometres the railway had been undermined or even swept away. But it had been promptly repaired—it is no difficult task to bank up sand and lay sleepers on it—but over those doubtful kilometres the train crawled slowly, while gangs of Arabs and Kabyle navvies stood aside to let it go by.

Storms in the desert! Last July the motor diligence from Ghardaia to Tougourt, both places over a hundred and fifty miles inside the Sahara, ran into one. The lightning and thunder were tropical, and hailstones fell, not such as dwellers in temperate climes know, but sharp-edged bars of clear ice two or three inches long, each enclosing a round, clouded hailstone such as is ordinarily seen. They pierced the tarpaulin cover of the diligence as though they had been bullets, they battered and bruised the driver's arms, hands and body until he was forced to pull up and wait for a couple of hours. And even when the storm had passed he was unable to proceed at once, for the ground for miles was slippery with the ice particles. Ice in the Sahara in July!

Near each railway station on the line to Tougourt there is at least one large oasis, if not more—for the oasis is the *raison d'être* of the station's existence. In many of them the villages are large and boast quite imposing mosques, the white minarets rising among the tall dark palms. The extent of the high walls of sundried bricks surrounding the crowded dwellings is surprising; as are the other evidences of prosperity in the vast number of palm-trees—close on two hundred thousand in some cases—the ground cultivation of vegetables under them, the herds of goats, sheep and donkeys, as well as the crowds that gather for the weekly markets.

Astonishing too, is the number of oases visible from the train all the way between Biskra and Tougourt. The popular idea that the whole Sahara is a vast, desolate, sandy desert inhabited only by wandering tribesmen is erroneous; for in other parts beside this which is served by the railway there are large oases with many villages containing a numerous settled population.

An oasis, as I have said, is simply a spot where water is found on the surface or more usually by sinking wells; for then irrigation will allow palms to grow, and where they are life can be supported. So villages of mud bricks spring up as if by magic. For the palm-tree means everything to the desert-dweller. It gives him almost his only food, the date and the edible pith. From the date is distilled a liquor something like anisette. Trees that do not bear fruit well are tapped near the leafy crown, and every morning the exuding sap is collected in earthen vessels tied under the incisions. When fresh it forms a harmless drink, but when fermented it is a strong intoxicant. "Lakmi," the Arabs call it; in India it is termed "toddy," and to produce it palms are extensively cultivated along the coast near Bombay. This tapping of a tree has a good effect on it, causing it to subsequently bear better fruit.

A date palm, although it does not produce a crop for the first fifteen or twenty years of its existence, is nevertheless a good investment; for it lives more than a hundred years, and even when dead its roots, trunk and leaves are useful for a variety of purposes. It is not usually grown from date-stones, but from slips. Palms are either male or female, and trees of the latter gender must be fertilised from the former.

They only fructify in the Sahara zone. The principal regions which produce dates in Southern Algeria are the Oued Rhir, the Ziban, the Souf, Ouargla, the Tidikelt, the Zousfana and the Saoura. There are very many varieties of this fruit. The finest quality, and the one usually exported for foreign consumption in cases, wooden and cardboard boxes, is the transparent Deglet-Nour.

The produce of the oases of the Souf and the Djerid is considered the best; and the crop is purchased entire by merchants even before the dates ripen.

The soft dates called Rhar, which the natives consume largely, are sold compressed in goatskins. The Horra and Degla-Beida are eaten by the bulk of the inhabitants of the Sahara and the Hauts Plateaux. Other varieties are the Mouchi-Degla,

Koutichi, M'hentich, M'tima, Alaoua and a host of others. The harvest season is in November.

The staple, if not the only diet of the nomads is couscous, dates and camel's milk. Only on rare occasions, such as feasts, are sheep slaughtered for food—and then they are roasted whole. But dates from their portability—they are packed tight in goatskins sewn up—form the principal nourishment of a wandering Arab; and without the palms the desert would be uninhabitable to him. But these trees require much water. Here the French come to the aid of the Arabs and sink artesian wells by machinery for them, naturally boring to depths that the old method of digging by hand could never reach. Indeed, all this land, and not only the Sahara, owes much to its rulers, who have developed its resources astonishingly. The man who thinks that the French cannot colonise should visit Algeria. He should see the farms, the cultivation, the vineyards of the northern provinces and the oases that are springing up in the desert thanks to French companies and the money they spend in developing them. It comes as a surprise to the tourist to see at a little wayside station in the Sahara the motor-car or the pony cart of one of their employees with his wife and children sitting in it. These vehicles look as out of place among the tethered camels, mules and donkeys as do their occupants in their European dress among the drapery and flowing robes of the Arab men and the picturesque though tatterdemalion figures of the female desert-dwellers with unveiled faces.

After El-Berd, where a solitary loopholed picquet tower rises above the desert and a few well-shaped Arab horses with gaily decorated high-peaked saddles were made fast to hitching-posts near the little station, there were several other stops before the train at last reached Tougourt. A real desert town this. Here one saw the bare, uncovered, unmistakable sand. Though around and about are many shady oases in which to hide among the palms, Tougourt stands up naked and unashamed against the sky, perched on a low hillock of loose sand, which drifts up against the deeply crenelated wall on one side of the arched gateways and on the other the barer, uglier one over which peep the flat roofs of the houses and the minarets of a score of mosques. It looks to-day much as it has for centuries, this Tougourt, brought in touch with civilisation at last; as the railway attests, as do the little Catholic church outside the town and the miserable horse dragging a small tram along narrow rails below the sand dune and up the one broad, deep-arcaded street that holds a hotel and a few offices. But nothing detracts from the Eastern look of the town. Certainly not the whitewashed arches and walls of this main street, at the head of which, backed by a hundred palm-trees rising behind white, open balustrades and bordered by arcaded, one-storied buildings with an occasional domed roof, is the market place.

Here the sellers, when not engaged in animated disputes with bargaining buyers, squat or lie full length on the ground, comfortably awaiting custom beside their wares. Piles of dried bush-stumps for fuel and bundles of coarse desert grass for fodder are for sale. On cloths are spread—for stalls there are none—dates, grain, native bread and flat cakes and cooked food. Patient donkeys stand with drooping heads. Camels bunched up on the sand survey the passers-by with supercilious, evil stare and fill the air with burbling complaints when urged to uncurl their long legs and rise. On Fridays the market is filled with them; for the desert carpet-weavers have come in with their weird, gaudy wares for sale, strips and squares of fascinating colours, blues, greens, reds, yellows, purples, magentas, in clashing, impossible contrasts, yet subtly harmonising in some strange way.

Unromantic though a market be, ordinary the actions of all in it, yet this market place of Tougourt is picturesque, and its tones of subdued green from the background of palms, of yellow from the sand that fills it, of white from the buildings and the dress of the chaffering groups, with over all the vivid blue of the Saharan sky, would delight a painter. Lazy, dishonest, immoral though the Arab may be—and I have never met anyone to defend him—the flowing lines of his robes give him a stateliness and a dignity to the eye at least.

After the market-place comes a square. On one side is a long, white, two-storied building of many-arched verandahs surmounted by a dome, the Bureau Arabe. Similar arcaded houses fill up two other sides; while the fourth is bounded by the grim, loopholed, bastioned wall of the fort and barracks in which the French Algerian troops are quartered. Above it a tall tower pierced for rifles and machine guns rises high in the air dominating town and desert, a sign for all, nomad or street-dweller, a warning symbol of the Dominant Power—"Lest They Forget."

In the square is a large, covered well with a stand-pipe from which gushes warm, almost hot water, springing up from a depth of over seven hundred and fifty feet where the French boring-tools had found it and discharging an amazing quantity of water every hour—water so strongly impregnated with magnesia as to have unpleasant effects on the Europeans in Tougourt—about fifty or sixty all told—who are obliged to drink it.

Opposite the fortified wall of the barracks is the Great Mosque—there are nearly a score of these edifices in the small town.

And now all picturesqueness ends; for the rest of Tougourt is just narrow, gloomy streets, mere lanes of loose sand, running between high, brown, sun-dried brick walls, blank, but for one small door for each house. If open this door allows a glimpse of a deep courtyard in which a camel is tethered or perhaps a palm-tree towers, hemmed in by mud-coloured buildings where external stairs lead up to the dwelling rooms over the stables on the ground floor. The streets, like all Eastern streets of private residences, are dull, for the town Arab will have no windows through which the outer world may pry into his home life. "He does not live in the street" as he says the European does.

Even the houses of the two great men of Tougourt, the Marabout or Holy Man and the Caïd—the secular chief—present the same depressing external aspect. But when I visited the latter a door in the wall led me into a bright little courtyard where a shapely white horse was tethered and a group of Arab and negro servants lay or squatted against the house. And the room in which, reposing on a white mattress and propped up by pillows, the caïd, suffering from a sprained knee, received me, was light and cheerful. And in it we drank coffee and discussed Pierre Benoit's "L'Atlantide"; for the author had spent three months in Tougourt when writing the book, and the caïd, a charming and educated man, *decoré*, and speaking French fluently, had known him well.

Tougourt has played its part in the history of the Sahara and could boast its Sultans, whose tombs stand lonely and ruinous in the sand outside the town. One dynasty ruled it from the fourteenth century to the nineteenth when Sultan Ben-Djellab-bou-Lifa acknowledged the French suzerainty. His young grandson, Abd-el-Kader-ben-Djellab, a mere boy, was the ruler in 1854 and was murdered by an ambitious relative, Ben-Sliman-ben-Djellab, who seized the power and joined forces with Mohammed-ben-Abd'Allah whom the French had driven out of Ouargla, another desert town and small state a hundred and seventy kilometres south-west of Tougourt. Against them the Algerian Government sent four very mobile columns under Colonel Desvaux, Commandant of the Sub-division of Batna, reinforced by the *goums* (native irregular contingents) of Biskra, Bou-Saada, Laghouat and Géryville under Commandant Marnier. The confederate Arab force was defeated at Megarine on November 29th, 1854, losing a thousand men; and the French entered and took possession of Tougourt on 2nd December.

I think of this as I leave the caïd's house and try to picture this small town and the waste of sand around it as an independent kingdom. A Saharan Sultan must have been but a very small potentate.

Legend tells that the Tougourt of to-day occupies a different site to the Tougourt of the past. North of it was the village of Tala, now in ruins, in which lived a beautiful courtesan named El Bahadja (La Joyeuse), for whose favour all the young men of Tala contended. Driven out of the village as an evil-doer she sought to enter Tougourt. Refused admission she was obliged to shelter in a hut of palm-branches hurriedly constructed by her lovers, who followed her in a band and pitched their tents around her dwelling. Shortly afterwards a very holy man, the Grand Marabout of M'Sila, came to Tougourt to beg for his religious school; but as the ruler and people of the town belonged to a different sect of Mahommedanism they refused him admission, too. But the Gay Lady was more charitable and sheltered the venerable greybeard when night found him stranded in the desert; and she and her young men showed him so much kindness that he blessed his hostess, and prayed, "Allah! protect El Bahadja! May her humble cabin become a palace and the inhospitable houses of Tougourt fall in ruins!"

And the marabout's prayer was heard. Civil war set the inhabitants of the town at each other's throat and eventually destroyed the Tougourt of that day. But La Joyeuse's cot had been replaced by a fine building; and other houses sprang up around it and developed into the Tougourt of our time.

The afternoon wanes. From the high tower of the fort one can gaze out over the desert, beyond the bare, brown village outside Tougourt, across the jagged tops of the palms in the oases around and watch the sinking sun fill the heavens with glowing reds and pinks and yellows.

Night comes swiftly, and the air is chill; so that I wear an overcoat as I walk to the little restaurant with the French aviation officer who was my fellow traveller and is to be my guest. But the dark sky is pierced with a million points of brightness, the stars that shine over the desert with a brilliancy that Europe never knows. And the Saharan day is done.

19

LEWIS GASTON LEARY, *SYRIA, THE LAND OF LEBANON* (NEW YORK: MCBRIDE, NAST, 1913), PP. 72–78, 80–84, 86–87

The land of UZ

To appreciate truly the significance of Damascus, one should approach it from the east, across the thirsty wilderness which stretches between the Euphrates and the Syrian mountains. The long, wearisome journey would be worth while if only for the first glimpse of the city as it appears to the wondering eyes of the desert-dweller. But the twentieth century visitor may be excused if he prefers to save time and strength by utilizing the railway. To-day there is even a choice of routes. He can travel to Damascus from the west comfortably, or from the south speedily. But the adverbs are not interchangeable.

We have already taken the slow, beautiful journey from Beirut across the two mountain ranges. The other railway between Damascus and the coast starts from the seaport of Haifa, at the foot of Mount Carmel, and follows at first a fairly easy grade through the historic Plain of Esdraelon to the Jordan Valley at Beisan. From here it runs northward along the river to the Sea of Galilee, then in a general easterly direction up the valley of the Yarmuk to the plateau of the Hauran, where the Haifa branch joins the main line of the Mecca railway. Although the distance to Damascus by this route is a hundred and seventy-seven miles, or almost twice that from Beirut, the journey takes no longer. But in warm weather it is not a very comfortable trip, for more than half the time the train is below the level of the sea.

From Semakh, which lies at the southern end of the Sea of Galilee six hundred feet below the Mediterranean, the railway ascends the Yarmuk gorge through the most wild and desolate scenery imaginable. The entire region northeast of Galilee is volcanic. Prehistoric flows of molten rock extended over large areas, and the subsequent erosion of the river has cut through a solid layer of hard basalt from ten to fifty feet thick, whose perpendicular black cliffs appear in striking contrast to the irregular outlines of the softer limestone beneath.

For two hours after leaving the Sea of Galilee we do not pass a human habitation; indeed, for the first few miles there is no evidence of vegetable life except now and then a small clump of bushes at a bend of the stream. As the train puffs slowly up the bed of the steep, twisting ravine, all that can be seen is the narrow torrent rushing madly along between white walls of lime or chalk, above these a smooth, regular layer of shining black basalt and, as we look straight up or down the valley, a few bare, brown mountain-tops showing above the nearer cliffs. After a while, however, oleanders appear along the riverside, and for mile upon mile their thick foliage and gorgeous flowers add the one touch of life to the wild, lonely landscape. We pass a strange monolithic pyramid a hundred feet high, which has been carved by some freak of the winter floods. A little farther on, a recent landslide has covered the bottom of the valley with black stones and soot-like dust. Even early in the morning it is hot and stifling in this breezeless trench below the level of the ocean.

As we rise higher, however, scattered olive trees appear among the oleanders by the riverside, and a few little patches of thin wheat are seen among the rocks. A small herd of black, long-haired goats are drinking in the stream. We are startled to behold a rude oil-well. A dozen men are gathered at each railway station, though the villages from which they have come are still invisible on the heights above us. Then the valley suddenly turns and broadens, and we see against the cloudless sky the clean-cut profile of the highland country toward which we have been so long ascending. The track now leaves the river's bank and, in great loops, quickly mounts the side of the valley. From the edge of the plateau there comes tumbling a magnificent succession of cascades, which finally roar under a railway bridge and break in spray at the bottom of the gorge far below us. Another broader waterfall drops in a solid sheet of silver from the unseen land beyond the level summit of the precipice. Our train twists up a last steep grade, straightens out on the level ground—and, after looking for three hours at the close cliffs which hemmed in a narrow valley, it gladdens our eyes to gaze now on the vast prospect which is revealed in the shimmering light of the noonday sun.

Before us stretches the Hauran, the ancient Land of Bashan, a rolling sea of soft brownish earth and waving wheat. From time immemorial this has been the chief granary of western Asia. Until we become accustomed to the new perspective, we can not distinguish a village or tree or living creature. Here and there a few apparently low hills show their summits above the horizon. The Arabs, who came from the high eastern desert, called this the *Haurân*, or "Depression," because it lies flat between the mountains. But to us who have climbed hither from a point 2,500 feet below, the broad acres of Bashan seem set far up among the lonely skies. An endless, level, undivided expanse of wheat; dim summits far away; fertility and spaciousness and freedom and strong, ceaseless wind—this is the Hauran.

Muzeirib, the first station on the plateau, is the terminus of the earliest railway from Damascus to the Hauran, which was completed by the French in 1895. During recent years this has suffered severely from the competition of the Hejaz Railway begun in 1901 by Abdul Hamid; for the Turkish line is somewhat cheaper, has better connections, and enjoys the odor of sanctity. In fact, its chief avowed object is ultimately to connect Damascus with Mecca and thus provide transportation for the multitude of the Faithful who each year make the pilgrimage to the holy city. Only Moslems were employed on the construction of this sacred railway, large numbers of Turkish soldiers were detailed as guards and laborers; and, besides special taxes which were levied, voluntary subscriptions for the pious enterprise were sent in from all over the world of Islam. On account of the revolution of the Young Turks and the troublous times which followed the enforced abdication of Abdul Hamid, no work has been done on the railway for several years. Already, however, it extends 823 miles to Medina, which is four-fifths of the distance to Mecca; but non-Moslems are strictly forbidden to travel beyond Ma'an, 285 miles from Damascus, without a special permit from the government.

Der'a, where we join the Hejaz main-line, has since the earliest days of Christianity been identified with Edrei, the capital of Og, the giant king of Bashan. Beneath the ancient citadel, which stands some distance to the south of the station, is a wonderful labyrinth of caves, with real streets and shops as well as dwelling-places. This underground city doubtless was intended as a refuge for the entire population of the capital in time of siege, but it has not been used for many centuries.

As our train now turns northward from Der'a, Mount Hermon comes into full view at our left, in all its splendor of towering summit and dazzling whiteness, and the lofty blue cone with its long streaks of summer snow stays with us for the rest of the day.

Thirty miles to our right, Jebel Hauran, also known as the "Druse Mountain," rises from the level sea of grain like a long, low island. At such a distance we find it difficult, even in this crystal air, to realize that the isolated mountain is really forty miles long and only a little short of six thousand feet high. It is one of the few localities in the region where are still found the once famous "oaks of Bashan."

There was just such a great wind from the wilderness the last time I went to Damascus. The Hauran bears a deserved reputation for coolness and healthfulness; but that day, as happens two or three times each summer, there was a sirocco. The wind was indeed blowing—blowing a furious gale of perhaps thirty-five miles an hour; but it came straight from the eastern desert and scorched as if it had been a blast from an opened furnace door. I did not have a thermometer with me; but, from sirocco experiences elsewhere, I should judge that the temperature in the train was not under a hundred and five degrees. The drinking-water that we had brought for the journey became warm and nauseating; but we put it to good use in soaking the back of our necks, where it evaporated so quickly in the dry, burning wind that it stung like ice for a few seconds, and then was gone. Strange as it may seem, the only other way to mitigate the heat was to shut the car windows and *keep the breeze out.*

There were fortunately some interesting incidents to enliven the long, hot ride over the monotonous plain. We did not see any of the renowned "strong bulls of Bashan," or any other cattle grazing on the plain, but we watched slow caravans bearing wheat to the coast, as they have been doing for millenniums past. They could never carry all the grain that this productive district might harvest, and the railways should prove a rich boon to the Hauran. We pondered curiously as to why the stations were never by any chance just at the towns and why the track should swing far to the right and left in great curves, as if it were ascending a difficult grade, when the only engineering problem involved in its construction could have been solved by laying a ruler on the map and drawing a straight line down the center of the level plain. A fellow-traveler explained to us that the course of the railway had not been determined by the usual considerations, such as economy of construction and the desirability of passing through the most densely populated districts, but by the amount of *bakhsheesh* which wealthy landowners would pay the government in order to have the line pass through their estates.

We stopped an unconscionable length of time at every station, for no evident reason; and when we did get ready to start there were so many vociferous warnings that very naturally none of them was heeded by the passengers who had got off for refreshments. So finally the rapidly moving train would be chased by a crowd of excited peasants, most of whom carried big bundles and wore long, hampering garments. Several were left behind at lonely stations. There would be another train—to-morrow! Of course, all the dogs ran after us. Provided they are well-fed, dogs and children are exactly the same the world over; and these were not the starved, sullen curs which lie in Oriental gutters, but were wideawake, fun-loving fellows who ran merrily alongside the train for a half-mile from the town, and had no difficulty in understanding our English shouts of encouragement. As we were pulling out of one of the stations, a very reverend, gray-bearded old farmer stole a ride on the running-board; but he misjudged the quickly increasing speed of the train, and, when he at last decided to jump off, rolled head-over-heels down the steep embankment. The last we saw of him, he was gazing after us with a ludicrously dejected countenance whose every lineament expressed stern disapproval of the nervous haste of these degenerate modern days.

As a rule the other travelers were too hot and tired to afford us much entertainment; but one new arrival, not finding a seat elsewhere, tried to force his way into the harem-compartment which Turkish railways always provide for the seclusion of Moslem ladies. The lord and master of the particular harem occupying this compartment resented the intrusion with such a frenzy of threatening gesticulation and insulting malediction that the members of our party who were unaccustomed to the ways of the East expected to see murder committed forthwith. The conductor, who interposed as peace-maker, was—as is usual on this holy railway—a Turk who knew no Arabic, and he consequently had great difficulty in determining what the quarrel was about; but the Syrians have a healthy fear of any one wearing a uniform, so the trouble was finally adjusted without bloodshed.

After we became accustomed to the peculiar features of the landscape we could now and then distinguish a village. Yet at a very short distance the largest settlements were blurred into the brown plain; for the houses are all built of a dull black basalt and, save for one or two square towers, the compact hamlets are hardly to be distinguished from rough out-croppings of rock. All of the dwellings look like deserted ruins: some of them are. All seem centuries old: many have been occupied for more than a thousand years, for the hard basalt seems never to crumble.

The extraordinarily rich earth of the Hauran is only disintegrated lava, and as we near the end of the plain we pass tracts where presumably more recent eruptions have not yet been weathered into fertile soil. Two or three miles to the east of the railway a long line of dark rock some thirty feet high marks the western edge of the Leja, which in New Testament times was known as the Trachonitis or "Rocky Place."

By this time most of the passengers in our coach have become very tired and irritable, though the loud breathing of some indicates that they have fallen into a restless slumber. Several are quite sick from the heat. At half-past five in the afternoon the sun has lost none of its midday glare, and the noisy wind from the desert still scorches with its furnace breath. On either side, the monotonous multitude of round black rocks strew the brown, burnt earth. The hills, which constantly draw in closer to us, seem as if they might have fair pasture-land on their lower slopes; but, save for the shining white dome of one Moslem tomb, they bear nothing higher than scattered grass and dusty thorn-bushes. We climb slowly over the watershed in the narrow neck of the plain, then speed swiftly down a steep incline; and, lo, we behold a veritable paradise of running water and heavily laden orchard trees, above which the glory of the setting sun gilds a forest of slender minarets.

Part 2

PATHBREAKERS AND STONE BREAKERS

Belgium, Holland, and colonies

20

E. H. DERBY, *TWO MONTHS ABROAD* (BOSTON: REDDING & CO., 1844), PP. 36–38

DURING our stay at Verviers we visit the rail-way station at the present terminus of the great Belgian chain. The line has been recently finished to this point, and the permanent buildings are still incomplete; but a large area has been purchased, and all the structures in progress are on a proper scale and of a substantial character. We are received by an official, who courteously shows us the buildings and cars. The latter consist of three classes, all short, and on four wheels. The first class cars are well padded, about five feet high, and divided into two compartments, each holding nine passengers, who face each other. The second class are covered, and have haircloth seats, but some have curtains instead of windows. The third class are open and divided into four parts, with side seats parallel to each other, like those of an omnibus, and carry forty passengers. The engines are of the English pattern, with six wheels.

At half past six, on the morning of the 9th, we take an omnibus to the depot, and purchase tickets for ourselves and baggage, for which a small extra charge is made. The charges are, for the first class passengers two cents per mile, second class one and four tenths, and third class eight tenths of a cent; and it is a gratifying fact to the philanthropist, that all attempts to advance these rates have diminished the revenue of the rail-ways, which pay a fair interest on the outlay, and bid fair to become very productive as the freight traffic, now in its infancy, becomes developed, and the lines completed.

Our train conveys 104 persons. Of these, 20, including a portion of our party, and many English, are first class; 26 second class; and 58, or more than half, third class. As the morning is clear and delightful, and I am desirous to see the country and the route, I take my seat in the rear car, with the third class passengers, and find there many well-dressed and respectable people. Beside me sits a very pleasant and intelligent priest, and a very polished gentleman with him, who converse with ease and fluency in French and Latin, point out to me many objects of interest, and make many inquiries about America. One of them styles the rail-way the *viam ferream*, which is certainly more euphonious than the *Chemnin de fer*, of France, or the *Isebar*, of Germany. The conductor, who speaks German, English, and French, and has but 1200 francs, or $225 a year, is as courteous and gentlemanly as any one I have ever seen in that office.

In a few moments after our train is arranged, the station-bell rings. The conductor, at the head of the train, sounds his bugle; the guard, at the other extremity, blows his bugle in reply, and we are in motion. We follow the valley of the Vesdre, a small stream like that of our Pontoosuc valley, and cross and re-cross the stream by frequent bridges, and pierce the spurs of the interlocking hills by tunnels, of which there are no less than eleven in the twenty miles between Verviers and Liege, one of which is more than half a mile in length. The country is broken, and resembles the Agawam and Valatie valleys, between Boston and Albany. We pass many chateaus, the residences of the nobility and gentry, and a large zinc manufactory, from which large supplies are sent to the United States. We travel slowly, on account of the gradients and curves: and, as there are no sparks, our seat is one of the most pleasant in the train. In the open car, with us, are many well-dressed females, who use parasols to shelter them from the sun. We enter the ancient city of Liege by a light and graceful stone bridge, on three elliptic arches across the Meuse, here five hundred feet wide. This structure shows the decided improvement of modern art, and is far superior to an ancient and heavy stone bridge above, of six arches, built two centuries since.

At Liege we engage a carriage, and drive for two hours through this fine old city, built principally of stone. We pass the quay, on the banks of the river, the theatre, the baths, in a fine building with a beautiful garden in front, many large squares, and enter the Court of the Palais of Justice. This venerable old palace is built around a hollow square, at least two hundred feet wide, was erected three hundred and twenty-five years since, and, in the time of Henry the Fourth of France, was described by the queen of Navarre as one of the finest palaces of Europe. It is still beautiful, and in fine preservation.

We visit St. Paul's Church, the interior of which is in exquisite taste; its size, 250 feet by 80; its gothic architecture, fretted and painted roof, rich altar, tessellated floor, and fine paintings, with the mellowed light which comes through the narrow windows, seem to predispose one to devotion.

We examine the largest and best arcade we have seen in Europe; a building nearly an eighth of a mile in length, admirably lighted by sky-lights above and by a large dome in the centre, and lined with many gay shops. We pass the market-house, and for half a franc purchase a basket filled with choice peaches, plums, and pears, and return to the depot in season to proceed to Antwerp by the noon train. We now number 20 first class, 12 second, 70 third class passengers. Many of the latter are ladies, who seek shelter from the sun under their parasols, of which I observed five or six in one car. In another, I noticed several clergymen, wearing three-cornered hats.

We ascend from Liege an inclined plane of two miles by stationary power, so well managed that few of our party observe any difference in our motion, or notice the change from the fixed engine to the locomotive at the summit. As we proceed, the country becomes more level, populous, and highly cultivated. We notice large fields of wheat stubble, oats, potatoes, clover, flax, and English beans, and frequent villages and church steeples. The rail-road is admirably built with the exception of the rail, which is an edge rail, on chairs apparently of not more than forty pounds to the yard. When the cuts exceed ten feet in depth, we notice a space of at least two feet between the drain and the bank, and the face of the cut divided into two slopes, one above the other, as a precaution against slides. Nearly all the road-crossings are on a level, and are made perfectly secure by a guard and turnpike bar. The guards at these points are all furnished with handspikes, and, as we pass, stand erect, and present arms like soldiers. With such discipline, remissness and inattention cannot often occur.

At Louvain our train has 36 first class passengers, principally English, 92 second class, and 120 third class. The average price paid by each person is about one and one sixth cent per mile. We soon reach Malines, the great central station, where the lines from Ostend, Lille, Antwerp, Liege, and other stations, intersect and exchange passengers. A most beautiful exhibition presents itself; five trains, for as many different points, are drawn up in parallel lines. The passengers, principally in open cars, with many females and children interspersed, in light colored dresses, have a most gay and lively appearance. From 1500 to 2000 passengers are assembled. For a few moments there is a rapid movement from car to car; but soon the interchange is effected, and train after train takes its departure. The whole system of Belgium is the most liberal, judicious, and admirably conducted in Europe; contributes most to the social intercourse and innocent amusement of the people, confers inestimable benefits on commerce, has been conceived by philosophic men, independent of and above the influence of narrow and grovelling minds and popular caprice. It does honor to the country, and deserves the imitation of enlightened nations.

At Malines we notice a preference is given for engine-houses of an oblong pattern, not far from sixty feet in length, with side windows, like those of our churches, reaching nearly to the ground. From Malines to Antwerp we proceed across a level country, highly cultivated, producing clover, beans, carrots, turnips, potatoes, and grain, and arrive at the station, without the ramparts of Antwerp, at 6 o'clock, P. M.

I remain, yours ever,

MASSACHUSETTS.

Antwerp, September 9, 1843.

21

W. C. DANA, *A TRANSATLANTIC TOUR* (PHILADELPHIA: PERKINS & PURVES, 1845), PP. 195–197, 216–219

It was important for me to ascertain, before reaching the Hague, the hours when the Picture Gallery there would be accessible—a matter which varies according as the King is present or not—also the distance to which the railway was completed, &c., so as to decide whether to proceed at once to Amsterdam, or remain that day at the Hague. I looked round me in the *diligence* to see what was the prospect of my being understood, should I attempt to make inquiry. Of eleven fellow-passengers, six were ladies; of the gentlemen, three proved themselves to be natives by their continual smoking, and all had a decidedly Dutch look. One, however, had a face, to my thought, more intellectual than the rest, which, with his dress and manner, induced me to think him perhaps a clergyman, or a Professor at Leyden, which place was on our route. At any rate, I determined to put the matter to the proof; so drawing out pencil and paper, I wrote in such Latin as the case admitted, an inquiry about the railroad, which, although a thing unknown and consequently unnamed by the classic Romans, might well enough be designated as *Via Ferri*, (or *ferrea*,) in imitation of the French "*Chemin de Fer*." I watched the countenance of the stranger, who sat at some distance from me, as the slip of paper reached him, and was gratified to find that my conjecture was correct, at least as far as a knowledge of the "communis lingua doctorum" was concerned. The information which I obtained from him enabled me so to adjust my plans as to get access to the Galleries, both at Amsterdam and the Hague, which otherwise would have been impossible. Let no schoolboy denounce his Latin grammar, as of no possible *practical* utility. It may yet befriend him where he little expects it. This brief intercourse with my learned friend established a sort of good feeling between us, which was attested by sundry bows and signs, in default of words, when he left the diligence.

How the Dutch, accustomed for ages to their canal boats, could bring themselves to tolerate the introduction of the fiery-footed iron steed, and to be whirled along at the rate of twenty miles an hour, is hard to be conceived. The speed of railway locomotion must have given a ruder shock to their ancient customs, than to those of any other nation, while, on the other hand, the perfectly level surface of their territory renders it peculiarly adapted to railways.

Some miles beyond the Hague, we reached the terminus of the railway from Amsterdam, and, entering the cars, were soon at *Leyden*, so celebrated for its ancient University, which numbers among its distinguished professors and scholars, Grotius, Descartes, Salmasius, Scaliger, and Bœrhaave. *Arminius*, the expounder of the system of theology that bears his name, was also a professor here. The university is rich in its collections in natural history, and numbers, at the present time, between six and seven hundred students. The country seat of Bœrhaave is in the neighborhood of Leyden, and still bears his name. In the Church of St. Peter is his monument, with this inscription—"Salutifero Bœrhaavii Genio sacrum."

Leyden is situated on that branch of the Rhine which alone retains its original name as far as the sea. Here it seems like a broad canal, making its way sluggishly to the sea-shore, where, for nearly a thousand years, a vast accumulation of sand, rolled up by a tempest, barred its egress till, in 1809, a canal with enormous sluice-gates was constructed, through which the river, no longer rolled back and stagnating on the level surface, is discharged into the sea. The most stupendous dykes in Holland are those raised at the entrance of this canal. At ebb tide the gates are opened by machinery, and thus the Rhine, or rather the sluggish branch which here bears its name, makes its exit.

AFTER several hours on the railway, as we were descending an inclined plane two or three miles long, Liege came in view, most beautifully situated in a rich valley, at the confluence of the rivers Ourthe and Meuse. It has a population of 66,000, and, unlike the other Belgian cities, is prosperous, having flourishing manufactories, particularly of fire-arms.

These and other facts are duly set down in the guidebook, but the romance of "Quentin Durward" is what chiefly makes Liege interesting to the tourist. I spent an hour in the inner court of what was once the palace of the Prince Bishop, erected in 1533. The colonnade round it remains entire; its stunted pillars, each carved in a style different from the others, bear some resemblance to the architecture of the Doge's Palace at Venice. While standing here, I thought of the scene so thrillingly described in the romance, when the princely prelate, with dignity "somewhat between the bearing of a feudal noble and of a Christian martyr," confronting the ferocious William De la Marck, sinks down murdered without a groan, at the foot of his own Episcopal throne.

The court of the palace is now surrounded by fashionable shops, where I saw a crowd of ladies examining the goods, of which there was quite a showy display. As I was leaving the place, a troop of little girls, all neatly dressed in white, came round me, the oldest with a cup in her hand, which she held out to me for a donation. Scandalized at such barefaced importunity in one so well dressed, I turned away in disgust, internally denouncing Liege as holding a bad eminence, even in beggarly Belgium. Instead of taking the repulse meekly, the little mendicants absolutely set up a cry against me, as if my refusal was something most unreasonable; and I should to this day have recollected Liege as famous for impudent beggars, had I not ascertained afterwards that it was a Catholic fete-day, and that these donations were solicited for the *Virgin;* so that the youthful solicitors, whom I had taken for common beggars, were in fact only active members of a sort of Juvenile Missionary Society. As it was too late to make the *amende honorable,* I could only moralize on the danger of hasty inferences, and resolve to be more than ever distrustful of appearances—an obligation which, if held sacred by foreign tourists in our land, would have suppressed many piquant anecdotes designed to show up our want of civilization.

After dinner a two story omnibus drove up, which was speedily filled with passengers, to the number of perhaps forty persons, with their baggage. The directress of the hotel, young, pretty, and well dressed, stood bowing and smiling at the door as we took our departure. The enormous vehicle had horses of commensurate size attached to it, and we went rattling over the pavements of Liege, those of us on the *promenade deck* having a very open prospect into the second story of the houses.

At the depot a vast crowd was assembled. Half the population of Liege seemed to be on the hill-side adjacent, while a respectable portion of the other moiety were securing seats in the cars. This section of the road had been opened but a day or two before; hence the excitement and the crowd. The distance to Verviers was nineteen miles, and there was a tunnel, on an average, to each mile; the work has been aptly compared to a needle run through a corkscrew. Being the last link in the chain of railway from the sea-coast of Belgium to the Rhine, the government has expended vast sums on a work so important. One minute a high hill, or rather mountain, would be directly before us, the next we would be darkness, and the next in the open valley again, having thus saved many a bend of the serpentine river, (the *Vesdres*) along the green bank of which the road principally lies. The cars were filled to overflowing, ladies, as well as gentlemen, standing after all the seats were filled. In the car that I was in, were ten or twelve of the young men of Liege, all in high spirits—but there was nothing rude or boisterous in their mirth—their demeanor was truly polite, and I could not but acknowledge to myself that a stranger in America, similarly situated, especially if he dealt with the English language, as I did with the French, would probably have had reason to complain of a different style of manners. It almost seems peculiar to the Anglo-Saxon race, to have their risibles irresistibly excited by any abuse of their mother tongue; while French, Italians, and others, will hear their language mangled and tortured to any extent, with the most imperturbable gravity and politeness.

English travellers are not generally popular on the continent; the repulsive and supercilious manners of the inferior class, who often affect a lordly style where they are unknown, exactly proportioned to their servility at home, has given the English a bad name, so that the truly well-bred of that nation, of whom it was my happiness to meet many on the continent, have not only a character to support, but one to redeem. I grew rapidly in favor with the young Liegois when they found that I was an American. When we reached the depot at Verviers it was quite dark, and every thing was in confusion, the small town being crowded full in consequence of the recent completion of the road.

22

COMPAGNIE DU CONGO POUR LE COMMERCE ET L'INDUSTRIE, BRUSSELS, *THE CONGO RAILWAY FROM MATADI TO THE STANLEY-POOL* (BRUSSELS: P. WEISSENBRUCH, 1889), PP. 106–110

The workmen of the railway

We class in two categories the workmen to be engaged: *Excavators* and *helpers* and *men of trade*.

For the recruitment of black excavators we may rely upon:

A. Men not belonging to the Independent State of Congo;

B. Natives of the State enlisted out of the railway region;

C. Natives of the cataract region.

A. The recruiting of the first category may be effectuated in several parts of Africa itself:

1° *On the western coast.* The *Krooboys*, stout workers, enlisted on the coast of Kron of Monravia at Cap Palmas. The railway from Loanda to Ambacca has found in this region their best workmen; a considerable number of them went even to the Panama: They know since a long time the Congo, as the State as well as commercial firms are employing them constantly. The salary of the Krooboy is from fr. 0.75 to 1.25. The transport will cost about 20 francs.

The *Why* enlisted lately in Liberia for the service of the Independent State of Congo are docile and devoted servants. A large number of them may be obtained. Their wages are the same as for the Krooboys.

The *Haoussas* enlisted on the Slave-Coast, principally at Lagos, were especially enlisted as soldiers. Nevertheless at several times, more particularly at Leopoldville in 1883 and at the time of the transport of the *Ville de Bruxelles*, they have been employed in earthwork, with very satisfactory results. The wages of an Haoussa are fr. 1.25 per day. His transport costs 30 francs.

The *Loangos* and *Cabindas* have been employed at all times in the factories of the Congo and in the establishments of the State on the lower river. They are very available workers so much the more disposed to be rendered to the Congo,

135

as there the find themselves in the midst of tribes using nearly the same language as themselves, and as everywhere on the river they are meeting countrymen. This people engage on the spot, so that no transport is to be paid; their wages vary from fr. 0.50 to 1 franc per day.

The portuguese government enlist at Mossamedes workers for the planters of S. Thomé. These workers are highly appreciated.

2° *On the eastern coast of Africa* the State have enlisted *Zanzibaris* and *Caffers*. The Zanzibari, although he excells in no kind of work, complies with any of them; he is more or less proper for any trade and possesses remarkable aptitudes to assimilate any work. He makes himself a carrier, excavator, mason, carpenter and even a blacksmith, if necessary. The Caffer has many of the qualities of the Zanzibari, besides docility, although he has less force of resistance. After all they are very valuable auxiliaries, who always may be obtained in great number.

Their wages are 25 francs per month, more the travelling-expenses which amount from 125 to 150 per head.

B. *Natives of the State enlisted out of the cataract region.*—The principal center of recruitment known up to now is to be found with the *Bangalas*. It would be useless to repeat all what has been reported by the most reliable traveller about these workers. The results will speak for themselves. Actually the Bangala is accustomed to change his residence in order to enter the service of Europeans. It is now a habit for them, as it is since time immemorial for the Krooboys on the western coast, for the Wanyamonozi, for the Zanzibaris on the other side of Africa. Such movement will continue increasing, as every contingent who return at home consolidate the confidence, and covetousness is excited by the sight of the wages they bring with them. Thus the ground is admirably prepared for recruitment, and we may advance without hesitating that these tribe will supply a great number of hands. The Bengalas are stout and intelligent; they have proved to be good excavators, who work with animation and emulation.

The actual wages of a Bangala are 1 1/2 *laiton*, the actual value of which in Europe is from 12 to 13 centimes; this figure will not be long increasing.

C. *Natives of the cataract region.*—Finaly in the very cataract region, numerous workers may be enlisted. Conclusive experiment have been made on the subject and the only objection made up to now was the question: Shall the black engage for that kind of work out of his habits? Whoever has been observing african matters since some years knows very well that this objection does not stand. The native of that region is a carrier, but he has not been always a carrier. He became a carrier because it was the only kind of work proposed to him first; now, when he was asked to put themselves to the heavy waggons of the *Stanley* he did not fail, he did not refuse such new kind of work. At Manyanga, then at Lukungu and then at Lutete more than a thousand of them have been enlisted every time in less than eight days.

In spite of such proof the same objection has been made again as, at the end of 1887, the *Ville de Bruxelles* and the *Roi des Belges* were to be transported. They said: the natives of the Northern bank will not drag the waggons. Nothing of that

COMPAGNIE DU CONGO POUR LE COMMERCE ET L'INDUSTRIE

kind happened: the negroes of the right bank were not more obstinate than those of the left river and the heavy waggons arrived at Isanghila dragged exclusively by natives. Even a great number of them were employed in repairing the road, and they did not feel more reluctant to that work than to any other.

In fact the important problem of manual labour in that region has been resolved from the very day, when the first native transported a parcel for an European. At present every thing can be obtained with tact and money.

Men of trade.—Black men of trade are to be engaged rather exclusively among the non-natives. The english possessions of the Gold-coast will supply a great number of masons, carpenters, blacksmiths, stokers properly acquainted with their trade. A rather considerable number of them has been employed by the independent State and generally have complied well. Wages are from 75 to 125 francs per month.

Carpenters and masons are to be found also among the Cabindas; the wages are slightly inferior, as the worker is generally less clever. They are paid from 50 to 75 francs per month.

It would be easy also to recruit masons in the Angola province, where the rate of salary is nearly the same.

Finally among the Zanzibaris and the Cafers many men of trade may be met with; at all events, as has been stated above, this people possess great aptitudes to assimilate such trades, so that they may be employed under the survey of other clevers workmen.

Conclusion.—We think that the manual labour will be met with in Africa and principally in the Congo itself. This is a rather important matter. For, if we can leave in the very country the greatest portion of the wages, we shall make it rich before working it.

23

E. D. MOREL, *RED RUBBER: THE STORY OF THE RUBBER SLAVE TRADE FLOURISHING IN THE CONGO IN THE YEAR OF GRACE 1906.* WITH AN INTRODUCTION BY SIR HARRY JOHNSTON (NEW YORK: THE NASSAU PRINT, 1906), PP. 91–103

Public works and the price thereof

"What does the native receive in return for all this taxation? I know of absolutely no way in which he is benefited. Some point to the telegraph. In what way does the telegraph benefit the native? Those who live near the line have to keep the road clear for nothing, and in tropical Africa that is not an easy task. Others point to the scores of steamers running on the Upper Congo. In what way do they benefit the native? Here and there along the river natives are forced to supply large quantities of firewood for an inadequate remuneration. Others, again, point to well-built State stations. In what way do they benefit the native? They were largely built and are now largely maintained by forced labour. Then others point to the railway. It is a splendid achievement of engineering skill and pays large dividends to shareholders, but in what way does it benefit the thousands of natives on the Upper Congo?"—J. H. WEEKS, for twenty-five years a missionary in the Upper Congo, in a letter to the author, dated Monsembe, December 24, 1903.

I COME to the third claim. The Congo Administration has undertaken the construction of public works and buildings. "Elegant" stations have been erected along the banks of the upper river. That is quite true. No one has ever denied it. Some of the public edifices at Boma and Matadi on the lower river are quite as substantial as those which are to be met with in other administrative centres of the West Coast of Africa. But who has paid for their erection? The Congo native. Whose labour is it which has reared them from the ground? The labour of the Congo native. Whom do they benefit now that they are there?

The Congo native? The Congo native who is "entitled to nothing"? The Congo native who owns neither his land, nor the fruits of the soil (which he alone can gather), nor his labour?

If the Congo native does not benefit from the existence of these fine buildings which his labour has constructed and paid for; if their existence merely facilitates the plunder of his country and the exploitation of his person by the occupants of them, in what sense can their construction be claimed as evidence of "civilisation"?

To maintain such a thing would be to make use of an argument which no longer passes muster in the world. It is out of date by two thousand years.

Go *behind* those fine stations, those camps of military instruction, those Government-run plantations. Go *behind* them into the forest and the bush. Mingle with the people of the land. Witness their abiding desolation, their daily griefs. Wander among ruined homes and poverty-stricken hamlets, where once flourished prosperity and ease. Look how the grass almost conceals the village paths once so clear and clean; weeds overhanging the now crumbling huts; sud invading the river frontage once filled with cassava steeping-pits—that sud where the mosquito and the tsetse love to breed, the purveyors respectively of malaria and sleeping sickness, whose dread ravages sweep increasingly through the land, finding ready victims in a broken-spirited and ill-nourished people, broken by long years of grinding tyranny, ill-nourished through the workings of a system which demands for its multitude of agents the staple food-stuffs of the country. Where are the stores of brass rods, the numerous live-stock which were once the pride and wealth of these primitive communities? Arbitrarily seized, the Commission of Inquiry is fain to admit, as it records the "incontestable impoverishment of the villages." Where are the native industries which once gave pleasure and occupation to these people—iron-ware, brass-ware, rude pottery, basket-making? They have "decayed," says the report of the Commission—decayed, as everything worth preservation has decayed and withered beneath the breath of Leopoldian civilisation. "It is hard to tell how these people live."

See these men in whom the very manhood seems stamped out dragging themselves back from the bush at the day's end after a weary search through partly submerged forest, knee-deep, waist-deep in fœtid swamp, for the accursed juice of the rubber vine, that vine which they must find and tap in all seasons, in all weathers, whether the sap is rising or falling, always, ever, day after day the year round until death in some form—by violence, exhaustion, exposure, or disease, or mere weariness and sorrow—closes the term of an everlasting and—to them—mysterious visitation. See them at night in the forest, far from home, wife, and children, their interminable search not yet over, huddled together shivering under a few palm-leaves with a scrap of fire in their midst. The nights are cold in the equatorial forest. The rain invades their scanty shelter, and the night-wind chills their naked bodies racked with rheumatism and fevers, their minds a prey to superstitious fears in the impenetrable gloom made by the giant trees and matted creepers through which the sun never pierces, where malignant spirits are abroad—exposed, unarmed and helpless, to the attack of some roving leopard.

What thoughts are theirs! In the distant village wives and children live at the mercy of the capriciousness, cruelty, and lust of the armed ruffians set there by the white man: men fierce, all-powerful, speaking another tongue, tribal enemies perchance, or maybe the worst malefactors in the community, specially selected for that very reason as the most fitting instruments of oppression: men whose lightest word is law, who have but to lift a finger—they and their bodyguard of retainers—and death or torture rewards protest against the violation of the sanctuaries of sex, against the rape of the newly-married wife, against bestialities foul and nameless, exotics introduced by the white man's "civilisation" and copied by his servants in the general, purposeful, satanic *crushing* of body, soul, and spirit in a people—crushing so complete, so thorough, so continuous, that the capacity of resisting aught, however vile, slowly perishes.

Out there in the forest, the broken man through the long and terrifying watches of the night—what is his vista in life? Unending labour at the muzzle of the *Albini* or the cap-gun: no pause, no rest. At the utmost if his fortnightly toll of rubber is sufficient, if leaves and dirt have not mingled in too great proportion with the juice, he may find that he has four or five days a month to spend among his household. If so he will be lucky, for the vines are ever more difficult to find, the distance to travel from his village greater; then the rubber must be taken to the white man's fine station, and any number of delays may occur before the rubber-worker can leave that station for his home. Four or five days' freedom per month—that is the very *maximum* he can expect. Five days to look after his own affairs, to be with his family, and always under the shadow of the sentry's rifle. But how often in the year will such good fortune attend him? Shortage on one occasion only will entail the lash, or the chain and detention; worse, perhaps, if the white man has a fever or an enlarged spleen that day. And if he flinches? If, starting from an uneasy sleep there in the forest, when shapes growing out of the darkness proclaim the rising of another day, he wakens to the knowledge that his basket is but half full and that he must begin his homeward two-days' march betimes, not to miss the roll-call, his heart fails him and he turns his face away, plunging further into the forest, fleeing from his tormentors, seeking only one thing blindly, to get away from his life and all that it means—what will happen? Well enough he knows. Has he not seen the process with his own eyes? Father, mother, or wife will pay for his backsliding in the hostage-house. And whither shall he flee? The forest encompasses him on every side, the forest with its privations by day, its horrors by night. There he must live seeking such nourishment as roots and berries will afford. Shall he gain some other village in the hope that it may be a friendly one? But there will the sentry be also, and his doom as a "deserter" is sure.

Go *behind* those "coquettish" centres of "civilisation" where the superior Congolese official drinks, keeps his women, and superintends the shipment of the rubber in the river steamers bound for the Pool, the railway, and the ocean steamers. Go behind those outlying "Posts" where the subordinate Congolese official or

agent of the Government-controlled rubber trusts lives in discomfort and solitude –
unless his posse of savage and often cannibalistic auxiliaries can be called company—eating out his soul, losing hold on decency and dignity with the months,
harried by perpetual objurgations from the superior person in the fine station for
rubber, more rubber, still more rubber.

Go *behind* them—those out-stations—and in some covert place near at hand in
a clearing, surrounded by bush, hidden from prying eyes of prowling missionary
or chance traveller, you will come across it. A small, low-roofed building, opening
into another, where a guard of sentries keep watch and ward. This is the hostage-
house, one of the recognised institutions of the Upper Congo, like the *chicotte*, the
collier-national—otherwise the chain-gang—and the *matabiche*—otherwise the
rubber bonus. Inside, herded like cattle in a pen, cramped and suffocated, unkempt,
grovelling in filth and squalor—men, women, and children, chiefly women. Half-
starved, wholly starved at times—what a story the records of the Congo Courts
will tell if a substantial number of them are ever dragged to light! For the pestered,
unwrought subordinate white man in the out-station, grown callous, and habitually,
almost unconsciously, cruel, has other things to think about besides his hostages
and their victualling. It is as much as he can do, often enough, to feed himself
and his soldiers. Taught by his superiors to look upon the people of this regenerated land as brute beasts ere he sets foot among them, the daily task assigned to
him has bred a total disregard for human suffering. His mind has become simply
non-receptive to such ideas. Rubber is his god! His salary is a mere pittance, but
every ton of rubber from his out-station spells *matabiche*, and every month that
passes means possession coming nearer, and with it release from his surroundings.
Censure, if the out-put falls below the stated figure. Praise and advancement, if he
succeeds in maintaining or increasing it; . . . and *matabiche*. Rubber is his god! The
natives are but means to an end—and them he loathes. Ah! how he grows to loathe
them! Are they behindhand in their quota? Then they are robbing *him:* he who has
power of life and death over hundreds or thousands of men, women, and children!
Do they tremblingly urge that the vines are exhausted? They are defying *him!* He
knows it, and his fever-haunted brain devises fresh measures for their coercion. He
rereads his instructions, couched in terms of mingled cajolery and warning, and
he hardens his heart. Fevers, solitude, discomforts, excesses, the sense of omnipo-
tence grafted upon an indifferent *morale* and pernicious ideas inculcated by his
employers, the sense of mingled irritation and vanity excited by seeing fear, and
the deceit born of fear, in every face, the iron chains of the whole system of which
he has become the tool, and, in a sense, the victim—a system implacable, unal-
terable, machine-like, whose motive power, controlled and directed with genius
from a far-away European city, operates in the Equatorial forest with passionless
regularity—all this has made of him what he is, what he needs must be, lost to all
moral sense, impervious to emotions of pity or compassion.

"When an official begins to realise the *coulisses* of the Administration,
he is stupefied to have fallen so low in the social scale. He cannot ask

for his resignation because the *Recueil administratif* does not admit it. If he insists, and leaves his station, he can be prosecuted for desertion, and, in any case, will probably never get out of the country alive, for the routes of communication, victualling stations, etc., are in the hands of the Administration, and escape in a native canoe is out of the question— every native canoe, if its destination be not known and its movements chronicled in advance from post to post, is at once suspected and liable to be stopped, for the natives are not allowed to move freely about the controlled water-ways. The official must therefore finish his term, always obeying the *ukases* of the Governor-General and the District Commissioner, without the hope of being able to make known the miseries he is undergoing to the outside world, because in Boma there is a *Cabinet noir* for correspondence."

Look inside that hostage-house, staggering back as you enter from the odours which belch forth in poisonous fumes. As your eyes get accustomed to the half-light, they will not rest on those skeleton-like forms—bones held together by black skin—but upon the *faces*. The faces turned upwards in mute appeal for pity: the hollow cheeks, the misery and terror in the eyes, the drawn parched lips emitting inarticulate sounds. A woman, her pendulous, pear-shaped breasts hanging like withered parchment against her sides, where every rib seems bursting from its covering, holds in her emaciated arms a small object more pink than black. You stoop and touch it—a new-born babe, twenty-four hours old, assuredly not more. It is dead, but the mother clasps it still. She herself is almost past speech, and soon will join her babe in the great Unknown. "The horror of it, the unspeakable horror of it."

Every station, every "post," every "factory" of the rubber districts of the Upper Congo, and many in the food-taxed districts, has its hostage-house. The number of hostages detained is inscribed upon registers, and—so far as the out-stations are concerned—monthly statements on forms printed for the purpose and entitled, "*Etat des indigènes soumis à la contrainte par corps*," are forwarded in duplicate to headquarters. By careful reckoning of the number of stations and out-stations, the authorised number of hostages detained *per mensum* in each, and documentary evidence showing how that number is exceeded, it has been possible to compute that ten thousand human beings pass through the hostage-houses of one only of the vast rubber preserves of the Upper Congo in a single year. How many remain to die, or leave them only to die, is more difficult to compute.

The hostage-house is one of the most efficacious assets of the rubber slave-trade.

Sometimes with shameless boldness, but with some attempt at outward decency because the site is a more public one, the hostage-house flaunts itself openly and is a more pretentious and commodious building. This, on the premises of one of the "fine" and important central stations. And here you can see the prisoners as they march, roped, through the station to the abode which a beneficent Administration has caused to be erected for the purpose of stimulating a healthy desire to work among the natives of Central Africa. Slowly the procession winds its way through the station buildings—officers' bungalows, drying sheds for rubber, and so on. At its head walk four sentries fez on head, and cap-gun or *Albini* slung from their brawny shoulders. Behind them eighteen women—mothers, those whom motherhood will shortly claim, maids, girls of tender age. Some carry babies, or hold tiny children by the hand, for who shall feed these if left in the village behind? Faltering they come, casting fearful glances to left and right, "so terror-stricken that they cannot control the calls of nature." What is their offence? It is an offence by proxy, and a very grave one. The husbands, or the brothers of these women have failed to trap the weekly antelope required as part of the tax for the white man's table; or their supply of fresh fish is short—fish are not always abundant in all seasons in the same locality, but the Congo official and his soldiers require fish, and fish they must have; or the rubber has been of bad quality and insufficient in quantity. It is necessary to take these measures. The husbands will require their wives, and they will trap the antelope, they will find the fish, and they will improve their rubber supply. They are lazy that is all. If they do not—well the women will remain in their pleasant abode, fed generously by an Administration full of concern for their moral and material welfare. Should delay prove exaggerated and indefensible, it will be the painful duty of the official in charge to send a number of sentries to visit that village. Merely to visit it, of course. They will take their guns? Yes, but for self-protection. These people are wild, very wild. But, rest assured, the guns will not be used save under deliberate provocation; it would be contrary to the regulations. Ah! of course, if the regrettable necessity presented itself—why, then these poor brave sentries would have to defend their lives. The women in the house of detention? Well, no doubt they would be very happy to join the sentries' *menage*. And who knows? You observed the fifth in the line, she with the brass anklets? No? You English are strange people. She was pleasing, quite pleasing. "Distinguished magistrates" assured the Commissioners of Inquiry—says their Report—that the detention of women in hostage-houses was the most "humane form of coercion." Perhaps it is on the Congo, for there are many worse. But the Leopoldian conception of humanity, is the humanity of the human tiger thirsting, not for blood, but for rubber which presently—when flung from the hold of an ocean carrier (owned by an Englishman, plentifully be-starred and be-medalled) upon the Antwerp quay—shall be converted into gold.

Gold to pour into the lap of some favoured friend. Gold to be invested in undertakings "from China to Peru." Gold to rear palaces, pagodas, and monuments to the Emperor of the Congo in Belgian cities. Gold to purchase properties under brilliant Mediterranean skies. Gold to be hoarded in private treasure-chests of which none but the Royal owner holds the key. Gold to corrupt consciences and manufacture public opinion: to disseminate lying literature throughout the world, even on the seats of continental railway carriages.

I have stood on that quay of Antwerp and seen that rubber disgorged from the bowels of the incoming steamer, and to my fancy there has mingled with the musical chimes ringing in the old Cathedral tower, another sound—the faintest echo of a sigh from the depths of the dark and stifling hold. A sigh breathed in the gloomy Equatorial forest, by those from whose anguish this wealth was wrung. *They* knew not their merciful Emperor. Yet that echo took form of words in my mind. "Imperator"—it has seemed to whisper—"Imperator! Morituri te salutant!" (We who are about to die, salute thee, Emperor!) Perhaps it was because thoughts flew backwards five hundred years when to the sound of the same gentle pealing from the old Cathedral tower, the ancestors of this same people, which permits to-day its foreign monarch and his financial bodyguard to plagiarise in Africa the infamies committed upon its own citizens by the hirelings of another foreign monarch, fell in mangled heaps in the narrow streets of this very city. If there be a spirit in that tower which never dies—as legend somewhere has it—one can picture the cynical smile that flits across its shadowy features as, contemplating at once the rubber-laden quay and the escutcheon of the city with its severed hands, and thinking of the Congo toll—the toll of the handless stump—reflects of the world and its ways, "Plus ça change: plus c'est la même chose."

Yes. Go *behind* those fine stations cemented with the blood of black humanity, and see into the lives, read into the hearts of the people. Witness the degradation to which native life has sunk—that elderly Chief honoured in the eyes of his subjects, flogged and put to menial tasks, made to drink from the white man's latrine. In the social system of the African native the person of the chief is at once the father of the clan, its rallying-point, the centre to which it looks for guidance, the symbol of all that the clan venerates and regards as holy. The deliberate policy of "Bula Matadi" has been to break down that influence, in nine cases out of ten an influence for good, and of course put nothing in its place. Every feature of indigenous life which made for self-respect has been dragged in the mud of grinding tyranny and foul imaginings: natural instincts of dignity and decency undermined: indigenous laws for the localisation of disease rendered of no avail through the wholesale deportation of women, and the moving hither and thither of masses of soldiery. Public incest as a pastime to the brutal soldiery: things nameless, unprintable. Watch that procession wending its way through the tortuous bush track. Mourners—sons carrying the body of their father, murdered by one of the village sentries in a fit of caprice, to the white-man's station. The slain man was the chief of that primitive community. Moreover he was a "medal-chief." Surely in this case justice could be secured against the assassin. Impatiently the white man hears the story, and bids the bearers, through an interpreter, depart. The rubber was insufficient. It was not the first offence. The chief was responsible. "It is enough." As the men delay somewhat in taking up their burden, he sets his dog upon them. Watch, too, this son of a murdered father, begging from the murderer, permission to untie the body from where it hangs on yonder sapling, and give it decent burial. That permission will be granted him eventually, but on it will be founded a further pretext for extortion, and a goodly portion of the remaining family goods will pass into the sentry's hands. Note the gait of that youth as he limps painfully into the village square. He is a fine muscular specimen of humanity. What ails him? As he turns, the cause is clear enough. Down his broad naked back and loins, the blood slowly runs and drips upon the ground. Flies are buzzing round his shoulders. He has been flogged by the white man's orders for shortage. Fifty blows of the rhinoceros hide whip. He fared better than Bokoto of Wala, he explains to his aged mother as he reaches his hut—*he* got a hundred strokes, and had to be carried away.

Go *behind* those "fine" stations, which figure in the illustrated publications so obligingly scattered broadcast by the Press Bureau. Get from the lips of survivors the story of the "breaking" of their village. The narration takes you back to the Middle Ages, to the exploits of the Spanish *conquisitadores* in the West Indies. Go from village to village: from district to district. Leave the rubber zone and visit that fishing centre where the old men—the young are away getting in their fortnightly "tax"—will tell you, in their primitive simplicity, "our young men have no time even to make children. There is nothing before us but death." Get from the lips of the people everywhere the same story of misery and woe: here, when the weekly tax in food-stuffs have been paid there is nothing left but leaves to eat: there the chant of mourning for relatives slain in an affray with the sentries. Pass on through swamp and brushwood. There is another hamlet not far off and from its direction a confused noise arises, quickly to be distinguished as cries of terror, shouts, execrations. A man dashes past you running swiftly down the bush path you are now entering. Seeing you he doubles back and plunges into the forest. You come upon the scene. It is typical and commonplace. A white man in dirty clothes and straggling beard sits upon a stool. Before him stand several soldiers surrounding, or holding five women and a man, whom the official is angrily interrogating through an interpreter. He is taking the census of the village, and apportioning its "taxation," that is all. Other soldiers are busy looting the huts, coming out with armfuls of spears and knives, cutting down the plantations, or chasing with loud shouts the villagers who have fled panic-stricken to the bush. Multiply such scenes, such tales, such tragedies ten thousandfold, and you will only touch the fringe of a people's misery.

To men who have lived among them for many weary moons, and whose existence would long ago have been intolerable but for their faith in the Almighty, to a man who for years has been receiving the outpourings of these men's hearts in letters and in speech, and whom circumstances have given an insight—granted to few—into the European side of this unparalleled scandal and colossal human tragedy, until their hideousness has burned itself into his soul and scorched it, there is no "redeeming feature" in the public works constructed by King Leopold on the Congo, or in Brussels.

On the Congo, every mile of railway, every mile of road, every new station, every fresh stern-wheeler launched upon the water-ways means a redoubling of the burden on the people of the land. First because their labour and their labour alone, supplies the needed moneys and the needed muscles. Secondly, because these material evidences of "civilisation" serve but one purpose, that of facilitating the enslavement of the inhabitants, of tightening the rivets in the fetters of steel within whose pitiless grip they groan and die.

As for the handsome edifices raised by King Leopold in Brussels with the proceeds of this rubber slave-trade, I can find no words more fitting than those of Mr. Vandervelde uttered in the Belgian Chamber last March, to characterise them:

"I tell him that this money, these profits, these presents are shameful things because they are the result of the exploitation of a whole people."

24

REVEREND J. H. WHITEHEAD, 'REPORTS AND LETTER OF PROTEST TO THE GOVERNOR-GENERAL', IN E. D. MOREL, *RECENT EVIDENCE FROM THE CONGO* (LIVERPOOL: J. RICHARDSON & SONS, 1907), PP. 14–17

In the Lukolela region

We have received long and detailed reports from the Rev. John Whitehead, of Lukolela, as to the state of affairs in his district, also copy of a letter of protest he has despatched to the Governor-General. It will be remembered that an important report from Mr. Whitehead appeared in an Annex to the White Book "Africa No. 1," 1904.

Mr. Whitehead's first advices are dated 13th Nov., 1906, and deal mainly with the taxes in staple food supplies exacted from the native towns in his neighbourhood. They are particularly instructive inasmuch as they give some indication of the interpretation on the spot of the Reform decrees. One of the main provisions of these decrees is that the native is now only required to labour on behalf of the Administration or its *concessionnaires* forty hours *per month, i.e.*, sixty days per annum, instead of, as formerly, three hundred days per annum (as recorded by the Commission of Enquiry).

The Congo Reform Association has pointed out in a Memorial to Sir Edward Grey, that so far as the rubber districts are concerned a fall in the rubber output of three-fifths the quantity now exported would be the immediate result of the application of this regulation. In Mr. Whitehead's own district the tax is a weekly tax in *kwanga*, or native bread, each village having to supply to the Government post a specific number of loaves or balls of this food, which requires careful preparation. Mr. Whitehead, who has many years' experience of the country, estimates, after careful computation, that the payment of this tax at the present moment involves the villages in forty-five hours' labour *per week*, for which they receive the sum of 50 centimes (5d.) in trade goods from the Administration.

In addition to this labour entailed in preparation, there is the work of carrying the tax to its destination, for which no payment is made, and Mr. Whitehead says that "on an average each carrier has a journey of sixteen hours each week from the nearest village."

Natives kidnapped for five years' forced labour

Other parts of Mr. Whitehead's letter deal with the raiding of villages for railway labour:

"In May last," he writes, "a *chef de poste* of Lukolela, acting upon instructions from the District Commissioner, who also had instructions from the Governor, went into the inland district and secured twenty able-bodied young men (five from one village, Mibenga) and brought them to Lukolela, where they were transported to the railway works away at Stanley Falls. I made enquiries from an official some days ago in respect to them, and I learnt that they had been sent to work for five years; that this demand of the Government for workmen for public works can be made annually, and if refused can be affirmed by force. I believe this conscription of young men from this district for works in other and distant places is not admired by the officials of the district, for very urgent reasons, but it is persisted in from headquarters. The people in this district, and especially the wild people from the interior at Lukolela, cannot bear the change of climate and food; few are able to live, and fewer still return to their people again. Of the fifteen commandeered at Lukolela for the Vankerkhoven expedition towards the Nile in 1891, only two found their way back to Lukolela, and that only after desertion. There will be a boast of the great work of that railway soon, and how the Congo State built it will be forgotten. It is abominable cruelty to these natives, and yet it is for the 'Public benefit!' What is the 'Public' here?"

How rubber is obtained in the "Crown Domain"

The practice of the Administration in selecting certain villages, arming their inhabitants and setting them as rubber tax-gatherers over other villages, which has been largely adopted in recent years, is also referred to by Mr. Whitehead. He says:

"A year or two ago the people on the river and inland at Lukolela were disarmed of their flint-lock guns in a deceptive fashion, under the pretence of sending them to Stanley Pool to be marked, and to receive permits to carry arms. Sums of money were deposited by the natives on that undertaking. Neither money nor guns were seen again. But the other day a man, who came from an inland village which is really in the district of Lukolela, but has been put into the district of Lake Leopold II., sought my advice, and it came out that in that district the officers arm the chiefs of the various villages with cap-guns. (The one at Bonginda, I understand, has five of these guns, and they are given plenty of caps and ammunition.) The Administration had experience with a man from that neighbourhood—Lokolologanya—whom they used to browbeat the people until he got beyond their power, when he gave the Administration and the people around very much trouble. He attempted to enslave everybody right and left, and he led this same village successfully for a time, holding out against the Administration.

"And here they are arming the chief again! I am told it is the common practice in the district. This chief is compelling everybody, with these guns, to own allegiance to him, and he is doing it with the authority of the Administration behind him. The native who came to me for advice complained that this man had flogged his sister to death, and that when he went to the official of the Administration at Mbongo, the official said he was not there for talk but for rubber. Finally he told the man to go for rubber, and when he brought it to bring the chief with him. He now has the rubber, but the chief is threatening to shoot him if he comes within sight of him. He wanted to know what to do. I told him to return to the official and tell his story, and if he did not do anything in the matter to come to me again, and I would write to Boma. But what does it matter so long as rubber is got in the Crown Domain?"

Mr. John Whitehead's further reports

We have received the following further report from the Rev. John Whitehead, which is reproduced here as forwarded to Sir Edward Grey by the Congo Reform Association on 4th March. These reports shew that the natives of the Lukolela district are in a more wretched state than when visited by Consul Casement three years ago:

In a letter of protest to the Governor-General, dated Lukolela 29th December, 1906 (copy received by me on 1st March with a covering letter dated 31st December), the Rev. John Whitehead communicates a lengthy report as to the atrocious state of affairs prevailing in the neighbourhood.

Mr. Whitehead furnishes the fullest details in every case he deals with. The following is a summarised version:

The Lukolela region is under direct Government control, and forms part of what is now called the "National Domain" of the "Congo Free State," and from Mr. Whitehead's narrative the privileges of citizenship in the "National Domain" of this African "Free State" can be fully appreciated.

The food taxes

The crushing burden of the food "taxes" form the principal subject matter of Mr. Whitehead's protest. This, for example, is the position of affairs in the "small" Ngele district. This district was previously taxed *every fortnight* in 300 "bunches" or "lots" of fish, of a local value of 3,000 mitakos, or £6 5s.; or, multiplied by 26, £162 10s. per annum. As a remuneration for this "tax," the tax-payers received from a generous Administration a rebate of 300 mitakos (12s. 6d.), thus reducing the value of their annual "tax" in fish to £146 5s. They also had to supply thirty fowls and three ducks every month—the local value of a fowl being 2s. and of a duck 8s. 4d. The local value of this tax per annum was, therefore, to the tax-payer £51 12s. For this they were supposed to receive in return a rebate of £12 10s. The payment of this tax *involved a seven days' journey in a canoe*" to deliver it at destination.

Part 3

INCONGRUOUS *EISENBAHN*
Railways in Austria, Switzerland,
Germany, and colonies

25

J. G. KOHL, *AUSTRIA, VIENNA, HUNGARY, BOHEMIA, AND THE DANUBE* (LONDON: CHAPMAN AND HALL, 1843), PP. 156–158, 160

Railroads

It has often been matter of complaint, that the city of Vienna has not a more immediate connexion with the many rail and water roads radiating from it. The passengers by the steamboats complain when they find themselves compelled to leave their beds soon after midnight, if they wish to set off at five in the morning, and those by the railroads grumble equally at having to travel through the whole city, together with its suburbs and the villages beyond, before they can consign themselves to the energetic guidance of the locomotive. The various rail and steamboat stations lie two or three leagues apart, and some of them at that distance from the centre of the city. An incredible number of hackney carriages are constantly employed in transporting passengers to the several points. The magnificent terminus of the Vienna-Raab railroad lies at the extreme outer line of the city. The position is so lofty, that they might have continued the road to the very centre of the city without being in the way of the smoke of a single chimney. The terminus in that case would have reached about half way up to the summit of Stephen's Tower.

Before railroads were invented, many of the beautiful environs of Vienna were a forbidden Paradise to its citizens. Those who had no other means of conveyance at their command than what nature provided, never reached Baden, Stockerau, or any such distant point, from one year's end to another, or perhaps not in the course of their lives. Within the last few years the railroads have given them a key to these Elysiums, and at every opening of a new branch of road the newspapers of Vienna announce the fact in a style that might have suited some of Captain Cook's discoveries, new and most captivating descriptions of Stockerau, Briel, Helenenthal, &c., being put forth to entice people by thousands to the railroad.

The railroads have wrought a change in the whole environs of Vienna, and in the whole system of out-door pleasures. The Prater and the Augarten are lost, and comparatively empty now, when the seekers of pleasure can be carried away with so much ease to a distance of five or six (German) miles. The Prater had made the most extraordinary promises; it had announced a "Bacchus festival," to end with a faithful representation of the eruption of three volcanoes in Fernando Po. The three were to vie with each other in the splendour of their flames, and send forth smoke enough to darken the heavens. Preparations had also been made to blow up several masses of (pasteboard) rock. Nevertheless, the Prater was doomed to be deserted that evening, and the visiters were thronging to the railroads. On the other hand the invitations for more distant places of pleasurable resort were not less alluring. At Mödling, Strauss promised his newly-composed dances, "Country Delight," "Railroad Galopade," the "Naiads," &c.; and Lanner announced his musical conversazione, his "Eccentric," his "Reflex from the World of Harmony," to be given at Liesing. In Baden all sorts of "*Volksfeste*" were to take place. There was to be the "Dance for the Hat," a Milan dance, in which the ladies dance through a gate, and she whose transit falls in with a certain given signal obtains a hat by way of a prize. In the various "Arenas" (garden theatres), "The Bohemian Girls in Uniform," the "Elopement, from the Masked Ball," "The Maiden, from Fairy Land," and other attractive pieces, were advertised.

Around the last coach setting off for the Vienna-Raab railroad the people were thronging and steaming. "Pray, gentlemen, let the ladies go first," cried some voices in the crowd. "Yes, yes, the ladies first, the ladies first, they all say, and here am I shoved back again," cried a woman who had been pushed back from one of the carriages. She was launching in her despair into a high strain of eloquence when we invited her into our hackney-coach, and recognised in her, in spite of her shining kid-gloves, a Vienna cook. The cooks generally wear short sleeves, between which and their long gloves, a brown and scorched ring of an arm remains to reveal their calling.

The Vienna-Raab railway (now that its direction towards Hungary is given up, it will probably be called the Vienna-Trieste railway) is probably the most magnificent railway in existence. The terminus and intermediate stations are remarkable for their size and splendour. The waiting-rooms for the passengers of the first and second-classes are more like drawing-rooms than any thing else.

There are three classes of carriages; they are all extremely capacious, carrying not fewer than fifty-six persons. Besides these three classes, there are the, so called, "saloon carriages," furnished with looking-glasses, divans, tables, &c., and destined for persons of wealth and distinction. At present the lines of railroad are towards the resorts of pleasure, and have their names accordingly:—Mödling, Baden, Neustadt. The time will come when more important names will appear— the Adriatic, Venice, the East, the Levant, &c.

The banker Sina is at the head of the Vienna-Raab line, as Rothschild presides over the Vienna-Brunn line. At first the engineers were all Englishmen, but they have since been replaced by Germans. "The English have not the phlegm of the Germans," said a Vienna citizen to me, "they were rash, and careless, and many accidents were the consequence." The precautions observed on the Austrian railroads are so great as almost to counteract the main object of these roads— speed. Very slowly and very gradually the train is set in motion, countless are the whistles before it moves at all, and very moderate is the progress for some time. Long before they mean to stop, the speed is slackened, and astoundingly slow in its motion up to the terminus. It is true that if we could be assured that every new precautionary measure saved some lives, they could not be sufficiently commended, but the question will arise—do they really do so? It may so happen that the negligence of the lower functionaries increases in exact proportion with the extreme foresight of the higher. The surer the public is that precautions are taken by others, the less will they take care of themselves.

On the day I went on the Vienna-Raab railroad we had, in our train, fifteen carriages, full of people starting from Vienna in search of pleasure, consequently, seven hundred persons. We encountered similar trains several times, and, I believe, that the number of persons carried out that Sunday could not be less than twelve thousand. The direction of this railroad galopade was towards the plain at the end of the forest of Vienna. The hills are pierced by several valleys, beyond which lie the before-mentioned pretty villages of Liesing, Mödling, Baden, and others. Hundreds of men, women, and children, were disgorged by the train at the entrance of these valleys, and hundreds of fresh passengers packed in. Formerly a stranger required a week to visit all these vaunted places in their turn, now he can be whirled there, have a peep at them, and be back in a few hours.

We allowed ourselves to be complimented out of the carriage at Mödling, to enjoy the highly lauded views of "in der Briel." We found a dozen of asses ready saddled, standing at the station. One of the donkeys was named "Karl Wizing," another "Nanerl," and her gentle daughter "Sofi," so at least the juvenile drivers informed us. As we were just three in number, we chose these three animals, mounted them, and trotted away into the mountains. The father of the present Prince Lichtenstein first brought the neighbourhood of Briel into notice. He caused the naked declivities to be clothed with woods, paths to be cut, and the ground to be laid out with taste; adorned the summits with pavilions and summer-houses, built a magnificent seat in the neighbourhood, and abandoned the picturesque old ruins to the curiosity of the public. At this present time several yet wilder, woody and rocky valleys in the neighbourhood of Vienna are undergoing a similar transformation. Coffee-house civilization has put to flight the nymphs and dryads of the woods. The caves of the fauns have been fitted up for the sale of beer and wine, and where formerly a solitary lover of nature could scarcely force his way, the population of a whole quarter of the city are now gadding about in merry crowds.

Life in Baden has undergone a great change of late years. Formerly the emperor Francis lived here in the summer, and, like king Frederick William at Teplitz, assembled much of the great world around his person. Both places have lost by the death of those two sovereigns; nevertheless, now that the railroad brings, daily, thousands into the neighbourhood, and inundates it with smokers, drinkers, and cooks, the pleasures of the arenas have become of infinitely more consequence than those of the saloons. The baths will be great gainers. They are now within reach of many to whom they were before unattainable. Many invalids in public offices come with the first train, take a bath and return to the capital before their hours of business. Prince Puckler Muskau observes that, in Vienna, people talk about a "*lamprelle*," or a "*parapluie*," but know nothing about a *Regenschirm*. I also had opportunities enough of remarking the fondness of persons of the uneducated classes for sporting a few French phrases. While waiting with some hundreds of persons in the room appropriated to the second class, for the arrival of the train, I sat down near a very fat, very fine lady, who was parading her French to an acquaintance. "Comment vous portez vous?" said the lady. "Oh, ah, oui, bien," was the reply. "Prenez place ici, voulez vous?" "Non." "Pourquoi donc?" "Non! je, je,—Ah what shall I say, I don't know how to say it, but I'd rather stand," and hereupon he laughed out loud. "Il fait très chaud ici," persisted she. "Ay, you mean it is very hot, yes hot enough to stifle one." "Oui c'est trop," rejoined the fat dame, "it is *too* bad. If they would but collect the heat and put it into the engine they might save their firing."

The drive back, at eleven o'clock at night, was really brilliant, and the precautionary lighting of the road almost superfluous. The stations were illuminated with red and green lamps; the whole way along, lamps and torches were planted, and withal the moon shone resplendently in the heavens. Late as it was, we met several trains, and, without any exaggeration the engines were piping and whistling as numerously along the railroad as so many mice in a granary.

It was one Sunday afternoon that I walked into the streets to see what aspect the city bore at that time of the day. The workday and morning tumult had quite subsided, the constant "*Ho! ho!*" of the hackney carriages, and the "*Auf!*" of the car-drivers were silent, for 20,000 of the inhabitants of Vienna were rolling over the newly opened railway to the newly-discovered Paradise of Stockerau, and 20,000 were flying by the Raab road to Mödling, Baden, and the other valleys of the forest of Vienna; 50,000 more were gone into the country for the summer, and another 50,000 were gone after them for the day, to forget the troubles of the week in their society.

26

JOHN W. CORSON, *LOITERINGS IN EUROPE* (NEW YORK: HARPER & BROTHERS, 1848), PP. 222–227, 234–239, 263–266

WHEN I rose next morning and began to look about me, I found myself decidedly in a new country. The immense round earthen stove in the corner of my room, like the pipe of a steamer—the little feather-bed, too short at the head and not long enough at the foot, that had been over me instead of under me, and that it had so puzzled me to balance in my sleep—the fat, blooming landlady—the bill the most moderate on the Continent—the peasant houses with thick walls and low roofs— the broad people with little caps—the hearty, kind good morning (*guten morgen*)— the straw-colored beer in long glasses—the ornamented pipes, and the smoke that came from them—were all German. It was a still wintry morning, and the sun was glistening brightly on the deep snows of the surrounding hills. I walked out to try and get a near view of an old ruin belonging to the ancient counts of Cilly, once the lords of all Carinthia; but the snow chilled my ardor.

The railroad that (if they can tunnel or scale the Alps between) is intended to be completed from Vienna all the way to Trieste, now reaches as far as Cilly. On applying for my ticket at the little station-house, I noticed on the engine the name of the maker, "W. Norris." I recognized it immediately as the mark of our enterprising countryman; and the unexpected meeting with the slightest memorial of home in the wilds of Styria was enough to cause quite a thrill.

As in our rapid flight by railroad, we came to the more level country, the temperature became much milder. There was an air of plenty and domestic comfort about the dwellings of the rural population that was quite pleasing. We crossed the Drave and halted at Marburg on the opposite bank, and, skirting in places the frontiers of Hungary, traversed a well-cultivated region, and stopped, at last, at Gratz, the capital of Styria. It contains a scientific institution with lectures, and a museum, for the study of natural history, founded by the pariotic and greatly beloved Archduke John.

Forsaking the pomp of courts for the dress and manners of his favorite Styrians, this prince has married the daughter of a postmaster, encountered in one of his hunting excursions, and, by living familiarly among them, and encouraging every laudable enterprise, has succeeded in acquiring immense influence.

INCONGRUOUS *EISENBAHN*

Styria is still as famous for its excellent iron as it was in the time of the Romans. There is a legend among the miners, that, at the expulsion of the Romans by the barbarians of the North, the Genius of the Mountains appeared to the new-comers, and said, "Take your choice: will you have gold for a year?—silver for twenty years?—or iron forever?" They wisely accepted the last.

Gratz is a very cheery city and delightfully situated. The necessaries of life abound, and living is said to be cheaper than in any other city of Europe.

Taking the cars again, we crossed the Mur, and pushed rapidly on to the mountain pass of the Sömmering. Here we were unpacked from the cars and transferred to carriages drawn by horses, with which, in three or four hours, we scaled the mountains, and took the railroad again on the other side. All the passengers seemed inveterate smokers. There was a regulation posted up in the cars obliging all persons to use pipes secured with a cover or lid from causing accidents by fire, and forbidding smoking, except with the consent of the company; but the inhalers being an overwhelming majority always ruled. It was intensely cold, and the atmosphere inside the cars was at times perfectly thick and dismal. Though never yet a partaker, I have always enjoyed the sight of the pleasure of smoking in others. I can conjure up the faces of dear friends that have never beamed so kindly, never seemed so contented with this sorrowful world, as when, after a social repast, or in the dim twilight, softly as the sighing of a fairy, curled from their lips wreaths of peaceful smoke. But my liberal sentiments were in vain, and, more than the most delicate German lady, I coughed and panted for an open corner of the window. Indeed, the ladies seemed to have admirably disciplined themselves to the puffing propensities of their partners.

At last, we reached Vienna in the midst of a furious snowstorm. I escaped from the cars, and took up my quarters at a clean, spacious hotel, as I fancied in the city. It was only the *Vorstadt*, a sort of outer city, extending like an immense suburb a little distance round the ancient walled city proper. Between this outside city and the inner one, there is an immense pleasure-ground a quarter of a mile wide, laid out with walks, and ornamented with trees, and extending like a belt round the whole of the old city. It is used for military exercises and other purposes, and gives Vienna a different appearance from any city in Europe, constituting an immense breathing-place, as it were, for the citizens. After crossing this broad, vacant space, you come to a ditch some twenty or thirty feet deep, inside of which are the defenses of the old city walls that anciently resisted the Turks; and you enter by gates and gloomy passages into the Paris of Germany. Within, all is bustling gayety. Only with the evidences of the lively pursuits of pleasure, there is more of stately magnificence than in the French capital. It is situated in the flat basin of the Danube, about two miles from that noble stream. The streets are narrow but very cheery, the shops splendid, the houses massive and lofty, and the streaming of gay throngs and the dashing of rich equipages through every passage and square of the central or old city keep the stranger in constant excitement. Before the entrances to the numerous dwellings of the nobility resident in Vienna, you see in winter a livery greatcoat lined with fur, surmounted with huge bear-skin collars, and stuffed with tall, red-faced porters, standing passively all day long. You are soon reminded, too, that it is the capital of a large empire, by meeting in the streets the dress and physiognomy of some dozen different nations. Germans, Bohemians, Poles, Hungarians, Greeks, Italians, Dalmatians, Tyrolese, and all the intermediate varieties, are curiously blended. Encircling the whole of the old city is a mound of earth, some fifteen or twenty feet high, two or three rods in width, and faced externally with a stone wall. It was this fortification which saved the city in two sieges by the Turks. Since its capture by Napoleon it has been leveled on the top, and forms a delightful dry pleasure-walk for all classes, from royalty downwards. It served me for a daily promenade the greater part of the winter. There is scarcely a better chance for a stranger at this season to get a general glance at the Viennese than at the hour when it is most crowded.

Almost the first features that strike the attention of a stranger with the Austrians, and the Viennese in particular, is their air of contented gayety. The latter, indeed, have a proverb, "One lives to live" ("*Man lebt um zu leben*")—and they zealously observe it in their own way. Austria is a wine country; food, clothing, the necessaries, and even the luxuries of life are exceedingly cheap. The government, for political purposes, carefully assists in providing for the amusement of all classes. Vienna is, perhaps, the most musical city in the world. I have heard nearly the whole assembly in one of their Catholic churches join with the organ in chanting a beautiful and difficult anthem; and the leading attraction in Vienna for years has been Strauss's famous band. The whole population, too, appear to let off their exuberant spirits through their heels. More than one half of the placards you see in the streets are of music and dancing. During summer, the citizens are said to go out to the beautiful environs of Vienna to waltz in the open air. In winter, the rich gather in splendid halls; the poor meet merrily at the smaller places, or rush to the shows and dancing of the "Elisium," a fairy cavern beneath the city; and on a frosty morning, the very children in the streets may be sometimes seen frisking about to measured steps to keep themselves warm. As in all popular assemblies in Austria, the police are sure to be always present at these festivities to preserve decorum.

I shall never forget the expression of blank astonishment in the faces of several Viennese friends, at different times, as I tried to explain to them the conscientious scruples which many of the religious community in our own country have to such light amusements. The stranger is often surprised with the warmth of heart and generous hospitality of the Austrians, and, in fact, all the Germans.

One is struck at first, too, with their ceremonious yet sincere politeness. It is a mortal offense any where in Austria to enter into any apartment, office, or establishment without being uncovered. Some members of the royal family visiting the manufactory of a friend doffed their hats to the humblest of the workmen. More than French politeness, the German seems unaffected and earnest. It is amusing to witness the formidable bows and interchange of civilities between two postillions meeting in a café. The higher classes often mingle with the common people with much freedom. Happening to meet some of the Austrian nobility quietly paying their respects to the social circle of a friend, I was struck with their good-natured communicativeness, and the ease with which they moved in a mixed company.

One day after dinner, a friend, as recreation, gave me a lecture on German titles. An ordinary married lady is addressed simply *Frau* (woman), or, more politely, *Madam;* if of a higher grade, *Gnädige Frau* (Gracious Madam); if the husband have a government office she takes the title of her husband with a feminine termination, as Madam Directress, Madame Judgess, Madame Generaless. In speaking to an unmarried lady, you say *Fraulein,* or the French *Mademoiselle.* Gentlemen have an abundance of high-sounding appellations, from plain *Mein Herr,* to *Herr Von* (ranking the English Esquire), *Rath* (Councilor), and many others, depending on the grade or profession up to the different orders of nobility. It is customary to address persons by titles above their real rank, and to be profuse with compliments. Some of the more exquisite of these are really curious. In Vienna you frequently hear, as a parting salutation, or courteous acknowledgment to a lady, "I kiss your hand, gracious madam;" and in a courtly way the action is sometimes suited to the word.

THE Danube has been a famous stream for crossing and fighting upon, from the time of Trajan to Napoleon. We passed over by steam on a railroad bridge at daybreak; and the only enemy we had to fight was a terrible frost, which seemed as if it would shrink us to mummies, and made us draw up our limbs like an assemblage of turtles. It froze our very curiosity. We passed the battle-field of Wagram with scarcely courage to look out into the penetrating air. One can easily conceive that in the same latitude as you go inland toward Prussia the cold increases. I have tried the winter of some of our most northern states and Austria, and I give the premium to the frost of Vienna. One finds natural causes for the habits of most nations. I came latterly to consider it quite proper that the Austrians should have extensive earthen stoves, and double windows, and indulge in the luxury of elegantly-tanned sheep-skin overcoats, with the wool inside.

We passed through many little towns and villages with hard German names, and traversed a portion of Moravia. In the cultivated open country here were more evidences of extensive ownership and the effects of the feudal system than in any other country yet visited. Vast unfenced fields were often observed, over which game were frisking, without a human dwelling in sight. Here and there was seen a village of inferior little houses, all of a size, inhabited probably by the tenants of some neighboring nobleman. Prince Lichtenstein, one of the richest of the Austrian nobility, is said to have an estate extending in one direction a distance of two hundred miles.

The railway upon which we were traveling, like all the others in Austria, belongs to the government. It extends from Vienna to Prague, in Bohemia, and it is intended to have a branch completed to Austrian Poland.

Toward evening we arrived at Olmutz. It seemed a sleepy sort of place, full of old houses, beer-shops, soldiers, and guarded with formidable dikes, bastions, and strong walls. The Swedes nor any other enemy will hardly take it easily the second time. At the time I made numerous inquiries about the prison of La Fayette.

At last I was delighted to find an old man who, with a rough Bohemian accent, I understood to say, had known the illustrious prisoner. It was a mistake—my German had not yet come to maturity, and I had misunderstood him. He was like the man who, being asked if he knew German, replied, No—but he had a cousin who played on the German flute. My friend had a relative who knew La Fayette's prison. Sauntering among the fortifications about sunset, I happened to meet a couple of Austrian officers, to whom I mentioned the object of my search, and stated that I was from America. They politely referred me to a moldering bomb-proof pile inside of a very strong fortress a few rods distant. It seemed uninhabited, and was roofed above with earth. One could easily conceive that in its damp, low cells, the sufferings of the illustrious patriot must have been very severe.

To be on the spot to start by the train at a very early hour, I removed in the evening to a respectable-looking, quiet inn, at the railroad station, about a mile out of the city. Happening to go down into the traveler's room rather late in the evening, I encountered a sight very often to be seen at the inns frequented by the country people in Germany. Men, women, and children, of the poorer class, unable to pay for a bed among the aristocracy above, were lying in their clothes in groups upon straw scattered over the floor. It was a bitter cold night, and I could not just then smile at the scene, grotesque as it was, for pity.

Taking the cars bright and early, we whirled all next day through a pleasant country, and at sunset came in sight of the spires of Prague. We entered the city by crossing the hill where Ziska, the blind Hussite chieftain, led out his valiant band to a camp fortified by the assistance of the women and children of Prague, and from which he descended, against fearful odds, to defeat the Emperor Sigismund, the betrayer of Huss. Except Edinburgh, I saw no city in Europe that approached in the grandeur and romance of its position to Prague.

It is situated in a valley encompassed like an amphitheatre with bold eminences, and traversed by the River Moldau; and the numerous turrets, domes, and spires that rise, tier above tier, from the water's edge, give it something like Eastern splendor. Loftier than all the rest, and looking boldly over the city from the brink of a precipitous hill, towers the ancient palace of the Bohemian kings, the Hradschin. It is larger than the Imperial Palace at Vienna. My first impulse upon gazing at it from the other side of the town was to climb up the hill where it stood. To do this I had to cross the magnificent old bridge over the Moldau, upon which stands the famous statue of St. John of Nepomuk. The saint, as the story goes, was confessor to the queen aud having refused to divulge the secrets confided to him was secretly drowned by being thrown from the bridge into the river. A miraculous light, however, revealed the situation of the body to the people, and it was removed, and, in later times, transferred to a silver coffin in the cathedral. The latter edifice is upon the same hill, and close to the palace, and derives its chief interest from the immensely rich shrine of this most popular saint. I never saw such a profusion of precious metal as is contained in the several good-sized statues of angels and other ornaments about the tomb. They are said to contain in all the incredible amount of nearly two tons of silver. And this forms only part of the treasures of a shrine now, perhaps, the richest in the world. More than eighty thousand pilgrims at a time have been known to gather from the surrounding countries within late years, to celebrate the great festival of the saint in May. The walls of the cathedral must have been originally of great strength, as it is said that during the bombardment of the city by Frederic the Great, in the Seven Years' War, it served as a mark for his cannon, and received more than a thousand balls.

Near the palace, also, once resided the Danish philosopher, Tycho Brahé, who was astronomer royal to the munificent Rudolph II. Beneath the palace walls are two obelisks, marking the spot where the cruel ministers, who counseled the persecution of the Bohemian Protestants, in a tumult, were thrown from a window at the height of some eighty feet, and preserved by a dunghill; and thus, in a slight affray, began the conflict which ended in the terrible Thirty Years' War.

Few things interested me so much in Prague as its university, distinguished as one of the most ancient in Europe and as the scene of the labors of John Huss and Jerome of Prague. In the height of its glory it is said to have been frequented by the almost incredible number of forty thousand students of several different nations, and some regulations affecting the privileges of the foreigners within its walls, were the means of driving away some thirty thousand pupils in a single week, and founding the universities of Leipsic, Heidelberg, and Cracow. It was through some of the Englishmen frequenting the university that Huss is supposed to have become acquainted with the doctrines of Wickliffe.

One of the students, seeing I was a stranger, politely showed me into the library. It was crowded with busy, silent readers, and a librarian, with a bunch of keys and a black gown, beckoned me to explore with him its rich treasures. There was one of the first Bibles ever printed; and there were the celebrated theses of John Huss in his own handwriting. But the most interesting relic of all, was a manuscript Hussite liturgy discovered, as the librarian told me, in destroying one of their ancient places of worship. It was found to have been executed at the cost of the different trade-companies of the city, and was beautifully illuminated with paintings, the subjects of which were taken mostly from the Bible and the life of Huss. One series of these illustrations was very remarkable. It consisted of three small pictures on the margin of the same page, representing the progress of the Reformation. The first represented Wickliffe, striking a spark with flint and steel; the second Huss, blowing a little kindling fire; and the third Luther, holding up a blazing torch. Beneath was a picture of Huss intrepidly looking up in the agonies of death amid the flames and surrounded by fierce-looking persecutors at Constance.

One afternoon I took a stroll into the Jews' quarter, known, in the expressive German, as the *Judenstadt*. It is one of their oldest colonies in Europe, and the persecutions and massacres of earlier times, and hereditary prejudices at the present, have helped keep them a distinct people. They are now no longer locked up in their own streets at eight o'clock in the evening, and they are even allowed their own schools and magistrates. As in every Jews' quarter, there are the same intelligent, hard faces, and there are the same streets of old clothes and smallwares, and now and then, as you saunter carelessly along, you are perhaps half startled at seeing, leaning archly over some little counter, the beautiful form of some bright eyed and dark-haired Naomi or Rebecca. The Jews of Prague boast of the most ancient synagogue in Europe, it having stood, as they allege, a thousand years. After a diligent search for the sexton, I gained admission to the most curious, dark, and dingy place of worship I ever beheld. The windows were exceedingly small; there was some religious scruple against any kind of cleansing, and the walls and high roof were blackened by time and the smoke of the lamps and torches that for days together are sometimes burning during their more solemn services. There were the curiously-wrought lamps and furniture exhibiting the mysterious number seven, and reminding one of the descriptions of the Old Testament, and in the place of the altar of a church was a sacred inclosure for the holy books of the law. Separated from the body of the synagogue, and communicating with it only by apertures through the wall about the size of an ordinary pane of glass, was the apartment to which the females only were admitted.

Not far away was their spacious ancient burial-ground. I wandered a while in this lonely place, brushed away the snow from some of the little heaps of stones, brought one by one as tributes to departed friends, and gazed vacantly on the curious symbols and the Hebrew characters engraved on weatherbeaten, crumbling gravestones. It is crowded to its utmost capacity. More than a century has elapsed since the last interment. The talkative guide explained the epitaphs on some, pointed out the more imposing monuments of their dignitaries and rabbis, and, with something of a look of pride, as I thought, showed me the grave of a Jewess who, by some freak of Fortune, had married a prince, and had preferred in death to sleep with her people.

BLESSINGS be on him who invented railroads. Next to balloon-flying, or some other means in which I am equally inexperienced, they seem to afford the most comfortable way of traveling in cold weather. Posting over the rough ground is no comparison.

It is true, that, except the select few within the car, you see little of the people, and your recollections of the country are something like Milton's description of the voyage of Satan to Earth—rather misty. But who ever tasted happiness in this world that had not its drawback? And the calm pleasure of sitting like a philosopher, and without the motion of a hand or the quiver of a wing, flying over the beautiful earth, like a spirit, is necessarily fleeting; and the impressions of the scenes through which you pass are easily effaced.

The railroad from Berlin to the mouth of the Elbe had been finished but a few days previous, and instead of a jolting, tedious ride over a weary level for nearly two hundred miles, I found myself, on a fine brisk morning, sitting quietly in a car, waiting for the last whistle of the conductor, and expecting to sup in Hamburg.

Our route lay through the flat territory of the principality of Mecklenburg Schwerin, famous for its geese, horses, and other animals, the more fleet from having never to go up hill. It is a part of that vast plain, here less barren, that skirts for hundreds of miles the southern shore of the Baltic, and extends into Russia. Scattered over this every where are numerous granite boulders of various sizes, brought apparently by some violent cause from a distant mountain chain. They have rather puzzled geologists. Some have fancied they were floated there upon icebergs, loosened and thawed at the time of the Flood; and others have thought that the Baltic once covered all this plain, and that rocks from the mountains of Scandinavia, upon flakes of ice, might have been ferried over and deposited.

We passed near the place where the poet Körner, the German Tyrtæus, fell in rallying his countrymen against the French, but a few hours after composing the celebrated "Sword Song," and was buried by his companions in arms, beneath a spreading oak.

Just at sunset we came to the pleasant environs of Hamburg, and in half an hour, with a cheerful party of Germans, I was duly established at an hotel.

Next day I had a delightful ramble though this old-fashioned commercial city. It will be remembered it was anciently a leading member of the powerful confederacy of the Hanse Towns. In some parts the houses have a very antiquated, odd appearance, as though they had stood for centuries. But these are quite eclipsed by the beautiful edifices rising from the ashes of the late fire. Its havoc must have been immense, as, with all the resources of the first seaport of Germany, a large space is still desolate.

The city is built at the junction of a small river, the Alster, with the Elbe; and the former stream is dammed so as to form an extensive basin, around which is a beautiful promenade, termed, in the expressive German, the "Maiden's Walk."

Happening to be out just after sunrise, I could not help noticing the dressy appearance of the servant girls out making their purchases for the day. It is customary for them not to appear in the streets except in the gayest attire, and it is rather amusing to see their provision baskets, shaped like little coffins, nicely enveloped in the folds of a splendid shawl, and borne by hands garnished with kid gloves.

But the most curious costume you meet in the streets is that of the female peasants from a settlement in the neighborhood, supposed to have been an ancient Dutch colony. Their dresses are queer as the most heathenish robes of savage people in a child's picture book, and their hats look as if the original idea had been taken from the top of a mushroom or the inverted form of certain dishes in a dairy.

When the water in the Elbe is low, the large London steamers are sometimes detained some eighty miles below at the mouth of the river, and this being strongly threatened at the time of our visit, a party of us embarked on board a smaller English steamer for Hull. Large quantities of floating ice impeded our progress, till at last we caught a glimpse of the port of Cuxhaven, and soon after were buffeting a rough sea in the German Ocean.

The voyage usually varies in length with the weather. At day-break of the third day we entered the mouth of the Humber. We had left winter in Germany to find decided spring in England. It was the beginning of March and yet it seemed like an April day. Soon after, the sun rose, and we landed in Hull. The hum of one's mother-tongue seemed delightfully welcome. It was a lovely Sabbath morning; and the stillness of the streets, the closing of all the shops, the ringing of the bells soon after, and the cheerful and yet sedate groups bending their way at a given hour to the churches, all contrasting with the dissipation and gayety of the day upon the Continent, strongly reminded me of home.

Next day I took an early stroll through the town. The situation of Hull at the head of a fine estuary, and its numerous communications with the interior, make it the first seaport of the north of England, and its docks, filled with shipping, covering a dozen acres or more, attest the activity of its commerce. Of late its trade in the Greenland whale-fishery has considerably declined.

Soon after, in company with a fellow-passenger, a kind, intelligent German, who needed the assistance of an interpreter and guide, a party of three of us set out by railway for the south. The rich, finished aspect of the country, neatly hedged and ditched every where, the broad, sleek-looking cattle and sheep grazing in the fields, and the neat cottages and stately old mansions, scattered thickly over the country, quite captivated our German friend. Passing through the pleasant towns of Selby and Rotherham, we came to Chesterfield. The spire of one of its churches has a very singular appearance, looking as if it had been built of some yielding material, and been twisted round two or three times, and then pulled slightly to the westward. From this we pushed on to the pleasant ancient cities of Derby and Leicester, and joined the great Northwestern or Liverpool line at Rugby.

Anxious to get on, from pressing engagements, we took the first upward train, and in the dusk of the evening the houses and the smoke began to thicken, the conductors to search for some suspicious character on board, and we soon after were liberated at the immense station in Euston Square.

By nine in the evening I was in a distant part of London, enjoying the society of delightful friends.

27

RACHEL HARRIETTE BUSK, *THE VALLEYS OF TIROL: THEIR TRADITIONS AND CUSTOMS, AND HOW TO VISIT THEM* (LONDON: LONGMANS, GREEN, 1874), PP. 148–149, 168–170, 327

The advance of the iron road has not stamped out the native love for putting prominently forward the external symbols of religion. I one day saw a countryman alight here from the railway, who had been but to Innsbruck to purchase a large and handsome metal cross, to be set up in some prominent point of the village and it was considered a sufficiently important occasion for several neighbours to go out to meet him on his return with it. Again, on the newer houses, probably called into existence by the increased traffic, the old custom of adorning the exterior with frescoes of sacred subjects is well kept up. This is indeed the case on many other parts of the line; but at Fritzens, I was particularly struck with one of unusual merit, both in its execution and its adaptation to the domestic scene it was to sanctify. I would call the attention of any traveller, who has time to stop at Fritzens to see it: the treatment suggests that I should give it the title of 'the Holy Family *at home*,' so completely has the artist realized the lowly life of the earthly parents of the Saviour, and may it not be a comfort to the peasant artizan to see before his eyes the very picture of his daily toil sanctified in its exercise by the hands of Him he so specially reveres?

An analogous incident, which I observed on another occasion, comes back to my memory: it happened, I think, one day at Jenbach. The train stopped to set down a Sister of Charity, who had come to nurse some sick person in the village. The ticket-collector, who was also pointsman, was so much occupied with his deferential bowing to her as he took her ticket, that he had to rush to his points 'like mad,' or his reverent feelings might have had serious consequences for the train! So religious indeed is your whole *entourage* while in Tirol, that I have remarked when travelling through just this part in the winter season, that the very masses of frozen water, arrested by the frost as they rush down the railway cuttings and embankments, assumed in the half-light such forms as Doré might give to prostrate spectres doing penance. The foot-path on to Hall leads through a continuance

of the same diversified and well-wooded scenery we have been traversing hitherto; but if time presses, it is well to take the railway for this stage, and make Hall
or Innsbruck a starting-point for visiting the intervening places.

North Tirol—unterinnthal (right inn-bank)

The railway station, as if it dared not with its modern innovation invade the rural
retreat of primitive institutions, was at a considerable distance from the village,
and we had a walk of some fifteen or twenty minutes before we came within reach
of even a chance of breakfast.

My own strong desire to be brought quite within the influence of Tirolean traditions perhaps deadened my sensations of hunger and weariness, but it was not so
with all of our party; and it was with some dismay we began to apprehend that
the research of the primitive is not to be made without some serious sacrifice of
'*le comfortable.*'

Our walk across the fields at last brought us to the rapid smiling river; and
crowning the bridge, stood as usual S. John Nepomuk, his patient martyr's face .
gazing on the effigy of the crucified Saviour he is always portrayed as bearing
so lovingly, seeming so sweetly all-enduring, that no light feeling of discontent
could pass him unrestrained. Still the call for breakfast is an urgent one with the
early traveller, and there seemed small chance of appeasing it. Near the station
indeed had stood a deserted building, with the word '*Restauration*' just traceable
on its mouldy walls, but we had felt no inclination to try our luck within them; and
though we had now reached the village, we seemed no nearer a more appetising
supply. No one had got out of the train besides ourselves; not a soul appeared by
the way. A large house stood prominently on our right, which for a moment raised
our hopes, but its too close proximity to a little church forbad us to expect it to be
a hostelry, and a scout of our party brought the intelligence that it was a hospital;
another building further on, on the left, gave promise again, because painted all
over with frescoes, which might be the mode in Schwatz of displaying a hotel-
sign; but no, it proved to be a forge, and like the lintels marked by Morgiana's
chalk, all the houses of Schwatz—as indeed most of the houses of Tirol—were
found to be covered with sacred frescoes. At last a veritable inn appeared, and
right glad we were to enter its lowly portal and find rest, even though the air
was scented by the mouldering furniture and neighbouring cattle-shed; though the
stiff upright worm-eaten chairs made a discordant grating on the tiled floor, and
a mildewed canvas, intended to keep out flies, completed the gloom which the
smallness of the single window began.

It is the border town against Bavaria, and is consequently enlivened by a
customs office and a few uniforms, but it is a poor place. I was surprised to be
accosted and asked for alms by a decent-looking woman, whom I had seen kneel-
ing in the church shortly before, as this sort of thing is not common in Tirol. She
told me the place had suffered sadly by the railway; for before, it was the post-
station for all the traffic between Munich and Innsbruck and Italy. The industries

of the place were not many or lucrative; the surrounding forests supply some employment to woodmen; and what she called *Dirstenöhl*, which seems to be dialectic for *Steinhöl* or petroleum, is obtained from the bituminous soil in the neighbourhood; it is obtained by a kind of distillation—a laborious process. The work lasted from S. Vitus' Day to the Nativity of the Blessed Virgin; that was now past, and her husband, who was employed in it, had nothing to do; she had an old father to support, and a sick child.

28

ROBERT L. JEFFERSON, *A NEW RIDE TO KHIVA* (NEW YORK: NEW AMSTERDAM BOOK CO., 1900), PP. 32–43

By the blue Danube

THE blue Danube was decidedly yellow when first I saw it. Still, one mustn't be too hard or too cynical, for have we not our own silvery Thames? And if the Danube was muddy at Ratisbon, so is old Father Thames everywhere, except above Reading.

But here it was, the Danube at last, whose course I was to follow as far as Buda-Pest, whence, while the river went south to flow through fair Roumania, and past the bloody battlefields made by the Russo-Turkish war, I should go north-east into the land of the Carpathians.

On Sunday morning, to the chiming of the bells of Ratisbon, I pedalled out once more into the country. Off to my left the fast-flowing river ran its course. Ahead of me stretched a flat and sterile-looking land, although, in the dim distance, the rugged outlines of the hills of the Austrian Oberland showed clear and distinct. The road was fair enough, and with the wind behind I had no difficulty in making Straubing in good time. But the wind, though kind, brought misfortune. Clouds scurried across the sky. The "blue" Danube, yellower than ever, raced and seethed along in veritable ocean waves. Rain fell, and at Straubing I was housebound.

A black and gloomy sky, a moaning wind, and streets swimming in rain-water! That was the outlook when I pulled out for the Austrian frontier next morning. It was work indeed to push my machine through the sodden clay and sand which formed the roadway. Everything looked bleak and deserted; and as I splashed through some village there would be no sign of life, unless it were a brood of geese muddling by the roadside, or some mire-caked pig grunting and nosing through the ooze. Dogs would yelp occasionally, and make futile efforts to get at me, but the mud would be too much.

Sometimes I caught a glimpse of a peasant sheltering beneath the overhanging eaves of his cottage, diligently smoking his pipe, and regarding me, as I splurged along, with a look of stolid wonderment. Out in the country I would perchance overtake a rumbling waggon, the heavy oxen steaming and straining at their laborious task, the driver enveloped in sacks, and ever smoking. Sometimes I would pass a benighted Bavarian tramp, who, with shoes slung over shoulder, and whose jaunty green cap looked sadly bedraggled, slouched miserably along. The drizzle of the morning became in the afternoon a perfect downpour. In a tiny and squalid village I sought shelter, and in sheer disgust abandoned the idea of getting to Passau that night.

Bavarian villages may never be noted for being up to date. This one in particular was a mere collection of brick and timber huts, standing now in a sea of mud. There was a *gasthof* of diminutive proportions, in the one room of which twenty or more rain and beer-soaked peasants were indulging in a carousal. They stared askance at me as I entered, my mud-covered mackintoshes streaming.

The reek of Bavarian tobacco, the all-pervading smell of Bavarian beer, the humid odour of unwashed Bavarian clothing caused me to gasp. Friendly but blear-eyed men came to me with their mugs that I might refresh myself. The proprietor generously pushed an old man out of his seat in order that I might have a place. A foaming mug of beer was placed before me, and I had received a Bavarian welcome—all they had to give. Rough, uncouth, unwashed, yet kind, these Bavarians are not bad fellows to a stranger. "Money I haven't got," says the child of the Danube bank, "but everything else is for you."

An accordion with one or two leaky notes squeaked out a monstrous melody, and a heavy peasant flopped into the middle of the room to give us a sight of his Terpsichorean capabilities; round and round he wheeled to the admiration of the onlookers. The room was thick with smoke, hot and stifling. Once I went to the door to get a breath of fresh air, and to note with chagrin the persistently descending rain, the scurrying clouds, and the mist on the hilltops ahead.

The afternoon was waning when, rain or no rain, I set out intent on reaching Passau that night. To stop in that village when a lively and bustling town was only twenty miles away was not an agreeable prospect. I couldn't get much wetter, and my poor bicycle was a mere mass of revolving mud.

Night settled down, and the steady downpour became a storm. Lightning darted across the black expanse of the heavens, thunder rolled and boomed. The rain eased now and again, only to return with tropical intensity. Once from the brow of a small hill I caught a glimpse of welcoming lights ahead: the sheen of electric lamps playing on the surging waters of the Danube.

On my right side ran the railway, and five miles from Passau a mail train came thundering along. As it passed I saw, within the brightly-lit carriages, indistinct heads of people reclining in ease and comfort on warm cushions. Then the train was gone in a blaze of sparks and light, and I shivered and jerked heavily at the pedals.

But everything has an end, and an hour later, when in borrowed clothes I was doing justice to an ample dinner and tasting my first Hungarian wine, I became a little happier. I was now on the Austrian frontier, and to-morrow would leave the land of the Deutscher Kaiser for that of Franz Joseph, Emperor of Austria and King of Hungary. Kind friends in Passau told me horrible stories of the inhospitality of Austrians and the barbarous tactics of Hungarians, but I ate much salt with my food and the stories, for I had already learned that race hatred here in the Danubian provinces is deep and lasting.

"When you get to Neuhaus," said the proprietor of the *gasthaus*, "you have got to cross the River Inn by a small bridge. Half of the bridge belongs to Bavaria, and the other half belongs to Austria. In the middle of the bridge is an Austrian customs-house, and there you'll have to pay sixty marks duty on your bicycle— that is, if they catch you. If I were you I'd just get across that bridge as hard as ever I could go, dodge the guard, and there I'd be, and not a penny to pay." Such excellent advice as this was not to be treated lightly. An hour after leaving Passau I came in sight of the River Inn, and at Neuhaus, the last Bavarian town, drank my last glass of German beer.

Even as the proprietor of the Passau hotel had advised, I rode hard up the slope of the Inn bridge, saw, but took no notice of, the blue and white and black and yellow posts of Bavaria and Austria side by side, and with a clear run before me, for the bridge was deserted, put on a spurt, and began to congratulate myself I was all right.

But I reckoned without my host. I heard a hoarse shouting behind me, and as I careered on down the slope of the bridge saw a soldier in the middle of the road waving his arms excitedly. There was no help for it. I jammed on the brake and rode peacefully into custody.

"Donnerwetter!" cried the soldier. "What do you mean by riding past the customs?"

"Donnerwetter!" cried I. "What do you mean by stopping me?"

But Germans don't waste time in argument. The soldier hauled me back to the customs-house, where half a dozen stern and severe officers looked at me as if I were a criminal of the deepest dye. I at once assumed an utter ignorance of the German language, and only smiled when they commenced their tirade of abuse. I spoke to them in English and shrugged my shoulders, produced my passport, and sat down on the kerb.

They gave me up as a bad job at last. An aged functionary affixed a leaden seal to my machine, another one handed me a paper and demanded sixty marks. Sixty marks he got, and I was bidden to "be off." It is evident that dodging the customs does not command respect.

And I was in Austria! A land built up of ten nationalities, where race pride and race hatred are more rampant than in any other corner of the earth. A fair enough land for him who comes unbiassed and unprejudiced; and such was I, for I cared little for the internal strife between Bohemian, German, Pole, Hungarian, Crotian, Slavonian, Bosnian, and all the rest of them who go to make up Austria. Hills there were ahead of me, which I should have to cross, and these commanded all my attention for the nonce. Politics were for those who made them; for me the country was simply as it impressed me.

INCONGRUOUS *EISENBAHN*

My first two days in Austria were pleasant enough. Improved weather made the going easy, and I passed Linz, Melk, St. Polten, and came within measurable distance of the city of Vienna. Only one incident served to give colour and romance to my ride, one of those incidents which might occur even in England, but which far away from the old country always wear a more serious aspect. Now and again some enthusiastic local cyclist would turn out to give me a lead. I should be a curmudgeon to look a gift-horse in the mouth, but sometimes I have wished that *some* of the local cyclists would not turn out at all. Some fifty miles or so west of Vienna I struck a small village, and while consuming a humble repast in burst a perspiring cyclist, who immediately made known to me that he intended to accompany me for twenty kilometres.

He was a good sort, but rode a German-made racing machine, with a gear approaching a hundred inches. He criticised my mount severely, and could not understand how on earth I should have selected such a heavy bicycle for my ride instead of having a racer.

The road out of the village was hilly and terribly loose. For five kilometres the course wound round and round, but ever upwards. At length we came to the top, and saw below the smiling valley of the Danube and the great rolling hills beyond. Now the way descended abruptly, and we went spinning down at a spanking pace, the wheels crashing and skittering through the rubble and loose stones which bestrewed the surface. My companion was leading me by about five or six yards, when, with a suddenness which was hair-raising, his machine crumpled up like a piece of paper and he went flying through the air.

Another moment and I should have been foul of the wreck, but instinct caused me to wrench round my handle-bar. The back wheel skidded in the loose stuff; I missed the wreck by bare inches, bounded up the embankment on the side of the road, struck against a telegraph post, and went head over heels four feet below into a dry ditch, with my machine on top of me.

For a moment I thought the bicycle must be smashed. I was up instantly, and my joy was great to find that nothing was broken. I climbed out of the ditch and saw my companion sitting in the middle of the road surveying with sorrowful eyes the jumbled-up mass of metal and rubber which represented his racer. Poor fellow, he was sad enough. I went on to the next village and sent a cart out to fetch him and his broken machine, and that done, pursued the even tenor of my way, more than ever determined not to ride too near a German-built racer in future.

Nearing Vienna the roads became miserable in the extreme. For the last ten miles they were quite unrideable, and I was forced to foot it. Tramping is slow work, however, and I took to the footpath, which made decent running. I was three miles from Vienna when a policeman hauled me off and inquired, politely, at any rate, what I had got to say for myself.

"I didn't know it was forbidden to ride on the footpath," said I, with a stare of blank astonishment. "I am a foreigner, and you haven't any notice boards saying it is prohibited to ride here."

"You are a foreigner, yes, and you look like an intelligent man, and an intelligent man should know that it is forbidden to ride bicycles on the footpath anywhere. Yes, that is the way to Vienna. Please don't do it again."

I accepted the rebuff, trudged steadily through the sand of the roadway, and an hour later was in the whirl of the traffic of Austria's capital.

29

E. H. DERBY, *TWO MONTHS ABROAD* (BOSTON: REDDING & CO., 1844), PP. 20–32, 34–36

We leave our trunks at the rail-way station, and drive through a pleasant street to a hotel to dine, and, after dinner, walk to the station, which occupies a large area outside the city gates. Here a large engine-house, with a vaulted roof, is in the course of construction, with other spacious buildings for freight and passengers, all of a showy and costly character. The rail is of the bridge, or inverted *U* pattern, like the new rail of the Baltimore and Ohio line, and laid on longitudinal sills. The engines and cars are all short, and of the English pattern. The first class cars are like a gentleman's carriage. The second class have glass windows and haircloth seats. The third class have covers and seats. The fourth class are like open freight-cars, with rails, against which passengers may lean. The conductors wear wallets, in which they carry tickets, and keys to lock in the travellers.

Our train conveys four first class passengers, who pay two and a half cents per mile; twenty second class, paying one and three quarters cent per mile; and nearly forty third and fourth class, who pay, on an average, about one cent per mile. Our fuel is coke; the stations permanent, but too expensive. On our way we pass a long train of passengers, nearly all of whom are third and fourth class—classes which furnish the principal revenue of the line. And here let me notice, that the omnibus fare, from the rail-way to the hotel, is usually in France and Germany but eight cents of our currency for each passenger, with his baggage, and there is little doubt, if similar rates were introduced here, it would diminish that sharpness of competition so annoying to every one who travels.

The route of the rail-way, from Carlsrhue to Heidelberg, is across an intervale country, and eminently favorable. Our speed is about twenty miles per hour, and at eight P. M. we reach in safety the 'Hotel of the Court of Baden.'

Yours, truly,

MASSACHUSETTS.

Heidelberg, September 5, 1843.

At nine P. M. we reach Frankfort, after a pleasant drive of fifty miles, at a very moderate expense. The city is full of strangers, assembling for the annual Fair; and with much difficulty, after visiting several houses, we secure apartments for the night at a principal hotel. We take our coffee in a spacious hall or coffee-room, where we see ladies and gentlemen sipping coffee, completely enveloped in tobacco smoke. We find our host and his attendants speak English, and are very courteous; and after a night's repose rise at five A. M. to take the rail-way for Mayence.

The station for Frankfort is out of the city. As we approach, we observe an elegant stone building, at least three stories high, and two hundred feet long, with a flower-garden and carriage-way lying between it and the highway.

The omnibus deposits us, with our companions and trunks, in the open air at a small door, on the principal front, within which every article of our baggage is to be weighed, and if in excess over fifty pounds, the overplus is to be paid for as freight. When this process is completed you enter a ticket-office and purchase a ticket, and then follow your baggage through the building and across an open court to long sheds in the rear, running at right angles from the main building. In these the cars are stationed; and you discover, to your surprise, that the main edifice is for clerks, not passengers, and is a useless barrier between the omnibus and the cars; for the expense and annoyance of weighing and moving the baggage must equal all that is gained for the freight of it, to say nothing of the exposure of the passengers to the weather.

The rates of fare are moderate, the charges for the first class passengers about the same as on our roads; for the second, third, and fourth classes, much lower. We have but three first class passengers, while there are six cars well filled with the other classes, pride yielding to thrift. The country is populous, the soil light; we notice flax, orchards, mowing, and less tobacco than yesterday. We accomplish our twenty miles in an hour and five minutes, and drive across a bridge of boats to the steamer at Mayence.

Yours, truly,
MASSACHUSETTS.
Mayence, Sept. 7, 1843.

At an early hour in the morning of September 8, we drive to the rail-way station and take the cars for Aix-la-Chapelle; the distance is forty-three miles. The station is like those I have described, but in other respects the rail-way resembles the Boston and Worcester; the rail, the curvature, and the country remind me of our line to Worcester. The cars are of three classes;—the first class padded and glazed; the second covered, cushioned, and curtained; the third class is open, and supplied with seats. The charges are, in American currency, $1.44 for the first class, $1.08 for the second, and $0,72 for the third. In our train we have 10 first class passengers and 70 second and third, and the average price paid is not far from one dollar for each passenger. We pass over a rolling and sometimes broken country, producing oats, grass, and potatoes. We observe several large cuts, embankments, and tunnels, with severe gradients. At one point our engine, of a light English pattern, nearly stops from lack of power. We notice guards at all the road-crossings, which are on a level, and reach Aix-la-Chapelle in two hours and three quarters from the time we left Cologne.

The entrance to Aix-la-Chapelle is very pleasing; the rail-way descends rapidly by a long and magnificent viaduct; and the city, with its spires, turrets, and white buildings appears embosomed in a beautiful country of alternate swells and valleys of the most vivid green. The depot is a large building three stories high, but presents nothing worthy of comment, or of copying.

On our arrival at Aix-la-Chapelle, we find the diligence for Belgium is not to leave for two hours, and suppose we have ample time at our disposal to ride through and examine this beautiful city; but to avoid detention we determine first to secure our seats, and for this purpose drive to the office of the diligence. We arrive there, and are deposited with our trunks in a hollow square, and find ourselves encircled by at least an hundred passengers, and their baggage.

A scene occurs it is almost impossible to describe. We apply for seats in the *coupée*, but are told that we cannot have them until our trunks are weighed and certified. We discover in one corner a scale surrounded by trunks, and a crowd of travellers, each urgent for priority; a scale which is to receive successively, trunks, valises, boxes, and carpet-bags without number. We divide our party into four detachments, one to see that every thing is carried to the scale, one to take the certificate of each article, another to see they are not separated afterwards, and a fourth to engage if possible a private carriage. After many delays our articles are weighed, but some mistake is made by the weigh-master, and a part must be weighed again; at length the certificates are signed, and we apply for our tickets, but are told we can have *no places* except in the *rotunde*. But we have tried this once on a dusty road, and we urge, that we have spoken early for the *coupée*, and if we cannot have it will look for a private carriage. At this moment our detachment, No. 4, reports, that he has found a private carriage; when, to our dismay, five or six porters seize our trunks and carpet-bags, and bear them away to as many different diligences, alike heedless of remonstrance, reproof, and resistance. In this posture of affairs, the ticket-seller informs us, that he will give us a carryall, and assures us, that we may rely on finding our baggage safe at the custom-house on the frontier. As soon as we are free, at the last moment, we are told our passports must be inspected, and two of us engage a guide and hurry to the bureau of the police. While we are gone, although it still lacks ten minutes of the hour for our departure, our coachman mounts the box, gives one of the three seats of our carriage to a lady and her child, insists that he cannot wait, and begins to drive onward. A douceur of a few francs induces him to stop. We fortunately arrive in a few moments, and are on our way before the appointed hour, and thus, in this annoying manner, we waste two hours, and lose the privilege of seeing Aix-la-Chapelle.

We reach the custom-house on the frontier; the diligences and other carriages are drawn up in a line, the trunks and packages are arranged in front of the office, opened and inspected by a very courteous set of officials, but one of value, the property of Col. W—, containing specie, letters of credit, and important papers, is missing. The other trunks are replaced, our coachman refuses to wait, mounts his box, cracks his whip, and begins to move onward. We are compelled to submit; and, on attempting to enter, find another passenger has been admitted, and has taken one of our seats. The new-comer, however, on reading the expression of our faces, retires to the back seat and holds the child, and we are again in motion. Amid all our perplexities, however, our attention is drawn to the magnificent works of the new rail-way from Aix-la-Chapelle to Belgium; it crosses a broken country by tunnels and viaducts on a gigantic scale; the designs are striking, and the masonry of the most massive and enduring character; the work, admirably executed, promises to last for centuries. Great pains have been taken with the high embankments, which are faced or paved with stone, to preserve them. We arrive at Verviers, and determine to stop there for redress.

I remain, as ever,

MASSACHUSETTS.

Verviers, September 8, 1843.

30

SAMUEL LAING, *NOTES OF A TRAVELLER, ON THE SOCIAL AND POLITICAL STATE OF FRANCE, PRUSSIA, SWITZERLAND, ITALY, AND OTHER PARTS OF EUROPE*, SECOND ED. (PHILADELPHIA: CAREY AND HART, 1846), PP. 165–169

The railroads, from which the Germans promise themselves exaggerated and imaginary advantages, belong to the objects for which Germany perhaps is not yet ripe as an industrial community. All her cross-country roads, and a great portion of her main roads between her most important cities, are in a wretched state, scarcely passable, and roads are altogether wanting through districts where roads should be. The extent of the country is itself a natural impediment to the multiplication and goodness of roads. The difficulties thrown in the way of communication from place to place by the passport system, and the town-duty system, and the monopoly by the governments in a great part of Germany of posting trade, coaching trade, parcel carrying trade, in short of all transport over the roads, reduce all internal traffic to the minimum amount with which society can exist. It is of little importance to get from Frankfort to Mayence, or from Leipsic to Dresden, on a railroad, if all the veins and arteries which should feed this railroad are shut up, and choked with mire and sand. The want of roads, and of free traffic and competition on such roads as are, will long retard any considerable development of industry in Germany, and the formation of that home market, that mutual exchange among men of the products of their industry, which exists from the facility and cheapness of transport and supply. Railroads may even do more harm than good, in the present state of Germany, to her industrial progress in general, by absorbing that capital of governments, or individuals, which would have been applied, with more advantage, to improving the old main roads, and opening up new; to laying that foundation of transport and communication through every district of a country, upon which alone, commercially speaking, railroads can subsist. A railroad is like a horse, very profitable and enriching to the individual who keeps him, provided there is plenty of productive labour for the horse to do; but very unprofitable, and impoverishing, if the individual has no work for his horse but to drive about on him for curiosity or pleasure. It is still an undetermined question whether railroads can be used with advantage for the conveyance generally of goods. Such valuable goods in small compass, as may be sent from Manchester to Liverpool, or from Birmingham to London, afford no rule to judge by, the cost of carriage being trifling compared to the value of the package. But can the manufacturer not seated immediately on a railroad, transport his coals, his bricks, his lime, his timber, his iron, and all his bulky machinery and raw materials, with advantage on railroads? He is seldom in a pressing hurry for these, but sees beforehand for some time what he wants of such materials or means, so that speed in their transport is no object, but cheapness is; and if the railroad cannot transport them cheaper, he will prefer the common road, because he has no reloading them to bring them to the spot where they are required. This practical question is not yet determined in England; but evidently the railroad can only aid, and not supersede the use of good roads; and is itself comparatively valueless to a country, unless it is fed by a system of good roads all around, and free trade and competition of transport on them. The most enlightened commercial men you meet with in Germany seem not a little fanciful in talking of the vast commerce, and industrial prosperity, to be founded on railroad communications. The transport of passengers on their pleasure tours in summer, and to and from the watering places, is the only business at present on the railroads; and however useful and profitable to the shareholders the amount of this transport may be—and from the nature of the country, the German railroads have cost the shareholders very little, compared to the usual expense of construction—it adds but little to the internal trade and industry of the country in general, or even of the towns it runs through. It is not, as in England with her railroads, an addition to the facilities which harbours, docks, shipping, a network of admirable main and cross-country roads spread over the land, and an unrestricted unquestionable freedom of movement on them for man and goods, give to industry; but here the railroad is to be a substitute for, instead of an addition to, all these preliminary steps to a high national state of industry and wealth. This will end in disappointment; and the rational and attainable objects of the German commercial league, the supply of their own wants by their own industry in the first place, be defeated by straining after objects not attainable—such as a great manufacturing for a foreign trade, without sea-ports, shipping, or secure access to the foreign markets—and not desirable, if attainable by forced efforts and encouragement, until they spring naturally from the overflowings of a great home market for the products of their manufacturing industry.

It is by raising the condition of the people—their civil and political condition, by removing all the trammels of the military and functionary system upon their personal freedom of action and industry, and by the establishment not only of roads, but of free transport and competition of individual industry on them without any kind of government interference, that the true objects of the German league must be obtained. A hundred Frankforts or Leipsics in Germany would not spread wealth and national prosperity; for look at the country a couple of miles from the gates of either of these cities, and you find the roads as impassable, the country people as non-consuming and non-exchanging, and industry as dead, as if these cities had no existence. It is a change in the social economy of Germany that is needed, more than an increase of her class of capitalists. If they are already driven to manufacture for the foreign consumer, before the home consumers are half supplied with what they might consume, it is clear there is something unsound in the project of beginning to build the national prosperity of Germany under the commercial league, upon a basis which is without and not within the country. Such a change in the social economy of 26 millions of people who have but one principle at present in common—that of producing as much of what they consume individually, by their own time and labour, and buying as little of it as possible,—is not to be accomplished suddenly. It must be the gradual operation of time, of unrestricted intercourse among men, and of civil and political liberty, as it has been in England. The German commercial league, if carried on with the haste, and to the extent, and for the objects which the excited minds of even prudent people in Germany call for, and are eager to rush into, will prove a delusion as ruinous as the Mississippi scheme, as devoid of any solid basis, and which the first blast of war will dissolve.

According to every true German, the league is to be the grand restorer of nationality to Germany, of national character, of national mind, national greatness, national everything, to a new, regenerated German nation. They are to spin and weave themselves into national spirit, patriotism, and united effort as one great people. They are to have colonies, if a continent can be discovered for them to colonize—an independent flag for their commercial league, if the naval powers agree to recognize a nonentity as an effective neutral power on the high seas—and a navy, too, if the Rhine would breed seaman, and Cologne build ships of the line, instead of a dozen or two of river barges. These are innocent evaporations of a foggy atmosphere of mind often found among Germans, through which small things appear great, and ideas are taken for realities. Yet the most sensible of the newspaper editors of Germany lend their columns to such day-dreams. The stern reality amidst these childish fancies of the German patriots who ever look to the ideal future, and never to the real present, is, that at no period in modern history have the civil rights and free agency of men in their moral, religious, and industrial relations been more entirely set aside in Germany—at no period have their time and labour been taken from them by governments and local authorities so uselessly and unreproductively for the people, as since the conclusion of the last war. While all that forms the spirit, independent feeling, and moral existence of a nation, and all that forms the wealth and industrial prosperity of a nation, are kept down by military organization and interference by edictal law, regulations, and functionarism, to a kind of Chinese state of society, German writers dream of national independence, national spirit, national action in European affairs, for the German population. The emancipated negro population in our West India colonies enjoy in reality more civil and political rights, more free agency, as moral beings, in their religious, social, and domestic relations—have their time and labour more entirely to themselves, and at their own free disposal without the interference of government through its civil or military functionaries, than the great mass of the labouring class in Germany. The German commercial league may produce a decided alteration in this abject social state; but it begins at the wrong end with its renovation of Germany, if it only encourages the increase of a body of commercial or manufacturing capitalists, on the one hand, supplying the foreign consumer, and a mass of helpless operatives, on the other hand, thrown into misery whenever the foreign consumer cannot or will not take the usual supplies; and does not begin with laying a sound foundation for a home German market and home consumpt for German production, by setting free the industry of the people, and by abolishing the military restraints on their free agency and productive powers. There are good seeds sown by this great movement. It is a powerful demonstration of the will of the people for a common object, and of the people of capital and experience—of the weightiest people of a society. It can only fail of attaining the object, of raising German industry and well-being, by aiming at such an impracticable object as that of making the league an acknowledged political power, and by such impracticable means as that of getting a flag, a fleet, colonies, and all the idle fancies which scholars and newspaper writers pin upon the one wise and attainable object of the league—the raising a home market for industry first, and a foreign market afterwards as a secondary outlet for the products of a manufacturing body of operatives.

31

NATHANIEL PARKER WILLIS, *RURAL LETTERS AND OTHER RECORDS OF THOUGHT AT LEISURE* (NEW YORK: BAKER AND SCRIBNER, 1849), PP. 288–289

The railroad from Leipsic to Dresden runs a gauntlet of ghosts, for it passes over fields that have been the great arena of the battles of Europe; scarce a rood of the seventy miles, probably, that has not drunk the blood of the victims of "glory." As there are no fences, and this part of Germany is almost a dead level, it looks like one broad prairie, specked here and there with females laboring in the fields, or sheep watched while they graze, by a family of women and children. It strikes an American oddly to see no farm-houses, no barns, and no cottages. He wonders where the laborers live who cultivate so carefully this vast garden. And it seems most repugnant to our idea of the charm of rural life, to arrive, every five or ten miles, at a little, pent-up, crowded, wretched village—like a cancer cut from the noisome heart of a city—and find that here live, in propinquity economical for their masters, the laborers whose toils extend for miles around, and who have a day's work in getting to and from the scenes of their labor, besides the evil of constant absence from home and certain exposure to unfavorable weather. It is, perhaps, partly a result of these customs, so hostile to a *home*, that the women of the agricultural class in Germany are on a level with beasts of burthen—doing all the drudgery of field-labor, while their husbands loiter with their pipes about the beer haunts of the town, acting rather like farm-overseers, while the females of the family are farm-laborers.

You see, every where, groups of women doing men's work in the fields, and seldom a man employed, except in driving a horse, or in some of the more agreeable kinds of farm labor. Public opinion in America would make any rural neighborhood "too hot to hold" a man, who should degrade his "women-folk" to the condition of females in the agricultural class of Germany.

In any weather better than an equinoctial storm, I should have felt a poetical compunction at crossing, for the first time, as famous a river as the Elbe, at the skipping speed of a rail-train. Its banks looked wintry and unattractive, however, and the tall castle of Meissen, (once a monarch's residence, and now a manufactory of porcelain,) looked drearily worthy of its latter destiny. The fourteen miles hence to Dresden, give the eye a most welcome relief from the flat country of which it has become weary. The grouped hills along the shores of the Elbe are bright with villas and with the sparkle of decorative culture, and, from a short distance, Dresden looks more Italian than German. It was easy to see, even at this season, that it must be, in summer, the most lovely of halting-places for the traveller. With some trouble in holding on to our hats and cloaks, we scrambled from the terminus to the hotel, taking our first impression of the world's great china-shop, in a gale of wind thoroughly raw and uncomfortable. On the way, I called my brother's attention to the small market-carts, which were invariably drawn by women and dogs, or women and a donkey, harnessed together. The women had broad girths over the breast and back, and drew with all their might, as did the dogs—the donkey alone requiring whip or encouragement. The three animals were apparently on a complete level of treatment and valuation.

32

MARK TWAIN, *A TRAMP ABROAD* (HARTFORD, CONN.: AMERICAN PUBLISHING COMPANY, 1899), PP. 24, 103, 547–549

In a short time the shrill piping of a coming train was heard, and immediately groups of people began to gather in the street. Two or three open carriages arrived, and deposited some maids of honor and some male officials at the hotel. Presently another open carriage brought the Grand Duke of Baden, a stately man in uniform, who wore the handsome brass-mounted, steel-spiked helmet of the army on his head. Last came the Empress of Germany and the Grand Duchess of Baden in a close carriage; these passed through the low-bowing groups of servants and disappeared in the hotel, exhibiting to us only the backs of their heads, and then the show was over.

It appears to be as difficult to land a monarch as it is to launch a ship.

When we got down town I found that we could go by rail to within five miles of Heilbronn. The train was just starting, so we jumped aboard and went tearing away in splendid spirits. It was agreed all around that we had done wisely, because it would be just as enjoyable to walk *down* the Neckar as up it, and it could not be needful to walk both ways. There were some nice German people in our compartment. I got to talking some pretty private matters presently, and Harris became nervous; so he nudged me and said,—

"Speak in German,—these Germans may understand English."

I did so, and it was well I did; for it turned out that there was not a German in that party who did not understand English perfectly. It is curious how wide-spread our language is in Germany. After a while some of those folks got out and a German gentleman and his two young daughters got in. I spoke in German to one of the latter several times, but without result. Finally she said,—

'Ich verstehe nur Deutch und Englische,"—or words to that effect. That is, "I don't understand any language but German and English."

We left for Turin at 10 the next morning by a railway which was profusely decorated with tunnels. We forgot to take a lantern along, consequently we missed all the scenery. Our compartment was full. A ponderous tow-headed Swiss woman who put on many fine-lady airs, but was evidently more used to washing linen than wearing it, sat in a corner seat and put her legs across into the opposite one, propping them intermediately with her up-ended valise. In the seat thus pirated, sat two Americans, greatly incommoded by that woman's majestic coffin-clad feet. One of them begged her, politely, to remove them. She opened her wide eyes and gave him a stare, but answered nothing. By and by he preferred his request again, with great respectfulness. She said, in good English, and in a deeply offended tone, that she had paid her passage and was not going to be bullied out of her "rights" by ill-bred foreigners, even if she *was* alone and unprotected.

"But I have rights, also, madam. My ticket entitles me to a seat, but you are occupying half of it."

"I will not talk with you, sir. What right have you to speak to me? I do not know you. One would know you came from a land where there are no gentlemen. No *gentleman* would treat a lady as you have treated me."

"I come from a region where a lady would hardly give me the same provocation."

"You have insulted me, sir! You have intimated that I am not a lady—and I hope I am *not* one, after the pattern of your country."

"I beg that you will give yourself no alarm on that head, madam; but at the same time I must insist—always respectfully—that you let me have my seat."

Here the fragile laundress burst into tears and sobs.

"I never was so insulted before! Never, never! It is shameful, it is brutal, it is base, to bully and abuse an unprotected lady who has lost the use of her limbs and cannot put her feet to the floor without agony!"

"Good heavens, madam, why didn't you say that at first! I offer a thousand pardons. And I offer them most sincerely. I did not know—I *could* not know—that anything was the matter. You are most welcome to the seat, and would have been from the first if I had only known. I am truly sorry it all happened, I do assure you."

But he couldn't get a word of forgiveness out of her. She simply sobbed and snuffled in a subdued but wholly unappeasable way for two long hours, meantime crowding the man more than ever with her undertaker-furniture and paying no sort of attention to his frequent and humble little efforts to do something for her comfort. Then the train halted at the Italian line and she hopped up and marched out of the car with as firm a leg as any washerwoman of all her tribe! And how sick I was, to see how she had fooled me.

Turin is a very fine city. In the matter of roominess it transcends anything that was ever dreamed of before, I fancy. It sits in the midst of a vast dead-level, and one is obliged to imagine that land may be had for the asking, and no taxes to pay, so lavishly do they use it. The streets are extravagantly wide, the paved squares are prodigious, the houses are huge and handsome, and compacted into uniform blocks that stretch away as straight as an arrow, into the distance. The sidewalks are about as wide as ordinary European *streets*, and are covered over with a double arcade supported on great stone piers or columns. One walks from one end to the other of these spacious streets, under shelter all the time, and all his course is lined with the prettiest of shops and the most inviting dining-houses.

33

PETER ROSEGGER, *THE LIGHT ETERNAL* [THE ETERNAL LIGHT] (LONDON: T. FISHER UNWIN, 1907), PP. 246–248

6th September 1884.

This day has passed too. Now we are linked on to the great world by means of two iron lines. These rails, these iron lines, are humanity's signs of equality, I once heard say. On the 6th of September the first train arrived in the Torwald. It seemed to me, as I looked out from the loft of the Gral farm, as if I had never seen a train before in all my life. For I was looking with the eyes of my parishioners, who had never experienced one before. For it is not a mere sight; it is an experience. It burns through the brain like Fate, it alters the blood. People who vowed they would not take a step out of their way on account of that tomfoolery have come from great distances to see the first train arrive. The windows of Hotel Victoria, opposite the station, are crowded with people. The landlord demanded admission and the peasants gladly paid for it.

Crooked Christl has been hurrying up and down ever since the morning shouting at people: "Say your prayers, say your prayers that it may not come." And when the black monster was seen at the curve, and approached steaming and snorting, he shrieked wildly—"The hellish dragon, now it's come! Say your prayers, good people. Now it has come with all its might!"

The people were surprised that the steam carriage did not shake but came along smoothly and quietly.

"But it snorts like the devil," remarked one man, "and no wonder—if you look at all the houses it's dragging along after it."

Then they began to shout. All my parishioners, even the opponents of the railway waved their hats and handkerchiefs and screamed as loud as they were able. "Hip, hip, hurrah!" they cried, as the train with its eight wreathed carriages drew up inside the station. A number of strangers alighted. One man gave a speech from the step, but the shouting, music and salutes drowned every word. Even I felt a thrill; things like that do warm one. And yet I cannot help asking myself what is to happen next? The train has come too late to spoil the people. If it had come a few years ago, I should probably have said with conviction that the wolf had entered the sheepfold.

The sixty-seven-year-old Gral farmer and his mother sat beside me. The old woman did nothing yesterday and to-day but repeat prophecies which were circulated in this district in the time of her youth. "A time will come when they will hang heaven's lightning on to poles, and will build roads of iron. Then fire-spitting dragons will come, and they will be so great, that seven times seven knights will ride upon them, and then the end of the world will come." Others again had foretold that when the dragon appeared, people would have wings on their feet, and the walls would have ears, and flames would break forth from the flowers, and flames would not ascend but would go down to the earth.

Someone had ordered a jug of cider. Several people who were sitting there drank the health of the dragon that had made its appearance and will be visible now every day until the remotest times. Even the aged Gral mother raised her mug with a hasty hand, and stood as erect as her little withered-up body would allow. Her son pulled her sleeve: "Let us go, mother; let us go to bed."

"Now?" said the old woman in a loud voice. "Why, you stupid boy, we're just beginning to have some fun." When she had said that, she sank back against the wall, and when we wanted to ask her what was the matter—she was no longer living.

The old woman is dead. Soon everyone knew what had happened, and many thought the news even stranger than the entry of the steam horse. She was a hundred and odd years old. We had almost forgotten that she would die.

34

ADOLF FRIEDRICH (DUKE OF MECKLENBURG-SCHWERIN), *FROM THE CONGO TO THE NIGER AND THE NILE*, 2 VOLS. (LONDON: DUCKWORTH & CO., 1913), I, PP. 3–10, II, PP. 196–198

They were in London. The railway station looked inexpressibly dreary, with its long vistas ending in black shadow, its sickly lamps blinking like eyes that have watched all night and are weary, and its vast glazed roof, through which the grey dawn was beginning to glimmer.

It was yet too early to attempt to go to Mrs. Lockwood's house. They must wait at least a couple of hours. The vicar looked so worn, aged, and ill, that Maud tried to persuade him to seek some rest at the hotel close to the station, promising that he should be roused in due time. But he refused to do so.

"Sit here," he said, leading Maud into a waiting-room, where there was a dull coke fire smouldering slowly, and where a solitary gas-light shed a yellow glare over a huge, bare, shining centre table, leaving the rest of the apartment in almost darkness. "You will be safe and unmolested here. I must go and make some inquiries—try to find some trace——. Remain here till I return."

Maud thought she had never seen a room so utterly soul-depressing. No place would have appeared cheerful to her at that moment; but this railway waiting-room was truly a dreary and forlorn apartment. She sat there cowering over the dull red fire, sick, and chilly, and sad; listening nervously to every echoing footfall on the long platform without; to the whistle of some distant engine, screaming as though it had lost its way in the labyrinthine network of lines that converged just outside the great terminus, and were wildly crying for help and guidance; listening to the frequent clang of a heavy swing-door, the occasional sound of voices (once a man laughed aloud, and she involuntarily put her hands up to her startled ears to shut out the sound that jarred on every quivering nerve with agonising discord), and to the loud, deliberate ticking of a clock above the waiting-room door.

At length—how long the time had seemed!—Mr. Levincourt returned.

Maud started up, and tried to read in his face if he had any tidings of Veronica, but she did not venture to speak. He answered her appealing look:

"I have seen the station-master," he said. "They have not been here. I believe that much is certain. The man was civil, and caused inquiries to be made among the people—oh, my God, that I should have to endure this degradation!—but there was no trace of such people as I described. This man made a suggestion. They might have left the main line at Dibley, and either come to London by the other line, thus arriving at a station at the opposite end of the town; or—as I think more probable—have reached the junction that communicates with the coast railways, and so got down to the sea without touching London at all."

"O, Uncle Charles!"

"Come, my poor child, let me at least put you into a shelter where you will be safe from the contamination of our disgrace. You look half dead, my poor Maudie! Come, there is a cab waiting here outside."

As Maud moved towards the door to obey his summons, the light of the gas-lamp fell full on her pale face, and he almost exclaimed aloud at her startling resemblance to her mother.

It seemed to the vicar that the remembrance of his old love, thus called up at this moment, filled his heart with bitterness even to overflowing.

"O me!" he groaned; "I wish it were all over! I am weary of my life."

The cab rattled over the stones through the still nearly empty streets.

Maud's remembrance of any part of London was very vague. She had never even seen the neighbourhoods through which she was now being jolted. It all looked squalid, mean, grimy, and uninviting under the morning light. At last they came into a long street, of which the further end was veiled and concealed by a dense foggy vapour.

"What number, miss?" asked the cabman, turning round on his seat.

"What do you say?" asked Maud, faintly.

"What number, miss? This 'ere is Gower-street."

"O!" cried Maud, despairingly. "I don't remember the number!"

The cabman had pulled up his horse, and was now examining the lash of his whip with an air of philosophical indifference, like a man who is weighed upon by no sense of responsibility. After a minute or so, he observed, with great calmness, "That's ockkard; Gower-street is raythur a long street, and it'll take some time to knock at all the doors both sides o' the way." Then he resumed the examination of his whip lash.

"O, Uncle Charles, I am so sorry!" murmured Maud. "What shall we do?"

35

A. D. C. RUSSELL, 'THE BAGDAD RAILWAY', *QUARTERLY REVIEW* 235, 1921, 307–315

Art. 6.—The Bagdad Railway

FOR years men have been talking and writing of Mesopotamia and the Bagdad Railway; and bewildered with 'firmans,' 'irades,' 'concessions,' and 'kilometric guarantees,' have been left with the vague idea that, probably through the fault of the British Government, the Germans realised exceedingly successful commercial and financial results from their venture in Asia Minor. Now that the end of the War has rendered available information previously only accessible to Germans, it is consoling to be able to announce that, far from having made money over the Bagdad Railway, the promoters of that enterprise incurred losses which ran into millions, and that, even had the War not taken place, it is unlikely that the Bagdad Railway could ever have become a financial success.

The idea of linking up Mesopotamia with the Mediterranean by rail is of British origin. It dates back to the Fifties, when Colonel Chesney, R.E., who conducted the first accurate survey of Mesopotamia, suggested that the Euphrates Valley might be developed by giving it railway communication with the Syrian ports of Alexandretta or Suedia. The Englishman, however, turns instinctively to water rather than to land transport; and, although Mesopotamia did attract a certain amount of British enterprise, it was through Lynch's steamers, and not through Chesney's railways.

The first railway in Asiatic Turkey was built by a British Company and has remained under British control. This line received its concession in 1856, started from Smyrna, and ran up the Meander Valley to Aidin, and eventually beyond that town, being built in successive sections, each of which was worked and made a paying concern, through the consequent development of the surrounding country, before the next section was begun. The significance of this method will be seen when we come to deal with the construction of the Bagdad Railway. Unlike all other Turkish lines, the Aidin railway, as it is generally called, received no kilometric guarantee; that is, the Turkish Government did not promise to make up the revenues of the railway, should they prove insufficient, to an annual gross average return of a fixed amount per kilometre. This line has played a useful and profitable part in the development of Asia Minor;

but has never been able to exercise a political influence comparable to that of the younger companies.

French railway enterprise in the Near East has, on occasion, come into conflict with that of Germany; but, from a general point of view, it can be said that the Germans abandoned to French interests the railway possibilities of European Turkey and North-West Asia Minor; and to the Russians the Black Sea Coast, keeping for themselves the great road to the East, the road to Bagdad. Nor was this at first unwelcome to the British, whose ideas in regard to Turkey were still coloured by memories of the Crimean War. Already, since 1873, a railway had existed, running from Haidar Pacha, opposite Constantinople on the Bosphorus, to Ismidt, some 90 kilometres east. It had been built for the Sultan by Wilhelm von Pressel, a German engineer who played a great part in railway construction in Asia; but had been conceded to an English Company in 1880. The Ottoman Government, in 1888, bought out the original British Company, and granted to Herr Kaulla, the representative of the Deutsche Bank, not only the concession of the Ismidt Railway, but also that for the extension of the same railway to Angora. As a result of this, the Ottoman Railway Company of Anatolia came into being, with the Deutsche Bank as the directing force behind it and the German Government ready to assist by any means in their power.

The position of the Turkish Government cannot be understood without reference to the character and aims of the reigning Sultan. Abdul Hamid II, a man whose great ability has been seldom recognised, worked throughout his life in the pursuit of one ideal—Pan-Islamism, that is, the religious and political unity of Moslems all over the world. None of his predecessors had laid much stress on the Sultan's claim to be Commander of the Faithful and Successor of the Prophet. But after Turkey had lost the greater part of her Balkan possessions, and her cause in Europe began to appear hopeless, the idea of recovering elsewhere all, and more than all, that had been lost became particularly attractive. So far as religious primacy was concerned, Abdul Hamid's propaganda achieved speedy success. The establishment of Turkish Consuls-General in the British and Dutch East Indian possessions was the next step. Religious and political obedience are much more closely bound together in the Moslem than in the Christian world; and because the British ruled millions of Moslems in India, the Sultan abandoned the traditional Turkish policy of friendship with this country. On the other hand, it was obviously to British interest to confine the Sultan's authority as Khalif strictly to religious matters; in view of which circumstances, it is not surprising to find that, on Aug. 1, 1899, Herr Kurt Zander, of the Anatolian Railway, wrote to Herr Siemens, the Deutsche Bank representative in Constantinople: 'For the Sultan, the Bagdad Railway is solely a weapon against the English Khalifate policy.' On the other hand, Abdul Hamid was aware of the fact that German financiers were anxious to extend their operations towards the Persian Gulf, and had decided that, far from requesting the construction of the railway she desired, Turkey should be graciously pleased to grant on her own terms the petitions of those who desired to serve her. The success of this policy is acknowledged in a letter from Zander to Siemens of March 5, 1900.

INCONGRUOUS *EISENBAHN*

It was originally intended that the main line of the Anatolian Railway should run through Angora to Cæsarea, and continue through or near Sivas (there were several plans) to the headwaters of the Tigris at Diarbekir; and thence down the valley to Bagdad and the Persian Gulf. Von Pressel to the last maintained that this route, or one still more northerly, would have been preferable to that adopted. But the country was difficult, and Russia watched with jealous eyes any movement towards Armenia. As a result, the extension from Angora eastwards, though provided for in the fresh concession granted to the Anatolian Railway in 1893, did not materialise, but a new line from Eski-Shehir to Konia, the ancient Iconium, was built and opened for traffic in 1896.

Until this time the influence of the German Government had been mainly indirect. In 1898, however, William II paid his historic visit to the East, and associated himself immediately with the Sultan's Pan-Islamic ideas. It is instructive to compare the criticisms of 'Abdul the Damned,' in most of the Western Press, with the Kaiser's speech at Damascus on Nov. 8, 1898, when he assured 'The Sultan and the 300 millions of Moslems who venerate him as Khalif that the German Emperor is ever their friend.' The Kaiser also threw himself whole-heartedly into the idea of a Bagdad Railway, and came to regard the project as particularly his own. Not only did he personally bring pressure to bear upon the Sultan to obtain the granting of a concession for a line from Konia to the Anatolian Railway; but in August 1899, when receiving the Turkish Ambassador in Berlin, he said, 'Now then, get *my* railway down there finished for me.' ('Na, nun machen Sie mir da unten *Meine Bahn* fertig.') It should be noted that the German Government never quite realised the distinction between assistance and interference. The financial promoters of the scheme had frequently to complain that Baron Marschall von Bieberstein, the Ambassador in Constantinople, and Major Morgen, his military attaché, with entire disregard for economic considerations, interfered in matters that should have been regarded as strictly business. So great was the eagerness of the German diplomats that the business men in Berlin, in September 1900, wrote to inform their colleagues in Turkey of steps the Foreign Office had taken on behalf of those colleagues in Constantinople of which they themselves were not aware. Yet the Turks were secretly keener for the scheme than they pretended to be, and a letter of Zander's, dated April 11, 1902, describes the joy and relief of Zekki Pasha and another highly-placed Turkish official, when he said they might tell the Sultan that the affair could be managed.

A survey expedition went over the ground in 1899 soon after the Kaiser's visit. Not only were its chief engineers, Mackensen and Von Kapp, Germans, but the official German connexion was emphasised by the placing of the entire concern under the direction of Stemrich, the German Consul-General in Turkey. At the same time Major Morgen prepared a report on the strategic possibilities of the line. The survey party reported unfavourably on the Angora-Sivas route, and recommended an extension from Konia through the Taurus Mountains by the famous pass known as the Cilician Gates. This scheme was severely criticised by Von Pressel, who clung to his idea of a more northerly route, and it is now admitted that the prospectors vastly underestimated the difficulties of the Taurus region. Still, as it stood, their plan was considered feasible, and was approved by Berlin. Siemens was summoned to a conference at which the Emperor himself, Bülow, the Minister for Foreign Affairs, and Miquel, the Finance Minister, were present. Siemens reported that so far as concerned the financial and technical aspects, capital could be found and construction completed within about ten years; but that the political side was out of his hands. The Emperor, with the concurrence of both ministers, guaranteed the removal of any political obstacle. It was, however, considered desirable to obtain British co-operation, and necessary, therefore, to persuade the British, not merely to ignore, but actively to assist, an enterprise which possibly threatened their Indian Empire and certainly provided a means of evading their control of the Suez Canal. As for the French, they had a long record of influence in the Near East and large sums invested there—202 million francs in railways alone—and, apart from their natural dislike of the spread of German influence and trade, it was not impossible that they should desire an extension eastwards of the French Smyrna-Cassaba Railway, which had already reached the Anatolian line at Afion Kara-Hissar, though it was not yet joined to it. The 'international' character of the proposed railway was, therefore, insisted upon; and elaborate calculations were prepared, showing the saving in time that the new route would provide for mails and passenger traffic from Europe to India and the East generally. It was suggested that, by arrangement with the British, a fast ferry service should be established between the port of Koweit, on the Persian Gulf, and Bombay, and alternative plans were brought forward for a tunnel to be made under, or a bridge or train ferry established over, the Bosphorus. The British were to be told that in future they would be able to enter a train at Calais or Ostend, and leave it on the shores of the Persian Gulf; and the records of Russian and American railways were searched for instances of long-distance working. To quote the words of M. Huguenin, then Assistant-Director-General of the Anatolian Railway, 'It is agreed that we are to build a model line such as exists nowhere in Turkey, able in all respects to undertake efficiently an international service involving high speeds over the whole line.' It is true that Von Pressel maintained to the last that the cost of constructing a line fit to carry international expresses over the route chosen would be prohibitive. But he was not listened to; and it is certain that, once it was decided to continue the Anatolian Railway, the use of a narrower gauge for the newer sections, as urged by Von Pressel, was inadvisable. Still, the optimism of its promoters certainly exaggerated greatly the 'express service' possibilities of the new line.

The original proposal as made to the French was that 40 per cent. of the shares of the new concern should be reserved for French capital. A similar proportion was to be allotted to Germany, and the remaining 20 per cent. to other nations. In view of this, M. Constans, French Ambassador at Constantinople, and M. Rouvier, French Minister of Finance, favoured the new enterprise. The later German reports complain of the hostility of M. Delcassé towards them. But at the outset he was considered by those in France who disliked the enterprise to be too favourable to it. Needless to say, the Deutsche Bank took care that no real share in the control of the Bagdad Railway came into French hands; while the Germans obtained all they desired from the French—an absence of serious opposition; a certain amount of capital subscribed for the 'Bagdad' Turkish loans, and the assistance of the French representatives on the Turkish Public Debt Administration in the various financial measures, such as Consolidation of the Turkish Debt, and increase of customs duties, which were necessary to provide for interest on the Bagdad loans.

The German financiers set great store on British co-operation. So far back as 1889, Siemens had stated that 'the scheme was impossible without England,' and had written to Zander, 'The English must come in with us.' In 1900 he went to London in the hope of securing British co-operation. Certain English financiers were not unfavourably disposed to the scheme of a land route to India; but the proposed increase in customs duties met with considerable opposition; and Siemens, reporting this, added the comment, 'That ends Bagdad' (Damit fällt Bagdad), and wrote to Schrader, 'The Bagdad business seems to be lost. England will enter into no agreement without being pushed, and our politicians will not push her. Nevertheless, we must go on working in Constantinople; but every farthing of backsheesh is thrown away.'

The French comment at a later date, 'Londres ne veut pas; Berlin ne peut pas,' was already applicable. However, at the moment when the original capital was being subscribed, a determined effort was made to obtain British capital and assistance in the establishment of a terminus at Koweit on the Persian Gulf. On April 8, 1903, in reply to Mr Gibson Bowles, Mr Balfour gave the House of Commons to understand that the matter was under consideration, and that the suggestion was that 'British capital and control were to be on an absolute equality with the capital and control of any other power.' The subsequent refusal of Mr Balfour and Lord Lansdowne, then Foreign Secretary, to grant any official British co-operation was due to reasons explained in an article in the 'Financial Times' of April 17, 1903. It was there pointed out that, as Mr Waugh, British Vice-Consul at Constantinople, had already reported, there was absolutely no guarantee that the management of the railway would bear any relation to the nationality of the capital raised to build it. Indeed, though this was, of course, unknown in British circles at the time, Marschall von Bieberstein had sent a confidential memorandum to the financiers of the Deutsche Bank reminding them of the absolute necessity of keeping the power in German hands, and warning them that Berlin would tolerate no division of control. In any case, traffic to and from the new railway would have to pass over the Anatolian line, which already was under German control, and preferential treatment for German goods would thus be easy to obtain. As before, the proposed increase of customs duties aroused opposition in England. It was further pointed out that the Germans were keeping in their own hands the contracts for construction from which an immediate profit was expected, and that the nature of the country made it improbable that any appreciable dividend should be paid on the share capital for several years to come. Against this, only the possible political gain could be urged, with the eventual saving in time for the Indian mail, the importance of which was naturally questioned by British shipping interests.

Hence there were no British representatives among the directors of the new company. A certain amount of French capital was obtained, partly through Switzerland, and a pretence was made of French association in the directorate. M. Huguenin, of the Anatolian Railway, a French Swiss, played a leading part in the development of the new line as regards the technical railway side; but Gwinner of the Deutsche Bank, as President, and Testa, German representative on the Council of Turkish Bondholders, as Vice-President of the Board, enjoyed the real controlling influence.

On March 5, 1903, a concession for the construction and working of a railway from Konia to Bagdad, via Aleppo and Mosul, had been finally granted and signed. This authorised the Anatolian Railway Company to create a new company, to be called the Imperial Ottoman Bagdad Railway Company, with a capital of 660,000 Turkish pounds (15,000,000 francs). Ten per cent. of the shares were to be reserved for the Turkish Government, and the same amount for the Anatolian Railway. The failure to obtain the expected amount of foreign capital compelled the new company to depend very largely upon the Turkish Government. Turkey's finances were, however, at that time in a most unsatisfactory condition. So long ago as June 1898, Von Kühlmann, then Director-General of the Anatolian Railway, had written that almost all Turkey's financial resources were pledged for different purposes, and that, should she incur further obligations, any sudden emergency might lead to inability to meet railway guarantees. It is true that the succession of wars in which Turkey was involved between 1911 and 1918 could not have been foreseen. Nevertheless, in view of Turkey's existing liabilities it was hazardous to saddle her with the responsibility for an enterprise which involved an enormous expenditure of capital with an exceedingly problematical return. The Deutsche Bank group, however, did not know the extent to which 'strategical,' as against commercial, considerations were to be predominant. There were two logical courses—either for the Turkish Government to obtain from their German ally sufficient capital to build the strategical railway they considered necessary, lessening the cost by such profit on private traffic as they could get; or for a private company to build a line solely for commercial profit, choosing only such routes as gave promise of substantial traffic, and proceeding, as the Aidin Railway had done, by successive sections, each to become a paying concern before the next was begun.

Instead, a compromise was adopted by which a nominally private company, hoping to pay dividends to their shareholders, constructed a railway on purely strategical lines, often in wholly unprofitable country, on the strength of guarantees secured by a Turkish Government loan, which made that Government a partner in the enterprise, and entitled to the lion's share of any profits there might be. The attempt to combine business success with strategical considerations failed. The series of wars in which Turkey became involved naturally had an unfavourable effect upon business. But matters would not have gone so badly as they did, had the Bagdad Railway policy, from the outbreak of the Turco-Italian War onwards, been governed by strictly business considerations. Economic facts were disregarded in constructional plans. Pressed by the German Embassy on the one hand, and by the Turkish Government on the other, the business men sank deeper and deeper into the mire, ever hoping that better times would come and a larger measure of assistance be obtainable from the Governments concerned.

Part 4

ITALIA, ESPAÑA, LUSITANIA
Railways in Italy, Spain, Portugal,
and colonies

36

WILLIAM J. L. MAXWELL, *LETTERS OF AN ENGINEER WHILE ON SERVICE IN SYRIA IN CONNECTION WITH THE PROPOSED EUPHRATES VALLEY RAILWAY AND THE BEYROUT WATERWORKS* (LONDON: MARCUS WARD & CO., 1886), PP. 5–10

First period

[EDITOR'S NOTE.—On the 19th of July, 1870, Mr. Maxwell left London for Syria, under instructions from Mr. Telford Macneill, to make a survey of a proposed line of railway through the valley of the Euphrates for the promoters of that scheme. Mr. Maxwell's letters to his friends at home describe his journey from London and Paris, whence he travelled through France by the most direct route to Brindisi, crossing over Mont Cenis by Mr. Fell's wonderful mountain railroad. The Letters contain little worth putting in print up to this point, as in these days everybody goes to Paris, and most people are familiar with a still wider radius from home; but Mr. Maxwell's experience of the journey over the Cenis on the locomotive seems worthy of being printed, as that triumph of engineering adventure—so soon superseded by the more laborious work of tunnelling right through the mountain—is already forgotten. This will account for the abrupt commencement of the Letters. Writing from Brindisi, where an enforced delay took place, Mr. Maxwell gave a more detailed account of his experiences *en route* and his surroundings than he might otherwise have done. The real interest of the Letters lies in the description of Eastern places, people, and customs, and of the writer's experience in regions but little known to Europeans; but it has been thought well to print the narrative as connectedly as possible from the point where it is taken up.]

Brindisi, July 26th, 1870. . . . . . . The special feature in the railway over Mont Cenis is what is called the central rail. On steep parts of the railway, the central wheels grip the central rail laterally, and, as it were, climb up by it, as a boy would

ITALIA, ESPAÑA, LUSITANIA

climb a tree. This also keeps the train from getting off the bearing rails, as these wheels are fixed in front of all the carriages, as well as to the engine. This is absolutely necessary for rounding the sharp curves, and for descending the steep inclines.

Riding on the engine during the ascent was rough work; but the descent was beyond all description. In passing from the straight to the curved portion of the road, there is a lurch to such an extent that, if you have not hold of something, woe for you! My bones and muscles are sore yet from that ride, three mornings ago. In seventeen miles the railway descends 3,400 feet, so it is a continual down, down, down; swinging to one side, lurching to the other. Part of the way I found that, when approaching a sharp curve, it was easiest to grip the roof over the locomotive, and swing by my arms while passing on to the curve. The speed is close upon eight miles an hour. Dangerous as this system is, the old mode of travelling by *diligence* is still more so. I remember, crossing the Alps in deep snow, in January, 1865, on a sleigh, having felt much more frightened than on the Mont Cenis engine. Words fail to convey any idea of the grandeur and sublimity of the view; but to be on such a conveyance, with the scorching heat of the sun, as well as the furnace-fire, is not the best way to enjoy such a glorious prospect. The scenery on the Italian side is finer than on the French. On this side is also to be seen the wonderful industry of the natives. The little bits of cultivation on some of the hillsides could not be better described than by saying they look like a patchwork quilt.

Descending the steep incline, dashing across the carriage road, then re-crossing it in a few seconds, and looking upwards at the part of the railway on which the train had been a minute before, made one feel that there was wonderful daring in the man who first made the common road, and, again, that there was quite as much in introducing the steam horse to do the work of 150 mules. It is really a pity that the line has not been a pecuniary success; but it has demonstrated a principle, and it is to be hoped that some future lines will be laid down which will pay the promoters of this; for when the tunnel through the Alps is made, of course this railway will be broken up.

For most of the way to Turin, the railway runs in a valley, which at Susa is very narrow. For fertility, I never saw such a place. The natives have every means of irrigation, and the vegetation shows how attentive the husbandmen must be. The mountains are grand; houses are built on such elevations that they can only be reached occasionally, as it would be the work of hours to get up to them. In the valley the villages are numerous. Most of the houses are covered with rough, thin stones, put on without any squaring. How a watertight roof can be made with them surprises me. Each village has its chapel, with a rectangular clock-tower, many of which have mustard-pot-cover tops, made of sheets of bright tin, which, strange to say, does not get rusty. On some of the crags are ruins of castles; one, in particular, I call the key of the valley, although it stands in solitary grandeur on a mountain considerably lower than many on each side of it. On looking back at it when ten miles away, the sun was just tipping the hills to the right, and throwing a lurid glare behind the valley. The ruins stood out in bold relief: I never saw a more beautiful scene.

From Susa to Turin is about thirty-seven miles. Close to the latter, the country becomes comparatively flat, and upon a clear day, no doubt, a good view of the Alps is to be had; the heat, however, now gave a hazy look to everything. The station at Turin is the most elegant I ever saw. I think it is new since I was there in 1865, else I must have remembered it. The building is more like an exhibition palace than a station; much stained glass has been used, and the effect is charming. Turin is quite a new city, and is therefore laid out symmetrically. The total length of the great colonnades extends to miles; in these there are very fine shops, but I had some little trouble in getting a bottle of chlorodyne and another of citrate of magnesia. The purchase of these, and a few photographs of the Mont Cenis Railway, occupied a considerable time, and gave me much amusement, as I am sure it did to the vendors. A franc's worth of cigars—sixteen in number, and of very good quality—was another bargain, made with a fair maiden. There were some charming-looking ladies walking about in the colonnades, their dresses not differing much from home costumes, except that thin white tarlatan was all that covered the bust. High-heeled boots are fashionable here for men as well as women, and it is really pitiable to see the gingerly walk of some of the little fellows with heels two inches high.

I learnt at the hotel, from the landlord, that if I proceeded by the 8.40 train next morning, I could catch the boat to Corfu at 1.30 p.m. on Monday. This meant twenty-seven hours in a train!—but, feeling that I ought to do it, I did it; and here I am at Brindisi, with every prospect of waiting till next Friday; and consequently I am disgusted.

Out of Turin the scenery is pretty. Far away on the right can be seen the "Key of the Valley," with the great mountains of the Alps; and at the left are prettily-wooded hills, with neat villas peeping out between the trees. The vegetation, however, seems poor, and very different from that of the Susa and Mont Cenis valleys.

In the day's ride from Turin to Ancona there is very little variety. The Apennines are on the right, at a distance of perhaps twenty miles. Just coming from the Alps, they, of course, look tame; but, nevertheless, some are very fine, and the contour is prettily broken. We pass many interesting towns, many of them walled in and strongly fortified, the brickwork batteries topped with earthworks. Astri has an immense number of the levers for raising water, so often represented in Scriptural illustrations of the mode of irrigation used in the East. Some of the wells have no less than three over them. These are in the midst of fertile gardens, where the villagers may be seen in the cool of the evening watering the ground.

There is but one monotonous kind of scenery from Turin to Fumini on each side of the line. The ground is divided by trees, in rows, about twenty-five yards apart. The vines twine round these trees, and are carried across in festoons from one to the other. In the spaces between, ordinary crops, but principally Indian corn, are grown. Stubble in other parts shows where wheat and oats had been. There is no

ITALIA, ESPAÑA, LUSITANIA

pasture land, or at least very little. The few animals that are to be seen look all legs. The cattle are like deer, and the sheep like goats, with great long tails.

At Fumini, the blue waters of the Adriatic come into view, and nothing can be more uninteresting than the run along the shore, which continues until nightfall with very little variety. Ancona is a seaport of some importance, at which most of the Adriatic steamers call. I saw a group of Italian women here, the first attractive lot I had seen. They were ranged in a row along the railway fence, watching a trainful of soldiers depart. With black lace shawls on their heads, most of them looked like Spaniards; but here and there was a damsel in white, down to her very gloves and fan—I suppose as a sort of studied contrast. For four hours more we ran along the coast, with occasionally a piece of high land intervening, on which a strong castle was to be seen. The public road runs close to the railway; there is no fence, but here and there grow a few thorns, which, doubtless, are meant to take its place. On looking out at daylight, we had left the coast, and were running inland: a more uninteresting country could not, I suppose, be imagined. There were but few vines, and they looked stunted; and miles upon miles of figs and olives.

At Ancona, a military captain got in, with his wife, two children, and nurse. They had neat little pillows and sheets to put the children to bed; this they proceeded to do, and the babies slept soundly. On their getting out, the signora wished me "Bon voyage, signor," when I said, "The same to you, madam." She turned round on leaving the carriage, and said, "Thank you; I speak var little English; good-bye."

Towards the end of the journey, prickly pears and cacti, formidable-looking things, came into view, in growths of immense size. The leaves would pierce a man like a sword. These plants only flourish in great heat, and I never saw them before in the open, except at Athens. The houses here have nearly all flat roofs, so that I felt I was really getting into the East. The stone is all chalky, of a glaring whiteness, mixed with what looks like pumice. There were several navvies putting stone into wagons for ballasting the railway. The shovels used by these men were of most peculiar construction: I really do not know how they manage to fill wagons with such implements. The shovel is fixed on front of the shaft, just like a pickaxe; and this is the implement used for digging, or rather grubbing up the soil. It is wonderful to see how the natives work in the heat of the sun. The farm labourers have bare legs, their trousers only reaching to the knee.

At Brindisi, I drove to the hotel, a fine building, erected by the South Italian Railway in the hope of making the town as important as it once was, by turning it into the port for departure to the East, instead of Marseilles. From here to Alexandria is seventy-four hours by steamer; and, by putting on finer boats, they hope to reduce this time by twelve or fourteen hours. At present, I believe, a large portion of the English mails go this way. The hotel is not yet fitted up sumptuously, though no doubt it will soon be. A few words of Italian, picked out of Bradshaw, enabled me to get on all right; and here I am, waiting for my steamer, soon to leave the civilisation of Europe for the semi-barbarism of the East—that East which was, nevertheless, the birthplace of civilisation, and, what is more, of

Christianity itself. I regret the delay here, but cannot help it; and perhaps it is all the better for my health to reach the warmer regions of Syria by easy gradations.

I should have mentioned the system of irrigation in the country just traversed from daylight until my arrival here. It is by horse, mule, or donkey power. There is a large wheel, over which works a string of buckets; and as this string ascends, the water is brought up, and deposited in tanks. From thence it flows over the ground by rills.

37

LINA DUFF GORDON (LADY DUFF GORDON, CAROLINE LUCIE DUFF GORDON, MRS. AUBREY WATERFIELD), *HOME LIFE IN ITALY: LETTERS FROM THE APENNINES*, SECOND ED. (LONDON: METHEUN, 1909), PP. 12–14, 147–151, 174–175, 181–182

Another day it was a handsome and well-dressed woman of the middle class who supplied the human interest. She fell in among us, panting and evidently suffering from a storm of rage. Her sole luggage consisted of a basket of vegetables. She had never seen any of us before, but, with the curious mixture of secretiveness and confidence of Italians, she told us she had just run away from her husband, and unfolded every particular of conjugal difficulty. This virago had no tears in her composition; she gnashed her teeth and struck out at anyone who offered sympathy, until, worn out, she dropped her head upon her hands. The men patted her knees and jokingly rallied her on her sins: "You are no saint yourself, even if your husband has treated you like a fiend." This address calmed her, and for the rest of the journey she exerted herself to show us her many amiable qualities. But we none of us thought that her husband—"that devil in breeches"—would take the express train in pursuit of her.

Although the "good old coaching days" are over, the sense of adventure has by no means departed from Italian travelling. It is true that you go in a train, but you never can be sure when you may arrive at your destination, or what may happen to the luggage. The other day a friend found a porter reading "Paradise Lost," and spent a happy moment discussing its beauty, with the result that the trunks remained behind. "Will it not be the same if you get your things twenty-four hours hence?" asked the station-master. The Briton's reply was: "*No*, it will *not* be the same to me"; and the station-master looked puzzled. What a place for a rest cure, once native prejudice was conquered!

Certainly in Italy you never know when a train is likely to start, which must often bewilder the Italian, who makes heroic efforts to keep his watch with the sun. Often he arrives at the station punctually for a seven o'clock train and catches a five A.M. We soon learn too the time it takes, the declamatory conversations entailed, and the documentary evidence needed to show that you really are starting and have paid for the luggage. The other day, to take a ticket for a town three hours up the line, we waited an interminable time. The *Bigliettaio*, ducking his gold-braided cap through the guichet, triumphantly gave us a ticket with the name of the town written on in ink and a piece glued on which he had snipped off by mistake. We were told to be very careful not to lose the mended bit, as it was the most important part of the ticket. And how can one be angry when a broad smile greets a protest, and a *Pazienza, Signora*, is whispered in a soothing tone? Such toylike paraphernalia of travelling in the nineteenth century should only cause mirth. Some day, we are told, Italian railways, now under Government direction, are to become like any other railways, or even better, for electricity is Italy's great power. We shall then no longer arrive at our destination looking like so many charcoal-burners; but, alas! the feeling of a long pilgrimage to our Mecca will have departed. Already the first blow is dealt—the guard no longer sighs a shrill "toot-toot" through a toy-trumpet and says: "*Pronto, pronto, partenza*," in that cajoling voice which used to raise the spirits of the hurried traveller.

Courtship

THE *jeunesse dorée* of Brunella is represented by Mario, a young baker, who spends the whole of his time playing the flute and singing songs of passionate regret for "happy days long past." The plaintive strains rise and fall upon the hillside, as he wanders up and down and round the town followed by his boon companions, who provide him with a droning accompaniment on their guitars. His flute-playing is good, his singing execrable, but it produces loud applause. He throws back his head and half closes his eyes; his cheeks are flushed, and his even white teeth gleam beneath black moustaches, which, as an admirer once said, "are so neat that they seem as if they were painted." At any hour of the day you see him leisurely walking the streets, or sitting at a *caffè* playing cards, and always dressed in what the Brunellese call "English fashion"—a long ulster made of tweed with a check measuring several inches square. With the warm weather he discards this weighty garment, and reveals an elegant suit, cut, I am told, in the latest style. Everyone knew that this suit had come from "the most fashionable tailor of Florence," had cost three pounds, and would probably never be paid for. When the commercial traveller from this fashionable tailor arrived one day to collect money and new customers, Mario's friends carried him off to the topmost floor of one of their homes, where they remained with closed shutters until the traveller had departed, when they issued forth to play triumphal music. Mario leaves the baking to be done by his mother and aunt, who both look like shadows struggling with a too material world. Through the favour of the communal secretary, his intimate friend, he hopes to get a place in the Commune, which, in the town, is always the height of ambition. He will then earn three francs a day, in return for a little calligraphy lasting from ten to three. Most people, as well as himself, seem to forget that, young as he is, he possesses a wife and two children. The wife, however, often recalls her existence in an undesirable way. Mario married pretty but empty-headed Enrichetta when he was barely seventeen, and she just sixteen, so that they could only be married in the church. Lately it has been made more difficult to escape the civil marriage, which is the only legal one in Italy. Before three years were out Mario began once more his serenades, and neglected his young wife shamefully. But when Enrichetta ran away with a prosperous wine-grocer of Brunella, leaving Mario to be the laughing-stock of the place, he was well paid out. The "running away" was only a geographical expression, for it consisted in her walking into another house provided by the wine-merchant. Most Italians would have used their knives, but Mario is an easy-going fellow, not overburdened with courage, and his rival is one of the most important and prosperous of the Brunellese. So Enrichetta sits at her window, her beautiful, laughing face framed in the green shutters, while her "friend" spends most of the day on the doorstep of his shop, just opposite, smoking an immense Tuscan cigar and dreamily attending to his customers. Her boy and girl passing down the street on their way to school look up at her as to a stranger. "Thy little mother is dead," says the grandmother, stroking the girl's dark curls.

And Mario goes laughingly upon his way; the old and sensible people criticise and blame him severely; the girls hang out of their windows or rush to the door to see him pass. To many he is the ideal youth of their dreams. Alas for our little friend Zelinda; her head has been completely turned by Mario and his serenading. Only last year when she danced for us at the Fortezza she was but a child, and indeed she looks little more now, slender and straight of figure, with a plait down her back, and still wearing short skirts. And with what delight she would often accompany her father and us on a long country ramble, though she would keep silent and demure in all her enjoyment of the day. But her big dark eyes could flash out fire at times, and her clear, dark complexion flush with anger.

Mario has already proposed for her hand, and, as her father, an honest artisan, of course refuses to sanction such a match, there is rumour of an elopement. Sometimes when Zelinda stands at her window, listening to the music and answering the language of Mario's eyes, as he throws back his head and looks straight up at her, his wife appears at her window opposite. Directly he has turned the corner, like an enraged tigress, she begins to threaten a thousand maledictions if Zelinda— "a brazen-faced girl"—dares to accept the homage of her husband. Just as she is responding in all the facile eloquence of the Southerner, Marta, her elder sister, appears upon the scene, sharply closes the window, and locks her up to brood upon her transgressions. The sound of the flute comes from distant corners of the town, and from behind her green shutters Enrichetta hears her husband's song fall clear upon the night air:—

"Ah quei tempi felici! ah! che non tornano più!"

Since writing this a few months have passed, and what we all feared has happened. Mariannina came up one morning breathless with the news that Zelinda had eloped with Mario, and her family were broken-hearted. They had not taken any of the warnings seriously, and instead of sending the girl away to friends in the country, had only redoubled their watch over her. She had simply tossed her head and laughed, saying that she was not going to be so foolish as to run away with anyone. One who could have told them a good deal was the stout woman at the vegetable store just opposite their house; but they never suspected why Zelinda liked to run across the street to fetch their *verdura* every day, or why she scanned the cabbage leaves so critically. One evening, while all the family sat at supper, saying that she would go and change her dress—they were going to the theatre—she slipped downstairs, met Mario at the street corner, and together they quietly strolled up the Fortezza hillside. Sitting among the ilexes they looked down upon the station, and could see her father talking to the stationmaster, preparing to send endless telegrams in every direction, while one brother caught a train going up the valley, and another the down express. Then they laughed, and when all the town slept, they walked down the hill to Mario's house.

The town was, as it expressed itself, scandalised, not so much at the elopement, but at the effrontery of "that slip of a girl," who was not in the least ashamed at what she had done, but stood all day at Mario's window, nodding at her friends in the road below. There was much traffic in the street that day, and all the gossips of the place lingered about whispering.

Mario, now employed in a Commune some sixteen miles up the valley, had taken a train at dawn and eluded the father, who wreaked his vengeance on Zelinda, beating her till she was bruised.

Emigrants from Brunella

I BELIEVE that Italians are now beginning to see that emigration is not an unmitigated evil. Where population increases at the amazing rate as in Italy, and where, as yet, home industries cannot cope with the poverty of the land, it seems a sensible thing that some members of a family should seek their fortune and adventure abroad. For instance, a small peasant proprietor, who has a precarious income coming in from his farm of about eighty pounds a year, finds it very difficult to provide for his family of three or four sons and as many daughters; the situation becomes still more complicated when the sons marry and bring their wives to live in the paternal home. Two sons stay to work the land, one perhaps becomes a stone-mason or a worker in marble, while the most enterprising goes off to North or South America.

The desire for unknown wealth is spreading. In the backwaters of small Italian towns people at last are realising their poverty and the intense discomfort of their lives. This may mean the first rung in the ladder of ultimate prosperity. The United States and the Argentine Republic have become for Italians the promised land, where gold is to be picked up in the streets. If there were not a certain amount of fairy-like conception about the distant country and if the people realised fully the arduous toil and often great suffering entailed in the search for even a moderate fortune, few would be found to cross the ocean. Everyone knows the fuss an Italian makes when going a journey. I have seen two men embrace and bid each other an earnest farewell when the traveller was only going to join his regiment at a town two hours up the line. Here in Brunella our friends come to see us off at the station, when we are only going to shop for the afternoon at a neighbouring town, and there is much waving of hands and many a "*buon viaggio*;" and if we happen to miss the first train back, faithful Paolo is waiting anxiously at the station.

"I know all the world," says the pedlar who has journeyed through Italy. "He has travelled much," says a villager of a neighbour who has perhaps crossed over to France in search of work.

It is either dire necessity, or a desire to be a little better off and own a little land, which drives the Italian so far away from his beloved corner of Italy, to which, with few exceptions, he returns as fast as he can.

Their final success was due to an eating-shop and bar; but that such ill-educated and slovenly people should have succeeded in North America, or indeed anywhere, seems strange and hardly fair. Not better educated but full of natural ability is our local grocer, who set up his shop on the proceeds of his gains in America. At the age of twenty he fell in love with a girl living in the next town whose parents had entertained a higher ambition; but one night she dropped out of the window into his arms, and away they fled to New York. After that their history became a blank to even their intimate friends, until they returned a year ago, still quite young, very stout and very prosperous. They now sell Bologna sausage by the ton to all the countryside, and in the intervals drive out in a smart *baroccino* with a fast and high-stepping horse.

"Why do you not keep a carriage?" they ask us as they meet us trudging along the dusty roads; "it is very convenient, and one gets over the ground so fast."

And this prosperous grocer is not the only emigrant who has brought something of American restlessness into a quiet Italian town. Often a long absence makes the Italian critical of his native country, and uneasy among his old surroundings. This is especially the case among the younger generation, who on a visit to their parents soon weary for the land of their adoption. "Out there one lives, *c'è vita*," and so they return to the endless quest of fortune. In the train going up to the Bagni di Lucca one autumn, we came across an Italian family who were on their way home after some fifteen years spent in North America. They were well to do, if one could judge by the man's gold watch and immaculate black cloth clothes, and the woman's blouse of brocaded silk and marvellous garden erection for a hat. They were both genuinely overcome at sight of the familiar hills, and the wife began to draw a picture what perfect felicity it would be to her to live in a little house among the chestnut woods with a vineyard, a field, and a cow. Her handsome son and daughter, talking like pure-blooded Americans, and looking unmistakably Italian, crushed the idyl with all the severity of young people in their teens. They told her that, if that was her ideal, it certainly was not theirs, and that they would not come to see her, if she stuck herself down in a slow, little place in the mountains, where there were no trams and the railway was ever so far away. They proceeded to criticise everything around them, and to compare most unfavourably the backward customs of Italy to the modern delights of New York. It was amusing to watch the shocked expressions of these young puritans, because some peasants happened to be seeing to their vines on a Sunday, and the country had not put on a funereal garb. The mother looked frankly puzzled by her children, whose minds moved in a different sphere to her own; the father sat gazing out of the window at the Lucchese landscape.

38

EDMONDO DE AMICIS, *SPAIN AND THE SPANIARDS* (NEW YORK: PUTNAM, 1885), PP. 277–278

Cordova

ON reaching Castillejo I was obliged to wait until midnight for the train for Andalusia; I dined on hard-boiled eggs, and oranges, with a little Val de Peñas wine, murmured the poetry of Espronceda, chatted a trifle with the custom-house officer (who, by the way, made me a profession of his political faith: Amadeus, liberty, increase of salary of the custom-house officers, etc.), until I heard the desired whistle, when I got into a railway carriage filled with women, boys, civil guards, cushions, and wraps; and away we went at a speed unusual on Spanish railways. The night was very beautiful; my travelling companions talked of bulls and Carlists; a beautiful girl, whom more than one devoured with his eyes, pretended to sleep in order to excite our fancy with a sample of her nocturnal attitudes; some were making *cigarritos*, some peeling oranges, and others humming arias of *Zarzuela*. Nevertheless, I fell asleep after a few moments. I think I had already dreamed of the Mosque of Cordova and the Alcazar of Seville, when I was awakened by a hoarse cry:

"Daggers!"
"Daggers? In heaven's name! For whom?"

Before I saw who had shouted, a long sharp blade gleamed before my eyes, and the unknown person asked:

"Do you like it?"

One must really confess that there are more agreeable ways of being waked. I looked at my travelling companions with an expression of stupor which made them all burst out into a hearty laugh. Then I was told that at every railway station there were these venders of knives and daggers, who offered travellers their wares just as newspapers and refreshments are offered with us. Reassured as to my life, I bought (for five lire) my scarecrow, which was a beautiful dagger suitable for the tyrant of a tragedy, with its chased handle, an inscription on the blade, and an embroidered velvet sheath; and I put it in my pocket, thinking that it would be quite useful to me in Italy in settling any questions with my publishers. The vender must have had fifty of them in a great red sash which was fastened around his waist. Other travellers bought them too; the civil guards complimented one of my neighbors on his capital selection; the boys cried:

"Give me one too!"—and their mammas replied:

"We will buy a longer one some other time."

"Oh, blessed Spain!" I exclaimed, as I thought, with disgust, of our barbarous laws which prohibit the innocent amusement of a little sharp steel.

39

HENRY N. SHORE, *THREE PLEASANT SPRINGS IN PORTUGAL* (LONDON: S. LOW, MARSTON & COMPANY, 1899), PP. 307–314

There is scarcely a rood of ground over which the line passes, between Coimbra and Lisbon, but is associated with some affecting or tragic episode in that enforced migration of a populace before the devastating legions of France. And yet, in spite of what transpired, the landscape smiles as it did of yore, for that kindly old nurse, Nature, has swept away every mark and scar; and, but for the imperishable record of printer's ink, nothing would remain to remind one of the ghastly tragedy enacted here.

And so the hours drag on, as if the journey was interminable. I know there are people who complain of railway travelling in Portugal as wearisome. And so undoubtedly it is—if you are in a hurry. But you must never be in a hurry in the Peninsula. For there life is still held to be worth living, and, on that account, worth prolonging to the uttermost. And of all the ways of prolonging life, commend me to a railway journey in fair Lusitania. To enjoy it, however, to the full, the roving and impatient Briton must drop all preconceived ideas concerning the 'eternal fitness of things' in steam locomotion. He must commence by erasing the twin words 'quick' and 'hurry' from his vocabulary. For the only reply a self-respecting Portuguese fidalgo would deign to give an individual who hinted at the word 'hurry' would be the exclamation, uttered in a slow and dignified manner, 'Amanha!' which, being interpreted, means 'To-morrow!' And the nation conscientiously acts up to this rule of life by never doing to-day what can be put off till to-morrow.

Now it came to pass, about seventy years ago, that a bold British sailor called Napier—who was 'spoiling' for a fight of some sort—took it into his wild head to go campaigning in Portugal; and after fighting many battles against the usurper Dom Miguel, this bluff sailor bethought him of jotting down his experiences, wherein, amongst other brusque sayings, he had the effrontery to declare—in a moment of pique, begotten of some sad experience of native ways—that the Portuguese would never be a nation till the word 'amanha' was expunged from their language. But he was suffering from that essentially British complaint called 'restless energy,' which is anathema in southern lands.

To be sure, some folk might take exception to the number of stoppages and the apparent waste of time at small roadside stations where no one gets in or out of the train. But to me these halts are a never-failing source of delight. For, putting aside the question of sketching, or even of botanising, along the line while the train waits, there is both pleasure and profit to be derived from the spectacle of so many officials in gold lace and brass buttons, and with their caps decorated with miniature locomotive-engines wrought in gold thread, parading each station in a slow and dignified manner—almost bowed down with the burden of responsibility attaching to the duty of putting through one train a day each way. And then the mind wanders off into side-issues,—as, for example, how these magnificent functionaries employ their leisure moments—which, by the by, are neither brief nor infrequent; or how any railway company can manage to support such an incubus of officialdom and pay a dividend, supposing that it does pay a dividend, which in Portugal is too often to imagine a vain thing! *C'est magnifique, mais ce n'est pas la guerre!* or, as a British railway official would put it, 'It's grand, but it ain't business!'

At most stations you hear a shrill little voice calling 'Agua fresca! agua fresca!' and behold, a comely damsel, with red water-jar and glass, dispensing her limpid store to thirsty passengers. I have occasionally, when the demand was brisk, seen these young ladies running!—yes, actually running! think of that!—though, to be sure, I trembled for the consequences, expecting every moment to see the juvenile delinquent led away by a gilded official and consigned to a dungeon. Oranges and other sorts of fruit are hawked about, according to the season. But civilisation has not attained here to the tea-basket stage.

After the lapse of a decent interval the station bell is struck, once, twice, thrice, the last stroke being the signal for departure; and the train having gone, the gold-laced officials retire to their several lairs for a few hours' rest. I never saw any business going on anywhere; but perhaps the parcel and goods traffic is conducted under the cover of night. It often struck me, though, that if there was more work to be done the officials would not look so terribly bored and overburdened with dignity—then certainly would not willingly carry about such a weight of gold lace.

All the navvy work on the railways of Portugal is done by women—fine, muscular wenches they are too, many of them; and they carry the little baskets of sand and dirt beautifully poised on the head with infinite grace of deportment, chattering like magpies the while. It would be an insult to the human form divine to speak of these ladies as belonging to the 'weaker sex.'

Of the civility of the railway officials I cannot speak too highly. The person who asks to see your ticket—there is no 'demanding' tickets here—does so with an apologetic air, as if he were begging a very great personal favour; and having looked at the ticket—perchance snipped a piece out of it—the courteous official, instead of shoving it back into your hand without a word of acknowledgment, makes the return of it quite a graceful little ceremony, and leaves you enraptured.

The Portuguese are certainly a courteous race, and even railway officials have surrendered none of their native polish by accepting the badge of servitude. But then, of course, they are not flurried by unsympathetic inspectors and impatient guards who are worried with time-bills. An average speed of sixteen miles an hour allows the dull routine of duty to be carried on with proper regard for the dignity of the human race.

The official time-tables are an interesting study, for they show you what the official conceptions of travelling 'facilities' are in the ancient realm of Portugal. Take the journey, for instance, between Lisbon and the Liverpool of the north—Oporto. There are three trains each way during the twenty-four hours, but not one express. Two are what the time-table calls 'mixed,' and are considered rather slow even by believers in the 'amanha' doctrine of life,—they take from thirteen to more than fourteen hours over the pilgrimage, at an average rate of fourteen miles an hour. There remains, then, only one train for people in a hurry, and this 'flier,' by dint of skipping a dozen stations, manages to accomplish the trip in the record time of eleven hours. But then, of course, two hundred and fifteen miles is a serious undertaking for a descendant of Albuquerque, and it would be inconsistent with his sense of dignity to rattle over the miles at the rate we do. The average speed of this particular train is nineteen miles an hour, which quite accounts for the serious and anxious cast of countenance I observed amongst the officials as the time drew near for the passing of the 'flying Scotsman' of Portugal.

Comparing this with our own poor achievements, I find the distance but a few miles in excess of the longest express run without a stop—Paddington to Exeter, one hundred and ninety-four miles: time, three hours forty-five minutes.

The only other record run worth mentioning is that between Barreiro, on the south side of the Tagus, and Faro, the southern commercial metropolis. The distance is the same as to Oporto, and is achieved at the rate of sixteen miles an hour, or just under twelve hours. In this case only a single train runs each way during the twenty-four hours, and stops at every station.

Now, a recent British writer on Portugal gravely informs us that the Portuguese are essentially an adventurous nation, fond of travelling and full of enterprise. I often wonder if this was 'writ sarcastic.' A few minutes' study of the railway time-tables will show how much is being done at the present time in the way of affording scope for the national fondness for travel. That the spirit of enterprise is alive, however, is shown by the up-to-date management of the Lisbon-Figueras line, which actually runs an 'express' two days a week to Caldas da Rainha during the season. What more could the most exigent tourist want?

One result of the existing system of management is that visitors are entirely debarred from making excursions to places of interest along the lines and returning the same day. No 'pleasure-seeker' cares to drag himself out of bed to go to a place, say, twenty miles off, at four o'clock in the morning, and not get home again till midnight. And yet, that is what you must do in some cases. So few are the trains on any of the lines, that it is never considered necessary to have time-tables spread abroad. Every one knows quite well the hour at which the only train leaves and arrives, and that is all any one cares to know; and so, out of Lisbon or Oporto, it is the exception to find a time-table in the hotels.

As a further incentive to travel, several pages of the time-table book are taken up with particulars of 'circular tours' in Spain and Portugal, itineraries of routes and prices, etc., tickets for which may be obtained by any one confiding enough to deposit a sum of 'ready' eight days in advance. Personally, I wouldn't trust a Portuguese railway company with my oldest pair of shoes as a deposit!

As few of my readers have ever had the privilege of gazing on a 'Guia Official dos Caminhos de Ferro de Portugal' (Official Guide to the Portuguese Railways), I venture to offer a brief extract from one:—'WATER-CLOSETS.—Nos comboios directos que circulam entre Figueira da Foz e Villa Formoso ha water-closets com lavatorios, no fourgon do conductor. Em Pampilhosa ha gabinetes-toilette com retretos reservadas para homens e senhoras, a 30 reis por pessoa.'

Not being a holder—thank goodness!—of shares in Portuguese railways, their dividend-paying capabilities are a matter which interests me very little. But it is worth mentioning that every one 'engaged upon the business of the State'—a delightfully elastic term—is allowed to travel free or at reduced rates, a privilege which has proved such a wonderful incentive to travel, that no less than ten thousand persons are said to hold free passes over the State railways of Portugal.

From time to time a clamour is raised in the British Parliament on this very subject by patriotic M.P.'s, who desire to see free travelling for 'the chosen-of-the-people' introduced into our own benighted land. But just think of the whole six hundred 'wise men of Westminster' being let loose on our railways with their 'best girls'!—for, sure, no base Saxon Chancellor of the Exchequer, with a spark of chivalry in him, would deny the same privilege to 'their sisters and their cousins and their aunts'?—Begorra, no!

There is one thing which the peripatetic Briton will greatly miss here, and that is the poetry of the 'Pill-puff.' No big boards fleck the fair face of Nature in Portugal, bearing bewildering legends to cheer the traveller in his pilgrimage through the land. The simple inhabitants have not yet been educated up to that high pitch when the added beauty of the advertisement is felt to be essential to the complete enjoyment of Nature's charms. For, after all, Nature is a clumsy composer, and sadly needs helping along. Only the savage considers beauty unadorned as beauty still, and playfully chops off the heads of people who go about sticking boards on end.

When the fair Lusitanians have attained to a South Kensington system, and the croak of the art-student is heard in the land, and when all men can chatter 'art-jargon' for hours on end, and fall down and worship at the shrine of ugliness and decay, wear sad and bilious faces, and adopt the gait of the knock-knee'd and silly, and eschew the society of ordinary mortals of flesh and blood—why, then, they will be able to appreciate the dignity and beauty of the pill-puff, and will probably ordain that all their roads may be lined with illuminated texts, apropos of soap and other things. For of such is civilisation!

The shades of night had fallen ere we reached our goal. Our train was due at 8.30, but the Puffing-Billy and its Mahout were so worn out with their exertions

ITALIA, ESPAÑA, LUSITANIA

that a quarter of an hour had to be whiled away within sight of the station before a stray locomotive could be pressed into the friendly service of pushing us into the terminus. Here our friend met us, and very soon we were in his comfortable quarters overlooking the Estrella, whose noble pile looked more lovely than ever, the graceful dome gleaming like a mass of white alabaster in the clear moonlight.

40

JAMES JOHNSTON, *REALITY VERSUS ROMANCE IN SOUTH CENTRAL AFRICA* (NEW YORK: F. H. REVELL COMPANY, 1893), PP. 32–35

On landing, I began to realize how terrible was the heat on seeing a fox-terrier belonging to one of the newly arrived passengers being led along the street, when suddenly it wheeled round two or three times, gave a yelp, and rolled over on its back, dead. Fearing a like fatality befalling my bull-dog Gyp, I got her under shade and procured water for her as soon as possible.

The climate of Benguela has an evil reputation, and the odds are very much against the probability of its improving, chiefly because of the low-lying situation of the town, preventing proper drainage and favoring malarial exhalations. Within the past few weeks seven European traders have been cut off by hæmaturic fever. Few white men can live here for any length of time without frequent visits to their mother-country.

The streets are broad and well kept, with a row of trees on each side, mostly sycamores. The houses are built of adobe (sun-dried bricks) laid with mud; the roofs and floors are tiled. A large square forms the business center, where around each door we see crowds of natives who have brought from the interior ivory, wax, india-rubber, etc., receiving in exchange cotton stuffs, guns, gunpowder, beads, and "aguardente" (white rum).

By previous arrangement with my agent, Mr. Kammerman, manager of the Dutch House, I found several carriers waiting to take our personal baggage on to Catambella, a town some sixteen miles north, where our caravan was to be made up for the interior. We started in the evening along a fairly good road but for the deep sand and dust, and arrived at the Dutch House about ten o'clock. But this hasty retreat from Benguela proved ill-advised; for if we were in a hurry the shipping officials were not, and in a couple of days I had to return again to see my goods through, and then found that the greater part had gone on by the "Cazengo" to Mossamedes. Thus I had to wait several days until she returned; then two more were wasted in transferring them from the lighters to the wharf—a bit of business that would have been completed on the Clyde, the Thames, or the Hudson in half an hour.

Mr. Greshoff (also of the Dutch House) kindly took charge of all my papers and had everything passed through the customs without any trouble. But I had still to draw on my almost exhausted stock of patience, for now the packages were in the hands of the dilatory railway company, and although a track to Catambella was commenced six years ago, not more than half the distance is as yet completed. We were not surprised at this, after having had pointed out to us two brass guns lying in the sand near the wharf, for which carriages were ordered in 1790 and are still *expected.*

The navvies employed for the heaviest work in the construction of the railway are native women, many of them toiling along under the scorching sun with pick and shovel, or carrying rails, sleepers, spikes, etc., with babies strapped to their backs.

A large trade with the natives is carried on in Catambella, and during our stay of ten days we had an opportunity of observing its general character. The products of the far interior are bartered for the most common quality of cheap and trashy goods it is possible to manufacture—some of the calicoes resembling cheese-cloth, though not so strong; shoddy blankets; long flint-lock guns, with gas-pipe barrels, white-pine stocks painted red, and bound with numerous rings of tinsel; white rum, etc. The headmen of caravans receive much-appreciated presents in the shape of discarded military clothing, helmets, tunics, and overcoats, by way of encouragement to come again. It is no unusual sight to see those lucky individuals strutting behind their little company as they leave for the journey homeward—one trigged out in an old pair of '42 tartan trowsers and a helmet of the London police; another with a dismantled busby and a footman's swallow-tailed coat; next a silk tile and the scarlet tunic of a Highland soldier. Of course, in each case you must add Africa's national garment—the loincloth!

Every morning, without exception, caravans varying in size up to hundreds of natives come trudging into the town in long straggling lines, each carrier bearing a load on his or her shoulder or head of from forty to eighty pounds weight. The most pitiable sight it is possible to witness is the long procession, chiefly women, boys, and girls, limping along, footsore, with swollen ankles and shoulders chafed by burdens all too heavy for their emaciated bodies. A large percentage of these are slaves, bought in the interior by half-breed traders for a few yards of cloth, and return to their homes no more, being sold on putting down their loads at the trader's door. I saw a band of sixty such, each with a tin tag round the neck, being marched off to be shipped at Benguela for one of the Portuguese islands. Were *they* slaves? Oh no, only contracted labor. Just so. Or suppose we call them apprentices for life? What's in a name—so long as the letter of the law is evaded? Only this I know: that they were sold to their present owners at from three pounds sterling to six pounds per caput.

Long open sheds are provided in the yards of the houses at which the natives have come to trade, and after a few days these become loathsome in the extreme, from their crowded and unsanitary condition. The death-rate at best on the coast is very high, but add the filthy state of the kintouls, as these inclosures are called, and the mortality is fearful. Not a day passed that we did not see dead bodies, each wrapped in a bit of dirty cloth, tied to a pole and borne on the shoulders of two men to the top of the adjacent hill, where they are thrown over the other side, to be devoured by jackals and hyenas during the night, which is made dismal by their weird howls as they fight over their ghastly quarry. Deceased natives who have friends are carried out of town and buried by the wayside, so that for over a mile of the path to the interior there is scarcely a yard to right or left of the track that has not a grave.

Part 5

IRON ROADS TO THE IRON MOUNTAINS OF SCANDINAVIA
Railways in Sweden, Norway, Finland, and Denmark

41

EDWIN COOLIDGE KIMBALL, *MIDNIGHT SUNBEAMS, OR, BITS OF TRAVEL THROUGH THE LAND OF THE NORSEMAN* (BOSTON: CUPPLES AND HURD, 1888), PP. 78–86

The railway, which was completed in 1882, passes through the eastern part of the great mining district of Sweden, particularly rich in iron and copper mines, and also possessing lead, nickel, zinc, and a few gold and silver mines. The scenery is rather uninteresting, and the small villages of plain wooden houses have little to attract one's notice. At one place we saw, across the road near the station, a wooden building bearing a sign along its entire length, with this word in large capital letters, all of a size: "J. JOHNSSONSDIVERSHANDEL" (J. Johnson's variety store), which is as long a word as some of its German cousins.

On the Swedish time tables, a crossed knife and fork before the name of a station signifies that it is a meal station. Our first experience was at Storvik, where we arrived about four o'clock for dinner.

We entered a dining room, around which were arranged little tables covered with snowy linen; in the centre stood a large table, one end spread with the usual diversified collection of the *smörgasbord*, at the other were piles of plates, knives, forks, and napkins. The soup is brought in and placed on the central table; each one helps himself, and, taking it to one of the small tables, eats at his leisure; the soup finished you serve yourself with fish, roast meats, chicken, and vegetables, in quantity and variety as you choose, and return to your table. The servants replenish the supplies on the large table, remove soiled plates and bring tea, coffee, beer, or wine, as ordered, to the occupants of the small tables, but each one must serve himself from the various courses, ending with pudding and nuts and raisins. There was none of the hurry, bustle, and crowding usually encountered in a railway restaurant, but plenty of time was given for a quiet, comfortable meal, with no necessity for bolting your food.

For this abundant and well-cooked dinner the charge was forty cents,—tea, coffee, beer, and wine being extra. Your word was taken without questioning regarding the extras, as you paid for them and your dinner at the table from which the coffee was dispensed. The matter of payment was left entirely to the individual, and it never, apparently, had entered the manager's mind that one could easily have walked off, without first conferring with the woman at the coffee urn.

After dinner there was time for a short walk up and down the platform, and then we continued our journey through a country where the rail fences, red farm houses, pine trees, and abundance of stumps and rocks, made us imagine we were in Maine or New Hampshire, instead of on the other side of the "great pond." The scenery improved, and in places was beautiful, especially as we skirted the shores of a chain of lakes formed by the Ljusne river; and under a sky burning with the gorgeous coloring of a brilliant Northern sunset, we arrived at half-past nine at the little station where we were to take supper. Here was the same arrangement as at dinner, each one waiting upon himself, and a good supper of fish, hot and cold meats, eggs, tea and coffee was furnished for thirty cents, which is likewise the charge for a substantial breakfast.

There were few passengers on the train, and during most of the day we two had had a compartment to ourselves. There are no sleeping cars on the route, so as it was getting late we closed and fastened the doors of our compartment, drew the curtains to shut out the bright light of the Northern night, and lying on the long seats covered with our thick railway rugs slept undisturbed, until suddenly awakened by a loud rapping at our door. The train was in a station, female voices were calling to us in Swedish, and we sprang up anxious to learn the cause of this unlooked-for visitation. But when the door was opened, the dear creatures beat a hasty retreat the moment they saw us, and evidently were as surprised as ourselves at our meeting; as we soon heard their voices in a neighboring compartment, we knew they had found those they were seeking.

At five o'clock in the morning we arrived at Ostersund, where the train stopped for an hour. We paid four cents and entered a toilet room with marble wash-bowls, brushes, an abundance of fresh towels, and that article which is never furnished free in Europe—soap. After taking bread and coffee, and a brisk walk, we felt as fresh and rested as though we had passed the night in the state-room of a vestibule Pullman.

We had previously congratulated each other on having a compartment to ourselves; on resuming our journey, during the entire forenoon, we were the sole occupants of a whole car.

We skirt the shores of a series of lakes connected by rivers, and then through a dreary country ascend the range of mountains separating Sweden from Norway. We pass through snow sheds, and between high board fences built to keep the drifting snow from the track (both much simpler in construction than those along the roads crossing the Rocky Mountains), and in the midst of snow banks, enveloped in a thick chilling mist, arrive at Storlien, two thousand feet above sea-level, the last station in Sweden. We gather for the last time about the *smörgasbord* (we never saw it later in Norway), and a good dinner cheers us in our desolate surroundings.

Then we enter the Norwegian train of second and third class carriages, on the common European model of compartments entered from the sides, with the second class, in their fittings, fully equal to the first of many other countries, and begin the descent to the sea coast. The snow mountains are veiled by clouds, there is little vegetation, barren rocks are succeeded by marshy land and swamps, but soon we emerge from the mist into bright sunshine.

We are the only occupants of the second class carriage; the guard, who speaks English, opens the door as we arrive at a station and tells us how long we are to stop, and following the general custom we get out for a few minutes' walk, and to look at the natives.

We were both intently reading when the door opened and the guard made this startling announcement: "Gentlemen, this is Hell; we stop five minutes." We hastily left our seats to see the place against which we had been warned all our lives, hoping at least to refresh ourselves with a few glasses of sulphur water. No fumes of sulphur, no odor of brimstone greeted us, but instead, "a nipping and an eager air" enveloped the forlorn little settlement, even on that summer afternoon. Whatever *Hell* may signify in Norwegian, this place is decidedly different as regards climate from that of the same name mentioned in King James' version.

Descending from Hell the railroad runs for a long distance close to the edge of the lovely Throndhjem fjord, with its transparent waters, clusters of islands, and on the opposite side its deeply indented and darkly wooded shores, with a background of pale blue mountains. Then we roll into the most northern railway station in the world, and are in Throndhjem, a city of 23,000 inhabitants, the third largest city in Norway, situated on a line with the south coast of Iceland.

The houses are mostly built of wood, on very wide streets as a protection against the spread of conflagrations. At the head of a long street stands the cathedral, the most interesting edifice in the North. It is built over the burial site of St. Olaf, the Norwegian king who first introduced Christianity into his country, at the end of the tenth century. A succession of fires has destroyed the interior, which for years has been in process of restoration, and at the present time the nave, from the transepts to the west end, is given up to masons and stone-cutters, who are busy upon its reconstruction.

In one of the streets we saw throngs of peasants, who had come into the city to the weekly market, bringing butter and produce, besides an endless variety of cheeses, rolls of homespun cloth, and linen from the hand-loom. We strolled along the quays, interested in the shipping and the sea-faring men, and visited the finer buildings in the city, built of stone, occupied by shops with a fine display of goods; but we found the place chiefly interesting from its natural beauty and situation.

Our first impression of the Norwegians was a favorable one, for as we left the hotel and were vainly trying to find our way to a steamship office with an unpronounceable name, we asked a man both in English and German to direct us. Not understanding, but finding out where we wished to go from our pointing to the name in our guide book, he immediately turned and conducted us a long distance, and even when we were within sight of the building would not leave us until we arrived at the very doorway, when he politely touched his hat and disappeared before we had a chance to thank him.

During June and July Throndhjem is full of tourists, who take the steamer here for the North Cape and the regions of the midnight sun.

The steamers start from Christiania and Bergen, but most travellers, instead of taking the long and disagreeable voyage along the coast, go directly from Christiania to Throndhjem by rail, a distance of three hundred and sixty miles.

42

WILLIAM ELEROY CURTIS, *DENMARK, NORWAY, AND SWEDEN* (AKRON, OHIO: THE SAALFIELD PUBLISHING CO., 1903), PP. 118–124, 127–128

The kariol, the stolkiaerre, and the jernbanens

When one travels in Norway he is compelled to adopt primitive means of transportation, and that's the charm of it. There are plenty of rivers and lakes with "damp-sheep" upon them—that's the Norwegian word for steamboat—but if you want to go in any other direction you must take a carriage; or, if there are only two of you, a native cart called a stolkjaerre; or, if you are alone, a kariol, which is a sort of sulky. The arrangements are perfect and the roads are fine. Everything is under government supervision for the comfort and convenience of travelers; even the scenery, which is sublime. You can ride all day without a jolt, for the roads are as hard as asphalt pavement, and smoother than most of it, for in our cities the asphalt pavements generally have plenty of places that need repair. I suppose that when the United States is a thousand years old we will have such roads in our country, for good roads are the growth of centuries, and are not constructed by men in a hurry. Julius Caesar—or was it Hannibal?—started the good roads movement in southern Europe, and in Norway it began in the days of the Vikings. The national government there took charge of the highways in 1625 and has been extending and improving them ever since. It is generally the rule that the best roads are found in countries where their construction is difficult. You can drive anywhere on our western prairies, but through the Norwegian mountains a roadway has to be hewn out of the rocks.

The railway system of Norway is limited, but is gradually growing. The difficulties and cost of construction are so great, the population is so scattered and the traffic comparatively so small, that such enterprises have to be undertaken by the government—but, nevertheless, with the prudent and economical way they have of running things over there, they make even their railways pay. Two-thirds of the population live on the seacoast, where railways are practically impossible and useless because of the mountains and the fjords, except in a few favored localities, while in the interior the rugged mountains and the forests, the cold climate, the limited productiveness of the soil, the heavy snowfall and the thin and scattered population combine to make construction and maintenance very difficult and expensive and traffic very small. In 1901 there were 1,120 miles of railroad belonging to the national government, divided into thirteen different lines, most of them in the southern part of the kingdom, with their focus at Christiania. The chief trunk lines run south through Sweden to Copenhagen and furnish the main thoroughfare to Europe, and northward diagonally across the country to the ancient city of Throndhjem, a journey of eighteen hours. There is also a line to Stockholm. There were also 111 miles belonging to private companies.

The main roads belong to the government and represent an expenditure of 146,000,000 kroner or $40,000,000. The branch lines have been constructed by private corporations usually for their own convenience, to furnish access to lumber camps, manufacturing establishments and that sort of thing, and cost $16,000,000, making a total investment in railways for the entire kingdom of about $56,000,000 in our money, probably the most expensive transportation system for its mileage in the world. The ratio per area is only 0.9 miles to every 100 square miles of territory, while Great Britain has 17.2, France 12.2 and other countries of Europe comparatively the same. The ratio to population however, makes a much better showing, being 6.1 miles to every 10,000 inhabitants, while the ratio in Great Britain is only 5.2.

When the government builds a railway it requires the parishes it is intended to benefit to contribute 15 per cent of the cost in cash, in addition to the right of way. The remainder is paid from the public treasury, upon an appropriation by the storthing. The parishes sometimes raise the money by taxation and sometimes by subscription.

The gross revenue of the Norwegian government railways average 11,753 kroner per mile—about half from freight and the other half from passengers. The expense of maintenance in 1900 averaged $7,969 per mile, leaving a profit of 3,784 kroner per mile, or something like a total of $1,100,000, which is very large under the circumstances, and could scarcely have occurred under any other than Norwegian management, which considers a penny saved as good as a penny earned, and earns a great many pennies that way. The rates will average 2 cents a ton per English mile for freight and 5 cents per mile for passengers. The salaries of the officers and the wages of the employes seem to us amazingly small, and the repairs are carried on with a minuteness of detail which seems a waste of time and labor to those who are accustomed to large transactions. When a bolt is worn out somewhere a blacksmith belonging to the company makes another by hand instead of buying it at a hardware shop.

There has been a long controversy about gauges. All the original roads were narrow gauge, but broad gauge has been found to be more economical and advantageous, hence the new roads are built that way, and the old ones are changed as they require rebuilding. There are now 250 miles of new road under construction and 280 more contemplated, which will give a comparatively complete system. The chief road of importance under construction runs across the country east and west from Christiania and Bergen, the two largest cities, which are now reached only by steamship and carriages with a journey of from three to six days.

The new road goes through the mountains and presents many engineering difficulties. Two-thirds of the way the road-bed must be cut out of the mountain side, and there is a tunnel three miles long at a height of 2,820 feet above the sea level. The snow of winter is so heavy that it will be necessary to cover the tracks with sheds for a distance of nearly sixty miles. The construction is not only difficult but expensive, and although the distance is but 310 miles, it will be one of the most costly railways ever built. Sixty-seven miles of the line between Bergen and Voss on the western coast is already in operation, and it is a favorite journey of tourists, for the scenery is superb, although the traveler is in a tunnel one-tenth of the entire distance. There are forty-eight tunnels in all. A shelf has been hewn and blasted along the side of the mountains that inclose the celebrated Sorfjord.

The Norwegians call a railway a jernbane, literally "an iron path." Their cars are made on the conventional European pattern and are light and comfortable. They are furnished with toilet-rooms and run smoothly and noiselessly. Most of the trains are equipped with Westinghouse brakes, steam heat and electric lights. They run very slowly. Economy is studied in this respect, as in every other. There is a certain speed—say, fifteen or eighteen miles an hour—which can be maintained at a minimum consumption of fuel, and the Scandinavian railway managers have figured it down to a dot. They can haul a longer train a greater distance with a ton of coal than any other engineers, and the most scrupulous attention is applied to every feature of management, the tracks, the rolling stock, the station, the crossings. The crossing-keepers are usually women. A large number of that sex are employed by the railways. In Germany you find them as waiters on the dining cars.

The stops at the stations seem unnecessarily long to impatient Americans, but the time is utilized by the leisurely passengers in drinking big goblets of beer, and by the conductor in parading up and down the platform so that the patrons of the road can have an opportunity to admire his radiant uniform and fine shape. In Scandinavian countries the best looking men seem to have been selected for railway conductors and policemen and their deportment is decidedly different from what we are accustomed to. If you ask a question of a Norwegian policeman he will bring his heels together, give a military salute and stand in the attitude of attention like a soldier while he answers. He usually understands English too. Those who cannot are remarkably accurate guessers, and all take a friendly interest in your inquiries instead of giving you a short answer and a cold shoulder, like the policemen in our cities. They will walk to the corner to point out the house in the middle of the next block if that is where you want to go, and when you thank them for their attention you get another salute that makes you feel as big as a major general, or as if you had been mistaken for a member of the royal family. Railway conductors are equally polite and seem to understand that it is a part of their business to protect tender-footed travelers, as angels always look after good little boys.

IRON ROADS TO THE IRON MOUNTAINS OF SCANDINAVIA

It is a long, tedious trip from Copenhagen to Christiania by rail, but it it worse by water. The Skager-Rack is as bad as the Bay of Biscay or the English Channel. Two tides meet there, one from the North Sea and the other from the Baltic, and enter into a heartless conspiracy to make travelers miserable. The boats are clean and comfortable, but small, and have a triplicate-ellipitical-corkscrew motion that will make the toughest old sea dog bury his face in a pillow and wish that he had never been born. The consumption of food upon the vessels is less in proportion to their patronage than on any other line except those that cross the English Channel. When a steamer has forty passengers the cook never provides for more than four, for that is the usual ratio of crocodiles—and, of course, full board is charged against the rest. That is the habit of European steamers. When a voyage is rough and people are sure to be seasick, you pay for the regular number of meals in advance when you buy your ticket, and never eat them. If you are to have a smooth passage and a fierce appetite you are served a la carte and everything is charged extra.

Through sleeping cars run between Copenhagen and Christiania. They are divided into coops according to the ordinary European plan, some narrow with two berths, upper and lower, and some wide with bunks for four. First-class passengers pay 5 kroner for a bed, which is $1.40, and second-classers 84 cents, but I was not able to distinguish any difference between the accommodations, except that the 84-cent berths were upholstered in plain scarlet plush, and the $1.40 seats were finished in a pattern like a Persian rug; but, if I understand Norwegian accurately, they never put anybody in the upper berth over a first-classer, while the second-class compartments are packed full, according to the demand. At least that is what I gathered from an animated conversation with a porter who could not talk English and did not appear to get a very firm grasp on my Norwegian.

There is a universal language, however, which can be used in all countries. It is sometimes paper and sometimes coin; and, if you speak it fluently, you need have no anxiety or trouble. Give a railway conductor or porter to understand in that language that you want to be safe and comfortable, then retire to your compartment and take your ease. He will do the rest. He will see that you have everything that you need, and when you arrive at your destination will deliver you over to the porter of your hotel without a scratch or a stain.

You have to pay a krone extra for the trimmings in a Norwegian "slopwagen," as a sleeping car is called. The original price entitles you only to the privilege of stretching out on the seat wrapped in a dove-colored blanket belonging to the government. That is one of the national economies, but, by paying 28 cents more, the porter will bring a towel, a pillow and two sheets, and make up a bed.

Although Sweden and Norway are governed by the same king, both impose duties upon goods that cross the border, and there are custom-houses all along the line between them. The tariffs are low, and the inspectors are lenient to foreigners, but they are merciless to natives. A Norwegian customs inspector will sock it to a Swede if he finds a fish hook or an extra safety pin in his luggage, and the Swedes retaliate by searching every package brought over from Norway; but both pass the baggage of Americans or Englishmen without examination.

I was awakened in the middle of the night, as one often is, when something unusual is going on, and saw a giant in uniform feeling around among the traps that had been placed in the racks above my bed.

"What do you want? What are you looking for?" I exclaimed.

"Customs officer," he replied laconically, in good English.

"You have no right to come into a man's room like a burglar even if you are a customs officer," I said.

"English?" he asked, without taking any notice of my indignation.

"No. American."

"Anything dutiable?"

"No."

"Spirits?"

"No, don't drink."

"Cigars?"

"No. Smoked 'em all last night."

He then took a piece of chalk out of his pocket and marked each bag with a mysterious hieroglyphic. Then he began to feel around in the racks again.

"What's this?" he asked, hauling it down.

"Typewriter," I replied.

"What for?"

"I am an American newspaper correspondent, and I use it to write my letters."

"Open."

I unlocked the case and he examined it curiously, pressing his fingers on the keys like a child.

"For sale?" he asked.

"No, to use."

"Writing machine?"

"Yes."

"Good-night," he said calmly, as he chalked the case and left the compartment as noiselessly as he had entered it.

Norway is a narrow country like Chile, and when the rocks were passed around got more than its share. The coast is a succession of bold, precipitous cliffs, broken at frequent intervals by narrow bays called fjords, which extend their arms like devilfish into the mountains of the interior and fill the great canyons that have been made by glacial ice with still, dark, bottomless bodies of water. The surface of the interior is composed of parallel ranges of mountains divided by streams which generally flow eastward or southeastward. When people travel they are compelled to follow these water courses because the mountain ranges are impassable. The highest peak, Galdhöpiggen, has an altitude of 8,400 feet, and there are many others nearly as high. These mountains lift their summits far above the snow line and upon their slopes lie immense banks of snow and glaciers that form the striking feature of Norwegian scenery.

It has been impossible or impracticable to build railways through the mountain passes and hence travelers are compelled to retain the primitive methods and go across the country in carriages, which gives them a closer contact with the people, much better opportunities to study their habits and customs and home life and affords an outdoor experience and exercise that is good for both the body and the soul. No part of Europe and certainly no part of America is so fascinating. We have no system of excursions that will compare in interest and enjoyment with the carriage rides through the Norwegian valleys. Norway is not suitable for long walking excursions, as the distances are too great and the points of interest are too far apart, but the government, by providing a system of post horses, accommodates the traveler in a comfortable and convenient way and allows him to pass to his destination without unnecessary delay. He can go as rapidly as he pleases, and can stop as often as he likes, for the posting stations are seldom more than fifteen and often less than seven or eight miles apart.

From ancient times there has been a law in Norway requiring the land owners to furnish free transportation for the king and all who travel on his business. Private travelers can take advantage of the same privilege in return for a reasonable payment, the rates having been fixed as far back as the sixteenth century and seldom changed. The ordinary charge for one person is only about 7 cents a mile, but where the roads are very hilly an additional fee is required. There are nearly 1,000 "skyds-stationer," which are usually inns, although sometimes farmhouses, throughout the country. At some of them, called "fastestations," a traveler can obtain fresh horses within fifteen minutes after his arrival, but at the ordinary stations a proper time must be allowed for the "skydsskaffer," as the manager is called, to bring his horses in from the pasture. At every station there is a "skydsbog," a book in which travelers are required to enter their names and addresses, their orders and any complaints they may have to make concerning their treatment. These books are examined frequently by inspectors from the department of roads, who inspect the "skyds-stationer" whenever it is necessary to do so.

The Norwegian horse is a small, sturdy, stocky little fellow, about sixty inches high, hardy, gentle, enduring and a great climber. He looks like a percheron pony because of his heavy body and neck. He is not fast, but will take a heavy load along the road all day at the rate of six miles an hour up hill and down.

There are several breeds of cattle in Norway, and most of them are good foragers and equally good milk producers. The sheep are comparatively few, although it seems strange to the traveler that the vast ranges upon the mountain sides are not more utilized for flocks. I suppose there is a good reason for it, but I have not yet found out what it is. Up in the snow country reindeer are used for transportation purposes, and are kept in a domesticated condition. They live upon moss that grows upon the rocks, and paw it out with their hoofs from under the snow during the winter. By the census of 1891 there were 170,134 reindeer in Norway and only 150,898 horses. The cattle numbered 1,006,499 and the sheep and goats 1,689,982.

The national government builds the main highways, while the cross-roads are built by the parishes. The management is in the hands of a bureau in the national department of public works, and the maintenance falls upon the people who live in the neighborhood, under the supervision of a local inspector. Every farmer has a piece of road to take care of, according to the amount of land he owns, and at intervals slabs of cast iron are erected bearing his name and the section of the road he is required to keep in order. Thus every man's reputation is at stake in the neighborhood, and if there is a muddy place or a rut everybody knows who is to blame for it, and it cannot be laid to the county commissioners. On the outside of each road is a line of large blocks of stone set upright, which serve as a barrier to prevent wagons from going off into the ditch. There are 6,500 miles of main highway, and 11,000 miles of cross-road, or a total of 17,500 miles of roads in Norway, and the total expenditure upon them by the national and local authorities will average a million and a half of dollars every year.

The first cost of a road is usually about $3,000 a mile. They first dig an excavation about three feet deep, as if they were going to make a canal. On the bottom are thrown heavy blocks of stone, through which the water can filter, and occasionally there is a little drain to carry it off. Upon this is a layer of smaller stones, and then still smaller, until the surfacing is reached, which is macadam of pounded slate, mixed with gravel and stone.

43

FRANCIS E. CLARK AND SYDNEY A. CLARK, *THE CHARM OF SCANDINAVIA* (BOSTON: LITTLE, BROWN, 1914), PP. 153–156

TAMMERFORS, FINLAND, July 15.

MY DEAR JUDICIA,

Tammerfors is an inland city on the edge of the great lake region of which I wrote you in my last letter. I had to come here by rail, and perhaps you will be interested to know something about the railways of Finland. I must confess that as means of communication they cannot rival the steamers on the lakes and canals, but, as in most other countries, they are a very necessary evil, and, since in Finland they run on well-ballasted roads for the most part and burn fragrant wood instead of ill-smelling coal, their nuisance as smoke and dust producers is reduced to a minimum.

They are practically all owned by the State, and as the State is in no hurry to get its inhabitants from one place to another, or to get them out of the country, should they be bound to emigrate, the average rate of speed is not more than fifteen miles an hour. Even the express trains between Helsingfors and St. Petersburg are no cannon balls or "Flying Yankees," for a mile in three minutes and ten seconds is the best they attempt to do for the whole journey.

Still if you have time enough at your disposal you can travel a surprisingly long distance in Finland for a surprisingly small amount of money. The third-class fares (and the third class is patronized by the great majority of people) costs less than a cent a mile, and you can go clear around the east coast of the Gulf of Bothnia to its northern tip, if you are so disposed, and at Haparanda can almost shake hands with our Swedish friends, whom I visited in Luleå a few months ago.

I would not advise you to take a third-class car if you intend to take a long journey in Finland, for the hard, yellow, wooden seats get decidedly tiresome before you have jolted over a hundred miles of Finnish scenery. The second-class cars are entirely comfortable and even luxurious on the principal lines, and you can settle down happily in your plush, springy comfort, usually having a whole seat to yourself.

The first-class accommodations, as in Sweden, are only distinguished from the second by the placard on the door or the window and by your own inner consciousness that you have paid considerably more than your neighbors for the same accommodations. Most of the cars are more like our American cars than the ordinary European coaches, with an aisle down the middle and seats on either side, though the same car may be divided into two or three compartments with doors between.

The stations are modest, wooden buildings, and, except for the numerous signs of margarine, beer, and other comestibles with which they are decorated, I could readily mistake them for railway stations in northern New Hampshire or western Dakota.

One could never, however, mistake a Finnish railway restaurant for a similar institution in America. Here one sees no quick-lunch counter, no aged sandwiches made the day before yesterday, no greasy doughnuts or any impossible concoction misnamed "coffee." Here everything is neat, nice, and orderly. The coffee is sure to be delicious, for in the meanest Finnish hut, even in far Lapland, the proprietor would be ashamed to give you anything but a steaming and fragrant cup of their national beverage. With the coffee, and for the same price, you get an unlimited supply of little cakes or sweetbread, while if you want a full dinner of three or four courses, superbly cooked and elegantly served, it will cost you only two and a half Finnish *marks*, or about fifty cents, for a Finnish *mark* differs from a German *mark* in being of the same value as a *franc*.

Outside the station, in rows along the platform, I often see old women with baskets of apples or plates of fried meat or cakes, or loaves of coarse bread and bottles of milk, just as we saw them in that long journey across Siberia in the early days of the Trans-Siberian Railway. You remember how eagerly we used to race for the bread and milk stalls to get our supply before the little tables were swept bare by the hungry travelers? In Finland one does not have to be a sprinter in order to get his share of the food, for there is always an abundant supply at the restaurants. The old women on the outside, because of the cheapness of their wares, are largely patronized by the poorer people.

The notices in the stations and in the cars about smoking, spitting, putting your head out of the window, standing on the platform, and so on, are printed in six languages: Finnish, Swedish, Russian, German, French, and English, and the maps and diagrams and time-tables are so full of helpful information that no wayfaring man need go astray.

In one respect the Finnish railways differ from the Swedish, though they are such near neighbors. The Swedish trains glide away like the Arab when he has folded his tents, without making any fuss about it. No bell is rung, no whistle blown, no word of command given. The station master simply waves his hand when the exact second for departure has come, and unless you keep your eyes wide open, and your watch exactly with railway time, you are likely to see the rear car of the train vanishing in the distance while you make frantic but unavailing attempts to catch it. In Finland, on the contrary, there is no danger of your being left, for first the station bell rings, then it rings again, then the conductor blows his whistle, then the engineer answers him with the locomotive whistle, and by that time, everything being good and ready, the train will slowly get under way.

44

THEÓPHILE GAUTIER, *A WINTER IN RUSSIA*, TRANS. M. M. RIPLEY (NEW YORK: H. HOLT AND COMPANY, 1874), PP. 22–24

Schleswig

THE city of Altona, to which runs that flesh-colored omnibus that I have before mentioned, begins by an immense street whose broad side alleys are edged with little theatres and shows of divers kinds, suggesting the Boulevard du Temple in Paris; a somewhat droll souvenir on the frontier of the states of Hamlet, Prince of Denmark! It is true, however, that Hamlet himself loved players, and gave them advice like a journalist.

At the end of the suburb of Altona stands the station of the railway which leads to Schleswig, where I had business.

Business at Schleswig! Why not? What is there surprising about that? I had promised, if I should ever pass through Denmark, to pay a visit to a fair Danish *châtelaine*, a friend of mine; and at Schleswig I was to obtain the necessary directions for reaching L——, distant by a few hours' drive.

Imagine me, then, seated in a railway-carriage somewhat at a venture, having had much trouble in making the ticket-seller understand whither I desired to go, the German at this point being somewhat complicated with the Danish. Fortunately, some young gentlemen whom I encountered came to my rescue with a Teutonic French much like that in which Balzac's Schmucke and his Baron de Nucingen express themselves, but which was, for all that, most delicious music to my cars. They were so kind as to play the part of dragoman. When you are in a foreign country, reduced to the condition of a deaf-mute, you cannot but curse the memory of him who conceived the idea of building the tower of Babel, and by his pride brought about the confusion of tongues! Seriously, at the present day when the human race circulate like generous blood through the arterial, venous, and capillary tubes of railways in all parts of the world, a congress of nations ought to assemble and decide upon a common speech—French or English—which should be, like Latin in the Middle Ages, the universal human language; all schools and colleges should be required to teach it, each nation of course at the same time retaining its own native and peculiar tongue. But I leave this dream, which will be accomplished, I doubt not, at some not far remote future by some method which necessity alone can devise, and, meantime, cannot but felicitate myself that our own noble language is spoken, at least in some fashion, by every man, all the world over, who prides himself on being well-bred and well-informed.

Darkness comes on early, in these short autumn days, shorter here than in Paris even, and the level landscape soon disappeared in that vague darkness which changes the form and character of all objects. I should have done well to fall asleep, but I am a most conscientious traveller, and from time to time I put out my head, striving to see something in the gray light of the rising moon. Fatal imprudence! My cap was not secured, and the fresh wind, increased by the rapid motion of the train, which was going at full speed, took it off with all the dexterity of a *prestidigitateur!* For one moment I saw its black disk whirl in the air, like a star hurled from its orbit; a second later, and it was but a point in space, and I remained bareheaded and forlorn.

A young man who sat opposite me began to laugh quietly, then resuming his gravity, he opened his travelling-bag and drew out a student's cap which he begged me to accept. It was not a time to stand on ceremony; it was impossible to stop the train in order to procure other head-gear, nor indeed did the landscape have the appearance of being enamelled with hat-shops. Thanking the obliging traveller as best I could, I perched upon my cranium the minute cap,—taking good care, this time, to make sure of the strap—which gave me the air of a "mossy-head" of Heidelberg or Jena, well-advanced in the thirties, to say the least. This tragi-comic incident was the only one which signalized my journey, and from it I augured well of the hospitality of the country.

At Schleswig, the railway, which is to be carried further, goes a few rods beyond the station, and stops short in a field—like the last line of an abruptly interrupted letter! The effect of this is singular.

An omnibus took possession of myself and my trunks, and, with the feeling that it must of necessity take me somewhere, I confidingly allowed myself to be stowed in and carried away. The intelligent omnibus set me down before the best hotel in the town, and there, as circumnavigators say in their journals, "I held a parley with the natives." Among them was a waiter who spoke French in a way that was transparent enough to give me an occasional glimpse of his meaning; and who—a much rarer thing!—even sometimes understood what I said to him.

45

FINLAND JOHNSON SHERRICK, *LETTERS OF TRAVEL* (N.P.: N.P., 1905), PP. 79–82

Through Denmark to Prussia

WE spent the larger part of last week in Denmark and among the Danes. While that little Kingdom is a part of the Scandinavian peninsula and at one time was joined in government with Norway and Sweden, yet they are distinctively a different people speaking a different language. As soon as we crossed the line from Sweden we could notice that we were in another country and among other people. The barren rocks, the pine forests and the many acres of waste and mountainous lands of Norway and Sweden disappeared and instead were fertile fields, green meadows and fine growing crops. It was harvest time and the shocks of rye and wheat were thick upon the fields. The ground is level and we noticed no waste land. Some of the fields were being plowed for the purpose of sowing grass seed for a crop of hay next year. They grow no corn, and I did not see a hog in either Norway or Denmark. Neither did I see a mule. The railroads of Denmark are very good. They, however, unlike England, cross highways on grade, but they have a gate across the drive which is always closed in every country road when a train passes by. A little dwelling house is built close by every gate and the operator is a woman. As the train goes flying by she stands at her gate with never ceasing care for human life and sees that no one enters into danger. I am sorry to know that in my country there is little care of this kind and much less value placed upon human life.

I noticed in Denmark, as we rode by rail last Sunday that the people were generally at work on the farm as on other days. They seemed to be very busy plowing and harrowing the ground, cutting grain, mowing grass, hauling rye to stack, and in fact working just as we noticed them at work on any week day. We did not learn if this is the custom all the year or if it is only practiced during the harvest season, but I have noticed that in Europe generally, outside of England and Scotland, the Sabbath is not observed in as strict a way as by the people of Ohio. Foreign people do not live as fast as we do. They go much slower, seem to enjoy their leisure, and are very fond of company and sociability, and as you mingle with them you can't but think that they pluck many flowers of enjoyment along the pathway of life. Copenhagen, the capital of Denmark, is the largest city of Scandinavia. We spent a few days there and were much pleased with the city and its people. It is not as beautiful as Stockholm of Sweden, but much larger. Its chief attraction for all classes for sociability and entertainment centers in their most beautiful Tivoli grounds, which are said to be the largest and finest in the world. Although an entrance fee is charged, many thousands of people gather there every warm evening of the year. They seem to enjoy the cool breezes that ripple the leaves of acres of the most beautiful green trees, to promenade by the many tastefully arranged flower beds, by the artificial canals and crystal little lakes, and listen to bands of the very finest music is really charming. Tables are scattered everywhere beneath the trees, under canvas, and by the water's edge, with good seats, where one can sit, rest and be refreshed with food, drink and the dainties of the season; or you may sit on comfortable benches beneath the spreading trees, and see the well dressed and the elegantly attired promenade the winding paths that lead amid the beauties of nature, embellished by the art of man. Not only music everywhere, but other novel and entertaining amusements greet the visitor on all sides. Friends meet friends, and the hat is lifted whenever an acquaintance passes you by. Social enjoyment is unalloyed, good feeling is master of the hour, and happiness seems to reign supreme among all the people that gather there. Glistening from among the many trees, showering down from festoon hangings, illuminating the roofs and fronts of picturesque stands and booths, lining up the water's edge, and filling up every nook and corner of those vast grounds, are a countless number of Chinese lanterns and a hundred thousand incandescent lights of varied and beautiful hues, casting a mellow light of gold and purple upon the scene. This is the way the people of that city take their outdoor enjoyment. Men, women and children of every class and station of life mingle here, to eat, drink and be merry. This is the first place they direct a stranger to and they are very proud to tell you that there is no other place in all Europe as large, fine and grand as their Tivoli.

On last Sunday we bade goodby to this patriotic little kingdom of the Danes, to the people of the Scandinavian Peninsula (Norway, Sweden and Denmark) and crossed over the Baltic Sea, (where the waves were running wild and high) to the "Fotter Land" of our many German friends in America. To the land of Prussia that Frederick the Great made possible, and Kaiser Wilhelm and the "Grand Old Man," Bismark, made one of the strongest and greatest nations of the world. Their union with the old German States, and the capturing of Lorraine and Alsace from the French in 1876, secured for the German people, a powerful empire.

On the road from the Baltic Sea along the northeast coast of Germany to Hamburg, last Sunday afternoon, we saw quite a number of farmers hauling in their wheat, but all other common labor seemed to be suspended. At all stations along this road the people seemed to have a holiday. Men and women gathered where the train stopped and were passing their Sunday evening in a very social way. At every station where our train stopped, vendors of foaming beer came to the doors of the cars to offer it for sale. The voices that sang out "Beer, Beer," were heard above the din of every other commotion.

Part 6

RAILWAYS AMONG THE RUINS
Greece, Ottoman Empire (Turkey),
Czechoslovakia, and Serbia

46

MARK TWAIN, *THE INNOCENTS ABROAD* (HARTFORD: AMERICAN PUBLISHING COMPANY, 1875), PP. 417–418

A railway here in Asia—in the dreamy realm of the Orient—in the fabled land of the Arabian Nights—is a strange thing to think of. And yet they have one already, and are building another. The present one is well built and well conducted, by an English Company, but is not doing an immense amount of business. The first year it carried a good many passengers, but its freight list only comprised eight hundred pounds of figs!

It runs almost to the very gates of Ephesus—a town great in all ages of the world—a city familiar to readers of the Bible, and one which was as old as the very hills when the disciples of Christ preached in its streets. It dates back to the shadowy ages of tradition, and was the birthplace of gods renowned in Grecian mythology. The idea of a locomotive tearing through such a place as this, and waking the phantoms of its old days of romance out of their dreams of dead and gone centuries, is curious enough.

We journey thither to-morrow to see the celebrated ruins.

THIS has been a stirring day. The Superintendent of the railway put a train at our disposal, and did us the further kindness of accompanying us to Ephesus and giving to us his watchful care. We brought sixty scarcely perceptible donkeys in the freight cars, for we had much ground to go over. We have seen some of the most grotesque costumes, along the line of the railroad, that can be imagined. I am glad that no possible combination of words could describe them, for I might then be foolish enough to attempt it.

At ancient Ayassalook, in the midst of a forbidding desert, we came upon long lines of ruined aqueducts, and other remnants of architectural grandeur, that told us plainly enough we were nearing what had been a metropolis, once. We left the train and mounted the donkeys, along with our invited guests—pleasant young gentlemen from the officers' list of an American man-of-war.

The little donkeys had saddles upon them which were made very high in order that the rider's feet might not drag the ground. The preventative did not work well in the cases of our tallest pilgrims, however. There were no bridles—nothing but a single rope, tied to the bit. It was purely ornamental, for the donkey cared nothing for it. If he were drifting to starboard, you might put your helm down hard the other way, if it were any satisfaction to you to do it, but he would continue to drift to starboard all the same.

47

MRS. BRASSEY, *SUNSHINE AND STORM IN THE EAST, OR CRUISES TO CYPRUS AND CONSTANTINOPLE* (NEW YORK: H. HOLT AND COMPANY, 1880), PP. 354–357, 362–364

Adrianople

Famine is in thy cheeks,
Need and oppression starveth in thine eyes,
Contempt and beggary hangs upon thy back;
The world is not thy friend, nor the world's law.

Friday, December 6th.—We were called at 4.30 a.m. The elements certainly seemed to have conspired against our expedition to Adrianople, for the wind howled, and the rain came down not in torrents but in sheets. However, all arrangements had been made, so we determined to start—Mr. Bingham, Mabelle, and I; for Tom could not get away, having much business to attend to and much writing to do. George was late in coming off, and we nearly missed the train, having to row right across the harbour to Stamboul, and then to wade through a sea of mud, followed by a line of porters, to the station. There we found that there was some mistake about the saloon carriage; but we managed to make ourselves comfortable in a first-class carriage, in company with a gentlemanly Turk who spoke English, and a French lady who appeared to be in the habit of making frequent journeys between Adrianople and Constantinople, and consequently knew all the places on the road. We passed slowly through the town of Stamboul and its old walls, on to San Stefano, where one set of lines branches off to Tchekmedje.

Every station was crowded with Turkish soldiers, and was surrounded by a large encampment and many stores awaiting transport. The line meandered along near the edge of the sea and over salt marshes nearly all the way, by Baksais and Cattaldza. Some of the little gulfs were quite black with wild fowl and wild geese, which rose from the reeds and marshes in whirring flocks. At Tchorlou the train stopped to allow the passengers to dine. Sometimes there is not enough food for everybody, and as we had been warned of this we brought our own provisions and consumed them *en route*. This gave us time to walk about and see what there was to be seen, which was not much. The rain still continued to pour down, as if it would never stop. A long dreary road stretched away from the station to a distant town, while in different directions were several camps, hundreds of soldiers, and tons and tons of stores. It was here that, during the war, the Stafford House Committee did so much good by visiting the trains of wounded and sick soldiers, binding up their wounds, and giving them soup, wine, and water. What angels of mercy they must have appeared to the poor suffering wretches, who had been jolted and knocked about for days, untended and uncared for! There are no railway officials except the station-masters and those attached to the train: all the porters' work is done by soldiers, and they appear to perform their task well and civilly, though the stations are filthy beyond description. The carriages themselves look clean and comfortable, and run smoothly, so that the journey, though slow and monotonous, is not really fatiguing. The contract for making the line from Constantinople was taken at so much a mile, and its execution was not carefully looked after. The contractor consequently wandered about all round the country, in order to be paid for as many miles as possible, as well as to avoid bridges, viaducts, cuttings, earthworks, tunnels, or other expensive labour. In this way he contrived to add over fifty miles to the distance, besides making a very bad line, which is washed away whenever there is a heavy rainfall. It was a French *Christian* who did this for a Turkish *Mohammedan!*

We passed a great many villages that had been sacked, burnt, and destroyed by the Russians. At Lilli Bourgas we left the Turkish camps and soldiers behind, and passed through the Russian lines. The Russians seemed to take to porters' work just as handily as the Turks, only that they were a little more stolid and stupid. From this point it was quite dark, and I think we all slept till we reached Adrianople, soon after 9 p.m., where a friend kindly met us at the station. While we were talking to him at one door, a Russian soldier crept in at the other and tried to steal one of our bags. Luckily James, our new servant, saw him, and made him drop it, but the man escaped.

All round the station was a sea of mud; but as our friend had thoughtfully brought his carriage, we accomplished the few hundred yards' journey to the hotel in comfort. It was not a very inviting-looking place at the first glance. There were two large rooms full of Russians eating and drinking, a dirty stone hall, a staircase leading to a large square wooden upper hall full of Russian soldiers (officers' servants) making tea and smoking. Round it were about twenty little rooms, with thick walls and strongly barred doors, each containing a bed, washstand, and chair, and all scrupulously clean, well carpeted, and curtained. One bedroom had been turned into a sitting-room for us, and the table was prepared for dinner quite nicely.

From our windows we could see nothing but Russian soldiers, tents, and huts. All night long there was a constant rumble of forage, ammunition, and provision carts, fetching stores from the station. They say they have enough here for six or seven years—which does not look much like an immediate evacuation.

Saturday, December 7th.—A lovely morning after the rain. Even the poor street dogs, which appear to be more abundant than ever here, wagged their apologies for tails, shook their starved bodies, and licked one another in congratulation at once more seeing the sun shine.

We breakfasted at 8.30 a.m., and were ready for the carriage at 10 a.m. But it did not appear, and at last James got us a wretched little country vehicle, called a telika, very high, without springs, and with a sort of tilted roof, like that of a wagon, over all. There was one high step about two feet from the ground and two openings for doors, through which one was obliged to precipitate oneself head foremost on to the floor, trusting to be able to get right again when once fairly inside. There was no room to sit upright, and, with noses and knees touching, we were jolted over the most awful roads, sometimes with one wheel up in the air and the other in a deep hole, always in a sea of mud, which came over the steps. There were crowds of people, chiefly soldiers, besides carts and horses, all the way.

After leaving the consulate, we drove quickly back through the suburb of Tchergatasch, where many of the diplomats and rich people of Adrianople live, though all have a summer residence. After this came dinner, and then 'early to bed.' It proved a noisy night, for artillery and troops were moving constantly, nobody knows why or where. There has been a great exodus from Adrianople of Russian troops during the last few days.

It was impossible to sleep, and I lay and looked out of the window in the moon-light, and pictured to myself all the scenes of misery that had taken place at the station close by. Men, women, and children used to sit there for days in long lines extending nearly a mile on either side of the station, waiting for a passage by one of the few passing trains, clinging frantically to steps and buffers when carriages and cattle-trucks were full, only to be dragged away and left behind, or thrown off and killed at the first curve or sudden jerk. Carts went round every morning to carry a little coarse food, and to bring away the dead. One morning, after a severe frost and heavy snow, six cartloads of little children were carried away from among the crowds of refugees.

Sunday, December 8th.—We were called at 4 a.m., and found it very cold and dark. After a cup of hot coffee we went to the station, which was crowded with Russian soldiers. The country near Adrianople, which we had before passed in the dark, is much more interesting than that near Constantinople, which consists of nothing but bare marsh and moor land, with a few scattered villages, now, alas! burnt and abandoned. The train was very long, and full of Russian soldiers. At every station there were crowds of refugees waiting in the hope of obtaining a passage. At Koulleli-Bourgas, where we crossed a wide river, there is a branch line running up into the hills to Durcos, in the Balkans, through a country that looked quite pretty.

At Sidler-Tchiflik three men sprang on to the train just as it was starting, and clung to the carriage-doors. The guard saw them, but dared not push them off for fear of killing them, yet could not venture to stop the train on account of the delay this would have caused. He therefore beckoned to the men to creep slowly along the side of the carriages after him. It was a terrible walk, and made my blood run cold to see it. The poor men were wet, benumbed, and awkward. Each had a bundle on his shoulder—one on a stick, one on a gun, one on a sword. As they crept slowly along, hanging on for their lives, first one bundle, then another, dropped off, till at last, after an agony of suspense, they were safely landed in a cattle-truck, having lost the very little all that they possessed. A similar scene with but little variation was repeated several times in the course of our journey. At Tchor-lou, where we stopped three-quarters of an hour, the other passengers seemed to be enjoying a very good lunch. In two adjoining first-class compartments, sitting alone in solitary grandeur, were a Russian and a Turkish general officer, each on his way to inspect the troops under his command.

Constantinople was reached about 7 p.m., and we were met at the station by servants and sailors, who took our luggage straight on board.

48

OLIVE GILBREATH, 'MEN OF BOHEMIA', *HARPER'S MAGAZINE* 138, 1918–1919, 251–254

From staff-officers and from lean-muscled soldiers, the gigantic canvas of war *without* peace grew. Individually or by regiments, as soon as the opportunity offered, the Bohemians went over to the side of the Russians. One served four months in the Austrian trenches, another a year, one escaped at the end of eight days. Shuttled back and forth over Russia, sleeping on stone floors, eating sometimes (if the guard did not abscond with the funds, which he did two days out of three), bathing in wintry rivers, if at all, with never a change of clothing; their life in Russia is the old story not of Russian malice, but of Russian unpreparedness. The German prisoners often declared themselves Czech in order to receive better treatment, but the Russians could not be said in any case to have added to the luster of their hospitality.

From the fall of the old régime a new period dates for the Czechs. Prison doors swung open for the Slav as well as for the criminal, releasing them from prison, but not from suspicion. The one dirigible force for order east of the Carpathians was liberated, but they were still to eat bitter bread, for Czech regiments were forbidden, and at last, when they were formed, aeroplanes hovered over them lest they betray the country to which they had deserted. It is one of the little ironies of war of which this land of "unlimited impossibilities" is incredibly full. And more than ironical was that spectacular advance under Kerensky during the spring of 1917 from which the Allies entertained hope for a day that "Russia had still kick left in her," for the regiments which broke the German lines then and sent the enemy across the marshes were not Russians, but the suspected Czechs.

New blood temporarily stiffened the Russian army, but nothing could save it after the dismissal of discipline. It was fast breaking up, and as it crumpled the recruits from across the mountains separated themselves from the Russian soldiers and traveled south to assemble under their national leader, Professor Masaryk.

Doubtless when the men from Bohemia chose Kiev for their concentration they did not see in it one of the bloodiest scenes of the Bolshevik mania in south Russia. But such it proved to be. For a week in the early winter of 1918 the Bolsheviki bombarded it heavily, wrecking the quaint city gates and littering the streets with dumps of dead, and then they joined the Germans to march against it. The trans-Carpathian Slavs found themselves in the anomalous position of defending the rich old Russian capital against itself. And they did fight for Kiev until it was not a question of flight, but of direction and of how soon the Germans would envelop them from the north. Then they abandoned Kiev and began the hegira across Siberia.

Perhaps some day a complete account of this flight of an army across the waveless plains of south Russia and of Siberia will be rendered, and we shall understand. At present there are as many versions of the trek as there were travelers, and it is only fragmentarily—as it were, by flashes of lightning—that one sees the echelons struggling across the winter wilderness. On any question the French point of view is interesting. As General Paris, now representing France with the Czech army, told the tale in a candle-lighted drawing-room, terms stripped, it seemed a chapter from Cæsar's Gallic chronicles rather than that of a modern general.

"Flight, yes, but which direction? The west was closed. South toward the Black Sea or west over the Urals and across Siberia? We held a conference; it lasted hours in a peasant's smoky little hut. I feared treachery from the Magyar prisoners, but we decided to hazard Siberia. What else was there to do? Sixty trains were commandeered. The engines the men themselves put together as the Germans were closing in from the north. For eight days we had only a pound of bread a day. No more was possible; we were in too great danger. The first regiments got away with not too much difficulty, but every day the escape became more arduous as the Germans came nearer. The staff itself made off only in time, traveling in carts, walking. Sometimes the peasants in a village would drag us into a crowded inn to explain ourselves; it is a wonder that they did not kill us and end their suspicions. Penza and Bakhmach were the crucial places. The first trains passed Penza without trouble, but we knew that we should have to fight the Germans there and at Bakhmach. . . . I remember the first meeting with the Germans at Bakhmach. Our men were guarding a road down which came a big motor flying the Russian flag. The men stopped the motor and out stepped German officers, a tall blond colonel first. They were all shot. It was hard fighting at Bakhmach to shield the trains pulling out, and some were entangled there for three months. The Bolsheviki showed their usual bad faith. The Central Soviet had given us permission to pass, but Lenine and Trotzky soon began telegraphing the local soviets to put every hindrance in our way, to shunt us and divide us and hold the trains.

"And then came the order to disarm. To disarm! . . . You can understand that for the soldier that was a tense moment—to give up his guns, and to the Russians! Only thirty rifles were allowed to eight hundred men. We did surrender, however, except for a few hidden—you know. At one place where the guns of one of our regiments were to be turned over to the Russians, they had only to come, sign each his name, and take away a rifle. You can imagine it did not take our soldiers long to discover that. They cut the colors from their caps. Each man marched up to the officer, signed his name 'Ivan Feodorovitch,' 'Piotr Stepanovitch,' and took his rifle back again. . . . The advance regiments had no difficulty except to get trains. At Irkutsk, Professor Masaryk, chief of the National Council, started for Washington, and I came on ahead to arrange for transports to France. We came through without mishap, but the regiments following were not so lucky. It was the 26th that fought first at Irkutsk. When the train pulled into the station they were ordered to surrender all arms. The officers said it was necessary, but the men asked for fifteen minutes to decide. After five minutes, machine-guns were turned on them by orders *given in German.* The men dropped to the floor of the car like bats. Some of them crept off the train and along the ground. They killed the machine-gunners with bombs and stones and bare hands, and took the guns. In three seconds the guns were in their hands, and in fifteen minutes the whole station. They came through in safety. It was the first. From that time every regiment has had a fight at Irkutsk. Fourteen thousand came through—forty thousand are still out there somewhere. We left the sanitar train with guarantees, but we don't know. . . . There has been no news. . . . Nobody knows . . . "

"Nobody knows." These two words explain the return of the Czechs and begin the second book of the Bohemian epic.

The second book of the Bohemian epic—the opening page the clearing of Vladivostok. One reason for the return of the Czechs has been named; there was another. On guard one morning before dawn, British marines found the Bolsheviki exporting munitions to the Germans; the marines spoke no Russian, but they argued with English rifles. This was a prelude to the ultimatum to the Soviet and led to the action which overthrew the Bolsheviki, gave the most important port in the east into the hands of the Allies, and started the Czechs on their Siberian career.

The Soviet was surrounded and arrested on the morning of the 29th. By noon Bolsheviki were at a premium on the streets. At the big white staff headquarters across from the station, however, the Red Guard had concentrated for the main effort. Through a gray rain soldiers were marching in from the barracks, many without rifles, but each with a hand-grenade shining in his belt. A pallid fact on paper, hand-grenades, but they held a world of significance. The Allies had landed a patrol, but their attitude was tentative, to the immense grief of the marines. The hand-grenades meant that as the Czechs had fought their way through Siberia bare-handed, so they were taking Vladivostok and starting to the rescue of their echelons without rifles and ammunition, and also without artillery. A few Russian officers had joined them, one man in a uniform, with a civilian's hat, pumping a Lewis gun, and another, balanced on the station roof, sharpshooting, with the hat of reviving self-respect. In the main, however, it was conceded to be a Czech affair, and Vladivostok watched the professional despatch with feelings as varied as its politics. While the shops in the rear were being cleared of Bolsheviki the soldiers in gray occupied the station across the great square from the staff building. Since there was no artillery, the object was to drive the Red Guard away from the windows, so that the doors could be destroyed with hand-grenades. A face at a window and a puff of flame streaked the ominously empty square. The Lewis gun sputtered industriously. A few furtive figures tried to escape from the *krepost*, to be potted on the wet cobblestones. Once the Czechs, running across the cleared space at the sign of a white flag, were met by a treacherous bomb. Within half an hour of the time set by the officers, a grenade blew in the door and the building was rushed. A few German officers captured were marched away under British guard. Rumor pointed to a pool of blood where a deserting Czech tried to beat his brains out on the pavement; two were killed with rifle-butts. No one who saw the Czecho-Slovaks cut down their deserters can ever forget the ruthless rage of these trans-Carpathian Slavs. It was the most amazing feature of an amazing day. If a consensus of impressions could have been made they would probably have agreed that little "dove blood of the Slav" flamed in these Bohemian veins, and that there would be interesting news from the north.

By the time the long Siberian twilight closed down on the memorable Saturday, Vladivostok was non-Bolshevik. To what it was a prelude one could but wonder as one watched the soup-kitchens clattering into the great square. Soldiers squatted here and there in the fading light, tired groups. The crowd had begun to move vaguely, the dusk dimming the bright colors of their blouses and kerchiefs. The Golden Horn took down its shutters and Vladivostok went home to dinner. At the station a different scene was being enacted. Box-cars stood on the tracks, swallowing men into their interiors, as they had stood once before emitting them; row after row crawled into the lantern-lighted cars, piling up on bare planks. By the time the Russians had settled comfortably to the gaieties of "Mlle. Houp-la," the Bohemian echelons were already moving out to the north.

Within twenty-four hours the guns captured in the Vladivostok arsenal, lacking certain small but important parts while in the hands of the Bolsheviki, owing to Japanese forethought, were on the road. But in the mean time, immediate action being imperative to prevent a concentration at Nikolsk, the Czechs made their first attack without artillery. And a costly attack it was, a part of their mad heroism. Had lack of equipment held them, however, the wind and the rain of a season ago would now be whitening their bones on the plains of Russia and Siberia. They take it as a matter of course that they must capture as they go, wrest from the enemy himself the material to defeat him.

Issues, at present, are shaping rapidly in the east. The calendar travels a week overnight. Since the Czechs vanished into the north many events have occurred. The lost sanitar train has arrived from Habarovsk. The echelons have disentangled themselves, have taken Irkutsk and moved two days farther east to the corner of Lake Baikal. The scant news which comes by messenger indicates that the situation there at Baikal has developed seriously. Four thousand men are trapped without ammunition; food is to be had only from Irkutsk; railway tunnels along the road are blown in. Apparently the echelons have reached a position from which they are unable to advance, else they would move to a station two days east, where telegraphic communication might be established with Peking. But winter has advanced until it is only a few weeks away.

The Allies have come, too, since the Czechs departed, and not too soon if the echélons are not to perish. Vladivostok now takes on the atmosphere of a populous and militant Port Said. Troops are constantly departing for the front; French *casquettes* drink coffee in the little gardens; British officers are stiffly hunting the baths; "The Dollar Princess" ("*po Russkī*") plays nightly to rows of American khaki. A British transport is here from Hong-kong, a French ship from Saigon. The Japanese are here with white gloves and limousines and more troops than they care to confess. The Americans are here, not pretty, but serviceable, with mules and prairie-schooners. The railway engineers who have been playing pinochle in Nagasaki until, to quote them, they are "as jumpy as old maids," are here, living on Kerensky gold, imploring work. The Salvation Army is here. All the materials for a campaign are here in embryo, and much more will follow. From the size of the shadows, the events started by the Czecho-Slovaks are big ones. "The Queen of the East" promises to fulfil her name. The trans-Siberian— that thin line of communication between east and west, whose traffic, pouring Siberia's myriads of troops into Europe and feebly emitting *emigrés*, chronicles the history of Russia – will again see moving into Siberia the paraphernalia of war, men in khaki with modern guns, as during the first year of the conflict it saw millions of clumping gray figures with black bread under their arms, and shaggy little ponies, streaming along its length to fight for the White Czar.

What is the meaning of the Allies in Russia? No one can say with assurance. The Czechs have constantly and consistently affirmed that they have no wish to fight the Russian people, and they have, with the utmost caution, kept free from entangling alliances. The Allies have been equally definite, in their separate proclamations, declaring their intentions not to interfere in Russian internal affairs. Both by Czech and Allies, Russia has been handled with velvet gloves—assured of her territorial integrity, of her inalienable right to choose her manners and her morals, of her liberty, the color and stripe of her destiny. She has been promised everything—money, food, shoes, even commissions! She has been as delicately flattered as a woman; humored, clothed, and fed like an orphaned child; coddled like a sick man; wept with over her past; exalted for her virtues; promised a future; cursed for her sins; distrusted; pitied and held in contempt; supported; speculated upon; believed in with little visible reason, as no other nation in the world. And how will she respond?

The landing of the first troops evoked a storm of words and pamphlets; "the bourgeoisie had betrayed Russia, sold her to the foreigner." A student at the Far East Institute began an oration: "To-day England lands troops; war has begun with England."

To-day the Russian is a little tired. "What is to be done?" he asks. The stamp of the old régime is still upon him. But the mood of to-morrow?

As this leaves Vladivostok the opening of the Siberian railway to Irkutsk is practically accomplished, and if to Irkutsk, then to the Urals, since the Siberian government holds the line from Irkutsk westward. The optimist seems to have seen the situation more clearly than the pessimist. There will certainly be a strong movement to reach the Czechs in Russia fighting about Vologda and toward Archangel. And of all this two months ago there was not a sign or a vestige. To contrast the Bolshevik days with all this movement of war for saving Siberia is to have an admiration, which can hardly be exaggerated, for that disciplined, determined band who less than five months ago emerged from the steppe. What will yet be in Siberia no one knows. But whatever it is, the Czecho-Slovaks have been the motive power.

49

MARY HEATON VORSE, 'MILORAD', *HARPER'S MAGAZINE* 140, 1919–1920, 256–262

THE rain fell in Mitrovitza and thinned the streets of women and little girls, and it was as though it washed the color from the world, for the women of Mitrovitza wear trousers of orange and vests of green, while their head-dresses are saffron and pale yellow. No women in all Serbia are as brilliantly dressed as the Jewish women of Mitrovitza. They look equivocally at the men from their long eyes, for the town is a sink where the races and tribes of the Balkans meet. Here they eddy and swirl about one another; then they stream out over the roads through Albania to Montenegro. They go south to Uskub and north over the mountainous paths of the Great Retreat. Here come the Albanians from the hills in their white homespun clothes, braided boldly in black with the slash of their red sashes around their waists, while the soldiers of France and England meet those of Serbia in all the streets. Some come to Mitrovitza and see in it a great and wicked city and drink of its wickedness; and some see in it a lost and vicious little hole, a town part Turkish, part Albanian, and part Serb. For here begins the welter of the irreconcilable hates of Macedonia.

I walked past the shop where the Albanians were weaving rugs; past the bazaars, outside of which hung kerchiefs of scarlet and green and white and lemon and orange; and over the bridge, looking for bread for my journey. Turkish women, black even to their veils, hurried past me in hasty stealth. A cart drawn by water-buffalo waggled by. I stopped at the bread-shop, where the old Turk, in a well-wound turban, white stockings on his feet, sat cross-legged beside his piles of round, flat loaves.

A coal-black "madagash"—a French Colonial—his red fez on his black head, asked, in Serbian, "How much the bread, Turko?"

At a little distance a little boy stood watching me. He was dressed in rags, but so is half of Serbia. His gaze, uninsistent, speculative, and suffering, did not leave me, so I went to him and asked him if he were hungry, at which he shook his head, settled himself closer within his rags, and slopped off, the mud clinging to his big *opankas*.

I passed him again as I turned my back on the town, its strolling soldiers, its swarming boys, its tortuous byways ankle-deep in mud, and its white minarets.

The station, like all those of Turkish towns, was distant from the city and isolated as a pest-house, for the Turk feared and mistrusted the railway and kept the abomination as far away as he could.

No train was ready; no engine was in sight; nothing indicated the departure of the Uskub train but the groups of soldiers standing patiently in the rain by the track, which stopped with finality near some ruins. Some were in ragged overcoats laden with equipment-packs holding out their overcoats like bustles. Some were in mustard khaki—cloth bought from the English. Some in horizon blue, bought from the French—a nondescript, rag-tag army, bronzed, lean, formidable, and composed of gentle, innocent men.

Time passed; the slate-colored rain fell as the little engine puffed up noisily, as though to look at us, and puffed away. Groups of people laden with bundles and boxes came down the hill. They were wet and forlorn, and gradually they filled up the station-agent's room. I sat on my duffle-bag; the woman from Madnavo sat on her valise, her head in her hands, and the Turk from Mitrovitza huddled in the doorway.

The soldiers began to talk to pass the time.

"Where do you come from?"

"From Belgrade."

"On foot?"

"How else?"

"I go to Nish—"

"I have not seen my family for eight years—"

"I go to Salonique—"

A light feeling of friendship moved among us—a fresh breeze that cleansed the air, stagnant with waiting. They began to laugh. A soldier in horizon blue came up to me.

"Have you any one to carry your bags, *sestra?* No? Then I charge myself with them."

The Turk from Mitrovitza sat on his bundle and sang. The air smelled of wet clothes, of garlic, of packages of food.

The engine puffed up again; some of the soldiers climbed into the wagons. We still waited. The ragged boy I had seen in town stood on the platform. Presently he began to cry. He cried without violence, but as though the hopelessness of life had made his tears well over. The soldiers gathered around him, kind in their curiosity. "Why do you cry, *mali?*" they asked. He cried on disconsolately, without answering.

Then his story dripped out slowly, like rain falling. He raised his head and looked at the soldiers and talked without emphasis, with the manner of recounting the inevitable. There was no protest and no hope in his voice.

"He is an orphan. He has no one—he has no one at all," they reported.

The women clucked sympathetically: "Poor *mali*, poor boy!"

"He was going to Uskub to look for work, and now he has not money enough, he finds. He can get nothing to do, no place to stay in Mitrovitza."

The women rested kind eyes on him, hands went to pockets, soldiers brought out money.

"Here, *mali*—"

The boy stood looking out over the railway. He was twelve or thirteen; his grotesque rags once had been men's clothes. On his head was a battered cap. His face was brown and sharpened with hunger. His eyes were like a dog's, wistful and frightened and set far apart. The rags of his homespun coat dripped about him—his torn socks were pulled over his trousers, Serbian fashion—and on his feet were *opankas*, a sort of moccasin tied on with thongs, these, too, man's size.

He seemed so lost and so forlorn that a chill crept over us. He stood there unconscious, his gaze lost in the distance, isolated by his dirt, unattached, humble, standing a little bent, as though the weight of life were too heavy for him to bear. All at once the day was more cheerless, the station seemed the remotest place in the world. We shivered a little and moved restlessly about. We could not forget him, though he made no demands on us, did not even notice us. He did not ask our friendship or our attention, but stood there in the fading light, waiting humbly. He seemed not like a child, but a symbol of the lost children, crawling miserably over the roadways of the world, sleeping, as he had recently done, in the mud of ditches.

Our chatter flared up and died, for always our eyes went back to him and to his somber significance. I went up to him with a soldier in horizon blue who spoke French with me.

"Ask him where he comes from?"

"He come from Stenia," the soldier translated. "His father fell in the first offensive. His mother died of typhus. Then he worked for a farmer for nearly three years. He was a poor man. When his son came back he could keep the boy no longer. He paid him and told him to find work in some other place. That was soon after New-Year's. He has been looking for work for nearly two and a half months—they do not want such little boys."

He told his story monotonously, without emphasis, without protest, with very faint gestures of his grimy hands. He told it with a deadly air of indifferent matter-of-factness. A common tale.

I could not bear his isolation. I suffered from his loneliness.

"Please ask his name." I said for I felt if I knew that it would save me from his seeming to be a symbol of the desolate company of children disinherited by war.

At the soldier's question, the boy turned to me.

"Milorad Bachinin," he told me.

We straggled slowly to the train. The troops entrained in the carriage. We got into a box-car—the little group of soldiers and civilians who had made of one another the friends of an hour. We disposed ourselves on the floor; we pulled our blankets over us.

RAILWAYS AMONG THE RUINS

"*Sestra*, sit here. So you shall be out of the draft."

"*Sestra*, let me arrange your things. Are you comfortable so?"

"Gospodja Draga, draw up, draw up. Do not leave us for strangers!"

Laughter and talk. The bleak box-car became an encampment and its cold walls were warmed by friendship. The boy sat down on a bale of goods; delicacy made him withdraw himself. He was so dirty that in any other country he would be a pariah, but here no one made him feel this.

The conductor came among us encamped on the floor, perched on bales, done up in Pirot rugs, or sitting on our bags.

"Who are you traveling with?" he asked Milorad.

"With the American *sestra*," he answered, without hesitation, pointing at me.

The conductor nodded. The soldier in horizon blue smiled.

"A quick lad—children are not supposed to travel alone," he explained.

We undid valises; we opened musettes and packages and began to eat our supper. Every one remembered Milorad.

"An egg, *mali?*"

"Bread, *mali?*"

"A bit of meat, *mali?*"

He ate hungrily, smiling at me across the others, searching my eyes at each gift of food, as though to say, "I have an egg, *sestra*—bread." He must share these happinesses with me.

The night wore on. We had long since lighted our candles, and they made long shadows.

Milorad sat always on the bale of goods, isolated by misfortune. He sat relaxed, his dark eyes fixed on nothing, a forlorn picture of the fatherless. I turned away my head, and then I was conscious that he was looking at me, and we smiled across the others' heads.

"What will become of him?" asked Gospodja Draga. She asked it impersonally of the world of Serbia, of America. "What will become of Milorad Bachinin? If he were a little older—but twelve and not strong—there is little enough work now." He sat disturbingly quiet and mutely asked all of us, "What will become of Milorad Bachinin?" Will he go on from town to town, asking for work at doorways, cold, hungry, more and more beaten, more and more despairing? The train rattled on in its slow progress.

"What—will—become—of—Milorad Bachinin?"

"If I had him in Mladnova," said the soldier in horizon blue, "I would give him a home." He was dark and swift of motion, eager toward life, eager to help, eager to talk. Love of life and of laughter shone from him. "I have a little commerce in Mladnova. A store—that boy would help."

"A great help—a good thing for you," they answered.

"But how to get him back from Uskub?"

"Yes, how?" they agreed, with resignation.

"I may have to walk from Metrovitza—two hundred kilometers. He could never walk so far, poor boy!"

258

The night wore on. Some slept in abandoned attitudes at the other end of the car. Some soldiers drank too much and sang monotonously and noisily.

Milorad sat there, a hunched, grotesque figure, bobbing with fatigue; his shadow waggled about with monstrous levity in the candle-light. Suddenly I had to know what would become of Milorad Bachinin.

"Is it true?" I asked the soldier, softly, for Gospodja Draga slept. "Will you really take him?"

"If I could bring him back," he assured me. From Mitrovitza there is no railway. The back of Serbia is broken and no railway joins the north and south, so those going to Belgrade must walk or get taken by chance camions.

"I'll see you get taken by camion, the Red Cross or the English," I promised.

"Then it's settled. I take the lad." He smiled at him.

"Will you go with him?" I asked Milorad. He looked at the soldier gravely.

"I will go," he answered, but without a smile, his eyes on me.

The floor of the car became littered with people lying in the awkward abandon of sleep, as though slain on the battle-field of fatigue. The hoarse shouting of the guards brought us startled to our feet. We had arrived. We reeled out under our burdens on our unsteady feet, walking along like people hypnotized, sleep-walkers. My soldier in horizon blue carried my things.

"How shall the boy find you?" I asked.

"We'll find each other," he said, with his easy assurance. "We'll meet on the streets. Every one goes up and down the main street in Uskub."

"And does he understand where to find me?" I asked him.

He turned to Milorad. The boy looked at me very earnestly, a long look, as though he were trying to make up for his lack of words, and made his reply with his grave eyes always fixed on me. And then the station which had sucked us into its dim interior spewed us forth onto the dark streets.

I expected that he would be there waiting for me the next morning, but the street was empty of him. I thought somehow that he would find me and that he would be anxious about himself, about his clothes, for I had promised him new ones, and as to whether I had gotten transportation for him. Then I went out, down through the main street of Uskub.

There were shops where Albanians sold curded milk; shops with round Turkish bread, Greeks selling sweets that looked like poison—candy of bright green, candy of cerise. Yet the Turkish children eat them without dying. And farther, threading the crowd, are the closely veiled Turkish women, swathed in black robes; red-fezed bootblacks clamored impudently; donkeys and buffalo-carts, and the Jugo-Slav soldiers—volunteers from America—in their neat-blue uniforms. Through the shifting pattern of Turk and Christian, of Serb and Albanian, through all the multicolored rags that clad them, I searched for Milorad.

He had disappeared, and so had all the company of the night before. The soldier had gone and the woman from Mladnavo; they had gone, nor could I find one of them, although all day my eyes sought through the shifting tide of people which eddies and breaks perpetually over the bridge.

The town was empty to me and full of fear. What would become of Milorad Bachinin was my business, nor would the thought of him leave me as I went about my work in storehouse and hospital. Always my eyes sought through the crowds for his dumpy figure clad in unclean rags, and vague fears hunted through my mind. I looked for him perpetually in that little shuffling group of misery that waited, wanly hopeful, before the Red Cross headquarters.

Next morning my eyes sought for the thousandth time the group of faithful little boys perpetually waiting against the high yellow wall opposite. He was standing there, drawn apart from them, leaning against the wall, which was something adversity had taught him when it taught him that boys are cruel to misfortune. His somber eyes were fixed on the door.

I saw him before he saw me, as he stood there in an attitude of terrible patience; his arms were crossed on his breast. One could see how weary he was. He had perhaps slept all night outside the station gate and got up to wait when the first ox-cart creaked up with its load. Then he saw me and came flashing toward me; his clumsy coverings could not hide his swift beauty. The joy he felt, the darting swiftness of his lithe young body triumphed. His flight to me was like a leaping, happy animal.

"*Sestra!*"

"Where did you sleep, Milorad?"

"In a *cafana*."

"Have you eaten?"

He nodded, his eyes still on me.

"Your soldier—have you found him?"

He shook his head and spread out his hands. He had never trusted this promise; now he relinquished it with the fatality of the abandoned. My Serbian had run its short course. I called to one of our English-speaking soldiers.

"Explain this paper to him," I said. "There is a letter to the English military at Mitrovitza and one to the Americans. He is to go in the first camion of ours that comes through with his *voynik*."

Milorad nodded, folded the paper, and hid it carefully among his rags.

"He is to watch continually for his soldier." He nodded again. "This afternoon he is to come here and go with me for fresh clothes, to the Red Cross storehouse, and he is to go with me now to town."

I was leaving before light next day for Salonika, and I wished him to have something for the journey.

"*Sestra*, he says he would like to know your name," the soldier told me. Milorad repeated it carefully, as though committing to memory something precious.

He looked up at me. "My sister—*moya sestra!*" he said, and then my name. What love there was in that voice! Then we went along, Milorad repeating to himself, over and over, my first name, which was all he could remember, and then, "*Sestra—sestra—sestra*," like a song, the most caressing song in the world. It came from the center of the heart of love. He was singing it to me, so unconscious that he didn't even know that his happy lips were busy with this song of his. Some time I listened to him, while the spectacle of Uskub—its soldiers, its beggars, its Albanians, and Turks—flowed before my eyes, as though hastening to some incredible masquerade.

I changed my French money in the shop of an old Jew who had in his window gold from every land; rubles and sovereigns, Turkish coins I didn't know, and golden louis. And when I would have given Milorad this money, he held his hand up in a gesture faint, imploring, deprecating.

"Not money—not from you, my sister—only love—forget I am a beggar," the little gesture said; it was faint, protesting, lovely. He who needed all things could bear to take from me only the things of the spirit. He wished me not to think that he was a beggar.

We had a wordless battle of coaxings, of smiles, and since he could not say no to something I wished, he took it, still with his deprecating protest, and then gently, almost as with reverence, he took my hand in his and pressed it to his brown cheek.

He looked up at me and love streamed from his eyes, and the radiance of it transfigured him. He was so happy that he walked along in a sort of quiet ecstasy. He was so happy that it hurt me to look at him.

He had never wanted, he had never suffered, he had never hungered, he had never been unhappy. We exchanged swift looks full of mutual understanding. We laughed together over the droll things in the street, and wondered over the width of the river and the vastness of the town, the height of the minarets pointing their white fingers to heaven, for Milorad had never been in a big town before. He had never been happy before.

What had happened? Why were we so happy in walking down together through the harlequin crowd in Uskub streets?

I had not the answer; it came to me only with tears. Now I was happy, and my happiness had no name and no reason. I was happy with a deep content; drinking in the warmth and loveliness of the moment, not looking forward with the fear of to-morrow, with even knowledge of to-morrow cast out.

I record this as the high moment, higher even than when we got his clothes at the Red Cross store-room, walking proudly ahead of the crowd waiting for distribution.

I was so happy that I forgot during all that afternoon that I must say goodby to him that night. And then, as I called a soldier to interpret for me, it came to me as a frightful and unbelievable fact.

"Tell him that I am to go to-morrow to Salonika," I said, "and he must look for his soldier. If his soldier doesn't come, he shall stay here with the American mission."

In answer to this he had something to say. Putting his hand upon the soldier's arm, he talked to him with eager confidence. I saw pity growing in the soldier's face.

"He says it is better that he shall go with you. He says he is sure his *voynik* will not come. He says he wishes to go with his *sestra*."

A numbness came over me. What could I say to him? How could I explain? What use to tell him that I was reporting at Salonika for orders, that I might be sent to Rumania or Greece, that all this was out of my hands. I knew he would not understand, for all places were equally near and equally distant to him. He knew nothing about orders, or passports, or the thousand restrictions. He was talking again eagerly.

"He says many boys like himself have been sent to foreign countries. He says let him go with you. He will work for you. He says it is better for *you* that he goes with you!"

And I—I could do nothing but take him by the shoulders and speak to him in English and kiss him and explain again through my soldier that he must try to find the man who might take him to his home, and that the people in the Red Cross would look out for him if he did not go.

I was still stupefied with sleep when I left my home next morning. The city wore the livid face of dawn, when coming life and the approach of death have so close a resemblance. The same damp wind cut our faces that had greeted us when we arrived. The weary men and women who trickled down the street walked like somnambulists. Some drove animals which staggered as though laden with fatigue. Rain fell in a light drizzle.

We drew up to the station, and from the dusk came Milorad's swift figure. Had he waited all night? I do not know. I only know that my heart expected him. He ran to me smiling, and yet tense with anxiety. I knew what was in his mind. I knew that he thought I could not leave him since he could not leave me.

"Ask him if he has looked for his *voynik*," I asked the officer with me.

Again Milorad made that faint gesture of his—of relinquishment, of negation. He had never expected his *voynik*. He had always known that this home was illusion. He began helping the soldiers with my bags and bundles, plodding ahead, the drizzle of rain crusting his new coat in minute drops.

He clasped my hand and put it to his cheek with that lovely gesture of his as he said to me, "*Sestra, sestra!*" but I knew that my name meant, "Take me with you; I cannot leave you." He turned to the officer with me and spoke in a low voice rapidly, insistently.

"He says to let him go. He says it is better so. Do not go without him."

"Explain to him—make him understand how it is. Make him see that I'm not deserting him."

The officer talked to him earnestly, but Milorad looked only at me. Then, as our eyes held each other's, suddenly I understood both our joy and our pain. Suddenly I knew what miracle had happened to us.

I knew when he had looked at me first he had accepted me for his mother. He did not know this. He had no name for it. He had loved me when he first met me. All his being had gone out to me. Now I knew why I was so happy when we walked down Uskub streets together. We had recognized each other in the wide spaces of the world.

"Mother!" his heart had cried.

"Son!" mine had answered.

"Mother! Mother! Mother!" he had sung.

I had listened with the silent shining happiness that can never come from the song of a lover.

"I have needed you so, mother."

"I have loved you so, son."

"Mother, I looked for you in every face."

"Son, disguised in your rags, I knew you, and my heart leaped at sight of you."

We were strangers, and we did not speak each other's language, but the spiritual bond of mother and son was ours. Not a very good mother—not watchful enough, not patient enough; Milorad a boy on whom adversity had put its cramping hand, with no high courage, nor with the promise of much high endeavor—but to him the love of my heart flowed out, and in my heart were the things Milorad had found in none of the compassionate women of his own land. I loved him not for his goodness, but for his need of me, and because I must.

Now there came to him slowly the bitter knowledge that I, his mother, was leaving him to loneliness and misery. His pain welled over in tears, his sobs racked him and left him gasping. I have never seen a child feel such grief as that which bankrupted Milorad of hope. He had not believed I could go. He came to me and pleaded with me, his words rushing out in the torrent of his tears.

I did not need to know what he said; he was emptying his heart. He threw the treasure of his love before me, and his belief and his pain. People came up to comfort him. Then among the crowd came the woman from Mladnavo.

"Has his soldier not come?" she asked. "Then as I come up next week from Salonika he may come with me. Will you come with me, *mali?*"

He did not hear her; his eyes sought mine in the agony of his loss which shut out all other things. Slow tears came to the woman's eyes.

"I will be kind to him, *sestra,*" she promised.

"Listen, Milorad," I said. "Gospodya Draga will come for you next week."

He only knew I spoke to him. He only answered: "Take me with you."

The train moved. I could no longer see his face for my own tears.

He is safe; he does not walk the highways of the earth, nor sleep in ditches. He is not chased, hungry, from door to door. The woman from Mladnavo is good to him—but she is not his mother. Once by chance he encountered her; he knew her, he loved her; and for a happy moment our love flowed together. But when I look out over the implacable silence that divides us, I wonder if it would not have been better if we had not met. At night when I tuck my children in—my children, so safe, so secure—my children who have never had to weep for me, I wonder where you are, Milorad. I bless you, and I imagine you saying "*Sestra*" in your sleep.

Part 7

RUSSIAN PROLOGUES, DIALOGUES, TRAVELOGUES

50

THEÓPHILE GAUTIER, *A WINTER IN RUSSIA*, TRANS. M. M. RIPLEY (NEW YORK: H. HOLT AND COMPANY, 1874), PP. 236–242

Moscow

DELIGHTFUL as I found my life in St. Petersburg, I was still haunted with the desire to visit Moscow,—the real Russian capital, the great Muscovite city,—an undertaking which the railway renders easy.

Being now sufficiently acclimated not to dread a journey when the thermometer stands at $-12°$, when the opportunity of going to Moscow with an agreeable companion presented itself, I seized its forelock white with frost, and donned my full winter costume,—pelisse of marten, cap of beaver, furred boots coming above the knee. One sledge took my trunk, a second received my person assiduously wrapped; and here I am, in the immense railway station, waiting the hour of departure, which is set for noon, but the Russian railways do not pride themselves, as ours do, upon a chronometric punctuality. If some great personage is expected, the locomotive will moderate its ardor for some minutes, a quarter of an hour perhaps,—to give him time to arrive. Those who are going by the train are accompanied to the station by friends and relations, and the separation, when the bell strikes for the last time, never takes place without much shaking of hands, many embraces and tender words, often interrupted by tears. At times, even, the whole group take tickets, enter the carriage, and escort the departing one as far as the first station, to return by the next train. I like the custom; it seems to me a touching one; they desire to enjoy the society of their friends for yet a few moments longer, and to postpone, as long as they can, the sad moment of parting. In the faces of these mujiks—otherwise far from beautiful—a painter would have observed expressions pathetic by their simplicity. Mothers and wives, whose sons or husbands are going away—perhaps for years—in their deep and unfeigned grief, remind one of the holy women with reddened eyes and mouth contracted by suppressed sobs, that the mediæval artists represent along the way to Calvary. In divers countries have I seen inn-yards, when the diligence was leaving,—quays of embarkation,— railway-stations for departing trains,—but never, in any place, adieus so tender and so heart-breaking as those which I have witnessed in Russia.

The fitting up of railway-carriages in a country where the thermometer more than once in a winter goes down to thirty-five or forty degrees below zero, could not be expected to resemble that wherewith temperate climes are content. The hot-water tins, in use in the west of Europe, would soon contain only a block of ice, under the traveller's feet. The air rushing in through cracks around the doors and windows would introduce colds in the head, congestions, and rheumatisms. On Russian trains, many carriages united together and communicating by doors, which the travellers open or shut at will, form, so to speak, a suite of rooms, preceded by an ante-chamber and dressing-room, where the lesser articles of luggage may be placed. This ante-room opens upon a platform surrounded by a balustrade, which you reach by a stairway more convenient than the steps to our railway carriages.

Stoves, filled with wood, heat the compartment and maintain a temperature of 66° or 68°. The windows, listed with strips of felt, entirely exclude the cold air and retain the interior heat. You see, therefore, that a journey from St. Petersburg to Moscow, in the month of January, in a climate the mere mention of which makes a Parisian shudder and his teeth chatter in his head, has nothing really polar about it. You would be quite sure to suffer more in making the trip from Burgos to Valladolid, at the same time of year.

Around the sides of the first carriage runs a wide divan for the use of sleepy people and of those who are not afraid to cross their legs in Turkish fashion. I preferred the spring-seated arm-chairs with well-stuffed head-rests which are found in the second section, and installed myself comfortably in a corner one. Thus ensconsed, I seemed to myself to be, for the time, living in a house on wheels, rather than to be enduring the restraint of a public conveyance. I was at liberty to rise and walk about, to go anywhere in the compartment with the same amount of freedom enjoyed by the traveller on a steamboat,—a luxury of which one is deprived who is boxed up in a diligence, a post-chaise, or the railway carriage as it is still constructed in France.

My seat being selected, I left my travelling-bag to indicate and retain it, and, as the train was not ready to move, I walked a few steps along by the track, and the peculiar shape of the smoke-stack of the locomotive attracted my notice. It is coiffed with a vast funnel, which gives it a resemblance to those hooded chimneys that rise so picturesquely in profile above the red walls in Canaletto's Venetian pictures.

Russian locomotives are not coal-burners, like the French and those of the Western countries, but consume wood in all cases.

Logs of birch or pine are piled symmetrically upon the tender, and are renewed at stations where there are wood-yards. This makes the old peasants say that at the rate things are going in Holy Russia, they will soon be forced to pull down the log-huts to get wood to feed the stoves; but before all the forests are gone, or even all sufficiently near the railways, the explorations of engineers will have discovered some bed of anthracite or bituminous coal. This virgin soil must conceal inexhaustible wealth.

At last, the train moves off. We leave at our right, upon the old high-road, the arch of triumph of Moscow, stately and grand of outline, and we see fly past us the last houses of the city, ever more and more scattered, with their board fences, their wooden walls painted in the old Russian fashion, and their green roofs frosted with snow, for, as we leave the centre of the city behind us, the various buildings, which, in the fashionable quarters affect the styles of Berlin, Paris, and London, fall back into the national characteristics. St. Petersburg begins to disappear; but the golden cupola of St. Isaac's, the spire of the Admiralty, the pyramidal towers of the church of the Horse-Guards, the domes of starred azure and bulb-shaped tin belfries yet glitter upon the horizon, with an effect as of a Byzantine crown resting on a cushion of silver brocade. The houses of men seem to sink back into the earth, the houses of God to spring upward towards heaven.

While I was looking out, there began to appear upon the window-glass, as a result of the contrast between the cold air without and the heated air within, delicate arborizations of the color of quicksilver, which soon cross their branches, spread out in broad leaves, form a magic forest, and cover the pane so completely that the view is entirely cut off. There is certainly nothing more exquisite than these branches, arabesques, and filigrees of ice wrought with so delicate a touch by the hand of Winter. It is a bit of Northern poetry, and the imagination can discover Hyperborean mirages therein. However, after you have contemplated them for an hour, you become annoyed by this veil of white embroidery, through which one can neither see nor be seen. Your curiosity is exasperated at the idea that, behind this ground glass, a world of unknown objects is passing by, which will, perhaps, never come under your eyes again. In France, I should have lowered the glass without hesitation; in Russia, it would be perhaps a mortal imprudence so to do. Cold, the wild beast, forever lying in wait for his prey, would have stretched into the carriage his polar-bear's paw, and cuffed me, with all his claws unsheathed. In the open air, he is an enemy fierce, indeed, yet loyal and generous in his rough way; but beware of letting him within doors, for then it becomes a struggle for life; should but one of his arrows wound you in the side, it may be a long, hard struggle before you are a sound man again.

There was need, however, to do something about it; it would have been a great pity to be transported from St. Petersburg to Moscow in a box, with a milky square cut in it, through which nothing could be seen. I have not, thank Heaven! the temperament of the Englishman who had himself transported from London to Constantinople with a bandage over his eyes, removed only at the entrance of the Golden Horn, that he might enjoy suddenly, and without enfeebling transition, this splendid panorama, unrivalled in the world. Therefore, bringing my furred cap down to my eyebrows, raising the collar of my pelisse and fastening it close around me, drawing up my long boots, plunging my hands into gloves of which the thumb only is articulated—a real Samoyed costume—I made my way bravely to the platform in front of the railway carriage. An old soldier in military capote, and decorated with many medals, was there, looking out for the train, and seemed in no way inconvenienced by the temperature. A small gratification, in the shape of a silver ruble, which he did not solicit, but neither did refuse, made him obligingly turn his head towards another point of the horizon, while I lighted an excellent cigar obtained at Eliseïef's, and extracted from one of those boxes with glass sides, which exhibit the merchandise without the necessity of breaking the band which has been stamped at the custom-house.

I was soon compelled to throw away this pure Havana "*de la Vuelta de Abajo*," for though it burned at one end, it froze at the other. An agglutination of ice welded it to my lips, and every time I took it from my mouth, a bit of skin came off attached to the leaf of tobacco. To smoke in the open air with the thermometer at $-12°$, comes near being an impossibility; hence, conformity with the ukase prohibiting the out-of-door pipe or cigar is less difficult. In the present case, the scene unfolding before me was of interest enough to compensate for the small privation.

As far as the eye could see, a cold drapery of snow covered the land, leaving the undefined forms of all objects to be conjectured beneath its white folds, very much as a winding-sheet reveals the dead figure which it hides from sight. There are no longer roads, nor footpaths, nor rivers, nor any kind of demarcations. Only elevations and depressions, and those not very perceptible, in the universal whiteness. The beds of frozen streams are become only a kind of valley, tracing sinuosities through the snow, and often filled up by it. At remote intervals, clusters of rusty birch-trees, half-buried, emerge and show their naked heads. A few huts, built of logs, and loaded with snow, send up smoke, and are a stain upon the whiteness of this melancholy pall. Along the track you remark lines of brushwood planted in rows, destined to arrest in its horizontal course the white, icy dust that is moved along with frightful impetuosity by the snow-blow, that *khamsin* of the pole. It is impossible to imagine the strange, sad grandeur of this immense white landscape, offering the same aspect as does the full moon seen through a telescope. You seem to be in some planet that is dead, and is delivered over to eternal cold. The mind refuses to believe that this prodigious accumulation of snow will melt, and evaporate, or else return to the sea in the swollen currents of rivers; and that, some day, the spring will make these colorless plains green and dower-strewn. The low, overcast sky with its uniform gray, which is made yellowish by the white earth, adds to the melancholy of the landscape. A profound silence, broken only by the rumbling of the train over the rails, reigned in the solitude, for the snow deadens all sounds with its carpet of ermine. In all the wide waste there was not a person to be seen, not a trace of man or animal. The human being kept himself close behind the log-walls of his isba; the animal, deep in his lair. Only as we drew near stations, from some fold in the snow emerged sledges and kibitkas, the little dishevelled horses racing on the full gallop across country, without regard to the buried roads, and coming from some unseen village to meet the train. In our compartment there were some young men of rank going out hunting, clad for the occasion in touloupes, new and handsome, of light salmon-color, and ornamented with stitching in form of graceful arabesques. As I have before explained, the touloupe is a kind of caftan of sheepskin, the hair worn inwards, as are all furs in really cold countries. A button fastens it at the shoulder, a leather belt with plates of metal secures it around the waist. Add to this an Astrakan cap, boots of white felt, a hunting-knife at the belt, and you have a costume of truly Asiatic elegance. Although it is the mujik's costume, the noble does not hesitate to assume it under these circumstances, for there is nothing more convenient or better adapted to the climate. Furthermore, the difference between this touloupe, clean, supple, soft as a kid glove, and the soiled, greasy, shining touloupe of the mujik, is so great that no comparison between the two would be possible. These birch and pine woods that you perceive on the horizon as mere brown lines, harbor wolves and bears, and sometimes, it is said, the moose, a wild creature of the North, the pursuit of which is not without danger, and requires agile, strong, and courageous Nimrods.

51

LEO TOLSTOY, *ANNA KARENINA*, TRANS. NATHAN HASKELL DOLE (NEW YORK: THOMAS Y. CROWELL COMPANY, 1886), PP. 721–725

A BELL sounded, and some impudent young men of a flashy and vulgar appearance passed before her. Then Piotr, in his livery and top-boots, with his dull, good-natured face, crossed the waiting-room, and came up to escort her to the cars. The noisy men about the door stopped talking while she passed out upon the platform; then one of them made some remark to his neighbor, which was apparently an insult. Anna mounted the high steps, and sat down alone in the compartment on the dirty sofa which once had been white, and laid her bag beside her on the springy seat. Piotr raised his gold-laced hat, with an inane smile, for a farewell, and departed. The saucy conductor shut the door. A woman, deformed, and ridiculously dressed up, followed by a little girl laughing affectedly, passed below the car-window. Anna looked at her with disgust. The little girl was speaking loud in a mixture of Russian and French.

"That child is grotesque and already self-conscious," thought Anna; and she seated herself at the opposite window of the empty apartment, to avoid seeing the people.

A dirty, hunchbacked *muzhik* passed close to the window, and examined the car-wheels: he wore a cap, from beneath which could be seen tufts of dishevelled hair. "There is something familiar about that hump-backed *muzhik*," thought Anna; and suddenly she remembered her nightmare, and drew back frightened towards the car-door, which the conductor was just opening to admit a lady and gentleman.

"Do you want to get out?"

Anna did not answer, and under her veil no one could see the terror which paralyzed her. She sat down again. The couple took seats opposite her, and cast stealthy but curious glances at her dress. The husband and wife were obnoxious to her. The husband asked her if she objected to smoking,—evidently not for the sake of smoking, but as an excuse for entering into conversation with her. Having obtained her permission, he remarked to his wife in French that he felt even more inclined to talk than to smoke. They exchanged stupid remarks, with the hope of attracting Anna's attention, and drawing her into the conversation. Anna clearly saw how they bored each other, how they hated each other. It was impossible not to hate such painful monstrosities. The second gong sounded, and was followed by the rumble of baggage, noise, shouts, laughter. Anna saw so clearly that there was nothing to rejoice at, that this laughter roused her indiguation, and she longed to stop her ears. At last the third signal was given, the train started, the locomotive whistled, and the gentleman crossed himself. "It would be interesting to ask him what he meant by that," thought Anna, looking at him angrily. Then she looked by the woman's head out of the car-window at the people standing and walking on the platform. The car in which Anna sat moved past the stone walls of the station, the switches, the other cars. The motion became more rapid: the rays of the setting sun slanted into the car-window, and a light breeze played through the slats of the blinds.

Forgetting her neighbors, Anna breathed in the fresh air, and took up again the course of her thoughts.

"*Da!* What was I thinking about? I cannot imagine any situation in which my life could be any thing but one long misery. We are all dedicated to unhappiness: we all know it, and only seek for ways to deceive ourselves. But when you see the truth, what is to be done?"

"Reason was given to man, that he might avoid what he dislikes," remarked the woman, in French, apparently delighted with her sentence.

The words fitted in with Anna's thought.

"To avoid what he dislikes," she repeated; and a glance at the handsome-faced man, and his thin better half, showed her that the woman looked upon herself as a misunderstood creature, and that her stout husband did not contradict this opinion, but took advantage of it to deceive her. Anna, as it were, read their history, and looked into the most secret depths of their hearts; but it was not interesting, and she went on with her reflections.

"Yes, it is very unpleasant to me, and reason was given to avoid it: therefore, it must be done. Why not extinguish the light when it shines on things disgusting to see? But how? Why does the conductor keep hurrying through the car? Why does he shout? Why are there people in this car? Why do they speak? What are they laughing at? It is all false, all a lie, all deception, all vanity and vexation."

When the train reached the station, Anna followed the other passengers, and tried to avoid too rude a contact with the bustling crowd. She hesitated on the platform, trying to recollect why she had come, and to ask herself what she meant to do. All that seemed to her possible before to do, now seemed to her difficult to execute, especially amid this disagreeable crowd. Now the porters came to her, and offered her their services; now some young men, clattering up and down the platform, and talking loud, observed her curiously; and she knew not where to take refuge. Finally, it occurred to her to stop an official, and ask him if a coachman had not been there with a letter for Count Vronsky.

"The Count Vronsky? Just now some one was here. He was inquiring for the Princess Sorokina and her daughter. What kind of a looking man is this coachman?"

Just then Anna espied the coachman Mikhaïl, rosy and gay in his elegant blue livery and watch-chain, coming towards her, and carrying a note, immensely proud that he had fulfilled his commission.

Anna broke the seal, and her heart stood still as she read the carelessly written lines:—

"I am very sorry that your note did not find me in Moscow. I shall return at ten o'clock."

"Yes, that is what I expected," she said to herself, with a sardonic smile.

"Very good, you can go home," she said to Mikhaïl. She spoke the words slowly and gently, because her heart beat so that she could scarcely breathe or speak.

"No, I will not let you make me suffer so," thought she, addressing with a threat, not Vronsky so much as the thought that was torturing her; and she moved along the platform. Two chamber-maids waiting there turned to look at her, and made audible remarks about her toilet. "Just in style," they said, referring to her lace. The young men would not leave her in peace. They stared at her, and passed her again and again, making their jokes so that she should hear. The station-master came to her, and asked if she was going to take the train. A lad selling *kvas* did not take his eyes from her.

"*Bozhe moï!* where shall I fly?" she said to herself.

When she reached the end of the platform, she stopped. Some women and children were there, talking with a man in spectacles, who had probably come to the station to meet them. They, too, stopped, and turned to see Anna pass by. She hastened her steps. A truck full of trunks rumbled by, making the floor shake so that she felt as if she were on a moving train.

Suddenly she remembered the man who was run over on the day when she met Vronsky for the first time, and she knew then what was in store for her. With light and swift steps she descended the stairway which led from the pump at the end of the platform down to the rails, and stood very near the train, which was slowly passing by. She looked under the cars, at the chains and the brake, and the high iron wheels, and she tried to estimate with her eye the distance between the fore and back wheels, and the moment when the middle would be in front of her.

"There," she said, looking at the shadow of the car thrown upon the black coal-dust which covered the sleepers, "there, in the centre, he will be punished, and I shall be delivered from it all,—and from myself."

Her little red travelling-bag caused her to lose the moment when she could throw herself under the wheels of the first car: she could not detach it from her arm. She awaited the second. A feeling like that she had experienced once, just before taking a dive in the river, came over her, and she made the sign of the cross. This familiar gesture called back to her soul, memories of youth and childhood. Life, with its elusive joys, glowed for an instant before her, but she did not take her eyes from the car; and when the middle, between the two wheels, appeared, she threw away her red bag, drawing her head between her shoulders, and, with outstretched hands, threw herself on her knees under the car. She had time to feel afraid. "Where am I? What am I doing? Why?" thought she, trying to draw back; but a great, inflexible mass struck her head, and threw her upon her back. "Lord, forgive me all!" she murmured, feeling the struggle to be in vain. A little *muzhik* was working on the railroad, mumbling in his beard. And the candle by which she read, as in a book, the fulfilment of her life's work, of its deceptions, its grief, and its torment, flared up with greater brightness than she had ever known, revealing to her all that before was in darkness, then flickered, grew faint, and went out forever.

52

THE PHOTOGRAPHY OF SERGEI MIKHAILOVICH PROKUDIN-GORSKII (1863–1944), PROKUDIN-GORSKII COLLECTION. LIBRARY OF CONGRESS PRINTS AND PHOTOGRAPHS DIVISION. WASHINGTON D.C.

Figure 52.1 Steam Engine with Prokudin-Gorskii carriage in background. 1910.

Figure 52.2 On the handcar outside Petrozavodsk on the Murmansk railway. 1915.

Figure 52.3 Uneven tracks near the Ladva Station on Murmansk railway. 1915.

Figure 52.4 Bashkir Switchman. 1910.

Figure 52.5 Peasant Girls of the Russian Empire. 1909.

Figure 52.6 Bashkir woman in a folk costume. 1910.

Figure 52.7 Catholic Armenian Women in customary dress. 1905–1915.

Figure 52.8 Georgian women in holiday attire in the park of Borzhom. 1905–1915.

53

MAURICE BARING, *RUSSIAN ESSAYS AND STORIES*, SECOND ED. (LONDON: METHUEN, 1909), PP. 1–24, 52–55, 63–70

A journey in the north

I STARTED at night. The battle for a place in the third-class carriage was fought and won for me by a porter. A third-class carriage in Russia is not at all uncomfortable if you have a thick blanket, because every passenger has a right to the whole length of a seat. Three people can sit on the seat but only one can lie on it. The other two lie in berths above you or below you, as the case may be. At the end of the seat is a passage, and then there are further seats stretched horizontally across the windows. The seats are made of wood, and if you have a thick blanket and a pillow they are quite as comfortable as any other bed.

The differences between railway carriages in Russia and in England is that the Russian carriage is broader and bigger. Every carriage (whatever the class) is a corridor carriage. The first class is divided into separate compartments, but in the second and third class there is no partition and no doors dividing the corridor from the seats occupied by the passengers.

When you first step into the third-class carriage it is like entering pandemonium. It is almost dark, save for a feeble candle that gutters peevishly over the door, and all the inmates are yelling and throwing their boxes and baskets and bundles about. This is only the process of installation; it all quiets down presently, and everybody is seated with his bed unfolded, if he has one, his luggage stowed away, his provisions spread out, as if he had been living there for years and meant to remain there for many years to come.

This particular carriage was full. The people in it were workmen going home for the winter, peasants, merchants, and mechanics. Opposite to my seat were two workmen (painters), and next to them a peasant with a big grey beard. Sitting by the farther window was a well-dressed mechanic. The painter lighted a candle and stuck it on a small movable table that projected from my window; he produced a small bottle of vodka from his pocket, a kettle for tea, and some cold sausage, and general conversation began. The guard came to tell the people who had come to see their friends off—there were numbers of them in the carriage, and they were most of them drunk—to go. The guard looked at my ticket for Vologda and asked me where I was ultimately going to. I said "Viatka," upon which the mechanic said: "So am I; we will go together and get our tickets together at Vologda." The painter and the mechanic engaged in conversation, and it appeared that they both came from Kronstadt. The painter had worked there for twenty years, and he cross-questioned the mechanic with evident pleasure, winking at me every now and then. The mechanic went into the next compartment for a moment, and the painter then said to me with glee: "He is lying; he says he has worked in Kronstadt, and he doesn't know where such and such things are." The mechanic came back. "Who is the Commandant at Kronstadt?" asked the painter. The mechanic evidently did not know, and gave a name at random. The painter laughed triumphantly and said that the Commandant was some one else. Then the mechanic volunteered further information to show his knowledge of Kronstadt; he talked of another man who worked there, a tall man; the painter said that the man was short. The mechanic said that he was employed in the manufacture of shells. They talked of the disorders at Kronstadt last year. The painter said that he and his son lay among cabbages while the fighting was going on. He added that the matter had nearly ended in the total destruction of Kronstadt. "God forbid," said the peasant sitting next to me. No sympathy was expressed with the mutineers. The painter at last told the mechanic that he had lived for twenty years at Kronstadt, and that he, the mechanic, was a liar. The mechanic protested feebly. He was an obvious liar, but why he told these lies I have no idea. Perhaps he was not a mechanic at all. Possibly he was a spy. He professed to be a native of a village near Viatka, and declared that he had been absent for six years (the next evening he said twelve years).

From this question of disorders at Kronstadt the talk veered, I forget how, to the topic of the Duma. "Which Duma?" some one asked; "the town Duma?" "No, the State Duma," said the mechanic; "it seems they are going to have a new one." "Nothing will come of it," said the painter; "people will not go" (he meant the voters). "No, they won't go," said the peasant, cutting the air with his hand (a gesture common to nearly all Russians of that class), "because they know now that it means being put in prison." "Yes," said the painter, "they are hanging everybody." And there was a knowing chorus of "They won't go and vote; they know better." Then the mechanic left his seat and sat down next to the painter and said in a whisper: "The Government—" At that moment the guard came in; the mechanic stopped abruptly, and when the guard went out the topic of conversation had been already changed. I heard no further mention of the Duma during the whole of the rest of the journey to Vologda. The people then began to prepare to go to sleep, except the peasant, who told me that he often went three days together without sleep, but when he did sleep it was a business to wake him. He asked me if his bundle of clothes was in my way. "We are a rough people," he said, "but we know how not to get in the way. I am not going far." I was just going to sleep when I was wakened by a terrific noise in the next compartment. Some one opened the door and the following scraps of shouted dialogue were audible. A voice: "Did you say I was drunk or did you not?" Second voice (obviously the guard): "I asked for your ticket." First voice: "You said I was drunk. You are a liar." Second voice: "You have no right to say I am a liar. I asked for your ticket." First voice: "You are a liar. You said I was drunk. I will have you discharged." This voice then recited a long story to the public in general. The next day I ascertained that the offended man was a lawyer, one of the "bourgeoisie" (a workman explained to me), and that the guard had, in the dark, asked him for his ticket, and then as he made no sign of life had pinched his foot; this having proved ineffectual, he said that the man was drunk; whereupon the man started to his feet and became wide awake in a moment. Eventually a gendarme was brought in, a "protocol" was drawn up in which both sides of the story were written down, and there, I expect, the matter will remain until the Day of Judgment.

I afterwards made the acquaintance of two men in the next compartment; they were dock labourers and their business was to load ships in Kronstadt. They were exactly like the people whom Gorki describes. One of them gave me a complete description of his mode of life in summer and winter. In summer he loaded ships; in winter he went to a place near Archangel and loaded carts with wood; when the spring came he went back, by water, to St. Petersburg. He asked me what I was. I said that I was an English correspondent. He asked then what I travelled in. I said I was not that kind of correspondent but a newspaper correspondent. Here he called a third friend, who was sitting near us, and said, "Come and look; there is a correspondent here. He is an English correspondent." The friend came—a man with a red beard and a loose shirt with a pattern of flowers on it. "I don't know you," said the new man. "No; but let us make each other's acquaintance," I said. "You can talk to him," explained the dock labourer; "we have been talking for hours. Although he is plainly a man who has received higher education." "As to whether he has received higher or lower education we don't know," said the friend, "because we haven't yet asked him." Then he paused, reflected, shook hands, and exclaimed: "Now we know each other." "But," said the dock labourer, "how do you print your articles? Do you take a printing press with you when you go, for instance, to the north like you are doing now?" I remarked that they were printed in London, and that I did not have to print them myself. "Please send me one," he said; "I will give you my address." "But it's written in English," I answered. "You can send me a translation in Russian," he retorted.

"English ships come to Kronstadt, and we load them. The men on board do not speak Russian, but we understand each other. For instance, we load, and their inspector comes. We call him 'inspector' (I forget the Russian word he used, but it was something like skipador), they call him the 'Come on.' The 'Come on' comes, and he says 'That's no good' (niet dobrò), he means not right (nié harosho), and then we make it right. And when their sailors come we ask them for matches. When we have food, what we call 'coshevar,' they call it 'all right.' And when we finish work, what we call 'shabash' (it means "all over"), they call 'Seven o'clock.' They bring us matches that light on anything," and here he produced a box of English matches and lit a dozen of them just to show. "When we are ragged, they say, 'No clothes, plenty vodka,' and when we are well dressed, they say, 'No plenty vodka, plenty clothes.' Their vodka," he added, "is very good." Then followed an elaborate comparison of the wages and conditions of life of Russian and English workmen. Another man joined in, and being told about the correspondent, said: "I would like to read your writings, because we are a 'gray' people (*i.e.* a rough people), and we read only the *Pieterbourski Listok*, which is, so to speak, a 'black gang' newspaper. Heaven knows what is happening in Russia. They are hanging, shooting and bayoneting every one." And he went away. The dock labourer went on for hours talking about the "Come on," the "All right," and the "Seven o'clock."

Then I went back to my berth and slept, till the dock labourer came and fetched me and said that I had to see the soldiers. I went into the next compartment, and there were two soldiers; one was dressed up, that is to say he had put on spectacles and a pocket-handkerchief over his head, and was giving an exhibition of mimicry, of recruits crying as they left home, of mothers-in-law, and other stock jokes. It was funny, and it ended in general singing. A sailor came to look on. He was a noncommissioned officer, and he told me in great detail how the Sveaborg mutiny had been put down. He said that the loyal sailors had been given 150 roubles (£15) a-piece to fight. I think he must have been exaggerating. At the same time he expressed no sympathy with the mutineers. He said that rights were all very well for countries like that of the Finns. But in Russia they only meant disorders, and as long as the disorders lasted Russia would be a feeble country. He had much wanted to go to the war, but had not been able to do so. In fact, he was thoroughly loyal and *bien pensant.*

We arrived at Vologda Station some time in the evening. The station was crowded with peasants. While I was watching the crowd a drunken peasant entered and asked everybody to give him ten kopecks. Then he caught sight of me and said that he was quite certain I would give him ten kopecks. I did, and he danced a kind of wild dance and finally collapsed on the floor. A man was watching these proceedings, a fairly respectably dressed man in a pea-jacket. He entered into conversation with me, and said that he had just come back from Manchuria, where he had been employed at Mukden Station. "In spite of which," he added, "I have not yet received a medal." I said that I had also been in Manchuria. He said he lived twenty versts up the line, and came to the station to look at the people – it was so amusing. "Have you any acquaintances here?" he asked. I said "No." "Then let us go and have tea." I was willing, and we went to the tea-shop, which was exactly opposite the station. "Here," said the man, "we will talk of what was, of what is, and of what is to be." As we were walking in a policeman who was standing by the door whispered in my ear, "I shouldn't go in there with that *gentleman.*" "Why?" I asked. "Well, he's not quite reliable," he answered in the softest of whispers. "How?" I asked. "Well, he killed a man yesterday and then robbed him," said the policeman. So then I hurriedly expressed my regret to my acquaintance, and said that I must at all costs return to the station. "The policeman has been lying to you," said the man. "It's a lie; it's only because I haven't got a passport." (This was not exactly a recommendation in itself.) I went into the first-class waiting-room. The man came and sat down next to me, and now that I examined his face I saw that he had the expression and the stamp of countenance of a born thief. One of the waiters came and told him to go, and he flatly refused, and the waiter made a low bow to him. Then gently but firmly I advised him to go away, as it might lead to trouble. He finally said: "All right, but we shall meet in the train, in liberty." He went away, but he sent an accomplice, who stood behind my chair, and who also had the expression of a thief.

After waiting for several hours I approached the train for Yaroslav. Just as I was getting in a small boy came up to me and said in a whisper, "The policeman sent me to tell you that the man is a well-known thief, that he robs people every day, and that he gets into the train, even into the first-class carriages, and robs people, and he is after you now." I entered a first-class carriage and told the guard there was a thief about. I had not been there long before the accomplice arrived and began walking up and down the corridor. But the guard, I am happy to say, turned him out instantly, and I saw nothing more of the thief and of his accomplice.

A railway company director, or rather a man who was arranging the purchase of a line, got into the carriage and began at once to harangue against the Government and say that the way in which it had changed the election law was a piece of insolence and would only make everybody more radical. Then he told me that life in Yaroslav was simply intolerable owing to the manner in which all newspapers and all free discussion had been stopped. We arrived at Yaroslav on the next morning. I went on to Moscow in a third-class carriage. The train stopped at every small station, and there was a constant flow of people coming and going. An old gentleman of the middle class sat opposite to me for a time, and read a newspaper in an audible whisper. Whenever he came to some doings of the Government he said, "Disgraceful, disgraceful!"

Later on in the day a boy of seventeen got into the train. He carried a large box. I was reading a book by Gogol, and had put it down for a moment on the seat. He took it up and said, "I very much like reading books." I asked him how he had learnt. He said he had been at school for one year, and had then learnt at home. He could not stay at school as he was the only son, his father was dead, and he had to look after his small sisters; he was a stone quarrier and life was very hard. He loved reading. In winter the moujiks came to him and he read aloud to them. His favourite book was called *Ivan Mazeppa*. What that work may be I do not know. I gave him my Gogol. I have never seen any one so pleased. He began to read it—at the end—then and there, and said it would last for several evenings. When he got out he said, "I will never forget you," and he took out of his pocket a lot of sunflower seeds and gave them to me. As we neared Moscow the carriage got fuller and fuller. Two peasants had no railway tickets. One of them asked me if I would lend my ticket to him to show the guard. I said, "With pleasure, only my ticket is for Moscow and yours is for the next station." When the guard came one of the peasants gave him 30 kopecks. "That is very little for two of you," the guard said. They had been travelling nearly all the way from Yaroslav; but finally he let them be. We arrived at Moscow in the evening.

While talking with a person who had had a lot to do with the workmen in Moscow, I was told that they had been much demoralised by the extreme Revolutionary Party, and that now they preferred doing nothing and living at the expense of others to working. "The other night," my informant told me, "a friend of mine, a hospital nurse, was waked at midnight by two workmen whom she knew well, and had always known to be most respectable men. 'What do you want?' she asked. 'We have come for Brownings,' they said (Colt pistols). 'I haven't any Brownings,' she said. 'Are you not afraid some other hooligans might come and rob you?' they asked. 'No,' she answered; 'but what do you want Brownings for?' 'We are going out *expropriating*,' they said, as quietly as if they had remarked that they were going to their dinner. She then argued with them until four in the morning, and saw that in any case they did not go out expropriating on that night." But this word "expropriation" put into vogue by the revolutionaries, has had a disastrous effect on the working classes, who think they have only to stretch out their hands and take by right anybody else's property.

I travelled back to St. Petersburg in a third-class carriage, which was full of recruits. "They sang all the way (as Jowett said about the poetical but undisciplined undergraduate whom he drove home from a dinner party) bad songs,— very bad songs." Not quite all the way, however. They were like schoolboys going to a private school, putting on extra assurance. In the railway carriage there was a Zemstvo "Feldsher," a hospital assistant who had been all through the war. We talked of the war, and while we were discussing, a young peasant who was in the carriage joined in and startled us by his sensible and acute observations on the war. "There's a man," said the Feldsher to me, "who has a good head. And it is sheer natural cleverness. That's what a lot of the young peasants are like. And what will become of him? If only these people could be developed!" A little later I began to read a small book. "Are you reading Lermontov?" asked the Feldsher. "No," I answered, "I am reading Shakespeare's Sonnets." "Ah," he said with a sigh, "you are evidently not a married man, but perhaps you are engaged to be married?"

Just as I was preparing to sleep, the guard came and began to search the corners and the floor of the carriage with a candle as if he had dropped a pin or a penny. He explained that there were twelve recruits in the carriage, but that an extra man had got in with them and that he was looking for him. He then went away. Thereupon one of the recruits explained to me that the man was under one of the seats and hidden by boxes, as he wished to go to St. Petersburg without a ticket. I went to sleep. But the guard came back and turned me carefully over to see if I was the missing man. Then he began to look again in the most unlikely places for a man to be hid. He gave up the search twice, but the hidden man could not resist putting out his head to see what was happening, and before he could get it back the guard coming in at that moment caught sight of him. The man was turned out, but he got into the train again, and the next morning it was discovered that he had stolen one of the recruits' boxes and some article of property from nearly everybody in the carriage, including hats and coats. This he had done while the recruits slept, since when they stopped singing and went to sleep they slept soundly. Later in the night a huge and old peasant entered the train and crept under the seat opposite to me. The guard did not notice him, and after the tickets had been collected from the passengers who got in at that station the man crept out, and lay down on one of the higher berths. He remained there nearly all night, but at one of the stations the guard said: "Is there no one for this station?" and looking at the peasant, added: "Where are you for, old man?" The man mumbled in pretended sleep. "Where is your ticket?" asked the guard. No answer. At last when the question had been repeated thrice, he said: "I am a poor, little, old man." "You haven't got a ticket," said the guard. "Get out, devil, you might lose me my place—and I a married man. Devil! Devil! Devil!" "It is on account of my extreme poverty," said the old man, and he was turned out.

The next morning I had a long conversation with the young peasant who, the Feldsher said, had brains. I asked him, among other things, if he thought the Government was right in relying on what it calls the innate and fundamental conservatism of the great mass of the Russian people. "If the Government says that the whole of the peasantry is Conservative it lies," he said. "It is true that a great part of the people is rough—uneducated—but there are many who know. The war opened our eyes. You see, the Russian peasant is accustomed to be told by the authorities that a glass (taking up my tumbler) is a man, and to believe it. The Army is on the side of the Government. At least it is really on the side of the people, but it feels itself helpless. The soldiers are afraid of being punished. If they could act together like they did at Kharkov this summer (a regiment mutinied there and all the troops sent to quell the mutiny joined the mutineers) all would be over in a day—and the Government will never yield except to force. There is nothing to be done." And we talked of other things. The recruits joined in the conversation, and I offered a small meat patty to one of them, who said: "No, thank you. I am greatly satisfied with you as it is, without your giving me a meat patty."

The theft which had taken place in the night was discussed from every point of view. "We took pity on him and we hid him," they said, "and he robbed us." They spoke of it without any kind of bitterness or grievance, and nobody said, "I told you so." Then we arrived at St. Petersburg.

Down the Volga

ON the way to Ribinsk my carriage was occupied by a party of workmen, including a carpenter and a wheelwright, who were going to work on somebody's property in the government of Tver; they did not know whose property, and they did not know whither they were going. They were under the authority of an old man who came and talked to me, because, he said, the company of the youths who were with him was tedious. He told me a great many things, but as he was hoarse and the train made a rattling noise, I could not hear a word he said. There were also in the carriage two Tartars and a small boy about thirteen years old, who had a domineering character and put himself in charge of the carriage. The discomfort of travelling third class in Russia does not consist in the accommodation, but in the fact that one is constantly waked during the night by passengers coming in and by the guard asking for one's ticket. The small boy with the domineering character—he wore an old military cap on the back of his head as a sign of strength of purpose—contributed in no small degree to the general discomfort. He apparently was in no need of sleep, and he went from passenger to passenger telling them where they would have to change and where they would have to get out, and offering to open the window if needed. I had a primitive candlestick made of a candle stuck into a bottle; it fell on my head just as I went to sleep, so I put it on the floor and went to sleep again. But the small boy came and waked me and told me that my bottle was on the floor, and that he had put it back again. I thanked him, but directly he was out of sight I put it back again on the floor, and before long he came back, waked me a second time,—and told me that my candlestick had again fallen down. This time I told him, not without emphasis, to leave it alone, and I went to sleep again. But the little boy was not defeated; he waked me again with the information that a printed advertisement had fallen out of the book I had been reading, on to the floor. This time I told him that if he waked me again I should throw him out of the window.

Later in the night a tidy-looking man of the middle class entered the carriage with his wife. They began to chatter, and to complain of the length of the benches, the officious boy with the domineering character lending them his sympathy and advice. This went on till one of the Tartars could bear it no longer, and he cried out in a loud voice that if they wanted beds six yards long they had better not travel in a train, and that they were making everybody else's sleep impossible. I blessed that Tartar unawares, and after that there was peace.

The comfort of travelling third class in Russia is that there is always tea to be had. One would need the pen of Charles Lamb to sing the praises of Russian tea. The difference between our tea and Russian tea is not that Russian tea is weaker or that it has lemon in it. I have heard Englishmen say sometimes: "I don't want any of your exquisite Russian tea; I want a good cup of strong tea." This is as if you were to say: "I don't want any of your soft German music; I want some nice loud English music." It is a question of kind; not of degree. You can have tea in Russia as strong as you like. The difference is not in the strength, but in the flavour and in the fact that it is always made with boiling water, and is always fresh. But if you put a piece of lemon into a strong cup of Ceylon tea and think that the result is Russian tea you are mistaken. Russian tea is an exquisitely refreshing drink, and I sometimes wonder whether tea in England in the eighteenth century, the tea sung of by Pope and of which Dr. Johnson drank thirty-six cups running, was not probably identical with Russian tea. It certainly was not Ceylon tea.

Towards ten o'clock in the morning we arrived at Ribinsk, and there I embarked on a steamer to go down the Volga as far as Nijni-Novgorod. I took a first-class ticket and received a clean deck cabin, containing a leather sofa (with no blankets or sheets) and a washing-stand with a fountain tap. We started at two o'clock in the afternoon. There were few passengers on board.

It is a pungent and aromatic incense which pervades the whole atmosphere; warm and delicious and filled with the whole essence of summer. It is intoxicating and comes over one like a great wave, a breath of Elysium; a message, as it were, from the great white fields. And the night with its web of stars, and the dark waters, and the thin line of the far-off banks, make one once more lose all sense of reality. One has reached another world, the nether-world perhaps; one breathes "The scent of alien meadows far away," and one feels as if one were sailing down the river of oblivion to the harbours of Proserpine. And this wonderful sweetness comes, I ascertained, from the new-mown hay, the mowing of which takes place late here. The hay lies in great masses over the steppes, embalming the midnight air and turning the world into paradise.

In reaching Astrakan one is plunged into the atmosphere of the East. On the quays there is an infinite quantity of booths containing every kind of fruit and a coloured herd of people living in the dust and the dirt; splendidly squalid, noisy as parrots, and busy doing nothing, like wasps. The railway to Astrakan is not yet finished, so one is obliged to return to Tzaritsin by steamer if one wishes to get back to the centre of Russia. I pursued this course; and from Tzaritsin took the train for Tambov. The train started from Tzaritsin at two o'clock in the morning; I arrived at the station at midnight, and at this hour the station was crammed with people. Imagine a huge high waiting-room with three tables d'hôte parallel to each other in the centre of it; at one end of the hall a buffet; on the sides of it under the windows are tables and long seats padded with leather, partitioned off and forming open cubicles. These seats are always occupied, and the occupants go to bed on them, wrapped up in blankets, and propped up by pillows, bags, rugs, baskets, kettles, and other impedimenta. The whole of this refreshment hall is filled with sleeping figures. There are people lying asleep on the window sills and others on chairs placed together. Some merely lay their heads on the table d'hôte, and fall into a profound slumber. It is like the scene in "The Sleeping Beauty in the Wood," when sleep overtook the inhabitants of the castle. There are a bookstall and a newspaper kiosk. The bookstall contains—as usual—the works of Jerome K. Jerome and Conan Doyle, some translations of French novels, some political pamphlets, a translation of John Morley's *Compromise*, and an essay on Ruskin— a strange medley of literary food. At the newspaper kiosk the newsvendor is so busily engrossed in reading out a story which had just appeared in the newspapers of how a saintly peasant killed a baby because he thought it was the Antichrist, that it is impossible to get him to pay any attention to one. He is reading out the story to an audience consisting of the policeman, one of the porters, and a kind of sub-guard. The story is, indeed, a curious one, and has caused a considerable stir; and I intend to relate it at a future date.

The journey to Tambov was long; in my carriage was a railway official who drank tea, ate apples, and sighed over the political condition of the country. Everything was as bad as could be. "It is a heavy business," he said, "living in Russia now." Then, after some reflection, he added: "But, perhaps in other countries, in England for instance, people sometimes find fault with the Government." I told him they did little else. He then took a large roll out of a basket, and, after he had been munching it for some time, he said: "After all there is no country in the world where such good bread can be got as this." And this seemed to console him greatly.

The sunflower season has arrived. Sunflowers are grown in great quantities in Russia, not for ornamental or decorative purposes but for utilitarian purposes. They are grown for the oil that is in them; but besides being useful in many ways they form an article of food. You pick the head of the sunflower and eat the seeds. You bite the seed, spit out the husk, and eat the kernel, which is white and tastes of sunflower. Considerable skill is needed when cracking the husk and spitting it out to leave the kernel intact. This habit is universal among the lower classes in Russia. It occupies a human being like smoking, and it is a pleasant adjunct to contemplation. It is also conducive to untidiness. Nothing is so untidy in the world as a room or a platform littered with sunflower seeds. All platforms in Russia are thus littered at this time of year.

Another slight episode which gave me food for reflection happened in the train on a small line between the town of Kharkov and a neighbouring village. I was going to the town of Kharkov for the day; it was only half an hour's journey. I was in a third-class carriage; there were not many passengers, and most of them were railway guards off duty, two peasants, a soldier, and a monk. The monk had no sooner entered the carriage than he began a theological discussion. Now, as soon as the train started, although I was sitting quite close, I could not unfortunately follow the intricacies of his argument for the noise made by the train, but whenever the train stopped at a station his words were plain. And the drift of the matter was this: that all the passengers in the carriage were uniting to express to him in forcible language that priests in general, and monks still more (and himself in particular), were lazy, worthless, good-for-nothing scoundrels, and deceivers into the bargain. The soldier said, and his words received universal approval, that every one who was not a born fool knew that there was one God, the same for everybody, and that all men were equal before Him, and that consequently there could be only one real religious faith (namely, a belief in God), and that all the rest was the invention of priests. By "the rest" it subsequently became plain that he meant the Devil and the tenets of the Orthodox Church in general and of any other Churches. The monk, on the other hand, said that the Devil was intensely real, and that every man was followed by angels, who were constantly fighting the Devil for the soul of the man. Now, the soldier, and three guards off duty who were taking part in this discussion, starting from the premise that there is only one God, one faith which consists in the belief in this one God, and that all priests are liars, worried the monk with questions and attacked him in every possible manner. They accused him of begging in the first place; they would be ashamed of doing such a thing, they said. Then the soldier asked him if he had seen the Devil. The monk said, "Yes, often." "Where is he?" said the soldier. "It would be most interesting to see him."

Then when the monk stood up for the Orthodox faith the soldier said: "You say it is the only faith. You lie, because I have been told there are any number of other Churches, and each of them says its faith is the true one. For instance, the Jews have an entirely different faith, and this proves that all priests are liars; because God is the same for everybody."

At last the monk said that everybody attacked him and nobody stuck up for him, and he retired into another corner of the carriage, followed by the soldier, who went on with the argument, and afterwards repeated his main thesis to me separately, namely, that all priests were deceivers, because God is the same for everybody. Therefore there could be only one religious belief were it not for the lies of priests. But what struck me in this matter is a thing which has repeatedly struck me among Russians of the lower class, namely, their broad common sense in religious matters. "Mysticism," Mr. Chesterton once wrote, "was with Carlyle as with all its genuine professors only a transcendent form of common sense. Mysticism and common sense alike consist in a sense of the dominance of certain truths which cannot be formally demonstrated." Now the Russians of the lower class seem to me often the genuine professors of mysticism, because their mysticism is simply common sense. And it is this very fact which seems to me to lead people astray when they discuss the religion of the Russian peasant. For instance, you often hear people bewail the *superstition* of the peasant which makes him devote so much attention to paper and wooden images. Again, I have read in an English book on the Russian peasant that the peasant's habit of perpetually crossing himself, his respect for images, and his prayers are purely mechanical and therefore meaningless, because they are often interrupted by, or simultaneous with, jokes, laughter, and the business of life. Now this union of the practice of the outward signs of religion with the business of everyday life, this interruption of a prayer by a conversation, this sign of the cross made before a theft seem to me all to derive from the broad common sense which is at the root of their belief, and which, as Mr. Chesterton says, is synonymous with mysticism.

Because if your belief in God is solid and based on great rocks of common sense it is not extraordinary that your outward expression of your allegiance to the great fact should be mechanical. For instance, if you are the loyal subject of the King, you mechanically take off your hat when he drives past you in the street or when you see the colours of his Army go by, and nobody says, if at that moment you happen to be whistling a comic song or thinking of the North Pole, that your action is hypocritical, insincere, or meaningless. But it is exactly the same in the case of the peasants; the outward expression of their religion is as mechanical as possible, but it is mechanical because their religious feeling is true and right and not because it is insincere and false.

I will end by telling two stories which exemplify the common sense which lies at the root of the Russian peasant's religion. The first story happened at Kharbin. It was Easter, and the soldiers wanted Mass said for them. There were two priests. One priest had been engaged by some officers and the second priest was drunk. A soldier was relating these facts, and some asked: "Well, did you have to go without your Mass?" "Oh, no," said the soldier, "we went to the priest who was drunk and we pulled him out of bed, and we said: 'Say Mass, you devil' (and a lot more uncomplimentary expressions), and he said Mass." This story shows that the soldiers regarded the priest partly as an instrument to say Mass and partly as a man. They differentiated between the two, and the instrument had to perform its divine office whatever happened to the man, whose good or bad qualities had nothing to do with the case. This seems to me gloriously sensible.

The second story happened somewhere down in this government. A Socialist arrived in a village to convert the inhabitants to Socialism. He wanted to prove that all men were equal and that the Government authorities had no right to their authority. Consequently he thought he would begin by disproving the existence of God, because if he proved that there was no God, it would naturally follow that there should be no Emperor and no policemen. So he took a holy image, and said: "There is no God, and I will prove it immediately. I will spit upon this image and break it to bits, and if there is a God he will send fire from heaven and kill me, and if there is no God nothing will happen to me at all." Then he took the image and spat upon it and broke it to bits, and he said to the peasants: "You see God has not killed me." "No," said the peasants, "God has not killed you, but we will," and they killed him. And thus an act was committed which was one of common sense or of mysticism.

Part 8

STRATEGIC RUSSIAN RAILWAYS, RESOURCES, AND REPRESENTATIONS

54

GEORGE DOBSON, *RUSSIA'S RAILWAY ADVANCE INTO CENTRAL ASIA; NOTES OF A JOURNEY FROM ST. PETERSBURG TO SAMARKAND* (LONDON: W. H. ALLEN & CO., 1890), PP. 71–73, 102–104, 109–113, 125–132, 139–144

As far as Vladikavkaz I had been ninety-two hours in trains, and I now had before me a journey of 132 miles byroad across the mountains in order to reach the railway of the Transcaucasus. The tedium of this long railway journey had thus far been greatly relieved by the conversation and information of many interesting fellow-passengers, for the Russians, as a rule, are very sociable travellers. It would, indeed, be strange in a country of such vast distances, where railway travellers are often thrown together in one compartment for three or four days at a stretch, if they all hid themselves behind newspapers and never uttered a word to each other. In fact, it would be difficult to find a newspaper in the provinces beyond Moscow capable of engrossing attention to this extent. The Russian traveller prefers to talk, and is quite uneasy and miserable until he finds somebody who will reciprocate. He has no craving for railway literature, even on the longest journeys. His favourite pastimes are talking and smoking, or card-playing. Nothing is more rare in Russian trains than the reading of books or newspapers, but a provoking inquisitiveness takes its place, and induces the Russian to seize upon every opportunity of plying his fellow-passengers with questions until he has perfectly satisfied himself as to their business and destination. In my case the first example of this characteristic trait was afforded by a Moscow merchant, who was the first to inform me, rather to my surprise, how little personal interest was being taken among the class to which he belonged in the important railway event on the other side of the Caspian. In spite of the emphasis put upon the commercial importance and prospects of Russia's first great railway in Asia, none of the celebrated merchants of St. Petersburg and Moscow were to be present at the *fêtes* in Samarkand—not even those who have become famous for their semi-political caravan trade with the Asiatic border countries. Certain committees of the Exchanges in the two capitals had been invited, but apparently none of the members had accepted the invitation. The idea of making merry over the opening of the railway was apparently no business whatever of the Government, and the invitations were entirely the private concern of Generals Annenkoff and Rosenbach. As it turned out, the guests who, with great difficulty, eventually found their way to the Samarkand terminus of the Transcaspian Railway formed, with one or two exceptions, a kind of family party of General Annenkoff's.

The people of this district, as far as one could judge from the specimens lounging about at the railway stations, are chiefly Persians. Groups of swarthy, unkempt individuals stood about on every platform, with heavy black sheepskin caps, and beards painted dark saffron or deep red. In Baku I was surprised to see the legs of their droshky horses dyed with the same pigment, which made me think at first that the animals belonged to a circus. At many of the railway stations there were natives on duty in Cossack uniforms, shouldering muskets or repeating rifles, which showed that Russia had also organized these Persians into something of a militia or police force; while it was evident, by several officers met with in the train who were pure Persians, serving as chief police masters of districts, or in other positions of command, that they were not excluded from the local executive and administration. They all wore the same long Circassian dress,—that sartorial badge of the close and genial link between the Russian and the Asiatic, which is seen on the Cossacks who guard the Tsar at St. Petersburg, and on the Turkoman Khans who surround Colonel Alikhanoff at Merv. In a country of so many intermingled types and languages, it was not easy to recognize in these men the Russified natives of Iran.

When I got out of the train at Baku I was at once taken in charge by the police. The assistant of the police master was waiting for me on the platform and calling out my name and nationality in order, as he politely stated, to acquaint me with the news, of which I was already aware, that there was no just cause or impediment to my further progress into the Transcaspian. He then recommended me to go to a certain hotel, and kindly had my luggage put into a droshky. I had some scruples, however, as to the convenience of following this police advice in the matter of hotels, and so had myself driven to quite a different hostelry. This independent line of action, it turned out, was calculated to lead to some annoyance, for I had not long been in the hotel of my own choosing when another police officer made his appearance, who seemed quite ignorant of the special orders received from St. Petersburg on my behalf, and requested me to hand over my passport. I lost no time in going to the Steamship Company's office, and, to my utter disappointment, found that the steamer which the agent in Tiflis had positively assured me was to start that very afternoon, had been countermanded, and there would not be another boat for two days. This was a good example of the dependence to be placed upon any kind of information in Russia, even in matters of business. The representative at Baku blamed the agent at Tiflis for not knowing better, but officially-subsidized steamship or other companies in Russia are not bound to be precise with the public. Among all the five or six steamboat and shipping companies of Baku, there was not a single craft, under sail or steam, going to Oozoon Ada for forty-eight hours. After all I had heard of the great traffic and daily transports across the Caspian since the construction of the Transcaspian Railway to the Amu Darya, I was very much struck with this fact, especially on an occasion when one would have expected even more than the usual number of vessels to be running on account of the inauguration of the last branch of the railway.

Oozoon Ada and Krasnovodsk

WE reached the Bay of Oozoon Ada, the Caspian terminus of the new Asiatic Railway, early in the morning, after a fair voyage of about 132 miles in nineteen hours. The aspect of the place was extremely wretched and melancholy,—hardly an encouraging introduction into a new country, although some amends were made for the barren and blighted character of the landscapes by the beautiful fine weather and a cloudless sky with 100 degrees of Fahrenheit in the shade.

The train was timed to start at six o'clock in the evening, which entailed another whole day's delay, and this time in such a miserable and uninteresting waste, that most of the passengers preferred to stay in the steamer until the hour of departure. Instead of six o'clock, it was nearly midnight before the train actually did leave, as the one due from the opposite direction had first to be waited for; and there had been no communication either way for several days in consequence of the rails near Kizil Arvat and other places having been washed away by the floods. A whole day was certainly too long to inspect this bivouac on the edge of the desert; and its description may be summed up in very few words. Eighteen low, and narrow wooden piers jutting out into the water round a semicircular and sandy bay, with one or two larger and stronger landing stages belonging to the steamship companies; a few dozen sailing brigs, barges, and smaller craft; two or three steamers at anchor; with straggling rows and clusters of flimsy wooden houses, huts and warehouses, the whole enclosed by a background of bare hills and mounds of light yellow sand. Such is a picture of Oozoon Ada as I first saw it. The hurriedly built settlement had a very ephemeral and unsubstantial appearance, and in no way corresponded with the fanciful description of a Russian newspaper writer who had filled it with imaginary fine streets and squares. There was the green painted dome of the indispensable wooden church, dedicated to St. Michael the Archangel, or, as the Russians here, with very appropriate significance, prefer to call him, St. Michael, the Archistrategist; and large sheds for the weekly market or bazaar had also naturally been provided. The other wooden buildings now comprise sixty houses, one bad lodging-house, a few stores, including one for the sale of ready-made Vienna clothes, and one *dookhan* or Caucasian wine-shop. The small business of the place, such as it is, has, of course, been taken in hand entirely by Armenians from the Caucasus. The principal shipping and mercantile firms represented are "Lebedeff," "Droojina," "Nadiejda," and Koodrin and Company; and the inhabitants number from 800 to 900 souls. The railway station, which has a buffet, is situated nearly a quarter of a mile from the landing-place, and passengers have to trudge ankle-deep through the hot sand to get to the platform; but the trains from the interior are run round the bay from the station to the head of the steamboat pier. During violent storms of wind the fine sand flies into one's face like spray, and nothing can prevent it from irritating the eyes and penetrating through the clothes to the skin. Sometimes ports of the bay, deep enough for all ordinary vessels, get sanded up to within five or six feet of the surface, and the floating dredger has to be set to work before the deeper draught steamers can reach their accustomed anchorage. This is precisely what happens in the Amu Darya and other Central Asian streams that are gradually disappearing under the sand. At the same time the sea occasionally floods the houses near the water's edge, and this necessitates the raising of some of them upon piles. General Annenkoff is now about to construct a stone dam, or quay, on the north shore to prevent these inundations. At the time of my visit there was no fresh water supply at Oozoon Ada, as the condensing machine, which generally worked day and night, was out of order, and water had to be brought by every train in large vats, or cisterns, on wheeled platforms all the way from Kazandjik, 120 miles off.

The appearance of this dismal shore was not always perhaps so overpoweringly dreary as it is at the present day. If at this point the mighty stream of the Oxus, freighted with the wares of India and the East, once found an outlet into the Caspian Sea, the aspect of the desolate seaboard has probably undergone as striking a change as that in the course of the river itself. The part of the coast on which is situated the Caspian terminus of the Central Asian Railway now consists of a complicated and fantastic labyrinth of salt lagoons, the pale, green reflections from whose glassy surface contrast agreeably with the light yellow of the sandhills on the numerous islands and peninsulas which they form.

One can imagine the surprise of Annenkoff at the appearance of this Commission with Colonel Shebanoff as one of its principal members. It was at the same time reported that the construction of barracks and other official buildings at Oozoon Ada had been suspended by telegram, in consequence of the determination to extend the railway to Krasnovodsk. The Commission completed its work and returned to the capital, whither it was soon followed by General Annenkoff, who continues down to this day to express the most sanguine confidence in the perfect security of his precious creation. Nothing officially has transpired; but I am inclined to believe that the Krasnovodsk extension, although pretty certain to be made in the end, will not be undertaken for some time to come.

The train from Askabad which was to take me from Oozoon Ada to Samarkand, came in between ten and eleven at night, and started back again five or six hours behind time to begin with, as soon as the exchange of passengers had been effected. I was told there was not a single first-class carriage on the entire line, and such is the case up to the present day, with the exception of one or two special coaches reserved for General Annenkoff and the Governor-General. At the end of the train there was one very high double-storied waggon, second-class below and third on the top. There was no other second-class compartment, the rest of the train being made up of third and fourth-class cars. Several of the closed trucks, used indiscriminately on all Russian railways for cattle or troops, and marked "Eight horses or forty men," were filled by persons who found them much cooler. An official informed me that there were as yet only about 1,000 waggons and sixty locomotives for the entire distance of 900 miles, but these numbers have since been increased to 112 locomotives, 70 passenger carriages of second and third-class, 1,146 closed goods waggons, 570 open trucks, 62 water cisterns on trucks, and 82 tank-cars for petroleum. Many of the locomotives are always under repair in consequence of the sand getting into their wheels and machinery. As the Bokharan branch was not yet opened, there were no through tickets for Samarkand, and passengers could only book as far as the Amu Darya. I should not omit to mention that strict Mahommedan travellers have been specially thought of, and provided with separate waggons, lettered in two languages. A Persian time-table and guide has also been published by General Annenkoff, with a fine portrait of the Shah, for the purpose of inducing the Shiite Mahommedans to avail themselves of the Russian Railway in their pilgrimages to the holy city of Meshed.

Oozoon Ada to Geok Tepé

When I left Oozoon Ada it was a clear moonlight night, and the sandy desert could be comfortably surveyed from the rear of the train through the end door of the two-storied car which took the place of a brake-van. As we dragged along at the moderate rate of thirteen or fourteen miles an hour, the lone and desolate outlook recalled my school-day visions of the Great Sahara. I could compare this howling wilderness with nothing else that I had ever seen or read of; and all that was wanting to complete the picture were the bleached ribbones of camel skeletons protruding through the yellow sand. After the noble and elevating scenery of the Caucasus, this violent contrast was all the more melancholy and depressing. The only signs of human kind on this part of the road were two or three *kibitka* tents, seen between the hills, and half-buried in the sand. A French acquaintance boasted of having descried a jackal sneaking along in the distance, but I am pretty sure that it was only a stray dog, for no other animal would be likely to follow man into this wretched region. I do not believe there was a single other quadruped at Oozoon Ada, nor a single wheeled vehicle of any kind off the railway sidings; so that the traveller with luggage had reason to be thankful for the strong Persian *hamals*, who are able to wade through the hot sand with weights on their bent backs almost as heavy as the ordinary load of a camel.

The train first finds its way through a cutting between the sand dunes at a certain gradient, and then passes over the long dam or sand bank, which is very well laid across the estuary or lagoon that separates the island of Oozoon Ada from the peninsula of Dardja. This narrow trail of the water-flanked line is the only instance throughout the length of the railway, as far as my observation went, of the use of good stone rubble to strengthen the sides of the embankment. The thin telegraph posts seemed very infirmly stuck into the sandy bottom of the water along the side of this dam, and looked as though they would require frequent attention.

Farther on we passed several pools of presumably briny, and decidedly blood-red water, which probably accounts for the origin of the name of Krasnavodsk, in native nomenclature Kizil-Soo, both meaning red water.

The first halt of the train is at the little station of Michael's Bay, which was the original terminus and landing-place from Baku and Astrakhan, but is no longer used as such on account of the shallowness of the harbour. Here the train has to retreat a few hundred yards in order to reach the platform bordering the first rails laid down in the Transcaspian. The first part of the twenty-five versts, or seventeen miles, to this station presents nothing but shifting sand driven up by the winds into hills of all shapes and sizes, destitute of vegetation, and interspersed with salt lakes and pools. At Michailofsk the sand hillocks are varied by the kitchen middens of the former settlement, which has now entirely disappeared, and a rough wooden cross or two mark the sites of human graves. Nothing else has been left, except the small station building, and two or three scattered wooden houses belonging to the half-dozen employés.

Morning dawned upon us near Bala Ishem, and we soon saw the last of the Great and Little Balkan mountains, between which the train had passed during the night; while in return for this loss to the view we came in sight of the steep, rugged range of the Kuren Dag, continued opposite Kizil Arvat by that of the higher Kopet Dag, rising 6,000 feet above the sea. These mountains, which form the natural frontier of Persia, run parallel with the railway on the south for 350 miles, until the line bends off near Dooshak on its way to Merv. When one sees the sterile and lifeless character of their Northern or Russian slopes, it is no longer surprising that the Turkoman enemies of Russia preferred to remain and accept defeat upon the open plains, rather than retreat into their mountain recesses and imitate the opposition of the Caucasus. . . . There is a reasonable prospect, however, that the coal recently discovered at Penjakent, thirty to fifty miles from Samarkand, or the seams long worked at Hodjent, may be made available by the extension of the railway to Tashkent; so that the line may not be always dependent for its fuel upon petroleum.

At the station of Kazandjik, the first freshwater source from the Caspian, and eleven miles from another station misnamed Oozoon-Soo, "Long water," where there was not a drop of water to be had from any local supply, we heard of passengers ahead of us having had to wait as long as three days until the repairs on the inundated section had been completed. We afterwards passed the places where the damage had been done, between the small station of Ushak, or Ooshak, and Kizil Arvat, which is the first of the larger stations on the line; and there we saw the old rails bent and curled into all manner of shapes, lying hundreds of yards off from the line, where they had been thrown by the force of the water. I could never have believed in such hydraulic power on a perfectly level plain, had I not seen something more of the water's violence on my return journey, when I narrowly escaped the consequences of another destruction of rail and roadway. General Annenkoff had not then paid enough attention to this important matter. The line was not destitute of culverts through which the water would find its way in ordinary cases, but there were evidently far too few of these structures. Perhaps the Transcaspian Railway is not much worse off in this respect than many other Russian lines on which the traffic is often stopped for days together in spring-time by the floods from melting snows and swollen rivers; but this does not justify the appearance of floods on the rails in Central Asia, where they might be avoided. Without being a professional engineer, it was not difficult to see that there were many old waterways and depressions crossed by the railroad, which had not been provided with the requisite water passages; and although this defect had in some degree been remedied by trenches cut parallel with the road, about eight or ten feet broad and half as much in depth, there was still a great deal to attend to in this respect before the line could be pronounced perfect. After heavy storms, such as at that time burst over the mountains, the rain-water rushes and bounds across the plain in turbulent torrents and overflows these trenches in a very few minutes. Neither was there any ballast worth speaking of, which could offer the slightest resistance to attacks of this nature. With few exceptions, the rails have been laid down along the perfectly flat plain of alternating desert and oasis almost without any embankment whatever; and it struck me as well as several other persons, who like myself were travelling over it for the first time, that this must have been one of the most easily constructed railways in the world. There is not one tunnel along the entire distance of nine hundred miles; and the only engineering difficulties, properly so called, have been the bridging of the Amu Darya,—no slight undertaking, however,—and the two or three cuttings through the moving sands. These sand cuttings, it must be admitted, have been exceedingly difficult work, and quite out of the range of ordinary railway engineering. It would not be easy to say which has given the most trouble,—the making of them, or the keeping them open now they are made. A gentleman who helped to supply materials told me that one bit of the line at Michailofsk had to be re-made twenty times before the attacking sand could be finally held at bay; and in the meantime several barrels of fastenings completely disappeared beneath the sandy deluge. It certainly needed the discipline of the railway battalions to build these sections of the line; and the indomitable perseverance of a man like General Annenkoff was none the less necessary in directing the work. As to the other parts where no difculties or impediments existed, they might perhaps have been made more substantial and secure, had more money and time been devoted to them at the very outset; but the main considerations which guided the construction, irrespective of the pressure of military necessities, and the danger of Afghan frontier troubles, were cheapness and speed in getting the work done.

It was all the time a contest between General Annenkoff as the representative of the Minister of War, and the Minister of Ways of Communication, in order to prove which of the two could build strategical railways cheapest and quickest. This competition between the military and civil engineering departments had been going on ever since General Annenkoff built the Jabinsk-Pinsk line in Poland, which was severely criticized by the opposing authorities at the Ministry of Communications; but up to the present the energetic constructor of the Trans-caspian Railway has managed to hold his own, and even to get the better of his rival.

It seems strange to be writing about so much water in this desert country, which has been generally regarded as quite destitute of it; but my experience impressed me almost as much with the water nuisance, as it did with the dangers and troubles of the sand. I was told that these destructive floods had never been known before, and were quite exceptional. It was not the first time nor the last that the line has been inundated, but never to the same disastrous extent. Between Ushak and Kizil Arvat the damage extended over some six versts and a half. At one place every sign of the iron road was obliterated for 1,000 yards, as though there had never been any railway at all, while the rails and sleepers were carried half a verst away. It was a poor treat for General Annenkoff's daughters and their party to be on their way to Samarkand at this unfortunate juncture, though at the same time it was fortunate that the "representatives of all nationalities," so pompously proclaimed as having been present at the inauguration, only existed in the Russian imagination. Their accounts of the journey, had they been there, would hardly have been enthusiastic descriptions of triumphant railway progress. The General's relatives and French friends and admirers had to be carted through the water to Kizil Arvat, or wheeled there on trollies in the middle of the night, in order not to delay the opening of the Samarkand branch beyond the anniversary of the Tsar's coronation. They were first delayed at Kazandjik, where there is a tiny oasis supplied with water brought in canals cut by the Russians from a mountain stream into a reservoir, and then conducted two versts to the station through 4-in. pipes into six tanks, each holding 700 pailfuls. The Oozoon Ada-Kizil Arvat section is supplied with water from this station. There is also a very flourishing garden and a quantity of acacia, pistachio, and other trees planted as experiments. The belated guests had plenty of time during three days here to visit a cotton plantation and small house, with bathing accommodation, belonging to Prince Khilkoff, and occupied by the engineer of the section.

55

C. E. BIDDULPH, *FOUR MONTHS IN PERSIA AND A VISIT TO TRANS-CASPIA* (LONDON: KEGAN PAUL, TRENCH, TRÜBNER & CO., 1892), PP. 112–117

No greater proof of the absolute confidence which the Russian Government has in the demeanour of the population of Bokhara could be found than in the fact that the Political Resident there occupies quarters in the very midst of the town with a guard of only twenty Cossacks maintained evidently more for show than for protection, as the only troops procurable, in case of any emeute or disturbance, would be from Samarcand, whence they could not be brought under a delay of at least twenty-four hours. The Bokhara of history, with its horrible associations of the sufferings endured there by our own fellow-countrymen, may thus be considered as completely a myth of the past as any Greek legend; it only existed at all in the light in which it appeared in past ages, owing to its inaccessibility and the consequent impossibility of bringing anything more than a moral influence to bear upon it,—a fact which its barbarous rulers were fully aware of. Now that it is traversed by roads and railways, and overawed by European troops, it is not different from any part of the India of the present, and we, of all nations, are the last that should indulge in maudlin and sentimental regrets over the barbarities and abominations of the regimé which has ceased to exist; rather should we offer our hearty congratulations to the introducers of the change as benefactors, to no slight extent of the human race.

The difficulties attending the construction of the line of rail from the Caspian to Samarcand, and its maintenance in efficient working order, would appear to have been alike made too much of. That it evinced a spirit of the greatest resolution and enterprise to commence a work of such a magnitude, through so barren and apparently profitless a region, is beyond question; but once that the work had been commenced, the only difficulty to be encountered was in bringing forward the materials from Europe, and, as far as the line beyond Askabad was concerned, laying them down with sufficient speed to attain the object required, which undoubtedly at the time was of a strategic nature, for the course taken as far as the Merv oasis is over country as level as the plains of the Punjaub, with the exception of the first thirty or forty miles. The only real difficulty encountered has been in the crossing the tract of country intervening between the Merv oasis and the banks of the Oxus. For the first sixty miles or so of this extent, the sand hills of which it is composed, are stationary, and evidently in the spring covered with rank vegetation, the remnants of which could be seen in the withered grass and stalks of plants with which the surface was strewn. Underneath the surface too, where it had been cut through, could be seen a layer of closely matted roots, which extended to a depth of from two or three feet in most places; the obstacle offered to the carrying of the line of rail through these sands must, to all appearance, have been trifling. After traversing these, the railway enters upon what are termed the "Moving sands," that is, those which, throughout the year, are destitute of any vegetation at all such as would bind them together, and are thus in constant motion, being wafted to and fro, according to the quarter from which the wind happens to be blowing at the time. These, in the first case, must have occasioned a great deal of trouble in the laying down of the line, but now that this has been completed, and, moreover, well ballasted throughout, they present no further obstacle to the progress of the trains, as I was assured by several Russian engineers, than does the snow in the winter in most parts of Russia. In any case, the delay resulting from an accumulation of sand upon this portion of the line, which only extends for about thirty to forty miles, would not be of more than a few hours' duration. Whatever may have been the condition of this railway a year or two ago, it is now, to all appearance, most solidly and substantially constructed throughout the whole distance. This is probably owing to the fact that the Russians have been working steadily to improve it bit by bit, ever since its first opening for traffic; it is not indeed metalled throughout, but this has been done wherever there appeared to be any urgent necessity for it, as, for instance, through the stretches of sand referred to; and, doubtless, this work will be carried out gradually through its whole extent, as quantities of material were being quarried at various places, apparently for this purpose.

The weak point about the communication by rail is, as would be expected, the bridge over the Oxus, which, being constructed entirely of wood, must necessarily be liable to break down at any time in case of a flood, or in the event of its being exposed to any abnormal strain; but such an occurrence would not break off the connection with Samarcand to any serious extent, as abundance of rolling stock and material is available on the further side of the river, and passengers and goods could easily be conveyed across by boats. In any case, the interruption to through traffic occasioned by such an occurrence would be only of a temporary character, for the very fact of the bridge being made of wood, would facilitate its repair, abundant supplies of this material being kept in store for the purpose. The important part which this railway has played, independently of all other considerations, in consolidating the newly-acquired territories through which it passes, and pacifying the population contained therein, is beyond all estimation. As we have had ample experience of it in India and other similar parts of our possessions, the introduction of a railway acts like magic, in reducing to order the most turbulent and troublesome races, and such has been the case with the Turcoman and other inhabitants of these parts. Already cowed by sanguinary and disastrous conflicts, the civilizing influences of the railway and other innovations seem to have reduced them to a ready and willing submission to the rule of their conquerors, and completely diverted their thoughts from the old channels of rapine and bloodshed in which they had run for centuries, to the peaceful occupations of agriculture and commerce. The trains now traverse the entire distance of nine hundred miles from Uzun Ada to Samarcand in three days and two nights, or about sixty hours, and thus average a speed of fifteen miles an hour, including stoppages, or a running speed of about twenty miles an hour. This pace must frequently be exceeded, as the delays at the stations are very long, so that from time to time a speed of quite thirty miles must have been attained; there cannot thus be much that is faulty about the construction of a line of rail, which can bear constant heavy trains running over it at this rate.

The excursion of which I was a member was conducted under the management of the Compagnie Internationale des Wagons Lits, and nothing would offer a greater contrast to the experiences of former travellers, or furnish a stronger proof of the altered condition of affairs now existing, than the ease and comfort which characterized it throughout. From the moment of leaving Paris till that of arriving at Samarcand, the only hardship to be encountered was that of changing from one comfortable, not to say luxurious, sleeping car or saloon carriage to another, or to the saloon of a steamer. It seemed, indeed, as one passed station after station on the Trans-Caspian Railway and alighted for a cup of tea at that of Geok Teppe, or to breakfast, lunch, or dine, as the case might be, at those of Merv, Amu Darya, and Bokhara, and found there well-built and carefully-kept stations surrounded by bright little gardens, and containing all the necessary appurtenances of waiting-rooms, refreshment-rooms, etc., hardly possible to realize the fact that but a few years had elapsed since some of these had been the scenes of the most desperate and sanguinary encounters between the introducers of all these modern innovations and the barbarous inhabitants of the country, while others had only been visited at the risk of their lives by a few daring and intrepid explorers. Such, however, is the magic influence of modern science and civilization that, like a fairy wand, it reduces in a moment, as it were, the most savage and turbulent specimens of the human race to peace and submission, and causes houses and gardens and fountains to spring out of the very sands of the desert at its touch.

Comparatively little interest would be aroused in the breast of the traveller whose object it is to study the resources of the country and the social condition of its inhabitants, until he finds himself approaching the Kizil Arvat oasis, where, after traversing a weary stretch of sand and desert, such as is calculated to predispose him against the region to which he is receiving such an unpromising introduction, he makes his first acquaintance with the Trans-Caspian territory under its more favourable aspect; passing through patches of cultivated ground irrigated by streams of running water, he may descry far, far away in the distance, a jet rising from a fountain, which thus marks the position of the station. Here is a great railway depôt and changing station for engines, which, if the traveller's approach be made by night, he will find all lighted up by the electric light. The country through which the line of rail passes from this point onwards as far as Merv, reminds one very strongly of that traversed by the railway between Jacobabad and Sibi in Upper Sind, or Kutchi, as this particular portion is called. On one side the landscape is closed in by barren storm-swept ranges of mountains rising almost precipitously out of the plains, absolutely destitute, as far as is discernible, of the slightest trace of vegetation, while, on the other side, a boundless expanse of level ground stretches away to the horizon, as far as ever the eye can reach, without a hillock or a tree of any dimensions to break the monotony, of the view. The soil of these plains, moreover, seemed to be of a quality very similar to that of the Pat—as the vast extents of uncultivated land so familiar to the dweller in Sind are called—and, like the latter, apparently was possessed of the most extraordinary productive properties, for wherever water was available, appeared flourishing villages, surrounded by gardens and orchards, and fields, covered with crops of various descriptions; while, that the rest of the land as yet lying waste was possessed of similar powers of production, was proved by the fact that in places where the water had been allowed to run to waste, or had not been made use of, sometimes at great distances from any village site, the most luxuriant stretches of grass jungle had sprung up; and, again, that, where this was not the case, and no signs of the neighbourhood of running water at any time of the year were apparent, the whole of the surface of the ground was covered with the débris of grass and plants, which bore witness to the richness of the vegetation which it produced in the spring, after the melting of the snows and the winter rains, when the whole landscape is said to be one of the most brilliant green, dotted with flowers of every hue. That this might be the case could be easily imagined by an Anglo-Indian from the effect which may be seen to be produced upon the arid plains of Sind or the Punjab after the bursting of the monsoon, when grass and flowers spring up like magic on all sides. It is thus, as has been pointed out, a mistake to describe this region as a "desert," by which is generally implied a tract of country devoid of any productive capabilities, even under the most favourable circumstances. It is rather like the Punjaub, one containing, to a considerable extent, an alluvial soil, of an exceptionally high degree of fertility, which only requires a sufficient supply of water to be capable of an almost unlimited degree of development;—and there of course is the difficulty—for the only streams visible as far as the Tejend and the Murghab are paltry in their volume, and quite unequal to such a task, however much the present state of things may be improved by a more careful management of their waters, such as would enable the supply thus available to go much further than it does now, and perhaps extend it, by constructing artificial water-courses from the mountains to the south, in which all these streams take their source.

The analogy between the districts comprising "Trans-Caspia," that is, the extent through which the railway runs from the Caspian to the Oxus and Sind or the Punjab, exists, as may be expected, only as far as regards appearance and physical characteristics. The climates of the two countries will, of course, bear no comparison, and there is nothing more absurd than the impressions regarding that of India, which seems to prevail amongst the majority of Russians, officers and others, with whom we were brought in contact. Being, as they are, natives of an exceptionally cold climate, with no colonies or possessions such as would give them an idea of the degree of heat of which a tropical climate is capable, it seemed beyond their powers of conception to imagine a temperature higher than that which they were liable to experience in Trans-Caspia.

56

SIR HENRY NORMAN, *ALL THE RUSSIAS: TRAVELS AND STUDIES IN CONTEMPORARY RUSSIA, FINLAND, SIBERIA, THE CAUCASUS, AND CENTRAL ASIA* (NEW YORK: SCRIBNER'S SONS, 1903), PP. 231–235, 237

No foreigner, as I have said, lands at Krasnovodsk without special permission; Russia watches all strangers on her frontiers—and England's—hereabouts. Mine was obtained from St. Petersburg through the British Foreign Office before I started. The wooden pier was crowded with civilians and porters—Persian *hamals*—and, where the steamer was to touch, a group of uniformed police stood, with a military band behind them. When we were within a few yards the music struck up, and as soon as the gang-plank was in position the chief of police came aboard, and nobody else. The captain awaited him. Were there any foreigners on board? One—myself. My name? An official list was produced from a portfolio and consulted. *Pazholst!*—"If you please"—and I was politely invited ashore. In St. Petersburg it is the official pleasure to smile when you speak of special permission being necessary for the Trans-Caspian Railway. They take it seriously enough at Krasnovodsk. I may add that after this original formality—with the single exception of the Chief of Police, an army Colonel at Askhabad, who curtly summoned me to his office and kept me waiting for an hour and a half, and then charged me before all his subordinates with being in Central Asia without permission, the fact being that not only had I special permission but also the highest official letters of personal introduction to all the principal authorities—I received the greatest possible courtesy and assistance from the Russian officials everywhere, a courtesy going so far on one occasion as a mounted torchlight escort of Cossacks. It is, however, but natural that the Russians should be ready to show what they have done in Central Asia. They have every reason to be proud of it.

On the Trans-Caspian Railway there are two kinds of train—the train and the post-train. And the difference between them is that the latter has a restaurant-car and the former has not. The post-train has an extra passenger-carriage, and the train has several freight-cars, but the speed is the same and the discomfort is the same. For what the Russian railway service gives you in extra comfort on the magnificent Siberian Express, it takes out of you in extra fatigue and dirt on the Trans-Caspian. The train that awaited me was the post-train and consisted of five corridor carriages, the last being a restaurant-car, all of them painted white. The tender of the engine was an oil-tank, and behind it, on a flat truck, was an enormous wooden tub, to hold water, for in Central Asia there is little fuel, and water is the most precious commodity that exists. But a glance at the train raised a most painful suspicion, which a visit to the ticket office confirmed—there is not a first-class carriage on the Trans-Caspian Railway! It was not snobbery which evoked one's consternation at this discovery. A thousand miles of a slow, hot, dusty journey lay before me, and even in European Russia the prospect of a thousand miles in a second-class carriage would be far from pleasant, while in Central Asia, with ample experience in other lands of what a native crowd is, it was appalling. Let me say at once that it more than fulfilled all my expectations. The ordinary second-class, too, has narrow, flat wooden seats, with thin, hard cushions spread on them. After a couple of nights on one of these you are stiff for a week. There is a carriage which has stuffed seats, but it is half second and half third, and the toilette arrangements are all in the third-class half. Moreover, in the stuffed cushions are passengers without number who pay no fare. I still wriggle as I think of those carriages, for on one never-to-be-forgotten stage I became perforce what a recent Act of Parliament calls a "verminous person." Now, to go unwashed is bad, but to share your washing with third-class Russian Asiatic passengers is not only worse—it is impossible. Furthermore, while the railway authorities have separate third-class carriages for Europeans and natives, the second-class is open to both. Their idea probably was that the higher fare would deter the native passenger, but this is far from being the case, so prosperous has the sedentary Sart become under Russian rule. Therefore your carriage is invaded by a host of natives with their innumerable bundles, their water-pots and their tea-pots, their curiosity and their expectoration. They do not understand the unwritten law which reserves to you the seat you have once occupied; they dump themselves and their belongings anywhere, and they are very difficult to detach; they are entirely amiable; they follow your every movement for hours with an unblinking curiosity; and they smell strong. I hope I have nothing but good will for my Eastern fellow-man, and I assuredly often find him more interesting than people with white skins, but I have the greatest objection to passing days and nights crowded close with him in an over-heated railway carriage. And if I expatiate somewhat upon this minor topic it is because the Trans-Caspian railway journey is such a remarkable experience and affords such rare and vast interests, that everybody who can afford the time and money should take it, and the Russian authorities should do all in their power to make the actual travelling as tolerable as possible. As things are at present, I should not advise any lady to come who is not prepared for some of the most personally objectionable sides of "roughing it." Prince Hilkoff, however, Minister of Railways, is so prompt to make any improvement or to inaugurate any new enterprise that if this plaint should meet his eye it may well be that no future traveller will have occasion to make it. There is also one other little matter which calls for attention. Formerly the train at Krasnovodsk waited for the steamer from Baku. Now the local railway authority causes it to start precisely at three, even if the steamer is coming into harbour. So it has happened that the train has started without, a single passenger, while the wretched people arriving by steamer have had to pass twenty-three hours in some railway carriages, there being nothing of the nature of a hotel at Krasnovodsk. Such an absurdity should be corrected, but the fact that there is a railway here at all is so marvellous that every other consideration is insignificant beside it.

There is a strange medley on the platform before we start. Crowds of ragged porters, jostling and jabbering in Persian and broken Russian, and carrying huge bundles of native luggage tied in carpets; a few civilians—merchants and commercial travellers; Armenian "drummers," sharp and swarthy, for Persian firms; a score of officers in various uniforms; several soldiers sweating in heavy gray overcoats—they badly need a bath—and old, patched breeches of red morocco leather; three officers in the handsome green and gold of the *pogranichnaya strazha*, the frontier guards, soldiers and customs-officers in one; specimens of most of the natives of Central Asia; and myself, the only foreigner. There are no fewer than eleven parallel lines of rail, for either military purposes or freight accommodation, as may be needed. At three o'clock we start, and between the bare brown hills and the still blue sea the train runs slowly along for hours. It carries, as I said, its oil-fuel, and its water in a huge wooden tank on a truck behind the engine, for the country is a desert, and the stations are merely the little white houses of the employees, appearing as specks in the wilderness. The low indented coastline, within a few yards of our right, reminds me of the Mediterranean coast, between Marseilles and Nice, but here there are in every bay thousands of white-breasted ducks. For twenty-five miles the line runs across an absolutely barren plain; sunset finds us traversing a salty waste, dotted with scanty bushes, and when I look out of the window in the middle of the night, a bright moon shines on the same desolate scene. But at eight o'clock next morning comes a sudden thrill. Over a little station are written the magic words "Geok Tepe," and I rush out to see if anything remains to tell of the terrible battle and more terrible slaughter of 1881. Sure enough, on the opposite side of the line, only fifty yards away, is the whole story, and luckily the train is accidentally delayed long enough to enable me to make a hasty visit to the historic spot.

With a natural desire to perpetuate the memory of their own victories, the Russians have built between the railway station and the ruins a pretty little museum of white stone. In front of it stands a Turkoman cannon, captured by them from the Persians in one of their innumerable raids. This has its glorious story, too, for though it was mounted on the ramparts of Geok Tepe the Turkomans did not know how to use it, and, having captured some Russian artillerymen, they ordered them to fire it on their own comrades, or be slaughtered on the spot. The Russians loyally chose death. In the museum are portraits of Skobelef and the other commanders, and a collection of Turkoman guns and swords—poor tools against artillery and petroleum bombs, throwing the bravery of these nomad horsemen into still higher relief. I ran up the rough earthen steps leading to the shattered ramparts and looked through them at the busy station, the white train, and the groups of officers strolling up and down the platform. It was the advance of Russia at a glance.

Part 9

TEST OF THE RUSSIAN WILL
The Trans-Siberian Railway

57

ROBERT L. JEFFERSON, *ROUGHING IT IN SIBERIA* (LONDON: S. LOW, MARSTON & CO., 1897), PP. 1–11

The first day in Asia

THE short winter day was waning when the Chelabinsk train, seven days out of Moscow, sluggishly passed the big stone erected in a defile in the centre of the Ural mountain range, and which marked the geographical boundary of Europe and Asia. Since yesterday, when we had left the level plains of Eastern Europe for the uplands of the Urals, the pace had been tantalizingly miserable. Some people say that man can get accustomed to anything, but it absorbs an enormous amount of patience in getting accustomed to Russian railway travelling; the further eastward one goes, the slower becomes the pace, the longer the stoppages at insignificant stations, and the greater the demonstration—beating of tin cans, blowing of whistles, and ringing of bells—which accompanies each arrival and departure. But now, with Europe behind, the whole wealth of Asia before one, combined with the uncertainty of the unknown, and which was backed up by popular prejudice and travellers' romantic tales, the thinking man has food for reflection, and much of it.

We were rounding curves, sharp ones too, on a badly ballasted track, that caused the heavy Russian cars to oscillate alarmingly, notwithstanding the crawl at which we were proceeding. The views to be obtained from the carriage windows were superb, in spite of the wintry aspect which everything bore. It was January—time of deep snow, frozen rivers, and biting atmosphere—everything around (except the interior of the car) was wintry to the last degree. Snow piled up in great drifts on the sharp spurs of the mountainside; the branches of the melancholy birches bowing down with the weight of their snowy covering; icicles hanging in the crevices of the rocks, where, in summer, splashed a mountain cascade. Deep below us, in a narrow gorge, lay the tortuous course of a fast-flowing river, but now frozen to its very bed, and its surface cut and streaked by the runners of many sledges. Now and again we could catch a glimpse of some woodman's hut perched up on the hillside—a veritable house of snow, and as cold and bleak-looking as any one could think to see.

Hurtling violently around the corner, we pass a level-crossing, where stands a caravan of patient horses waiting to cross, with white frost hard on their shaggy coats, and icicles from their eyes and nostrils; a sheepskin-clad moujik, with fur hat over eyes and ears, and feet encased in huge felt boots, complacently puffing at a stunted *papiros*. Here, too, an old woman comes out to flag the train—a woman who looks, from the amount of heavy clothing she wears, more like an animated beer barrel than a human being, and on whose stolid visage is nothing except an expression of tremendous importance at the position she occupies in the service of His Imperial Majesty Czar Nicholas the Second.

Darkness fell; my three companions were asleep. The conductor came and inserted in glass boxes at each end of the long car two diminutive candle-ends, the wicks of which he lighted laboriously. He looked at the thermometer to see how far off roasting we were, and then, after gazing superciliously around, left us. The heat in the car was fearful, beads of perspiration stood out on the faces of my sleeping companions, and yet this is only the Russian way of doing things. The Réaumur glass outside showed thirty-six degrees below freezing-point; inside, the heat was sufficient to almost roast one. And thus for seven days had we sat and lounged, talked and read, and stewed gradually, with no greater diversion than the rush for the buffet at each station, an occasional row with some blustering traveller who would hustle us for places, or the periodical breaking down of the locomotive, which event occurred about once a day on an average.

It was impossible to read, for the light in the car was so dim that one could scarcely see a couple of yards away. The train jolted and groaned and jarred, the candles flickered and guttered, people in the adjoining berths snored, a child was wailing dismally at the other end of the carriage; the heat became more intolerable, and I thanked Heaven when, two hours after darkness had fallen, the creaking of brakes and the distant ringing of bells announced our immediate arrival at Chelabinsk—the terminus of the European system of the Russian State Railways.

The arrival of a train at a Russian station is attended with an amount of excitement which it is hard to associate with the usually stolid Russian. Particularly is this so in Eastern Russia, where railways are new and interesting. As the train slowly steams in, the assembled mob of sightseers and officials raise shouts of welcome—at least they seem to be. A man hard by the ticket-office performs a terrific tintinabulation on a large suspended bell. All the conductors blow whistles, while the locomotive syren goes off in spasmodic squealings. Slowly, but with many jerks and much grinding, the train comes to a standstill. But the passengers are not allowed to descend all at once. First of all the engine-driver must get off and shake hands with the first half-dozen men that happen to be hanging about near, no doubt receiving in return a sort of congratulatory address to the effect that he has got so far safely. Half a dozen gaily caparisoned policemen, in red hats with white cockades, and armed to the teeth with revolvers and swords, parade up and salute gravely. All the conductors get off—there seems to be quite a crowd of them. All salute a red-hatted, despotic-looking individual, who is gazing about with tremendous scorn and indifference, as if this sort of thing was very boring, although ten to one his heart is thumping with pride and excitement; for he is the stationmaster, salary one hundred pounds a-year, princely for him, indeed.

This individual, on thoroughly satisfying himself that beyond the possibility of the remotest doubt the train is really there, raises his hand as if he were about to pronounce a benediction, and instantly there belches from the heart of the mob a smaller mob of much-bewhiskered men in white aprons. These are the porters. These gentlemen throw themselves upon the train in a frenzy of hurry; tear open the doors, push, scramble, and fall over each other in their endeavours to get in first, and ultimately disappear from view. The crowd outside grows silent in expectancy; but the racket which proceeds from inside the train tells eloquently that the porters are doing their fell work. The cars now begin to disgorge boxes and men, bundles and women, baskets and babies, everything mixed up, everybody talking. The crowd outside parts, and the crowd *just* out slides over the slippery platform in a hard mass to the buffet doors. These always open outwards, and are generally just wide enough for a thin man to get in sideways. Then the crush commences. You are in the middle of the crowd with a corner of a box in your ear and four men standing on your feet. You worm and edge your way out of reach of the box and run your chest against the side of a kettle, blacker than the blackest hat, and which is tied around the neck of an evil-smelling moujik in front of you. Somehow the door gets open; the janitor inside scuttles, in order to prevent being swept off his feet. In we squeeze, and find ourselves in a long white-washed apartment, heated to a suffocating degree.

Down the centre of the apartment runs a long table covered with glasses, plate, and cutlery. Over on one side is a long bar, covered with smaller glasses and large bottles, mostly containing vodki, as well as at least half a hundred dishes of the *hors d'œuvre* style—sardines, bits of sausage, sprats, caviare, sliced cucumber, pickled mushrooms, artful dabs of cheese, raw radishes, smoked herring, and such like. For the nonce the crowd ignores the long table, equally so a kitchen-like arrangement in the corner where steams a heterogeneous mass of cutlets and "Russian" beef-steaks, and which is presided over by a couple of marvellously clean-looking men who are rigged out *à la chef*. Vodki is the lodestone of the arrived passengers. Each man gulps down a small glass of the fiery liquid, seizes a piece of fish, or sausage, or cheese, or whatever he may fancy or may be handy, and subsides to the big table, chewing vigorously. Energetic waiters pounce upon him, lay before him a big plate of the universal "stche," or cabbage soup, over which our Russian hangs his head and commences ladling away, apparently oblivious to its boiling heat or the feelings of the people around. The tables fill up. Great slabs of brown meat, floating in fat, are distributed with rapidity, and which are with equal rapidity demolished. Manners are delightfully absent. People jostle, growl, and gulp; smoke *papiros* and puff the smoke in each other's faces; or make the most disgusting noises with their mouths. At last, having got through several pounds of meat and fat, and drunk about six to eight glasses of lemon-coloured hot water, which is called tea, per man, the crowd lounges around in contentment, and waits patiently for the bell to announce the probable departure of the train—which may be anything in the region of one hour to four, or while there is a bit of food in the buffet uneaten.

What a relief to get out of such an evil-smelling mob and the heat and general nauseating surroundings, and, wrapt warmly in furs, to promenade the ice-covered platform! They have unscrewed the engine from the cars, and it has disappeared into the blackness of night on a search for wood and water. At one end of the platform the third and fourth class passengers, peasants of the humblest order, are huddled together—sitting or lying, some asleep, some laughing boisterously— a group of girls in their midst crooning forth a wailing song to the accompaniment of a harmonica, the national musical instrument of the Russian moujik. Over to the left, twinkling lights denote the town of Chelabinsk. Eastward all is black, save for the blinking of a signal light a mile away. That is the road to Siberia, and here is the commencement of the Trans-Siberian Railway.

58

JAMES YOUNG SIMPSON, *SIDE-LIGHTS ON SIBERIA; SOME ACCOUNT OF THE GREAT SIBERIAN RAILROAD, THE PRISONS AND EXILE SYSTEM* (EDINBURGH AND LONDON: W. BLACKWOOD AND SONS, 1898), PP. 147–149

Sleepers lay about everywhere—on a large central platform that occupied a considerable space, beneath it, on the supplementary shelves that skirted two of the walls, under them, even in the passages. They were often miserably clad, and slept in their clothes; others had partially disrobed or were stark naked. So thickly were they strewn that one had to pick every step: beyond a certain distance progress was impossible. And this is not distasteful to the Russian peasant; the Government lodging-houses, as well conducted as any in more Western lands, and cheaper than the ordinary lodging-house, are practically deserted in favour of the latter. These are the men you find in the overcrowded Siberian prisons; but the Petersburg Night Shelter surpassed anything I saw in the land of *tundra* and *taiga*.

The railway journey from Moscow to Nijni-Novgorod is the work of a night. Here the prisoners are embarked upon barges that are towed down the Volga and up the Kama as far as Perm. From this town they resume travel by train, and, crossing the Urals, descend on Tiumen. This last stretch of a day and night presents no hardship: the ordinary third-class car lighted by barred windows is a luxury compared with the horse-waggons in which the emigrants who pass along the Trans-Siberian Railway have to spend a week.

Tiumen is the first town in Siberia proper that greets the traveller when following the northern route. Its most interesting feature is the Forwarding Prison, of which no one has yet said a good word. It stands on an open piece of ground on the outskirts of the town: close by runs the railway, so that there is no difficulty in conducting the convicts from the waggons to their new quarters. The appearance is that of a rectangular three-storeyed building of whitewashed brick, rising out of a surrounding courtyard, which in turn is bounded by a high wall, erected in keeping with the prison as regards material and colour. Immediately to the right of the main entrance leading into the yard is a small edifice built on the wall, and used as a guardroom. Following the wall in its enclosing circuit, we find that on the next side, to the right of the main building, it supports the residence of the second-in-command, and farther on the gaily painted church. In the portion of the yard behind the prison is a large detached wooden barrack used only in summer as Peresîlni quarters, for it has no heating apparatus: it might hold 150 persons. Through a postern in the wall immediately behind the prison we pass into a new enclosure surrounded by the ordinary wooden palisade: it contains two recent log buildings, in one of which is set up machinery for grinding corn. Continuing our survey of the outhouses surrounding the main prison, we find on the third side a continuous line of single-storeyed log barracks, and before we come round to the front entrance again, we pass a two-storeyed building lying between it and the last of these outer Peresîlni barracks, being in close connection with the latter, although not on the same wall.

On the ground-floor of the main building are situated the *kontora* or office, a small *karaülnaya* or guardroom, and the clothes-store. Also, in a series of stuffy, poorly lighted rooms lying to the back, are the kitchen and bakery. Through the steam escaping from boiling caldrons we could see spectre-like figures, some of them stripped to the waist, gliding about over the rough brick flooring. And as the men and their existence, so was the labour of their hands. The bread here was poor and the *kvass* bitter compared with what we found in other prisons. Not far removed from this were the silent cells of correction. More will be said later about punishment as it figures in the Siberian prison system. Suffice it for the present that in this particular instance a gradational series of cells, perhaps half-a-dozen in all, opened off a corridor. There was the plain whitewashed cell, with plank-bed, and window out of reach. There was the smaller, bare, windowless cell with double doors—a hole. In one of the latter a refractory individual had been confined for seven or eight days, and when the doors were opened he blinked like an owl, and commenced a violent tirade on the *natchalnik*. "Why is he there?" "Because he disobeyed me"; and I confess my sympathies were all on the side of the official. The fare for those who have merited such dismal isolation is bread and water, and this system is found to prove effectual in the great majority of cases.

On the second flat was a great number of small rooms, some of which were crowded: one of them, which would have looked full with fifteen men, contained twenty-nine. The interiors of the rooms had a general appearance of cleanliness, and some of the walls had been recently whitewashed. In one of these *kameras* was a motley group of half-a-dozen dangerous-looking politicals condemned to hard labour. With the exception of an uncouth Jew, clad in a sombre frock-coat, who was deeply engrossed attending to a decrepit samovar, they belonged to that class of mischief-making Poles who live on the Austrian frontier and revel in intrigue.

59

ISABELLA L. BIRD, *KOREA AND HER NEIGHBORS: A NARRATIVE OF TRAVEL, WITH AN ACCOUNT OF THE RECENT VICISSITUDES AND PRESENT POSITION OF THE COUNTRY* (NEW YORK: FLEMING H. REVELL, 1898), PP. 239–244

The Trans-Siberian railroad

AFTER returning to Wladivostok, accompanied by a young Danish gentleman who was kindly lent to me by Messrs. Kuntz and Albers, and who spoke English and Russian, I spent a week on the Ussuri Railway, the eastern section of the Trans-Siberian Railway, going as far as the hamlet of Ussuri on the Ussuri River at the great Ussuri Bridge, beyond which the line, though completed for 50 *versts*, was not open for traffic. Indeed, up to that point from Nikolskoye trains were run twice daily rather to "settle the line" than for profit, and their average speed was only twelve miles an hour. The weather was brilliant, varied by a heavy snowstorm.

The present Tsar is understood to be enthusiastic about this railroad. During his visit to Wladivostok in 1891, when Tsarevitch, he inaugurated the undertaking by wheeling away the first barrowful of earth and placing the first stone in position, after which, work was begun simultaneously at both ends.

The eastern terminus of this great railroad undertaking is close to the sea and the Government deep-water pier, at which the fine steamers from Odessa of the Russian "Volunteer Fleet" discharge their cargoes. The station is large and very handsome, and both it and the noble administrative offices are built of gray stone, with the architraves of the doors and windows in red brick. Buffets and all else were in efficient working order. In the winter of 1895–96 only third and fourth class cars were running, the latter chiefly patronized by Koreans and Chinese. Each third class carriage is divided into three compartments with a corridor, and has a lavatory and steam-heating apparatus. The backs of the seats are hooked up to form upper berths for sleeping, and as the cars are eight feet high they admit of broad luggage shelves above these. The engines which ran the traffic were old American locomotives, but those which are to be introduced, as well as all the rolling stock, are being manufactured in the Baltic provinces. So also are the rails, the iron and steel bridges, the water tanks, the iron work required for stations, and all else.

Large railway workshops with rows of substantial houses for artisans have been erected at Nikolskoye, 102 *versts* from Wladivostok, for the repairs of rolling stock on the Ussuri section, and were already in full activity.

There is nothing about this Ussuri Railway of the newness and provisional aspect of the Western American lines, or even of parts of the Canadian Pacific Railroad. The track was already ballasted as far as Ussuri (327 *versts*), steel bridges spanned the minor streams, and substantial stations either of stone or decorated wood, with buffets at fixed distances, successfully compare both in stability and appearance with those of our English branch lines. The tank houses are of hewn stone. Houses for the employés, standing in neatly fenced gardens, are both decorative and substantial, being built of cement and logs protected by five coats of paint, and contain four rooms each. The crossings are well laid and protected. Culverts and retaining walls are of solid masonry, and telegraph wires accompany the road, which is worked strictly on the block system. The aspect of solidity and permanence is remarkable. Even the temporary bridge over the Ussuri, 1,050 feet in length, a trestle bridge of heavy timber to resist the impact of the ice, is so massive as to make the great steel bridge, the handsome abutments of which were already built, appear as if it would be a work of supererogation.

Up to that point there are no serious embankments or cuttings, and the gradients are easy. The cost of construction of the Ussuri section is 50,000 roubles per *verst*, a rouble at this time being worth about 2s. 2d. This includes rolling stock, stations, and all bridges except that over the Amur, which was to cost 3,000,000 roubles, but may now be dispensed with owing to the diversion of the route through Manchuria. Convict labor was abandoned in 1894, and the line in Primorsk is being constructed by Chinese "navvies," who earn about 80 cents per day, and who were bearing the rigor of a Siberian winter in well-warmed, semi-subterranean huts, the line being pushed on as much as possible during the cold season. For the first 102 *versts*, it passes along prettily wooded shores of inlets and banks of streams, and the country is fairly well peopled, judging from the number of sleighs and the bustle at the six stations *en route*. The line as far as Nikolskoye was opened in early November, 1893, and in a year had earned 280,000 roubles. The last section had only been open for eight weeks when I travelled upon it.

Nikolskoye, where I spent two pleasant days at the hospitable establishment of Messrs. Kuntz and Albers, is the only place between Wladivostok and Ussuri of any present importance. It is a *village* of 8,000 inhabitants on a rich rolling prairie, watered by the Siphun. It has six streets of grotesque width, a *verst* and a half long each. There is no poverty. It is a place of rapid growth and prosperity, the centre of a great trade in grain, and has a large flour mill owned by Mr. Lindholm, a Government contractor. It has a spacious marketplace and bazaar, and two churches.

It reminds me of parts of Salt Lake City, and the houses are of wood, plastered and whitewashed, with corrugated iron roofs mainly. A few are thatched. All stand in plots of garden ground. Utilitarianism is supreme. I drove for 20 miles in the region round the settlement, and everywhere saw prosperous farms and farming villages on the prairie, Russian and Korean, and found the settlers kindly and hospitable, and surrounded by material comfort. Nikolskoye is a great military station. There were infantry and artillery to the number of 9,000, and there, as elsewhere, large new barracks were being pushed to completion. An area of 50 acres was covered with brick barracks, magazines, stables, drill and parade grounds, and officers' quarters, and the military club is a really fine building. Newness, progress, and confidence in the future are as characteristic of Nikolskoye as of any rising town in the Far West of America.

The farther journey, occupying the greater part of two days and a night, except when near the swamps of the Hanka Lake, is through a superb farming region. Large villages with windmills are met with along the line for the first 30 *versts*, as far as the buffet station of Spasskoje. The stoneless soil, a rich loam 6 feet and more in depth, produces heavy crops of oats, wheat, barley, maize, rye, potatoes, and tobacco. Beyond Spasskoje and east of the Hanka Lake up to the Amur a magnificent region waits to be peopled.

Well may Eastern Siberia receive the name of Russia's "Pacific Empire," including as it does the Amur and Maritime provinces, with their area of 880,000 square miles, rich in gold, copper, iron, lead, and coal, and with a soil which for a vast extent is of unbounded fertility. When China ceded to Russia in 1860 the region which we call Russian Manchuria, she probably did so in ignorance of its vast agricultural capacities and mineral wealth.

The noble Amur, with its forest-covered shores, is navigable for 1,000 miles, and already 50 merchant steamers ply upon it, and its great tributary the Ussuri can be navigated to within 120 miles of Wladivostok. The great basin of the Ussuri, it is estimated, could support five million people, and from Khabaroffka to the Tumen, it is considered by experts that the land could sustain from 20 to 40 to the square mile, while at present the population of the Amur and Ussuri provinces is only ⅘ths of a man to the square mile!

Grass, timber, water, coal, minerals, a soil as rich as the prairies of Illinois, and a climate not only favorable to agriculture but to human health, all await the settler, and the broad, unoccupied, and fertile lands which Russian Manchuria offers are clamoring for inhabitants. To set against these advantages there are the frozen waterways and the ice-bound harbor. It is utterly impossible that an increasing population will content itself without an outlet for its produce. A port on the Pacific open all the year is fast becoming as much a commercial as a political necessity, and doubtless the opening of the Trans-Siberian Railroad four years hence will settle the question (if it has not been settled before) and doom the policy which has shut Russia up in regions of "thick ribbed ice" to utter extinction.

In the Maritime Province, Russia is steadily and solidly laying the foundations of a new empire which she purposes to make as nearly as possible a homogeneous one.

"No foreigner need apply"! The emigrants, who are going out at the rate of from 700 to 1,000 families a year, are of a good class. Emigration is fostered in two ways. By the first, the Government grants assisted passages to heads of families who are possessed of 600 roubles (about £60 at present), which are deposited with a Government official at Odessa, and are repaid to the emigrant on landing at Wladivostok. The industry and thrift represented by this sum indicate a large proportion of the best class of settlers. Under the second arrangement, families possessed of little capital or none receive free passages. On arriving, emigrants of both classes are lodged in excellent emigrant barracks, and can buy the necessary agricultural implements at cost price from a Government depôt, advice as to the purchase being thrown in. Each family receives a free allotment of from 200 to 300 acres of arable land, and a loan of 600 roubles, to be repaid without interest in thirty-two years, the young male colonists being exempted from military service for the same period. Already much of the land along the line as far as the Ussuri has been allotted, and houses are rapidly springing up, and there is nothing to prevent this fine country from being peopled up to the Amur, the rivers Sungacha and Ussuri, which form the boundary of Russia from the Hanka Lake to Khabaroffka, giving a natural protection from Chinese brigandage. In addition to direct emigration, large numbers of time-expired men, chiefly Cossacks, are encouraged to settle on lands and do so.

It would be shortsighted to minimize the importance of the present drift of population to Eastern Siberia, which is likely to assume immense proportions on the opening of the railway, or the commercial value of that colossal undertaking, which is greatly enhanced by the treaty under which Russia has taken powers to run the Trans-Siberian line through Chinese Manchuria. The creation of a new route which will bring the Far East within 6,000 miles and 16 days of London, and cheapen the cost of the transit of passengers very considerably, cannot be overlooked either. The railroad is being built for futurity, and is an enterprize worthy of the great nation which undertakes it.[1]

Note

1 I am very glad to be able to fortify my opinion of the solid and careful construction of this line by that of Colonel Waters, military attaché to the British Embassy at St. Petersburg, who has recently crossed Siberia, and desires to give emphatic testimony to "the magnificent character of the great railway crossing Siberia," as well as by that of another recent traveller, Mr. J. Y. Simpson, who, in *Blackwood's Magazine* for January, 1897, in an article "The Great Siberian Iron Road," after a long description of the laborious carefulness with which the line is being built, writes thus: "Lastly, one is impressed with the *extremely finished* nature of the work."

60

ANNETTE M. B. MEAKIN, *A RIBBON OF IRON* (WESTMINSTER: A. CONSTABLE, 1901), PP. 21–25, 110–118, 156–159, 166–172, 273–277

The Siberian express is a kind of "Liberty Hall," where you can shut your door and sleep all day if you prefer it, or eat and drink, smoke and play cards if you like that better. An electric bell on one side of your door summons a servingman to make your bed or sweep your floor, as the case may be, while a bell on the other side summons a waiter from the buffet. Besides the ordinary electric lights you are provided with an electric reading lamp by which you may read all night if you choose. Time passes very pleasantly on such a train, and it is quite possible to enjoy the scenery, for there is none of that fearful hurry that makes railway travelling so risky for body and nerves in Europe and America. Our average speed was about sixteen miles an hour.

At one end of the cheerful dining car was a Bechstein piano, and opposite to it a bookcase stocked with Russian novels; doubtless it will contain plenty of French and English books in time. On the fourth day we had an agreeable concert. Amongst the performers were a gentleman with a good tenor voice and two lady pianists of no ordinary merit. Three portraits adorned the dining car walls—those of the Emperor and Empress and that of Prince Hilkof—while ferns and flowers gathered by the way gave a homelike appearance to the whole.

We stopped at a great many stations; indeed on some parts of the route we seemed to get into a chronic state of stopping. At large stations there was often a halt of twenty minutes or half an hour. Passengers anxious for a change of fare seized such opportunities to dine at the station buffet. Card playing went on all the time and small sums of money were played for. If a Russian sits down to a game of cards, nothing but a matter of life and death will induce him to stir from it till it is finished.

"You have yet to learn what a Russian is worth when he's playing cards," said a German fellow traveller after I had waited two hours to get the name of an hotel from a young officer. As it was already midnight I gave up in despair and retired. The next day I got my information from the card player, but it was accompanied by no apology. There is a strange superstition among the lower classes that if a man can manage to get into his possession a piece, however small, of the rope with which a criminal has been hanged, he will always have luck at cards. A few weeks before we arrived there a man was hanged at Irkutsk, and a peasant, after endless trouble and exertion, secured a little bit of the rope, much to the envy of his relatives and friends.

The train was quite full. One lady about thirty years of age, who spoke French, told me she hated Siberia, and was only going to Irkutsk to sell some property. She intended to return to St. Petersburg by the next train but one; that is, in less than a fortnight, which meant twenty days of railway travelling and a journey of 8,000 miles within a month. Distance, like time, counts for nothing in Siberia. This lady thought us bold, if not rash, to travel without a revolver. "I always carry two," she said. Later on the Mayor of Vladivostok, who shared the next *coupé* with the manager of the Amur Steamer Company, took out his little pocket pistol and handled it fondly. "It saved my life once," he said. "You had better get one in Omsk if you haven't brought one with you." The Mayor told my mother a woeful tale of a fall he had had just before leaving St. Petersburg.

"I broke two ribs," he said, "and now I hear them crack every time I rise on the cushions of the train, which are too springy under the circumstances."

The conductor was a good-looking man in uniform. His position on the train seemed to be something like that of a purser on a steamer. We tried to find out from him whether there was any hotel at Omsk, and what sort of a place it was, but the only information we could extract was that it was warmer at Irkutsk than at Moscow. He knew nothing of Omsk, and could not even tell us when we might expect to arrive till we were within a few hours of the place.

After a day and two nights of steady travelling we came in sight of the Volga. All were eager to see something of the famous bridge over which we were to cross. Some, who feared they might not wake at 4 a.m., got up before daylight. I myself saw nothing of it then, but on another occasion when we passed at four on a lovely autumn afternoon I had a splendid view standing, while we crossed the water, on the platform between two carriages.

The Alexander bridge was named after Alexander II. It has thirteen spans of fifty sazhens each, a total length of six hundred and fifty sazhens and a distance of more than six hundred and seventy-four sazhens between its abutments. A sazhen is equal to seven English feet. It is built with stone piers on the double girder system with parallel chords and a roadway upon the lower chord. The rails are laid on metal beams. To us it was a bridge of delicate iron lace work closing over our heads.

Emigrants—lady doctors—Krasnoiarsk again

EMIGRANTS meet you at every turn on the Siberian railway and on the river steamers. Indeed I might almost say that we had them with us wherever we went. Russians are emigrating at the rate of 200,000 a year, and Minusinsk is one of the districts to which they are being sent in shoals. In cold weather we used to see them lying in "heaps" at the railway stations, sleeping away the time and keeping one another warm. When there was nothing better to do we amused ourselves by trying to guess to whom that pair of legs belonged, or whether this head belonged to a man or a woman. Wrapped in their winter sheepskins, to lessen their baggage, they would sleep sweetly while the powerful midsummer sun poured down upon their upturned faces.

Yet these poor creatures are by no means uncared for. To begin with, when, of their own free will, they make up their minds to emigrate, the Government allows them to send delegates ahead to inspect the land that is to be their new home. When these men return a final decision is made. On the frontier, at Cheliabinsk, all their passports are carefully examined before they are allowed to proceed. Whenever they have to wait more than a certain number of hours temporary shelters are provided. Those at Omsk are huts such as the Kirgiz live in. I was greatly mystified at first to see Russians going in and out of such dwellings.

Returning from Minusinsk to Krasnoiarsk we had for our companion on the steamer a young medical lady who had just accompanied a batch of emigrants from Moscow to Minusinsk. She had with her a large wicker basket in which she carried medicines, bandages and other articles that might be wanted. Her duties consisted in going a round of inspection every day. On the steamer she had to see that the babies got proper food, taste their milk, and see that they were fed with white bread, the ordinary black bread being too coarse for very young children. On one of her rounds she had discovered that a man was developing typhus. It had then been her duty to have him landed at the nearest spot to a hospital, and give him over herself to the care of the nurses. She expected to spend the following summer months in attending various batches on their journeys from Krasnoiarsk to Minusinsk. Another lady doctor was stationed in Krasnoiarsk to attend to the welfare of emigrants halting there.

The Government allows each man a certain amount of land, and this he is free to cultivate for ten years free of taxes. After that he becomes a regular citizen and pays his taxes like the rest. If he is very poor to start with, he may borrow thirty roubles, or some such sum, from the local official who has charge of Government money for that purpose. This he pays back by instalments as his worldly goods increase. There are some families who do not take kindly to the new life; they pack up their bundles once more and return to Russia. I wondered at first how it was that so many seemed to be travelling the wrong way. "Those are people who have changed their minds," I was told; "they are going home again." Now that they can travel by rail perhaps there are some who take the return trip for mere pleasure. Who knows? The carriages in which they travel are suited specially to these long journeys. Wooden flaps are arranged to form upper berths, and these they cover with their own bedding. So comfortable do they make themselves that they sleep the greater part of the way, and only wake for meals. Making my way through the central corridor of one of these carriages I felt as if I were walking between great cupboards, the shelves of which were packed with grimy humanity.

As for the souls of the emigrants, their welfare is also looked after by the Government. A church-railway carriage is hooked on to the end of the train when required, and a long-haired priest officiates. The church being very small the air soon becomes vitiated from the presence of such dirty people; none but an emigrant could stand it.

Great care is taken that those who have been neighbours in the old country shall continue to be neighbours in the new, and fresh arrivals are not allowed to interfere with those who were there before them.

At Omsk we made the acquaintance of a gentleman who is styled "Head of the Peasants." His business is to arrange with foreign markets for the purchase of their salt butter, corn and other agricultural produce. A large amount of the butter consumed by our London poor is made by Siberian peasants.

We found it a difficult matter to get away from Minusinsk, not because of the attractions of the place, but on account of the irregularity of the steamers. Hearing that one was due at five in the afternoon, and that after only an hour's delay it would start immediately for Krasnoiarsk, we drove down to the bank—there is nothing that can be called a wharf except a barge moored to the side—and, having dismissed our droshky, sat on some rough planks to await our steamer. It never came. After several hours had passed and the evening was getting dark and chilly, a peasant woman came and persuaded us to go back to the inn for the night. She managed to convey her meaning by shutting her eyes and leaning her head on her hand. The people who had seen us leave the inn smiled knowingly as they saw us return. Their faces seemed to say, "I told you so." This was very aggravating, but worse was still to come. The innkeeper came out to meet us just as calmly as if we had been new comers. He showed us, by pointing to the clock, that the steamer would start at five o'clock the next morning. We did not pay our droshky man, lest he should forget to call for us in good time. Lying down in our clothes, we spent a restless night and were thankful to hear the whistle of a steamer soon after daybreak. "There she is," I cried, and in another minute the droshky man was thumping at our door. I went out into the passage. The innkeeper lay there snoring, and did not seem inclined to wake. I roused him, however, and paid our bill. Then once more he and his wife bade us adieu. This time I said *dosvi danie* very politely, and gave the woman a larger tip, for I had a presentiment that we should meet again.

There lay the steamer; but how much smaller she looked than the one by which we had come! We began to have misgivings; but when we said "Krasnoiarsk?" in a questioning tone, to the men on the bank, they smiled and nodded. Thinking all was right, we told the droshky man to take our things on board. All at once the people shook their heads and tried to stop us. "Krasnoiarsk?" we said again, and again they nodded, but they would not let us go on board. As the steamer now showed signs of starting I grew desperate, and seizing my umbrella drew a line on the sand, and making a mark for Minusinsk and another for Krasnoiarsk, showed them where we wanted to go. Then an old peasant took the umbrella from my hand and added a branch line to my sand picture. At the end of the branch line he put a mark, pronouncing at the same time the name of a place I had never heard of. Then he turned and pointed to the steamer. At last we understood. The steamer's name was *Krasnoiarsk*, but she was bound for quite a different place, a a village on the Abakan! This time we felt painfully self-conscious as we drove back to the inn.

The following evening, at five o'clock, our steamer came at last. We went on board at once, but she did not start till five the following morning, thirty-six hours after the appointed time.

The name of this steamer was *Scotia*. She was originally a sea-going pleasure yacht, built in Scotland, but we found her a dirty, second-rate passenger boat. Still she was a tough little ship, for she was one of the two that braved the Kara sea and made their way from England to Krasnoiarsk. It rained a good deal going back, but we borrowed mackintoshes, and sat on deck most of the time. At one of the stopping places a pig ran swiftly down the bank and began swimming towards us; every one laughed to see its business-like air. Suddenly, when close to the steamer, after taking a good look at us all, it turned round and swam back to the bank as fast as it had come.

"Ah!" said a peasant who was leaning over the side, "he only travels first class!" (There were no first cabins on the *Scotia*, all were marked "second.")

What a nice change it was to get back to Krasnoiarsk and have eatable food once more! At Minusinsk there had been so little one could eat. The eggs were peculiar, bread, milk, and cream were sour, while a strange taste in the water spoiled the flavour of the tea we had brought from England.

At Krasnoiarsk we wrote our letters, and I took them to the post-office to be registered. The man insisted that the addresses must be in Russian, and as the only name I had learned to write in Russian characters was my own, I was obliged to register them to myself.

Travelling fourth class—Lake Baikal convicts

"ONE thing I must tell you," said a gentleman of Irkutsk as we sat at his hospitable board. "Your difficulties are only just beginning."

"We heard that in Moscow," I replied, laughing, "and it has been repeated to us in every town on our way."

"It is all very well thus far," continued our friend, shaking his head, "but now you will have to travel fourth class. There are no other carriages on the line; you will have to spend four nights and three days in the company of filthy emigrants, in very close company, alas! for the train will be crowded."

At the post office I met a Dutchman who was going the same way.

"It will be very rough travelling," he said. "I hope you have brought a letter from St. Petersburg?"

"Yes, we have a letter," I replied, "but how can that help us?"

"You had better take it at once to the station-master," was the reply; "he may be able to prevent your compartment from being overcrowded."

I at once took a droshky and drove to the station, a distance of two miles, for we were to leave at twelve that night for Lake Baikal, and there was no time to lose.

Not a soul at the station understood anything but Russian. However the station-master read the letter and reassured me with bows and smiles.

When the evening came we had kind friends to see us off, and just before starting had the good fortune to be introduced to some agreeable German-speaking tourists. These gentlemen were going no farther than to the other side of the Lake. Like every one else they did their utmost to discourage us. "There will be no porters to carry your luggage," they said. "You will have to carry it yourselves."

"We are taking no heavy luggage," I replied.

We passed the night in pleasant conversation, forgetting the hard seats in thankfulness that there were no emigrants in our division. At 5 a.m. we saw the Baikal. Then, in their efforts to help us, the tourists seized our baggage and lifted it out as soon as the train stopped, declaring that we might look in vain for porters at such a spot. At that very moment several of these useful personages hurried up and relieved our "Job's comforters" of their self-imposed task.

There lay the far-famed ice-breaker, puffing dark smoke from its three huge funnels, and standing so high above the water level that we shuddered to think how it would roll if caught in a storm. Of the storms that are to be met with on the Baikal we had heard enough.

Like the model we had seen at the Paris Exhibition, the ice-breaker had a great door in its stern with rails laid down to receive goods in their trucks direct without unloading. As this part was not yet in working order we found men busily unloading and disappearing with their burdens through the cavernous opening. Passengers who had hurried ahead to secure the best berths were returning with downcast faces; they had been told that they could not be admitted for an hour or more.

Just as we were preparing to sit down on our baggage and wait with the rest, a ship's officer came out inquiring for the English ladies. He told us that a first-class cabin had been reserved for us and proceeded at once to conduct us thither. The other passengers looked curiously after us as we disappeared within the great portals. Passing through the body of the ship, a large warehouse-looking place, supported on either side by elephantine pillars of iron, we ascended a skeleton staircase at the further end and found ourselves in quite another world.

Transbaikalia

A TRAIN composed of fourth-class carriages stood waiting for the passengers as they came off the ice-breaker. We got into a compartment and tried to keep it to ourselves, but there was no sign of starting, and more and more people kept coming in. Those who got there first took the lower places, and the rest clambered up on to the shelves above, which were three deep. At last those above us became an object of desire to two men of so dirty and unkempt an appearance that we became desperate. I put up my hands to ward them off, and cried "Conductor" in the most threatening tones I could muster. It was no use; they had gone into the next division, but only to climb quietly over into our shelves when they thought we were not looking. The sight of a wretched pair of feet hanging out over my head was too much for me. I rushed on to the platform, and addressed the first man in uniform I came across. This happened to be an engineer who had charge of that part of the line. As he spoke French I was able to explain what was the matter. He came with me at once to our compartment. The two men seeing him approach slid stealthily back the way they had come.

"This is not a fit place for ladies," said our new friend, looking round at our grimy companions—"and *English* ladies too! Oh, this will never do. I will arrange something better for you." Then he hurried off. In a few minutes he came back to say that he had ordered an engineer's private carriage to be put on the train for us. "You will have sleeping berths and a little room with a samovar, where you can make tea," he added; "but it will not be ready for two hours. I fear you must wait here till then."

The two hours seemed as though they would never pass, and the dirty men had climbed above us once more. At last, when it was getting quite dark, the engineer came again.

"I am very sorry," he said, "but a telegram has come ordering us to keep the carriage I promised you for an official from St. Petersburg, who is expected shortly. His Excellency, M. Iswolsky and his family, who passed through last week, took all the other carriages. What I can do for you I will. A captain and six soldiers have got a luggage van to themselves. If you don't mind sharing it with them as far as Stretinsk, I will have part of it curtained off for you."

"Anything, anything but this," we cried.

Once more he left us and we waited on. The night was getting chilly and rain began to come down in torrents. At length two men appeared with a lantern. They were the engineer and the conductor. The engineer gave my mother his arm, and they escorted us out into the rain and along the line to the last carriage on the train. The step was very high, but we clambered in.

How we blessed that kind engineer! With curtains from his own house he had partitioned off one corner of the luggage van for our use. The deal boards that had been put there for the soldiers were all we had to sleep on by night, or to sit on by day. But that was nothing so long as we had it all to ourselves. The size of our *coupé* was ten feet by eight. In the centre of the van was a stove with a chimney going through the roof.

"The captain thought you might be cold, so he made the soldiers light a fire," said the engineer, and we were most grateful for the genial warmth, for we had got wet as well as cold in coming across.

With heartfelt thanks we bade our deliverer good night, and the train started. It was just midnight.

Of course there was no going to bed for us that night, or for the three that followed. We lay down just as we were on our rugs, which we had folded as thickly as possible to take off the hardness of the eighteen inch boards. Oh, how our bones ached after ten minutes in one position!

My mother had the side nearest the curtain; a soldier slept on a similar board to ours on the other side of it, and she occasionally felt his elbow. We had a tiny window in the corner, so high up that to look out we had to stand on the seat. *Still, we had it all to ourselves.*

Three days and four nights we spent in that luggage van. The soldiers and their captain were kindness itself. They fetched us hot water and milk at the stations, and when we came short of bread gave us some of their own, which was brown, with sour lumps of uncooked dough here and there.

As the line was not yet open to the general public there were no buffets ready. We lived on bread, milk and tea. We washed our faces every morning with some of the water brought for tea. Happily we had neither dust nor extreme heat to contend with; for there was a gentle and continuous rain nearly all the time.

The next two vans to ours were prison vans. The windows were strongly barred, and instead of ordinary doors they had a sliding one in the side with a special lock.

Four of our soldiers sprang out the moment the train stopped, no matter whether there was a station or not, and stood with shouldered bayonets one on either side of each of the prison vans. Whenever I looked up at the prison bars I saw a cluster of children's faces peering out—hardly ever a man's face. The prisoners must have spent their time in sleep. There certainly did not seem much danger of their escaping. Once one of the soldiers picked some flowers and handed them in to the children. They stretched out their hands eagerly, and looked so pleased to get them.

For at least thirty-six hours heavy raindrops pattered unceasingly on the roof of our carriage. Every bit of low-lying ground had become a marsh, and the trees and bushes were heavy with water. The many streamlets that we passed were overflowing their banks. It was evening when the weather at last showed signs of change. Ahead of us the rain clouds had become a bright blue, which contrasted strangely with the brilliant green of the landscape.

Early on the morning of the third day we reached Chitá, and found it to be a flourishing town picturesquely situated among wooded hills. Many of the best houses, as I afterwards learnt, were hidden from view, and it was really a larger place than it looked from the station. We had introductions to people in Chitá, and had fully intended to spend a few days there, but the thought of leaving our cosy corner and having to travel for the rest of the way with emigrants was too appalling. We decided to go on in the luggage van, to which we had become quite attached, and not to break our journey again till we got to Stretinsk.

We were now travelling through the region known as Transbaikalia, which covers more square miles than the whole of the German Empire. Lying between Lake Baikal and the Upper Amur, it is bounded on the north by Yakutsk, a country of reindeer, frozen marshes, and unfriendly climate, and on the south and south-east by China.

Our train was to start for Vladivostok at 7 a.m., and it was a long drive to the station. I shall never forget the state of the roads: it was like driving over ploughed fields after rain.

At the station we recognized many familiar faces, amongst which were those of the brown-coated priest, the Moscow student and the actor. When people have been travelling together for weeks and weeks they meet more or less as old friends even if they have never exchanged a word.

As we walked up and down the platform we were struck with the great number of nationalities represented on it. Coreans dressed all in white with strange white headdresses, that made a striking contrast to their jet-black hair and dark yellow skins, were squatting on the ground in rows. Servian gipsies were walking about amongst the crowd and telling fortunes; Chinese and Japs were everywhere. One well-dressed Chinese lady stood quietly by the ticket office while her husband got the tickets. How she could balance herself on her tiny feet was a mystery.

There was a Circassian family from Tiflis all very good looking. The beautiful mother wore her thick black hair down her back in long natural curls, while on her head was a velvet cap, covered with a lace handkerchief which floated over her shoulders. Her handsome son-in-law was a priest. He had a bush of curly black hair and wore a long grey coat with loose sleeves. It was lined with bright purple silk.

The express train by which we travelled to Vladivostok was not so luxurious as the "train de luxe" by which we had travelled to Omsk. It was like an ordinary post train with a rough kind of dining car attached. At one end of the dining car was a buffet behind which stood two Jap boys always alert for orders. Down the middle ran a long table which was occupied half the time by passengers drinking beer.

I observed that the train seemed to be managed by soldiers rather than by the usual railway men, and that the stations were many of them quite military in appearance; whereupon I was told that this was because in time of war the Ussuri railway would become a military one, and it was necessary that the soldiers should have some practice in the management of it. Both at Khabarovsk and at Viasemska stations there were barracks and a railway battalion.

The country through which we now passed was very beautiful. There were hills and valleys and meadows all following one another in quick succession. The grass in the meadows was high, and amongst it were many kinds of lovely flowers that we had never seen growing wild before.

We stayed in the dining car till all the passengers except ourselves had had their lunch and gone back to their respective carriages. Then we drew our chairs close to one of the windows and passed several delightful hours feasting our eyes on the scenery and looking out for all the new kinds of flowers that were to be seen. We got quite excited over it as we pointed out each fresh blossom to one another. There was the purple, and the white iris, such as we afterwards saw to greater perfection in Japan; there were big yellow, red, and white lilies such as grow in our gardens at home, and there was a brilliant red flower, with clusters of blossom not unlike our common geranium. Some one got out and picked a bunch of them at one of the stations, and as they were placed in a vase on the buffet table we were able to examine them more closely; their petals were firmer than those of the geranium, and more waxlike.

Later in the afternoon, when we were refreshing ourselves with coffee served in glasses, the first we had tasted for nearly a week, we made the acquaintance of a

Russian officer who spoke English. He turned out to be a military agent. Colonel D—— was travelling with his adjutant, Lieutenant K——, and a Chinese servant. They had come by land from Port Arthur to Charbin in Manchuria, where they had crossed the unfinished railway and then proceeded by steamer down the Sungari to Khabarovsk.

"All was perfectly quiet," said the Colonel, "when we left Port Arthur, and we preceded the rebellion in each town by a few hours. At Mukden there was not the faintest indication of the approaching trouble, but at the very next town we stopped at, news reached us by telegram that Mukden was in arms."

"Things are looking very grave at Pekin," he continued, "and if I may be allowed to criticize the action of the English, French and Germans in the matter, I would say that it is nothing short of impertinence to send a small handful of men to set things right in the very heart of a country so powerful in men and arms as China! "I repeat it," he cried, getting quite excited. "It is *impertinence*, and the Chinese will look upon it as such and act accordingly."

61

LEO DEUTSCH, *SIXTEEN YEARS IN SIBERIA* (NEW YORK: E. P. DUTTON, 1905), PP. 140–144, 324–327

Our journey began on a beautiful morning in the middle of May when spring had just made its appearance in Moscow. The sunshine was bright and warm, and the scent of spring was in the air. Our mood was by no means in consonance with this aspect of outward things; but most of us elected to go on foot to the station. Our procession must have been an odd sight. Convicts with fettered feet and grey prison garb marched along beside other men and women in ordinary clothes. Most of us were quite young; few had reached middle-age. Of the twelve women in our party three were voluntarily accompanying their husbands to Siberia.

The last violent scene had depressed us all, and we traversed in silence the quieter streets of Moscow, where the few passers-by paused to look at us, and here and there faces stared from the windows. The station, which we reached after a short tramp, had been cleared of people; only some gendarmes, prison officials, and porters were on the platform. Police were keeping guard all round, and nobody who had not a special order was allowed through to the train reserved for us. When we "politicals" were established in the places assigned to us, a few persons—relations of the prisoners—arrived to say good-bye. The gendarmes would not let them come near to the carriages, and we had to shout our farewell greetings.

"Good-bye! Good luck! Don't forget us!" sounded from the barred windows.

"Keep up your courage! We'll meet again soon!" came back the response.

"Let us sing something together," called out somebody. We had formed a choral society in prison, and now started a song of Little Russia—"The Ferryman." Slowly the train was set in motion, and as we glided away the affecting strains of the beautiful melody accompanied us. Many could not restrain their tears, and sobs were heard which the rattle of the train soon drowned. With faces pressed against the bars of the windows we gazed back at Moscow as long as it could be seen. Then came the outskirts, and then our eyes were refreshed by the sight of broad meadows.

When we halted at the next station there were a good many people on the platform — peasants and workmen. Many of them came up to the carriage windows unhindered, and seemed to be offering things to us.

"Here, take it, in the Virgin's name!" said a voice close by me. I looked out, and was aware of an old peasant woman who held out a kopeck to me.

"I don't need it, mother; give it to someone who does," I said; and felt my heart warm towards this kindly old woman of the people.

"Take it, take it, my dear!" she insisted.

"Well, as a remembrance, then." I agreed; and I kept the little copper coin for a long time before I eventually lost it.

A whole chain of recollections was started in my mind by this occurrence, and I sank deep in thought. The further we went from Moscow, the sadder became my spirits; I felt as if I were leaving behind me there a host of friends I should never see again. I did not want to talk to anyone, but gazed silently out of the window. The line ran through a factory district; the stations were crowded, and along the railway banks we saw many groups of workpeople. Men and women in brightly coloured cotton garments stopped and called out after the train, making expressive gestures. Whether they knew us for exiles on our way to Siberia and meant to send us a message of sympathy I cannot tell. Perhaps it is the custom in that countryside, whence many prisoners are transported, to express in this way that feeling of compassion towards the "children of misfortune" so common among the Russian people.

On the following morning we arrived at Nijni Novgorod, whence we were to journey by boat to Perm, by the Volga and its tributary the Kama. Our party attracted much attention both at the station and on the way to the quay. The married and betrothed couples walked in front, arm in arm, and the rest of us followed, the escort surrounding us all. Two large cabins, one for the men and one for the women, were assigned to us on the big barge, which was taken in tow by a river steamer. Here we were rather comfortably lodged, and we were all in common allowed free access to the roomy deck, which was enclosed by iron netting at the sides and overhead. Food we provided for ourselves, and on that head had nothing to complain of, thanks to the kindness of our friends and to the provident care of Làzarev, our elected chief or *stàrosta*.

The voyage lasted some days; the weather was uninterruptedly fine; and we sat on deck from early morning till late evening, revelling in the charming scenes which passed before our eyes, on this giant among European rivers and on its tributary stream. Especially lovely was it towards sunset, when our choir, which boasted some exceptionally fine voices, would sing our favourite songs. As one sat, with head supported against the iron netting, and eyes following the shining ripples lit by exquisite fairy-like tints, the impression made on one by those beautiful sad songs was never to be forgotten. Gradually the colour would fade from the sky, and the stars shine down from a cloudless heaven, to be mirrored in the glassy surface of the great river; and everything around me—the river, the stars, the songs—would recall to my mind another royal stream, the mighty Dnieper, by whose banks my childhood had been spent.

"What are you thinking of? Why are you so sad?" on one such evening a young "administrative" asked me. She was a girl of about twenty, with whom I had become acquainted during the journey. We were soon engaged in intimate and friendly talk. She could understand my mood, and sympathised heartily. She was an unusually interesting creature of peculiar and, some might say, eccentric character, but of keen intelligence. She told me how she had come to adopt the principles of Socialism, and what kind of life she had quitted to join the revolutionary movement. Like so many others at that time, she had been possessed by the longing to do something for the people—the peasants. Where and how to begin she did not know, and she could find no one to advise her. She tried to discover some way for herself, and read everything she could get hold of that bore on the subject. At last, against her parents' wishes, she left her home in South Russia for Petersburg, where she hoped to find someone who could help her. In the course of her quest, and before she had arrived at any definite solution of the problems that perplexed her, she was arrested, and was now being sent to Siberia for three years' banishment. Like hundreds of others, this noble-hearted girl had expended her strength and sacrificed her happiness to no purpose, without benefit to others, without attaining her own peace of mind; a victim to the cramping and illiberal political conditions that reign in our native land. She died by her own hand in Siberia some time after this.

From Perm we were taken by rail to Ekaterinburg, where we arrived after a wearisome day's journey. Here we spent the night; and next day our party, consisting entirely of "politicals" with their escort, was to drive to Tiumen, the first town within the borders of Siberia. The construction of the Siberian railway was only just being begun, and the journey—now very simple—was then attended by all manner of difficulties.

We started at dawn, reached the river towards evening, and there camped out for the night. During the next few days we explored the locality, but in vain, and we were at last obliged to return from our fruitless errand. I then made further inquiries about the stone among the inhabitants of the place, many of whom were hunters, and therefore well acquainted with the surrounding country, and I promised a reward to anyone who could guide me to it; but it was not until nearly two years later that I heard a report of how two peasants from a neighbouring village had seen something of the kind. This rumour proved correct; and a gold-digger of my acquaintance undertook to guide me to the object of my search, making the expedition by sledge, as it was then winter.

The monument with the red inscription turned out to be not far from the spot where I and my friends had previously looked for it, but the dense forest undergrowth had hidden it from us. It dates undoubtedly from a very early period, and consists of a smooth perpendicular surface hewn in the rock, whereon curious signs and characters are drawn.

We made a careful sketch of the monument, and a photographer who happened to visit Kara subsequently took separate photographs of the whole stone and of the coloured characters. These I sent to Kuznetsov, with a detailed description, but I have never heard whether the meaning of the inscription has been deciphered.

When, in consequence of the imperial manifesto, I passed from the category of convict into that of exile, the change only affected my circumstances in that it deprived me of the right to an allowance from the State. Henceforward I was thrown entirely on my own resources, and the task of supporting myself was no light one. The population of Kara diminished steadily, and among others the family whose children I had taught for several years removed from the place. It was absolutely impossible to find any other remunerative occupation; my relations at home were sending me no money, and my affairs got into a very unsatisfactory state. I had a host of debts, and could expect assistance from no one.

Just then began the work in connection with the construction of the railway in the Stanitsa of Stretyensk, some hundred versts distant from Kara. I decided to migrate thither; and, the Governor having given me the necessary permission, I left Kara on the 20th of May, 1897.

The Stanitsa of Stretyensk, situated on the banks of the large and navigable River Shilka, was at that time the scene of much activity. The population had increased to between four and five thousand; there were some good shops and several business firms. The ordinary inhabitants, besides the Cossacks, were chiefly Jews; but the railway works had brought all kinds of people to the place—officials, clerks, contractors, etc.—so that Stretyensk had taken on more the appearance of a thriving town than of a mere Cossack village.

I soon found a post, and a comparatively good one, on the railway; my duties being to draw up the various orders, advices, and circulars, and to copy them out. But the yearning for a fuller life possessed me here even more than at Kara, partly induced by the more bustling life of the busy little place, partly by the total absence of any congenial society. In Kara I had had comrades with whom I could converse on every kind of topic; but in Stretyensk, though I knew nearly everybody at least by name, there was no single person to whom I could talk about anything beyond the most everyday matters. The principal, and almost the only, subject of conversation was money. The flow of capital into the country on account of the new railway had aroused in the inhabitants an almost incredible greed and a feverish desire of becoming rich. There were numbers of people who recoiled at nothing in the pursuit of this aim—cheating, dishonesty, even downright theft, were all in the order of the day; and the irresponsibility and arbitrariness of officials which prevails throughout Russia, and especially in Siberia, greatly assisted in undermining the morals of the population. Many large fortunes were made in an extraordinarily short time.

The only relaxations from this constant working and striving after riches were drinking and card-playing. Not only was there no library in the Stanitsa, but there was not even a school for the children of those who were not Cossacks, *i.e.* a greater part of the inhabitants. When I of necessity entered into the society of the place I felt myself in a world entirely strange to me, and utterly uncongenial. It was hardly possible for any, even intelligent, young man to escape being driven to drinking or gambling in such an atmosphere.

It is true that here I had the advantage of more freedom of movement than in Kara, and that I could go further afield. During the two years of my stay in Stretyensk I frequently made long excursions in different directions; and on these expeditions I became more closely acquainted with local conditions, and learned to understand the life of Siberia much better than would be possible from any amount of mere reading up the subject.

In the spring of 1899, while travelling, I met with a comrade of my own way of thinking, who had been exiled by "administrative methods." It was the first time I had met a Social Democrat newly come from Russia, and my delight may be easily imagined. We talked nearly all through the night, and I learned for the first time from him how great had been the expansion of our movement among the working classes during the last ten years, and how quickly the idea of Social Democracy had taken root in Russia. I was especially impressed by his account of its development among the Jewish workers in the western provinces.

Under the influence of the feelings aroused by this intelligence, my longing to return home sprang up with redoubled strength. This thought had been kept in the background during the last few years; but now it forced itself upon me with urgent insistence. What were the possibilities of the case? This question was hard to answer with any certainty. I had now been fourteen years in Siberia, and it was fifteen years since my arrest in Freiburg; in accordance with the terms of the last imperial manifesto, by which I was to benefit, I might go home after another seven years, and this term might conceivably be further shortened by some fortunate concatenation of circumstances. Once more to see European Russia, where I had not been as a free man for twenty years, was the most fervent wish of my heart; yet what warrant had I for supposing I should be still alive in another seven years? or that, being alive, I should actually be granted the privilege of returning to Russia? Life in Siberia became each year more irksome to me. I found it well-nigh impossible to remain in Stretyensk, and I determined to go further east, to the comparatively large town of Blagovèstshensk. After exerting myself for some time to obtain permission to do this, I at last succeeded, and in the autumn of 1899 I quitted Stretyensk.

I found myself much better off at Blagovèstshensk; I soon got employment on one of the two local newspapers, and the work was far more interesting than that to which I had hitherto been condemned. The society here, also, was much more agreeable, for the town contained many cultivated people, and also several comrades in our movement, political exiles like myself. The town possessed schools, a public library, a theatre, a telephone service—in short, so far as outward civilisation went, Blagovèstshensk stood in no way behind European towns of the same size, and was even in some ways more advanced.

62

LINDON BATES JR., *THE RUSSIAN ROAD TO CHINA* (BOSTON: HOUGHTON MIFFLIN COMPANY, 1910), PP. 71–74

In Irkutsk

THE train pulls slowly up to the white station-house at Irkutsk. A swarm of porters, *nasilchiks*, white-aproned, with peaked hats, and big, numbered arm-tags, invade the carriage. They seize each piece of luggage and run with it somewhere into the crowd outside. You, encumbered with your heavy coat, laboriously follow. Irkutsk station, more than any previous one, is crowded with passengers and Cossack guards. Train officials are shouting instructions, and every few paces a sentry is standing his silent watch. This is the transfer entrepôt for all through traffic, as well as the depôt for the largest and most important city of Siberia.

Threading the press on the platform, you struggle with the outgoing human current, and in time reach the big waiting-room of the first class. It likewise is crowded with a mass of people, and its floor is cumbered with heaping mounds of baggage. One of these hillocks is constructed from your impedimenta, which are being guarded now by a porter, apparently the residuary legatee of the half-dozen original competitors within the car. The man takes the long document that witnesses your claim to two trunks, and departs. Upon you in turn devolves sentry duty for the interminable time during which those trunks are being culled out from the baggage-car.

It is an exasperating wait, but the fundamental rule for Russian traveling is, "never separate from the baggage." The parcel-room here at Irkutsk held for six months a suit-case left by a friend to be sent to this traveler. The officials would not give it up to its owner or to any person save the forwarder, though he, oblivious to sequels, had gone on to San Francisco.

Like the rest, now, you camp, with the baggage in front of you, on the waiting-room floor. It is a very country fair, this station. At the far end is a big stand crowded with dishes, on which are cold meats, potato salad, heaps of fruit and cakes, sections of fish from which one may cut his own slices, boxes of chocolates, and cigarettes. All are piled up in heaping profusion. One can get a glass of vodka and eat of the *zakuska* dishes free, or while waiting he may buy a meal of surprisingly ample quantity and good quality at the long tables that run down the centre of the room. Most of the Russians order a glass of tea, and with it in hand sit down till such indefinite future time as the luggage situation shall unroll itself.

We move our baggage and join the tea caravan. Across the table is a slight, brown-faced man, with an enormous black astrakan cape falling to his ankles, and wearing a jauntily perched astrakan cap on his head. "One of the Cossack settlers," a friend from the train remarks. Beyond are half a dozen tired-looking women, with dark-gray shawls over their heads. Near them are men with close-fitting *shubas*, or snugly-belted sheepskin coats, fur inside, and rough-tanned black leather outside. Beside the lunch-stand are a couple of young men with huge bearskin caps, short coats, and high leather boots tucked into fleece-lined overshoes.

A general at one of the little side tables is talking volubly to a plump dame with furs, which are attracting envy from many sides. The lady merely nods between puffs of her cigarette, and sips her tea. A large fat merchant waddles past, wrapped in a paletot made of the glistening silvery skin of the Baikal seal. The room is stifling, full of smoke, and crowded with people. Yet no one seems to feel the discomfort, even to the extent of taking off the heavy outer coats, which, with the thermometer at twenty degrees below zero, they have worn on the sleigh-ride in, from across the river.

Your friends of the train, save those whose possessions were comprised in their multitudinous valises, are all here, fur-coated likewise and sipping tea, waiting, without a thought of impatience, for the baggage to be brought out.

At last appears your *nasilchik*. "They are got," he cries, and balances about himself, one by one, your half-dozen pieces of luggage. Through the noisy, gesticulating, thronging passengers and heaped belongings, he shoulders and squirms a way to the door and into the anteroom.

A couple of soldiers are good-naturedly hustling out, from the third-class waiting-room opposite, a little leather-jacketed and very dirty mujik.

"I did not owe seven kopecks. I cross myself. I am not a Jew," he loudly proclaims.

"*Nietchevo*," says the soldier. "Out with him just the same!" The peasants and crowd loafing alongside grin appreciatingly, as the mujik is escorted, collar-held, through the great doors.

The porter and yourself follow. A plunging line of sleighs, backed up against the outer platform of the station, extends far up and down the road. Their *isvoschiks*, leaning back, are shouting for fares. In sight are your two trunks. "How much to the Métropole?" you call. The legal fare across the river to the hotel is a rouble, but the Governor-General of eastern Siberia could n't tell how much it would be if you did n't bargain beforehand. "*Piat rubla!*" "*tree rubla!*" come hurtling from all sides.

It is for you to walk down the line calling in the vernacular, "fifty, seventy kopecks!" One of the drivers will eventually shout a fare which you feel able to allow, and the porter, who has been watching the bargaining process with keen interest, gives him the two trunks.

341

63

RICHARDSON L. WRIGHT AND BASSETT DIGBY, *THROUGH SIBERIA: AN EMPIRE IN THE MAKING* (NEW YORK: MCBRIDE, NAST & COMPANY, 1913), PP. 231–234

South of Kharbin you are still in a nominally peaceful region, but Manchurian China, with her Hoong-Hooses, is an uncertain pot on the hob and has an unpleasant trick of boiling over when one least expects it. So the Russian trackside guard houses, each with its handful of picked troops in garrison, are turned into very neat and serviceable forts, surrounded by high walls pierced with rifle slits and abutting in turreted bastions. The train, by the way, always carries military guards— a dozen strapping Cossacks from the garrison of Kharbin, armed with rifle, sabre and revolver.

In the dusk of the evening we came to the last little Russian station. On across the plain twinkled a blaze of bright lights: at that point, after the war, Japan amputated at the knee the leg on which Russia had taken her stand in southern Manchuria. Thus far may Imperial Russia run her trains and lord it over the natives, thus far and no farther. The track took a steep curve, and we rolled into Chang-Chun, one of the oldest and most picturesque railroad stations in the world.

The Russian train, lit only with flickering candles, pulls into a station flooded brilliantly with pink electric light shed by towering arc standards. Under the shadow of the platform roof the dusk is spangled with darting colored paper lanterns; every porter or tray hawker or railroad official carries his own gaudy Japanese paper lantern swaying at the tip of a short wand held in his hand. All about is a scurrying medley of Russians, Japanese and Chinese, and here and there an American, a Briton or a German overflowing with inquiries.

On the opposite track stands one of the fine trains of the South Manchurian Railway, brilliantly illuminated with electric light, modern Pullmans and beautifully upholstered sleeping coaches attached, a train almost indistinguishable from a modern American transcontinental limited. It is drawn by a powerful American locomotive with a tolling bell.

And above all things, you know a porter when you see one on the platforms of Chang-Chun. He is not one of those gorgeous, bebraided officials you take for a local chief of police, nor is he a tattered, shift-eyed coolie: most railroad porters in the East come under one or the other category. In nine-inch letters across the front of his blue canvas smock the Chinaman has PORTER—PORTER in good, clean, white, healthy, shouting English characters. He turns around and you get a back view. There it is again in letters nine inches high, PORTER. There is no deception about him. Wouldn't Ruskin have loved to have shaken him by the hand!

It was seven o'clock next morning when the train drew into Mukden. We took breakfast at the "Yamato," the station hotel. Gone now was the railroad refreshment room of the Russians with its oilcloth table covers, its messes of pickles and salt fish, its impossible coffee, and its wretched service. In its unlamented stead, Yamato hotels—fine, modern, airy buildings, with their luxury running to coolness and comfort in the place of gaudy wall papers and tarnished gilt tossed about by the pailful. Cosy wicker basket chairs, fern-embowered lounges instead of the crimson plush sweepings of the fake furniture factories of Paris and Moscow, tattered and scarred by drunken orgies. A restful atmosphere until you get your bill and find its charges equal to those of the most fashionable of New York hotels.

Mukden, of course, played an important part in the Russo-Japanese War. At this spot the tide of battle turned seven times. It also figured with sad prominence in the recent epidemic of pneumonic plague. Kharbin and Mukden were the two worst plague centers. Kharbin traced 172 deaths in one day and had well over 100 a day for weeks at a time. Mukden had about thirty deaths a day during her worst three weeks.

We at home sometimes wonder how a sphere of influence works, how the Japanese or Russians can maintain the whip hand of Manchuria while it is still a province of China populated by Manchus and Chinese and governed by a Chinese viceroy, who, by the way, has about as much real authority in his province as one of those red-capped porters has in the running of a great American railroad terminal. The matter is very simple. Here is your foreign railroad, built with foreign capital, worked by foreign employees, being financed in the working by foreign money.

The branch of the railroad between Manchuria on the eastern Siberian frontier and Popranitchnaia, the last station on the Maritime-Manchuria border, and the line south from Kharbin to Chang-Chun is known officially as the Chinese Eastern Railroad.

The building of this railroad was permitted by China; and she rashly sanctioned "railroad reservations" at certain points, bulbous swelling arteries along the railroad vein. China allowed a Russian "railroad reservation" at Kharbin where twenty-five years ago there was not a subject of the Tsar. So Russia built thereon a little town, and kept its population down until her position was sufficiently assured for her to come out boldly and enlarge that town until to-day it is the capital of northeast Asia.

The houses are all Russian. The police are largely Russian. Kharbin is so Russian that they dare to hang printed notices in hotels telling you to lodge your Russian passport for inspection at the Russian police station before you have unstrapped your trunks. The colossal impertinence of the thing—Russian police surveillance in the heart of a Chinese province! This passport request, however, is a sheer bluff. We refused point blank to discuss our business or chat about passports with the policeman they sent to pay us a call at the hotel. He smiled, shrugged his shoulders and departed. We were not bothered again during our stay of several days. Mr. Fisher, the American consul-general of Manchuria, put up a long fight at Kharbin during his residence in the city to establish the right of the American citizen to refuse to submit to this humiliating Russian police surveillance. The Russians hit back, literally as well as metaphorically, for the consul's life was made a burden to him, and on several occasions mud and stones were thrown at him in the streets.

Part 10

THE IRON ROAD MEETS THE SILK ROAD
Railways in Japan and China
Railways in Japan and China

64

NARRATIVE OF THE EXPEDITION OF AN AMERICAN SQUADRON TO THE CHINA SEAS AND JAPAN, PERFORMED IN THE YEARS 1852, 1853, AND 1854, UNDER THE COMMAND OF COMMODORE M. C. PERRY, COMP. FRANCIS L. HAWKS (NEW YORK: D. APPLETON, 1856), PP. 414–418

On the next day (March 11) a short conference was held by Captain Adams with the same Japanese officials in the treaty house on shore. He also bore a communication of the date of the 10th of March from the Commodore, addressed to the commissioners, in which the answer to the President's letter was acknowledged. The Commodore, while he expressed his satisfaction at the determination of the Japanese government to alter its policy in regard to foreign governments, at the same time stated that the concessions proposed were not enough, and that a written compact or treaty, with wider provisions, was essential. The chief points talked of were, the answer to the Commodore's notes in reference to the proposed treaty, and the privilege of going ashore. In regard to the former, they stated that a reply was not yet prepared; but as for the latter, the interpreter remarked, unofficially, that there would be no objection to the Commodore and his officers going ashore; but that if the permission should be general, difficulty with the people might ensue. Some general conversation followed in regard to the necessity of dispatch in the negotiations, Captain Adams stating that it was the Commodore's intention to send one of his ships to the United States, in the course of a week or so, to inform the government at home of the progress of the negotiations, that it might know whether it was necessary to send more vessels or not. The Japanese evinced some uneasiness at this statement, and asked, "Whether the Americans are friendly?" "Certainly we are," was the answer, and the conference closed in the most amicable manner.

The day agreed upon had arrived (Monday, March 13) for the landing of the presents, and although the weather was unsettled, and the waters of the bay somewhat rough, they all reached the shore without damage.

The following is a list of some of the various presents landed on the occasion:

1 box of arms, containing—

5 Hall's rifles,		
3 Maynard's muskets,		
12 cavalry swords,	Emperor,	
6 artillery swords,		
1 carbine,		
20 army pistols,		

2 carbines, cartridge boxes, and belts, containing 120 cartridges.
10 Hall's rifles.
11 cavalry swords.
1 carbine, cartridge box and belts, and 60 cartridges.

Boxes of tea, Emperor.
1 box of tea, commissioners.
2 telegraph instruments.
3 Francis's life-boats.
1 locomotive and tender, passenger-car, and rails complete.
4 volumes Audubon's Birds of America.
3 volumes Audubon's Quadrupeds.
Several clocks.
10 ship's beakers, containing 100 gallons whiskey.
8 baskets Irish potatoes.
3 stoves.

The presents filled several large boats, which left the ship escorted by a number of officers, and a company of marines, and a band of music, all under the superintendence of Captain Abbott, who was delegated to deliver the presents, with proper ceremonies, to the Japanese high commissioners. A building adjoining the treaty house had been suitably constructed and arranged for the purpose, and on landing Captain Abbott was met by Yezaiman, the governor of Uraga, and several subordinate officials, and conducted to the treaty house. Soon after entering, the high commissioner, Prince Hayashi, came in, and the usual compliments having been interchanged, Captain Abbott, with the interpreters, were led into the smaller room, where a letter from the Commodore and some formalities on the delivery of the presents were disposed of. The Japanese commissioner, after some discussion, fixed the ensuing Thursday (March 16) for an interview with the Commodore on shore, when they promised to deliver a formal reply to his notes in regard to the opening of the various Japanese ports insisted upon.

The presents having been formally delivered, the various American officers and workmen selected for the purpose were diligently engaged daily in unpacking and arranging them for exhibition. The Japanese authorities offered every facility; their laborers constructed sheds for sheltering the various articles from the inclemency of the weather; a piece of level ground was assigned for laying down the circular track of the little locomotive, and posts were brought and erected for the extension of the telegraph wires, the Japanese taking a very ready part in all the labors, and watching the result of arranging and putting together of the machinery with an innocent and childlike delight. The telegraphic apparatus, under the direction of Messrs. Draper and Williams, was soon in working

60 *ball cartridges*.
1 box books, Emperor.
1 box dressing-cases, Emperor.
1 box perfumery, 2 packages, Emperor.
1 barrel whiskey, Emperor.
1 cask wine, Emperor.
1 box for distribution.
1 box containing 11 pistols for distribution.
1 box perfumery, for distribution.
A quantity of cherry cordials, distribution.
A quantity of cherry cordials, Emperor.
A number of baskets champagne, Emperor.
A number of baskets champagne, commissioners.
1 box China ware, commissioners.
A quantity of maraschino, commissioners.

1 telescope, Emperor.
Boxes standard United States balances.
Boxes standard United States bushels.
Boxes standard United States gallon measures.
Boxes standard United States yards.
1 box coast charts.
4 bundles telegraph wires.
1 box gutta percha wires.
4 boxes batteries.
1 box machine paper.
1 box zinc plates.
1 box insulators.
1 box connecting apparatus.
1 box machine weights.
1 box acid.
1 box seed.
Large quantity of agricultural implements, &c., &c., &c.

order, the wires extending nearly a mile, in a direct line, one end being at the treaty house, and another at a building expressly allotted for the purpose. When communication was opened up between the operators at either extremity, the Japanese watched with intense curiosity the *modus operandi*, and were greatly amazed to find that in an instant of time messages were conveyed in the English, Dutch, and Japanese languages from building to building. Day after day the dignitaries and many of the people would gather, and, eagerly beseeching the operators to work the telegraph, would watch with unabated interest the sending and receiving of messages.

Nor did the railway, under the direction of Engineers Gay and Danby, with its Lilliputian locomotive, car, and tender, excite less interest. All the parts of the mechanism were perfect, and the car was a most tasteful specimen of workmanship, but so small that it could hardly carry a child of six years of age. The Japanese, however, were not to be cheated out of a ride, and, as they were unable to reduce themselves to the capacity of the inside of the carriage, they betook themselves to the roof. It was a spectacle not a little ludicrous to behold a dignified mandarin whirling around the circular road at the rate of twenty miles an hour, with his loose robes flying in the wind. As he clung with a desperate hold to the edge of the roof, grinning with intense interest, and his huddled up body shook convulsively with a kind of laughing timidity, while the car spun rapidly around the circle, you might have supposed that the movement, somehow or other, was dependent rather upon the enormous exertions of the uneasy mandarin than upon the power of the little puffing locomotive which was so easily performing its work.

Although the Japanese authorities were still very jealous of any intercourse on the part of the Americans with the people, and did all they could to prevent it, still there was necessarily a good deal of intermingling. The ships of the squadron were being daily supplied with water and provisions, for which the officials of the government had now consented to receive payment, but they insisted upon conducting all the regulations, and provided their own boats and laborers for the purpose. There was, however, what with the necessary passing to and from the ships with the supplies, and the arranging and working the telegraphic apparatus, and the toy railway, almost daily intercourse between the American officers, sailors, and marines, and the Japanese mandarins, officials and laborers.

The Japanese always evinced an inordinate curiosity, for the gratification of which the various articles of strange fabric, and the pieces of mechanism, of ingenious and novel invention, brought from the United States, gave them a full opportunity. They were not satisfied with the minutest examination of all things, so surprisingly wonderful as they appeared to them, but followed the officers and men about and seized upon every occasion to examine each part of their dress. The laced caps, boots, swords, and tailed coats of the officers; the tarpaulins, jackets, and trowsers of the men, all came in for the closest scrutiny; and a tailor in search of a new cut or a latest fashion, could not have been more exacting in his observations than the inquisitive Japanese, as he fingered the broadcloth, smoothed down the nap with his long delicate hands, pulled a lappel here, adjusted a collar there, now fathomed the depth of a pocket, and again peered curiously into the inner recesses of Jack's loose toilette. They eagerly sought to possess themselves of anything that pertained to the dress of their visitors, and showed a peculiar passion for buttons. They would again and again ask for a button, and when presented with the cheap gift, they appeared immediately gratified, and stowed it away as if it were of the greatest value. It is possible that their affection for buttons and high appreciation of their value, may be owing to the rarity of the article in Japan, for it is a curious fact, that the simple convenience of a button is but little used in any article of Japanese dress; strings and various bindings being the only mode of fastening the garments. When visiting the ships, the mandarins and their attendants were never at rest; but went about peering into every nook and corner, peeping into the muzzles of the guns, examining curiously the small-arms, handling the ropes, measuring the boats, looking eagerly into the engine-room, and watching every movement of the engineers and workmen as they busily moved, in and about, the gigantic machinery of the steamers. They were not contented with merely observing with their eyes, but were constantly taking out their writing materials, their mulberry-bark paper, and their India ink and hair pencils, which they always carried in a pocket within the left breast of their loose robes, and making notes and sketches. The Japanese had all apparently a strong pictorial taste, and looked with great delight upon the engravings and pictures which were shown them, but their own performances appeared exceedingly rude and inartistic. Every man, however, seemed anxious to try his skill at drawing, and they were constantly taking the portraits of the Americans, and sketches of the various articles that appeared curious to them, with a result, which, however satisfactory it might have been to the artists, (and it must be conceded they exhibited no little exultation,) was far from showing any encouraging advance in art. It should, however, be remarked, that the artists were not professional. Our future pages will show more artistic skill, than the rude specimens here alluded to would have led one to suppose existed in Japan. The Japanese are, undoubtedly, like the Chinese, a very imitative, adaptative, and compliant people; and in these characteristics may be discovered a promise of the comparatively easy introduction of foreign customs and habits, if not of the nobler principles and better life of a higher civilization.

Notwithstanding the Japanese are so fond of indulging their curiosity, they are by no means communicative about themselves. They allege, as a reason for their provoking reserve, that their laws forbid them to communicate to foreigners anything relating to their country and its institutions, habits, and customs. This silence on the part of the Japanese was a serious obstacle to acquiring that minute information about a strange people of whom curiosity is naturally on the alert to know everything. Much progress will, however, never be obtained toward a thorough knowledge of Japan, until some of our men of intelligence are established in the country in the character of consular agents, merchants, or missionaries, who may thus be enabled to acquire the language, and mingle in intimate social relations with the people.

The common people were found much more disposed to fraternize than were the Japanese officials. It seemed evident that nothing but a fear of punishment deterred the former from entering into free intercourse with the Americans; but they were closely watched by their superiors, as in fact the latter were by their equals.

In Japan, as in Lew Chew, probably, a closer intimacy would have ensued, during the visits of the squadron, with all classes, if they had been allowed to follow their own natural inclinations, and had not been so jealously guarded by the numerous spies. No one, even of the highest dignitaries, is intrusted with public business of importance, without having one or more associated with him, who is ever on the alert to detect and take note of the slightest suspicion of delinquency.

Kura-Kawa-Kahei, the prefect, and Yenoske, the interpreter, paid almost daily visits to the ships, and had always something to communicate in regard to supplying the vessels with water and fresh provisions, the arrangements for which were under their especial care. When they came on board, as they were subordinate dignitaries, they were not received by the Commodore himself, but by some of his chief officers, who were delegated for the purpose, and acted as his medium of communication with them. After one of these interviews, (March 14,) as Kura-Kawa and Yenoske were about taking leave, a Japanese official hurried aboard from Kanagawa, and, in a state of considerable excitement, reported that an

THE IRON ROAD MEETS THE SILK ROAD

American officer had passed through that town, and was walking very fast toward Yedo. His appearance, so said the messenger, was causing great excitement, and it was feared that unpleasant consequences might ensue. The Japanese officials, on hearing this, declared that the conduct of the Amercian officer was in violation of their laws and of the promises made to them by the Admiral. The Commodore, when informed of the fact, directed guns to be fired immediately, and a signal made recalling all boats and officers to their respective ships. He also prepared written orders, which were sent in different directions, commanding all persons belonging to the squadron to repair immediately on board. A copy of these orders was, on the instant, dispatched by the Japanese officials, then in the Powhatan, in pursuit of the American officer, reported to be on his way to Yedo.

65

LILIAS DUNLOP FINLAY SWAINSON, *LETTERS FROM CHINA & JAPAN* (LONDON: HENRY S. KING & CO., 1875), PP. 177–178, 181–183, 194–196

The Mikado is so anxious to break down all old customs, he has begun to take every opportunity of showing his hitherto sacred person in public. About a fortnight ago he opened the railway from this to Yedo, and on the approaching visit of the Grand Duke Alexis of Russia, intends to show himself again, so no doubt we shall have the pleasure of seeing him.

It seemed quite a novel sensation, finding ourselves once more travelling by rail, when, a few days ago, we paid our first visit to Yedo.

We started at 11 a.m., accompanied by Dr V., and found the train full of Japanese. They evidently now highly appreciate their new mode of locomotion, but we hear that the first day it was opened, though crowds assembled to see it, none of them would venture to travel by it. There are only three stations between Yokohama and Yedo, and the journey occupies about an hour. Passing through the well-cultivated country, yellow fields of ripe grain, large woods, and cottages half hidden among clumps of fine trees, we might almost have imagined ourselves in England.

Arrived at our destination we all got into Ginrikshas, each drawn by two men, one in front of the other, and the pace at which our *human tandems* took us over the very rough streets did, I assure you, necessitate a very firm seat, more especially at the corners round which they swung with a speed and sharpness which each time threatened to upset carriages and occupants. My lively young leader was evidently much diverted by the fits of laughter caused by this singular mode of progression, and of course went all the faster in consequence.

9th November.

I have now to record a second visit to Yedo, when C. D. acted as guide and interpreter. Without the latter it is by no means easy to get on, as "Pidgin English" is of little use, even with domestic servants, in Japan, and none whatever with the general population. Some little knowledge of the language is therefore absolutely necessary for those who reside in the country, though mere visitors like ourselves find a very few words go a long way. Were we remaining here, I should think it no hardship to be obliged to learn Japanese; it is very easy, and a soft, musical language, not very unlike Italian in the pronunciation of some words.

And now to return to our Yedo expedition. We thought this time, we should try the effect of being drawn by quadrupeds instead of bipeds. Accordingly we ascended into a high vehicle of the genus *break*, drawn by two horses, and in it were jolted over the streets till one felt quite imbecile, bodily and mentally; saw the temple at Asakusa, the largest in Yedo, very handsome, and gorgeously decorated with gold lacquer. A number of people were doing their "joss pidgin," and throwing alms into a trough with a grating over it, in front of the altar: the priests going through the usual ceremonies, which resemble so much those of the Romish Church.

In the extensive garden and grounds which surround the temple, we saw most curious specimens of the national skill in training plants (some of them not more than from one to two feet high) to assume the appearance of ancient trees. There were also some most grotesque wooden figures clothed in garments of chrysanthemum, and placed in all sorts of ridiculous attitudes. One, for instance, represented a boy tumbling head over heels, the different parts of his dress being formed by the foliage and flowers of different colours: the trousers brown or green, the coat yellow, and the waistcoat white.

A steam engine and railway carriage, nearly as large as real ones, were most perfectly modelled in the same way. The body of the carriage was green; yellow flowers formed the foot-board; the wheels were brown, and the windows some other colour. How these growing plants can be trained in such a marvellous manner baffles my comprehension; but the artists must not only possess skilful hands but infinite patience, as well as most grotesque imaginations.

In the same grounds there was also a large collection of birds and monkeys belonging to the temple. Of these the stork is considered the most sacred bird in Japan, and is to be seen represented on most of their lacquer-work.

Being one of their numerous fête days, the road to the temple was lined with gaily-decorated booths, where they were selling toys and all kinds of odds and ends, which looked more attractive in the distance than on closer inspection.

Again we mounted our exalted carriage, but had not gone far when a sudden jerk and the descent of one corner of our chariot to the ground, informed us that a wheel had come off, so out we scrambled amidst a large, and let us hope, sympathising crowd. Leaving our wrecked vehicle, we betook ourselves to Ginrikshas which I, at least, much prefer to our experience of Yedo carriages, as in them there is some novelty and amusement to make up for the unmerciful rattling to which one's bones are, in either case, subjected. *En route* to the station we passed through numerous fortifications, and over two moats which surround the castle, but supposing ourselves rather late for the train, we did not take time to visit the latter.

The ancient timber is one of the greatest beauties of Japan, and till lately it was contrary to law to cut a tree down without special permission, and planting a young one in its place. Now, unhappily, these restrictions seem to be removed, and it is sad to see the chopping down that is going on of many fine old monarchs of the forest. I am told of a very curious tree, something akin to the pine, the health of which is improved by imbibing iron. My informant had seen one which, having shewn signs of decline, was completely restored to health by having numbers of rusty nails driven into it.

23d November.

We were off early to the railway station to see the arrival of the Mikado; but his Majesty being late, we found it very cold waiting, and were much indebted to the kindness of Mr C., who ordered a fire in his room, and sent for breakfast.

By the time the Mikado appeared, it was raining in torrents; so he very wisely made up his mind to go quietly back to Yedo, and postpone the naval review to a more favourable day.

We all went on the platform to see him as he returned to the railway carriage, and admired his brave efforts to adopt the gracious manner of European potentates, and bow to each side as he passed along.

Just at the moment however, at which he approached our little feminine group, and we were preparing to receive him with our most graceful curtsies, his Majesty's courage failed, and he turned to the opposite side.

He is quite young, not above one-and-twenty, tall, but not handsome. I know not how better to describe his dress, than to tell you that he wore two articles of apparel resembling somewhat a *cassock* and *chasuble*—the former scarlet, the latter white, surmounted by what I think was a plume of black horse-hair: at all events it had the same effect, and stood straight on end from his head. On his feet, I need hardly mention, were the inevitable boots with elastic sides, which seem so fascinating to people of all ranks and ages in this country.

25th.—The sun made up for its absence on Saturday by shining brilliantly when the Mikado again arrived from Yedo to see the Russian ships, and show the fleet of Japan to the Russian Prince.

It was a very gay sight when his majesty arrived—the ships all decorated with flags—their yards manned, and the firing and answering salutes, from the English, French, Russian, and Japanese men-of-war. As our windows look out on the harbour, we had the benefit of the whole scene without any trouble.

Most of the day was occupied by the evolutions of the Japanese fleet, which is composed partly of vessels built by themselves, and partly of those bought in England. The Mikado in the meantime remained on board the ship of the Grand Duke, where, it is said, he was immensely pleased with a chorus sung by the Russian sailors. On his departure, the guns again boomed forth their farewell salutes, and we went to see him land, but this time, he did not vouchsafe any gracious bows to a crowd formed principally of his own subjects.

In the evening we went to a ball given by the German Club in honour of the Grand Duke of Russia, at which report said the Mikado had proposed being present; this, however, proved incorrect, but he sent some of his Ministers of State, who, no doubt, must have been much astonished at our foreign manners and customs.

66

ISABELLA BIRD, *UNBEATEN TRACKS IN JAPAN. AN ACCOUNT OF TRAVELS ON HORSEBACK IN THE INTERIOR*, 2 VOLS. (NEW YORK: G. P. PUTNAM'S SONS, 1880), PP. 26–32

Yedo

H.B.M.'s LEGATION, YEDO, *May* 24.

I HAVE dated my letter Yedo, according to the usage of the British Legation, but popularly the new name of Tôkiyô, or Eastern Capital, is used, Kiyôto, the Mikado's former residence having received the name of Saikiô, or Western Capital, though it has now no claim to be regarded as a capital at all. Yedo belongs to the old *régime* and the Shôgunate, Tôkiyô to the new *régime* and the Restoration, with their history of ten years. It would seem an incongruity to travel to *Yedo* by railway, but quite proper when the destination is Tôkiyô.

The journey between the two cities is performed in an hour by an admirable, well-metalled, double track railroad, 18 miles long, with iron bridges, neat stations, and substantial roomy termini, built by English engineers at a cost known only to Government, and opened by the Mikado in 1872. The Yokohama station is a handsome and suitable stone building, with a spacious approach, ticket offices on our plan, roomy waiting-rooms for different classes—uncarpeted, however, in consideration of Japanese clogs—and supplied with the daily papers. There is a department for the weighing and labelling of luggage, and on the broad covered stone platform at both termini, a barrier with turnstiles, through which, except by special favour, no ticketless person can pass. Except the ticket clerks, who are Chinese, and the guards and engine-drivers, who are English, the officials are Japanese in European dress. Outside the stations, instead of cabs, there are *kurumas*, which carry luggage as well as people. Only luggage in the hand is allowed to go free, the rest is weighed, numbered, and charged for, a corresponding number being given to its owner to present at his destination. The fares are, 3d class, an *ichibu*, or about 1s.; 2d class, 60 *sen*, or about 2s. 4d.; and 1st class, a *yen*, or about 3s. 8d. The tickets are collected as the passengers pass through the barrier at the end of the journey. The English-built cars differ from ours in having seats along the sides, and doors opening on platforms at both ends. On the whole the arrangements are Continental rather than British. The first-class cars are expensively fitted up with deeply cushioned, red morocco seats, but carry very few passengers, and the comfortable seats, covered with fine matting, of the 2d class are very scantily occupied, but the 3d class vans are crowded with Japanese, who have taken to railroads as readily as to *kurumas*. This line earns about $8,000,000 a year.

The Japanese look most diminutive in European dress. Each garment is a misfit, and exaggerates the miserable *physique*, and the national defects of concave chests and bow legs. The lack of "complexion" and of hair upon the face makes it nearly impossible to judge of the ages of men. I supposed that all the railroad officials were striplings of 17 or 18, but they are men from 25 to 40 years old.

It was a beautiful day, like an English June day, but hotter, and though the *Sakura* (wild cherry) and its kin, which are the glory of the Japanese spring, are over, everything is a young, fresh green yet, and in all the beauty of growth and luxuriance. The immediate neighbourhood of Yokohama is beautiful, with abrupt wooded hills, and small picturesque valleys, but after passing Kanagawa the railroad enters upon the immense plain of Yedo, said to be 90 miles from north to south, on whose northern and western boundaries faint blue mountains of great height hovered dreamily in the blue haze, and on whose eastern shore for many miles the clear blue wavelets of the Gulf of Yedo ripple, always as then, brightened by the white sails of innumerable fishing-boats. On this fertile and fruitful plain stand not only the capital with its million of inhabitants, but a number of populous cities, and several hundred thriving agricultural villages. Every foot of land which can be seen from the railroad is cultivated by the most careful spade husbandry, and much of it is irrigated for rice. Streams abound, and villages of grey wooden houses with grey thatch, and grey temples with strangely curved roofs, are scattered thickly over the landscape. It is all homelike, liveable, and pretty, the country of an industrious people, for not a weed is to be seen, but no very striking features or peculiarities arrest one at first sight unless it be the crowds everywhere.

You don't take your ticket for Tôkiyô, but for Shinagawa or Shinbashi, two of the many villages which have grown together into the capital. Yedo is hardly seen before Shinagawa is reached, for it has no smoke and no long chimneys; its temples and public buildings are seldom lofty; the former are often concealed among thick trees, and its ordinary houses seldom reach a height of 20 feet. On the right a blue sea with fortified islands upon it, wooded gardens with massive retaining walls, hundreds of fishing-boats lying in creeks or drawn up on the beach; on the left a broad road on which *kurumas* are hurrying both ways, rows of low, grey houses, mostly tea-houses and shops, and as I was asking "Where is Yedo?" the train came to rest in the terminus—the Shinbashi railroad station, and disgorged its 200 Japanese passengers with a combined clatter of 400 clogs—a new sound to me. These clogs add three inches to their height, but even with them few of the men attained 5 feet 7 inches, and few of the women 5 feet 2 inches; but they look far broader in the national costume, which also conceals the defects of their figures. So lean, so yellow, so ugly, yet so pleasant-looking, so wanting in colour and effectiveness; the women so very small and tottering in their walk; the children so formal-looking and such dignified burlesques on the adults, I feel as if I had seen them all before, so like are they to their pictures on trays, fans, and tea-pots. The hair of the women is all drawn away from their faces, and is worn in chignons, and the men, when they don't shave the front of their heads and gather their back hair into a quaint queue drawn forward over the shaven patch, wear their coarse hair about three inches long in a refractory undivided mop.

Davis, an orderly from the Legation, met me, one of the escort cut down and severely wounded when Sir H. Parkes was attacked in the street of Kiyôtô in March 1868 on his way to his first audience of the Mikado. Hundreds of *kurumas*, and covered carts with four wheels drawn by one miserable horse, which are the omnibuses of certain districts of Tôkiyô, were waiting outside the station, and an English brougham for me, with a running *betto*. The Legation stands in Kôjimachi on very elevated ground above the inner moat of the historic "Castle of Yedo," but I cannot tell you anything of what I saw on my way thither, except that there were miles of dark, silent, barrack-like buildings, with highly ornamental gateways, and long rows of projecting windows with screens made of reeds—the feudal mansions of Yedo—and miles of moats with lofty grass embankments or walls of massive masonry 50 feet high, with kiosk-like towers at the corners, and curious, roofed gateways, and many bridges, and acres of lotus leaves. Turning along the inner moat, up a steep slope, there are, on the right, its deep green waters, the great grass embankment surmounted by a dismal wall overhung by the branches of coniferous trees which surrounded the palace of the Shôgun, and on the left sundry *yashikis*, as the mansions of the *daimiyô* were called, now in this quarter mostly turned into hospitals, barracks, and Government offices. On a height, the most conspicuous of them all, is the great red gateway of the *yashiki*, now occupied by the French Military Mission, formerly the residence of Ii Kamon no Kami, one of the great actors in recent historic events, who was assassinated not far off, outside the Sakaruda gate of the castle. Besides these, barracks, parade grounds, policemen, *kurumas*, carts pulled and pushed by coolies, pack-horses in straw sandals, and dwarfish, slatternly-looking soldiers in European dress made up the Tôkiyô that I saw between Shinbashi and the Legation.

H.B.M.'s Legation has a good situation near the Foreign Office, several of the Government departments, and the residences of the ministers, which are chiefly of brick in the English suburban villa style. Within the compound, with a brick archway with the Royal Arms upon it for an entrance, are the Minister's residence, the Chancery, two houses for the two English Secretaries of Legation, and quarters for the escort.

It is an English house and an English home, though, with the exception of a venerable nurse, there are no English servants. The butler and footman are tall Chinamen, with long pig-tails, black satin caps, and long blue robes; the cook is a Chinaman, and the other servants are all Japanese, including one female servant, a sweet, gentle, kindly girl about 4 feet 5 in height, the wife of the head "house-maid." None of the servants speak anything but the most aggravating "pidgun" English, but their deficient speech is more than made up for by the intelligence and service of the orderly in waiting, who is rarely absent from the neighbour-hood of the hall door, and attends to the visitors' book and to all messages and notes. There are two real English children of six and seven, with great capacities for such innocent enjoyments as can be found within the limits of the nursery and garden. The other inmate of the house is a beautiful and attractive terrier called "Rags," a Skye dog, who unbends "in the bosom of his family," but ordinarily is as imposing in his demeanour as if he, and not his master, represented the dignity of the British Empire.

The Japanese Secretary of Legation is Mr. Ernest Satow, whose reputation for scholarship, specially in the department of history, is said by the Japanese them-selves to be the highest in Japan—an honourable distinction for an Englishman, and won by the persevering industry of fifteen years. The scholarship connected with the British Civil Service is not, however, monopolised by Mr. Satow, for sev-eral gentlemen in the consular service, who are passing through the various grades of student interpreters, are distinguishing themselves not alone by their facility in colloquial Japanese, but by their researches in various departments of Japanese history, mythology, archæology, and literature. Indeed it is to their labours, and to those of a few other Englishmen and Germans, that the Japanese of the rising gen-eration will be indebted for keeping alive not only the knowledge of their archaic literature, but even of the manners and customs of the first half of this century.

67

E. G. HOLTHAM, *EIGHT YEARS IN JAPAN, 1873–1881. WORK, TRAVEL AND RECREATION* (LONDON: KEGAN PAUL, TRENCH & CO., 1883), PP. 6–11, 101–112, 122–131, 211–213, 216–217, 247–249, 253–254

Our inspection of the railway; the concoction (purely as a pastime) of a design for altering the Yokohama terminus in case an impossible extension should be undertaken; the making of short excursions into the country that we might become acquainted with the customs of the people; a visit to Tōkiyō, to look at temples, the area devastated by the last great fire, the castle, and the engineering college; and several endeavours to acquire a taste for hot water with cherry blossoms in it, and for raw fish with soy, filled up part of our leisure during the ensuing three weeks, fortunately of faultless weather, while we were waiting for instructions. We also dined with the director, and tiffined with the chief; attended a performance by the Amateur Dramatic Society (Sheridan's "Critic," very well done); and partook of such other amusements as our acquaintances helped us to. But as this was not what we had come out for, we were glad to receive instructions to proceed to Kobe, and thence start up country on a survey of some difficulty for a projected railway across the mainland of Japan; and I fear I had contracted a pronounced dislike for the scene of our enforced idleness, after our long voyage out from England, before the *Colorado*, some days overdue from San Francisco, steamed into harbour, and our coast mail-boat, the *Golden Age*, that had been detained till she should arrive, at last stirred her lazy paddles and swung about her lofty deck-houses as she staggered away, rolling and pitching down the Gulf of Yedo, against a head-wind.

The run from Yokohama to Kobe takes usually about thirty hours; but we had an exceptionally long passage, leaving Yokohama at four o'clock on the afternoon of a Saturday, and dropping anchor about one o'clock on Monday. For about three hundred miles we retraced our track of three weeks before, and then turned northwards through the Kii channel into the Idzumi sea, a land-locked expanse of water communicating with the Inland Sea of Japan to the westward by the straits of Akashi about a dozen miles from Kobe.

As we steamed up towards the harbour, a range of snow-tipped hills, about three thousand feet high, confronted us; but these sank behind a lower and nearer range as we neared the land, and the white houses of the settlement came in view.

Then, having engaged our rooms, we proceeded further under the guidance of our friend to the railway offices, where we found our consignee, the Chief Assistant-Engineer, and sundry others of our own persuasion, and formed the centre of a procession from the offices to the club, taking the consulate on the way. We had of course to be registered as British subjects, and certified and rendered poorer in worldly goods to the extent of five dollars each; but it being now December, the worthy consul certified us as for the following year, such liberality well befitting his dignity as the best paid consul in Japan.

The idea we had formed from our observations in the neighbourhood of Yokohama, namely, that railway engineering in Japan was not as railway engineering elsewhere within our knowledge, was strengthened by what we saw at Kobe. The permanent buildings for the station and workshops were of iron, and had been designed upon the assumption that all the columns would be most suitably supported upon screw-piles; but when it came to erecting them, the screw-piles proved to be not quite long enough to reach the ground when the columns were fixed with reference to the intended rail level. So the structure was propped up in the air on temporary supports, while the ground was elevated, by means of concrete in blocks and sand filling, until the screws at the lower ends of the piles were reached and imbedded. Hard by we found one of the engineering staff despairing of getting into proper position a series of pegs intended to denote the centre line of railway, on a curve, because his theodolite was marked the wrong way round, as he said; but his resources were not by any means at an end, for in our presence he instructed his foreman to set the rails right, as near as he could, by eye alone, that he might get his centre line by measuring from them, and thus have no mistake as to the proper position of his future platforms!

Other funny things did we see that day and the next, and presently learned to keep our countenances under proper discipline; and, moreover, ceased to wonder at the alleged delay in completing the line. For it appeared that the only known way of passing a stream of water eighteen inches wide under the line, was to build a couple of walls that would have served for the abutments of a fifty-foot bridge, a foot and a half apart, and span the yawning gulf between them by means of beams sixteen inches square, of expensive timber, of sufficient length to have about a dozen feet at each end buried in the embankment behind the masonry. The walls were of finely worked granite, and must have cost a mint of money; but a structure of this description was to be found nearly every hundred yards.

Then we came upon two tunnels under rivers, justified by the peculiarity of the situation, but remarkable as being constructed for a single line only, while a third tunnel, a little further on, was made wide enough for a double line—the difference being explained by the statement that it had always been intended that the tunnels should be for a double line, but it was not found out while the two first were being constructed that they were not so.

On the second day we had a tramp through to Osaka, twenty miles, of which we rode four or five on a ballast engine. We crossed two considerable rivers by the railway bridges, already completed and wanting only the rails; and a third river we passed by boat, the bridge being yet unfinished. What with calling in upon three several engineers on the way, as in duty bound, and discussing with each of them the future possibilities of railway work, we found it falling dark as we arrived at the wilderness that was all yet achieved of Osaka station; but one of our party who had left England a few weeks earlier than ourselves, and had already paid a flying visit to Osaka, piloted us down to the foreign settlement at Kawaguchi (the word signifies river-mouth, but does not suggest the fact that the river Yodo has two mouths, neither of which are near the settlement), and then we fetched the French hotel.

Third year's work (1876)

EARLY in 1876, the surveying staff was broken up. Causes that had been at work almost from the time of our arrival in Japan, had first modified the sanguine ideas of the Minister of Public Works, and then extinguished the hopes entertained by the Railway Department, of the future of railway development in the country. The revenue of the country, drawn almost entirely from the laborious farming class, and burdened with the maintenance of the now useless and practically obsolete caste of fighting men, could not be made to yield a surplus, to be sunk in works not immediately productive, at all commensurate with the extent and variety of the claims brought forward to aid from the Treasury; and the proposal of a new foreign loan for public works was firmly rejected by the Ministry. In principle, the strategic value of a line of communication across the island was admitted, and it was therefore determined that the links connecting Kiyōto with the lake, and the lake with the west coast, should be kept in remembrance as having the first claim in case the expenditure of capital should be again found possible in that direction; but all else was indefinitely postponed. In fact, the extension from Kiyōto to Ōtsŭ, was only commenced in 1879, and the separate link between the lake and the sea in the following year.

The traffic on the first line opened, the suburban railway, connecting the capital Tōkiyō, with its port of Yokohama, which at the beginning had been very large, seemed to fall off unaccountably; and both that and the length already opened in 1874, between Kobe and Ōsaka, competed disadvantageously with the transport by water of all heavy goods. There was still the line between Ōsaka and Kiyōto in hand, without going any farther; and it was determined, after much vacillation, that the efforts of the Railway Department should be confined to this work for the time being.

The reduction of the engineering staff thus became necessary; and in the end of 1875 steps were taken to that end, some of them not well devised or immediately effective. We who had been appointed in 1873–4, with agreements for three years' employment, were not immediately concerned, though a tentative proposal came to us, suggesting that, "as men of honour, we probably should not desire to eat the bread of idleness." As, however, the possibility of such a state of things coming about as was now impending had been foreseen when we were appointed, and power reserved for the authorities to cancel our agreements without assigning any cause, upon payment of one year's salary, it was only necessary for us to remind them that the same was part of the consideration that had brought us to Japan, and thereupon leave them to take what course they thought fit; whereupon, it no doubt occurred to them, that as the said agreements had only about a year to run, they might as well have our services for their money; and so we heard no more of it.

But in other directions reductions were ruthlessly carried out, and employés unprotected by agreements were set adrift. I mention this because it should not be supposed that the old staff did not include several whose assistance our Chief would willingly have retained had it been possible to do so. The character of the change of policy, and the pressure it brought upon the Railway Department, however, from the end of 1875 onward, may be estimated from the fact, that from a full strength of twenty-five engineers and draughtsmen, reduced by death and retirements to twenty-two at the date just referred to, and again subsequently by another death and two retirements while the reductions by intent were in progress, the remainder after the expiration of all the three years' agreements only numbered five, two of whom belonged to the old staff, and these two again, dying in 1877 and 1878, were, though much regretted, not replaced; at least, not by additional engineers.

In the course of these changes, first Jimmy went away to Yokohama, to take charge of the line between that place and Tōkiyō; then Billy was called upon to take a length on the Ōsaka-Kiyōto line; Ned and Claude were "lent" to the Mining Department, and went off to the extreme south; James compromised with the Department and went home; Christopher returned to his friends; and only Charlie was left behind in Kiyōto, awaiting expiration of his notice. I had myself taken over charge of the railway under construction near Kiyōto, and had Charlie for a time as an assistant on the terminal station; but I was now, according to our official nomenclature, a "District Engineer" doing duty as a "Resident Engineer," my staff having evaporated, and except for seniority was just on a level with my old friend Tom, who was on the next length, and Billy who was half-way to Ōsaka. We all set to work to push forward our line to completion, and had a busy summer.

My length embraced a large quantity of bridging; arched flood openings to the extent of fifty spans of fifteen feet opening; girder flood openings and bridges, eleven spans of forty feet; two smaller girder bridges and numerous culverts; and the "big" bridge across the Katsura river, twelve spans of one hundred feet each. A great deal of work had been already done by my predecessor on the length, the earthworks and culverts being virtually complete, with about half the arched flood openings, and a good start made with the foundations of the rest of the bridging.

The key to the work was of course the big bridge, and considerable difficulty was encountered in sinking the foundation wells. The point of crossing was about half a dozen miles from the mouth of the gorge through which the river issued on to the plain, and the bed of the river was composed of gravel of all descriptions, from small shingle to good-sized boulders, brought down by the stream in times of flood, and more or less disturbed by every freshet. The actual bottom of the main stream was some ten feet below the level of the surrounding country, but the spaces within the flood-banks that were dry except in time of flood and partly cultivated, had been raised by successive deposits to an average of six feet above the fields outside the banks, and were themselves submerged at times to the extent of several feet in depth, the top of the river bank being some ten or twelve feet above the enclosed ground and nearly twenty above the fields. The main channel was somewhat variable both in position and depth, and the whole deposit permeated by water, which, when the river rose, leaked out through the foot of the flood-bank into the open country in many places, as the material of which the banks were composed was the same gravel, barely covered by vegetable soil, and strengthened by the roots of bamboos that grew all along the slopes. When the river was low, it drained the surrounding stratum of gravel, so that our foundation pits showed that the surface of the permeating water fell towards the channel; but this was reversed with every rise of the stream above an average level, when the surface of the water in the pits fell away from the river towards the flood-banks; and after the first few feet, all the excavation within the wells had to be done under water. My predecessor had devised a sort of circular dredge that acted very satisfactorily, but the difficulty was to keep the wells upright as they went down.

In many places the gravel was so hard, that the wells—great masses of brickwork twelve feet in outside diameter and two feet thick, bound together by iron rings and vertical rods—hung up on a mere shelf under the sharp cutting edge with which they were provided at the bottom, while the centre was excavated several feet below this edge; and the danger and difficulty lay in the runs made by the wells, sometimes without warning, when the supporting shelf gave way, and the difference of pressure owing to the great variability in the consistence of the stratum frequently forced the wells out of position. As this tendency increased with the depth of the excavation, it was necessary to keep a constant watch upon the dredging work, and use all possible means to keep the wells from sticking up. Until we were well below the bed of the stream, there was always a risk of a sudden flood producing a change in the direction of the channel, and scouring away the gravel so as to upset the wells; for the bed of the stream had many holes in it, that travelled about up and down the river, and the occasional approach of which to some of the wells was a source of great anxiety.

We worked night and day, when the weather permitted; and on the wells nearest the stream, even harder in bad weather than at other times, to get them down on to a firm bearing before the freshets came down; loading the brickwork at top with rails, so disposed as to correct any observed tendency of the wells to cant over. Many a rough day and night did I pass on the works, till we succeeded in moving some refractory well from an insecure position to a firm bearing, with the stream rising and roaring through our stagings. We had only one set of diving gear, and I had to send this away from time to time for Billy to use, on a lot of similar wells that he was sinking for the foundations of his flood-openings; but we worked amicably together, and did the best we could for each other. Our professional diver trained several Japanese, who seemed to take a delight in the work, and groped about in the darkness at the bottom of the wells, picking out the boulders from under the edge of the shoe, and coming up to the surface for a rest and a whiff of their tiny pipes every twenty minutes or so, with vivid descriptions of the particular state of some brute of a boulder that was holding up the well on one side; and then down they would go again, and work at him till he was dislodged, and they had to be hauled up sharp to the surface as the well began to move, and the water and gravel boiled up over the top of the brickwork, as the great mass settled down on to a fresh bearing below. Then the diving gear was shifted to the next well, and the dredger was set to work again at the bottom.

Gradually we got the upper hand of our troubles, as each pair of wells attained a safe depth below the bed of the stream, and was filled up with concrete. The upper works began to make a show, and it was curious to see the change in the aspect of the works, as the big wells disappeared, and for all there was to be seen above the surface we might have been working three months for nothing, till the plain brick piers were built up on the top of the buried wells, and the first of the iron girders were placed in position. By the time the later floods of July came down out of Tamba, the province beyond the hills, drained by our river, we were beyond all risk of anything but delay.

The work was much delayed when near completion, an erroneous idea having got abroad that the length was much behindhand, so that a push was made to get the line open up to the commencement of my length, and everything sacrificed to this, and my remaining work proportionately retarded. But after all I was only six weeks behind, and had a fair share of departmental help been given to me the whole length might have been opened simultaneously with a great saving in expense. As the Chief saw this, however, and did me ample justice, I was well satisfied.

We opened the line into Kiyōto on the 5th of September, the trains running to a temporary station near Tōji. As for the permanent terminal buildings, the designs for which were only placed in my hands in April, that was another affair, especially as they were of a rather ambitious character, as befitted the situation.

The summer was an exceptionally hot one, and so dry in the early months that there was a great loss of rice, owing to the deficiency of water when the seed was put down. As soon as the winter crops are partly cleared off the ground, each farmer makes a little nursery for his rice-shoots in a corner of his land, putting down the seed thick, and keeping it covered with shallow water, and nourished with manure, while he breaks up and levels the rest of his farm, arranges his banks, and brings in his water supply; then when the warm rains of early summer begin to fall he transplants the young shoots, some twelve or fifteen inches high, and separates them to a distance of about eight inches, so that what in the seed-bed covered only a space of a few square rods, suffices for as many acres in the field.

This year, however, the summer rains were very late and the country dry, and a good deal of rice perished in the seed-beds. I remember well going down to Ōsaka, on one of my frantic expeditions after material that seemed to hang on the hands of the transport department long after it should have been delivered on the work; going part of the way by road, and getting on to a trolly when I reached the rails, the coolies who shoved me along being mournfully eloquent upon the prospects of the season, explaining that rice was going to be so dear that poor people would lie down by the roadside and die, and the farmers be unable even to save seed for next season. They toiled along under the brazen June sky, with many a grunt and many a stoppage, so that I thought I should never get to Ōsaka—at least before nightfall; but lo! a little cloud "like to a man's hand" came out of the sea, and presently gathered on the flank of Rokkōsan, and grew black and spread over the western heavens, shutting out the cruel sun; while a little shiver, as of an awakening hope, went from field to field, and then a cry rang out from the villages that the long-expected rain was at hand. The toiling farmers put down their buckets beside the sick seedlings and bared their breasts to the rush of rain that swooped down from the hills. The yells of my coolies as the first heavy drops reached us were enough to bring the heart into one's mouth; and when the stinging shower struck them, they bent their backs to the work and whisked me along into Ōsaka at the rate of nineteen to the dozen, whooping with glee. I had to get through my business at head-quarters, and start off back by night, fearing a flood down the river; and sure enough the next day was none too long for us to get all snug at the bridge, before the water began to roar under our gangways and surge around the piers and stagings. Just below the bridge, a new channel was cut across one of the bends, wiping out the results of much labour in cultivation of the ground where the floods of former seasons had left their silt. We only lost a few sticks that broke away from their moorings; and some of those were afterwards recovered from the lower reaches of the river after the flood subsided. Yet another flood had we in the beginning of July, but I could laugh at it by that time.

Then came the hot season—late July and August—the river bed like a furnace, and my scamps of rivetters taking all the looking after I could give them. The day the line was opened to Mukōmachi, the station just short of my length, was a full one for us at Katsura. We had more than half the girders up, and I was disporting myself with a theodolite at the end of the bridge, giving lines for the adjustment of the rest, when suddenly I caught sight of a little blue smoke in the middle of a long thatched roof, over my stack of rail-balks. Whew! the men under the bridge thought I was fairly mad at last, probably, for an instant, as I bounced down amongst them and picked up a bucket of water for a shy at the blazing straw, and then thrust it empty into the hands of the nearest, turning him towards the river channel, with a kick behind to expedite him. But fire is no stranger in Japan, and in ten seconds every man was off the bridge and fighting for a bucket. I got little Musha, my head cadet, to organize a line to pass up the water; but the roof was dropping in blazing fragments on to the timbers beneath, so with a heave-yo! and a push with poles, hands, whatever we could get a bearing with, over it went to

366

one side, and the men swarmed on to the stack to fight the fire. The water began to come in, the logs were rolled over and drenched on every side layer by layer, and presently the tongues of flame ceased to dart up from out the chinks of the lower tiers, and there was a horrid stench of steam and charred wood and smouldering straw. Before twenty minutes were over, the last buckets of water were being smartly exchanged over heads and shoulders by the smutty and scorched monkeys who were dancing on the timbers; and then we all went off to repair damages, apply plaster and arnica and sweet oil, assume decent clothing, and get our tiffins.

In about an hour's time I was returning to the bridge, cigar in mouth; had exchanged a laugh with little Musha, who was trying to look as if he hadn't got a dozen yards of flannel twisted tight round his ribs where a post had caught him as he rolled amongst the logs; and just had my foot on the beginning of the upstream gangway, when two of the English foremen, the diver and a mason from Billy's length, who had come up for a holiday, met me; and one, touching his hat, said, "I'm sorry to inform you, sir, that Smith's drowned." I naturally asked "Where?" and was answered, "He's just below the old bridge, and we can't get him up!" "How long has he been in?" I shouted as I ran down the bank to the spot, thinking there might yet be a chance; but the reply, "About twenty minutes, sir!" sounded ominously in my ears. It was a deep hole under the bank, where half an old bridge, wrecked by the last flood, projected into the stream. Nothing was to be seen of him from above; but two of the native divers were already in search of him, and presently a shout from one of them, as he emerged and clung to the piling, brought a boatful of men out into the stream, one of whom leaning over the stem, caught at something under water; but it held, and he pulled the bows under, spilling all the crew into the river. They all scrambled out, and then one of the divers went down and released a foot that had caught in something, and the inanimate body of poor Smith was hauled ashore. We tried to revive him, but he had been in too long, and all efforts were fruitless.

Completion of the Ōsaka-Kiyōto railway—the great rebellion of 1877

THE opening days of 1877 were remarkable for the extreme uneasiness that was spread throughout all classes by the impending troubles. There were many who, mindful of the prestige of the great fighting clan of Satsuma, and believing to the full the rumours, not only as to the numbers of warriors ready to follow the lead of Saigo Takamori, but as to the disaffection of the shizoku throughout the empire, looked upon the overthrow of the existing government as a foregone conclusion; and counted the strength of the navy, officered and manned almost entirely by Satsuma men, as so much more weight to be placed in the scale that held the resources of revolution. There were among the foreigners in Japan many who also believed that if armed rebellion once broke out, it would be impossible to re-establish peace unless either the Satsuma leaders were victorious, or the whole shizoku class destroyed; and who justly looked upon this latter consummation as not within the bounds of reasonable probability. It was supposed that the standing army at the disposal of the government was inefficient; and that the policy of recruiting it from among the "heimin" or unprivileged classes would show disastrous results when the old fighting men arrayed themselves generally, as was expected, on the other side. The announced visit of the Mikado to Kiyōto, nearer by some three or four hundred miles than the official capital to the scene of the expected outbreak, was looked upon as a piece of bravado that was not likely to be actually carried out; and the preparations that were being made for a peaceful pageant, that of the State opening of the railway, to which all the representatives of foreign powers were invited, were supposed to be merely a blind.

How we did "jump around," as the Americans would say, that month of January! and by how many hours we were ahead of requirements at the last I should not like to say. The sort of "can't-be-helped" way of looking at things, that seems to be the normal state of Japanese officials, was changed for the opposite phase, during the prevalence of which every one gets hold of something and does something with it; a good and refreshing state of things, if only direction be not wanting to their efforts. It was required of us that we should have the permanent terminus ready at Kiyōto for the formal opening, if not for the arrival of the Mikado a few days earlier; and we were able to get our task finished and land his Majesty at the completed buildings.

The Emperor left Yokohama by steamer with an escort of vessels of war in the last week of January, and after being driven into the Toba anchorage for shelter, as heavy weather was met with, finally reached Kobe on the 27th, and was housed at the post office. We had notice to stop all traffic next day, and run a special train through to Kiyōto, which was done in due course, the whole length of the line being guarded by police, and the stations occupied by detachments of troops. No great parade was made otherwise, but our Chief rode up on the engine, and all the engineering staff in charge of the line accompanied the train. My first sight of the Mikado was at Kiyōto, where, after the train and the platform had been cleared, we were drawn up in line beside the door of the Imperial carriage; and our little Chief Commissioner, who had been riding with his Majesty, stood opposite to us as the Mikado stepped on to the platform and paused a moment. The Chief Commissioner said, "Gentlemen, I am ordered by his Majesty to thank you for your care for his safety to-day;" whereupon we all bowed, and blushed like pickled cabbage, and when we recovered saw the august cocked hat and coat-tails vanishing in the distance.

Next day we resumed the traffic as before, to the temporary station, and a crowd of officials of the household department took possession of the permanent building, and prepared it for the solemn function of the 5th of February. The offices were fitted up as withdrawing and reception rooms, and a sort of stage was built out in front of the station, carpeted and hung round with tapestry, with a gorgeous throne all proper. All the approaches were decorated, stands for spectators arranged, and curious devices set up, such as gigantic lanterns, dwarf Fujisans, ships, engines, etc., with Venetian masts, strings of lanterns and flags, and so on, and the same at both Ōsaka and Kobe. The saloon carriage upon which the energies of the locomotive superintendent and the carriage department had been concentrated for six months past, was secretly run up to Kiyōto by night, as a thing "that mote not be prophaned of common eyes," and No. 20 engine was painted and silvered up until she looked almost quite too beautiful, and the driver and stoker, even in their Sunday coats, were by no means congruous; so they were hidden in a grove of evergreen cunningly attached to the cab.

My little house at Ken-nin-ji was for the time almost in the midst of a metropolis of diplomatic talent; for the temple with its surrounding houses was made the lodging for all the ambassadors, and I never went in or out without feeling that I was a gross fraud, and that I ought to apologize to the crowd who congregated round the entrance gates and discussed my personal appearance audibly, supposing me to wield the power of Russia or represent the hauteur of Spain. These were of course the visitors from the country, as I was well enough known by most of the inhabitants of that quarter of the city, and had even been caricatured, with an enormous eyeglass and a very Roman-nosed waistcoat, by some local genius, upon the blank walls round the enclosure of the temple. I always suspected a certain shaven-pated blackguard, who used to come out of the chief priest's house and strike the hours upon the big bell, of this artless proceeding; he devoted so much time to watching me as I paced up and down under the trees with a cigar on fine evenings.

I had to make a special run down to Kobe, where I secured the last hat there was in the place, so as to make a fitting appearance at the impending solemnity. We had been warned that nothing less than dress coats and white chokers, with the regulation chimney-pot hats, would qualify us to stand over against the foreign representatives upon the platforms at Kiyōto, Ōsaka, and Kobe, subject to the gaze of thousands, while addresses were being presented and prayers recited. Of course some priests were mixed up in the matter, as indeed has been the case elsewhere than in Japan on occasion of railway festivities within my knowledge: for I remember a certain first sod, the turning of which, hard by the most insignificant of Sussex watering-places, involved a prayer, a speech to a toast, and a tearful collapse, from each of three rival parsons.

The morning, though bitterly cold until the sun was well up, turned out bright and glorious, and we soon warmed up as the Imperial train started away from Kiyōto, amid great firing of guns and shouts from the populace. We engineers had a compartment next the engine, with a friendly reporter and a pack of cards. At Ōsaka, a stoppage, and grave solemnities, firing of cannon, addresses, general enthusiasm, etc.; then en route for Kobe, where more solemnities were perpetrated and Admiral Véron and Mr. Thomas Brassey were presented, and the governor of the Hiōgo Ken lost his head first, and his cocked hat and his north point subsequently, and various impromptu alterations of the programme were attempted by an enterprising person who had been pitchforked out of some election committee into a consulship.

Then there was a grand scramble for lunch, laid out in a room thirty feet by twenty, for five hundred people, one hungry engineer, who had been up since half-past five that morning, getting a French roll and a bottle of beer for his share. The word was soon passed that the Mikado had had enough of it, and wished to get out of the way of Mr. Consul as soon as possible. So after a brief wait while that gentleman was being dodged round the passages, and at last shunted into a spare waiting-room, we started back, making the best of our way to Kiyōto without a stoppage. We arrived there safely, notwithstanding that we were turned through a siding at one station, instead of going by the direct line, insomuch that after charging the points at the rate of thirty-five miles an hour, we were not quite sure if we were all right for a few seconds: and afterwards were desolated by the barely averted destruction of our Traffic Manager's head against one of his own signal-boxes at Ōsaka, which would have spoilt all the fun we derived from hearing the ambitious consul's private address to the Mikado, read by our friend the reporter, who was the sole recipient of the document.

However, we did the forty-seven miles in an hour and thirty-five minutes; say a rate of thirty miles an hour all through, which was quite fast enough for our narrow gauge; and his Imperial Majesty was good enough to cut short the final ceremony at Kiyōto, so that we were free at half-past four or thereabouts.

The prettiest feature of the whole affair, to my mind, was the conduct of the country people all along the route. Wherever suitable ground could be found outside the fence, about on a level with the rails, spaces had been marked off to be occupied by the school-children from the various villages of the district; some of these spaces extended alongside the line for half a mile together. Each school was in charge of its teachers and the mayors and principal inhabitants of the villages, and as the Imperial train approached and passed the bands of eager girls or wondering-eyed boys bowed their heads and rose again, changing the bright field of expectant faces into an expanse of black polls, and then breaking out again with the flush of accomplished ceremony as the little ones clapped their hands and gazed after the vanishing train. The successive movement of the different corps of children had an effect like the passing of a summer cloud across a ripening cornfield.

Then we had yet another journey to make to Ōsaka, for on that evening a banquet was given to the principal government officials and local authorities, in the city hall, whereunto we were bidden; and here also was great enthusiasm. Our retiring director made a speech, in which he demonstrated that Tōkiyō and Kiyōto being each connected with a seaport, and the coast service of mail steamers being now in the hands of a Japanese company, the main trunk railway was as good as completed; and our Chief sang his swan's-song, and bade his staff farewell. A twenty minutes' oration by the editor of the *Choya-Shimbun*, who had come down from Tōkiyō with the rest of the distinguished visitors, received (on its conclusion) the most rapturous applause from both Japanese and foreigners, though I don't suppose the latter understood any part of it, except the "soré-kara" and "so-shité," which are about as much as if one should say "then" and "therefore." Towards the end everybody began to make speeches, and address our Chief Commissioner as "Your Excellency," on the strength of his appointment as Junior Vice-minister of Public Works, and the wise ones sought their hats and coats, and avoided the tumblers of champagne that were hospitably pressed upon the departing guests.

We all had to go to Kobe, as there was no train to Kiyōto; and somebody lost his boots on the way. It was for a time supposed that he had put them on the step to be cleaned, before he should get up in the morning, on entering the carriage; but at last they were found in the next compartment. And so finally we all got to bed and ended this eventful day.

While, however, enthusiasm and loyalty were in the ascendant in Settsu and Yamashiro, the ill-omened march of the Satsuma forces had already commenced, and Saigo had issued his proclamation that he would "attend the Emperor at Kiyōto, with ten thousand men, to present a petition." The government troops were already hurrying to Fukuōka, to seize the vantage ground of Minámi-ga-seki and bear back the tide of rebellion. The fortress of Kumamoto was invested, and the garrison, the only show of Imperial authority in Higo, were pent within their walls. And Kido was dying in Kiyōto, and his scared colleagues, the Ministers of State, were holding council by his death-bed.

But those who wish to read the story of the great rebellion of 1877, may find a far more complete account of its causes, purposes, and ultimate fate, in Mounsey's careful monograph, than could be attempted here. There they may read the story of the desperate valour and ungrudging devotion of life and fortune displayed by the adherents of a cause fore-doomed to failure, as was afterwards seen, though at first it was promising enough; of the steadfast face presented by the army, overmatched in the beginning, to its powerful adversary, till his progress was stayed and retreat compelled; of the lingering collapse of the rebellion, staining the mountain fastnesses of Hiuga with uselessly shed blood; of the waste of life and treasure that went on through that sad summer, till the 24th of September saw Kawamura reverently washing the severed head of his old friend Saigo Takamori, dead by his own hand on the slopes of the hill that was the scene of his first preparations, as of the final volley of his victorious opponents.

It is only, however, with side aspects of the rebellion that we foreigners in Japan had really to do; and it is not without satisfaction that one sees that the struggle was fought out in a fair field, between the representatives of two schools of political action that could not act together for their country's good; and that no hireling aid or outside scheme came into play, but that when all was over there was no one of the victors who could not honour his worsted foe, no survivor of the vanquished who was tempted to look for sympathy and charity elsewhere than to his countrymen, or to refuse from hands no longer unfriendly the aid of which he stood sorely in need. The Satsuma men who revolted put their all, as Satsuma men, upon the struggle, and lost; and are now merged in a wider nationality, accepted from the beginning by the wiser of their own kin.

Just as here in England we hear from time to time of small boys who aver that they put a piece of wood or iron in the way of a train, that they might "see the engine jump," so in Japan with children of a larger growth it is much the same story. Indeed, so far as my own experience and observation go, there seems great reason to believe that many obstructions are created by persons employed as watchmen or gate-keepers, for the mere pleasure of seeing the obstruction smashed into fragments by the charge of the powerful machine at the head of its train.

There is happily no instance of actual wrecking of a train by reason of such obstructions; but they were at one time so frequently met with, as to demoralize the staff, and even one or two of the English drivers were more than suspected of romancing in their reports of obstruction on the road—one of them had what almost amounted to a monomania on the subject.

One case that occurred while I was in charge at Tōkiyō, however, will always seem to me to be amongst the most remarkable of thoroughly understood events coming within a hair's-breadth of disaster. It was when we had a quantity of material for laying down the second line alongside the single line used for traffic; the timber sleepers were approximately in place, and the rails paired, but not fastened in any way. In the dusk of the evening—the time when such things almost invariably occur—some person, or perhaps more than one, lifted one end of a loose rail and carried it round, laying it across the nearer rail of the running line, pointing towards the next approaching train. It was then roughly propped in that position with some stones, to prevent it from slipping down if shaken by vibration from an approaching train; and formed an ingenious preparation for a hideous smash. Yet no smash occurred, though the train ran into the obstruction at thirty miles an hour, the driver only sighting it in the twilight as he came round the curve that terminated a few yards away from the spot.

What actually happened was this, as we traced it out by the marks on the engine. The life-guard on the off-side, the piece of iron specially designed to throw obstructions off the rail in advance of the wheels, caught the loose rail, throwing it round further across the line; owing to the far end of the rail being a little lower than the running line, there was a slight incline of the near end upward, that brought it against the inside framing of the engine, as it slewed round, just below the axle box of the near leading wheel, stripping a nut off a bolt securing the strap below the box. The sudden pinch slightly bowed the rail, and it glanced off, missing the wheel, and riding over the boss, or enlargement at the lower end of the brake-hanger in front of the near driving wheel, supported on which, and pushed sideways by the life-guard that had first come in contact with it, the rail was transferred bodily across the line, between the two wheels mentioned, and by the onward motion of the engine finally delivered clear of everything, on the near side of the road.

Such an occurrence was not calculated to make things pleasant for any one responsible for the safety of the public; and of course the Japanese authorities were just as anxious as I was. There was some very tall talk amongst the staff, and the propriety of converting a field adjoining the spot where the train was not wrecked into an execution ground for the occasion was mooted. However, it seemed that the most reasonable way of treating an outrageous crime was to show, if possible, to all interested, that justice need not deviate one step from her regular path in dealing with it, and that the penalty and its enforcement were common-place as well as inevitable; and this view found favour with those whose advice was likely to be most respected. Unfortunately we never caught our criminal; but the matter was a good deal discussed, and perhaps it is not strange that it was the last case of wilful obstruction of the railway for a long time; so that though no one was brought to justice, it would seem that the public conscience was stimulated.

We railway men were gladdened in the spring of this year 1878, by the news that a small extension of the railway system had been authorized. True, it was only about ten miles; but it represented a departure from the absolute quiescence entered upon a twelvemonth before.

Our Chief Commissioner, who though nominally holding the post of "third man" in the Department of Public Works, carefully eschewed all work not con-nected with his special branch, was for some two months in the capital making arrangements for this work, which indeed would have been earlier proceeded with had his previous exertions towards the same end been crowned with success. His frequent representations, and untiring efforts to give them a practical bearing, at last bore fruit in a sort of understanding that, though no extensive undertakings could be entered upon for some time to come, still a small amount of work might be kept in progress; as without some field for action there was great risk of los-ing the benefit he had made such great personal exertions to foster in his depart-ment—that was, the maintenance of an efficient staff of Japanese engineers and administrative officials qualified to undertake the construction and working of railways.

With this view even a small yearly extension of the railway system was of inestimable value, as a means of exercising and improving the Japanese staff, and keeping up the interest of practical work, without which the best and most active-minded of the staff could hardly be retained in the department. The new piece, small as it was in extent, would afford the required field for the acqui-sition of additional experience, and exercise of ingenuity in dealing with new classes of work, including as it did a tunnel through the range of hills bordering Lake Biwa on the south-western side, and a series of heavy inclines, the working of which would be an introduction to the conditions attending any future exten-sions in the more hilly parts of the country. So that when the Chief Commissioner returned to Osaka with his official authorization in his pocket, and with the neces-sary financial preliminaries settled, a gleam of sunshine seemed to fall upon the neglected department, that might be the herald of a better time than had latterly been experienced.

All this was planned for the 4th of November, and was to be forgotten before the return of the Mikado from his journey, expected about the 8th. But on the 4th it rained dismally, also on the 5th, likewise on the 6th; and I was just enjoying the prospect of getting at my official desk again (as the fun had to be given up) and making up arrears of work, when a fresh irruption of wild officials took place: the Mikado had determined to strike the railway at Kanagawa and return to Tōkiyō by rail. This was pleasing, after a fashion, for I had arranged to run a series of special

trains with materials for the works in progress, delayed on account of the forego-
ing trouble; and these I expected would all have to be countermanded. However, I
hung out my flags and assumed an air of festivity; and as it happened, perhaps on
account of some occult influence thereby set in motion, two of the ordinary public
trains were stopped to make room for the Imperial special, and my material trains
were only delayed an hour or two.

On the 9th, the Mikado arrived, his august consort coming down to the station to
meet him, and looking as solemn as if no jinks of any height to speak of had been
contemplated in his absence. She stood at the end of the platform to await him,
amid a group of attendant ladies,—some of whom, scandal said, were preferred
to herself,—made a low reverence to her lord as he passed with his immediate
suite, and fell into the procession just behind the bearer of the Imperial teapot and
spoons, entering her own carriage at the station steps to follow her spouse back
to the palace. Many thousand spectators were assembled, the Imperial Guards
drawn up, and all the chief officials who had not gone down to Kanagawa to meet
the Mikado there put in an appearance at the Shimbashi terminus. The spectacle
as a whole was rather imposing, and such displays are evidently popular with the
people of the capital.

I did not, however, get back into my offices for some days after this, as there
was a remote possibility that the fleet might be honoured after all by an Imperial
inspection; but the abiding foulness of the weather at last knocked the project on
the head for the season.

This November was an exception to the ordinary run of things. As a rule it is
the finest and most settled month in the year, a little frosty at nights, but bright
and clear when the sun is up. Sometimes the fine weather lasts through to the
middle of February with hardly a break; but that does not make a healthy season
in the large towns, as unless there is some kind of a fall to flush the surface drains
and carry away the refuse that favours the seeds of disease, a sort of epidemic
of low fever may be looked for. This month was fatal to another of our staff,
Theodore Shann, who caught cold by exposure to a chill after fast walking, and
had a recurrence of his bronchitis of the preceding winter, which weakened him
so much that he succumbed to an internal ailment of an organic kind, and left us
on the 28th. He was laid hard by his old friend John England, in the Yokohama
cemetery.

I had now to rely entirely upon my Japanese staff, to carry on the renewal
works and the doubling and maintenance of the line. The length was divided into
two sections, putting each in charge of a senior cadet as my representative, with
a senior foreman to assist him in the general arrangement of labour and materials, while an assistant foreman was attached to the outside work, and a Japanese
inspector of platelayers was "doubled" upon each of the two foreign platelayers.
Any special works, requiring continuous supervision on the spot, of which we
had many in hand, were placed in charge of the best men I could pick out for
the purpose, and made my own particular hobby. Very timid some of these good
fellows were at first, in their new places of responsibility, and their plaints of

"tak'ūsan ab'unai" (very dangerous) at the commencement of each new operation were amusingly sincere; but we did what had to be done without mishap, if at times a little the reverse of expeditiously.

The spring of 1879 witnessed another step in advance, in the railway management, by the introduction of native engine-drivers to work a portion of the traffic—a long contemplated change, which had been systematically provided for. It is true that between Tōkiyō and Yokohama the task of engine-driving is about as simple as it can be anywhere; but it behoved us to select and train our men properly, and in the result there have been but few instances of want of judgment on the part of the Japanese drivers. The curious view taken by the non-professional observer as to the dangers of such innovations, was well illustrated by a remark attributed to a gentleman who in his own line had to exercise some powers of investigation and judgment. He said that "it would be all very well so long as the train was on a straight line, but he doubted if any Japanese could be trusted to *steer* the engine round those curves!"

At first some acute inquirers amongst the travelling public were very keen to know which of the daily trains were still entrusted to Europeans; but as no casualties of any kind occurred to demonstrate the inferiority of the Japanese drivers, and as we found them not only steady and wideawake, as we knew beforehand, but also economical in the use of coal, oil, etc.—to say nothing of their lower wages, about one-sixth of those paid to foreigners,—the substitution was a source of legitimate satisfaction to all interested in the proper management and success of the railways. The unavoidable friction at the first starting of these arrangements, with a portion of the foreign staff, was well dealt with by the Locomotive Superintendents both at Kobe and Tōkiyō.

68

W. S. CAINE, *A TRIP ROUND THE WORLD IN 1887–8* (LONDON: G. ROUTLEDGE & SONS, 1888), PP. 159–164

On the following morning we all left Yokohama early, *en route* for Nikko, a journey of about 110 miles, of which 80 was by railway. Japanese railways are narrow gauge, about three feet wide, laid in double-headed rails on chairs and sleepers, and the train travels about 18 miles an hour. The stations are scrupulously neat and clean, and the rolling stock is very comfortable. The carriages are seated like omnibuses, with the first-class divided into three compartments, all communicating, and it is possible to traverse the train from end to end as in America. There are about 150 miles of railway now open in Japan, and some 450 more are projected, which will be built as soon as funds permit. English engine-drivers are employed, but the passenger and goods traffic is all managed by Japanese.

The line from Yokohama terminates at Tokio, and we had to ride in Jin-ricki-shas for three or four miles across Tokio to reach the station for Utsunomiya, our next stage sixty miles further on.

This journey was very full of interest, as the line passes through the finest agricultural district in Japan. It is densely populated, and the farms vary in size from half an acre to ten acres. Nearly every house we passed had pretty little gardens full of flowers, mostly chrysanthemums, now in all their glory, with quaintly-trimmed trees four or five feet high, tiny little water-falls and ponds, with toy bridges and boats. Some of these gardens looked exactly like a willow-pattern plate.

The soil is of magnificent quality and depth, and the whole country is running with clear streams of water, forming a complete system of irrigation. On most of the farms it is quite possible to get three crops in the year off the land. The main crop is rice, the staple food of the Japanese, and the whole country was yellow with the ripe grain, now being harvested. Every inch of the soil is cultivated. There are no hedges or ditches, the farms being divided by a small raised ridge about six inches high, which carries a little crop of its own on joint account for the two farmers whose land it divides. The soil is tilled by hand only. In a journey of eighty miles I only saw two horses, each engaged in drawing a small plough.

Most of the cultivation is done by a curious hand plough, which turns up a 3 ft. furrow every blow. The land seems capable of growing any crop that is put into it. Besides rice, I saw patches of tea, onions, daikons (a long white turnip, that seems a great article of diet everywhere), cauliflower, cabbage, beans, cotton, caladiums, buckwheat, ginger, carrots, barley, sweet and common potatoes, peas, beets, pepper, bamboos, tobacco, radishes, lettuce, maize, dhurra, celery, lotus (the seeds of which are a favourite food), artichokes, castor oil, and everywhere small clumps of yellow chrysanthemums, the flowers of which are boiled and eaten with much relish. Besides these ground crops there were orchards of mulberry-trees for silkworm culture, pears, cherries, plums, peaches, and persimmons, weighed down with golden fruit, a great favourite with Japanese of all sorts and conditions. These trees were all hung round with great bunches of rice straw, toughening to be plaited into hats and shoes. Not even in the best parts of Belgium is such perfect cultivation to be found as in this beautiful garden of Japan.

Four hours after leaving Tokio we arrived at Utsunomiya, the capital of a province, with a population of 25,000. We walked up to our quarters for the night, escorted through the streets by an admiring crowd of natives of all ages, who made huge merriment of our various peculiarities of dress, but with a good-natured politeness that took away the smallest trace of offence. I felt quite conceited at the special attention I received personally, due entirely to my six feet of height among a five-foot people. As we walk along, laughing groups run ahead and bring out their biggest men, whom they range alongside of me, driving them away with scorn as they fail to reach my gauge. My beard also receives much attention. One girl came up to me, bowed almost to the ground, and then pulled my beard, and ran away laughing.

The children are delightful and quaint beyond all description. The boys have their heads shaved, except odd little tufts on the crown and sometimes behind the ears, the little girls wearing their hair exactly as it appears on the twopenny fans so universal all over England. All the babies are bound on the backs of other children, and it is common to see a baby a year old tied on the back of a brother or sister three or four years old. Nothing is seen of the baby but its head, and the combination presents the droll appearance of a two-headed child. The baby is as jolly and laughter-loving as its bearer, and both grin and laugh in happy unison. All the children, great and small, laugh from crown to toe, are fat and well nourished, and are the happiest and jolliest children on the face of the earth. I never tire of the charming groups they make at every street corner. They swarm in every village like rabbits in a warren. Japanese children are the chief delight of their parents. I never saw such happy, well-behaved children. The only time I have ever heard one cry was when I came suddenly round a corner in some country village, when I fear they mistook me for the Red-whiskered Devil. They are never scolded or punished in any way, either at home or at school, and a parent who struck a child would be shunned as a monster. I do not, however, think this treatment would answer in England. I have heard the excellent qualities of

Japanese children ascribed to their vegetarian diet, but I must leave wiser dietists than I to settle that question. The Japanese love to turn their children out smartly dressed, with doll and fan, and the bright harmonious colours, the infinite variety of pattern and material, with the quaint cut of the garment added to their absurdly comical heads, plump faces, and beady-black eyes, yield never-failing amusement to us all.

69

LAFCADIO HEARN, *OUT OF THE EAST: REVERIES AND STUDIES IN NEW JAPAN* (BOSTON: HOUGHTON, MIFFLIN, 1899), PP. 275–279

VIII

The early morning train from Kyōto was in; the little station was full of hurry and noise,—clattering of geta, humming of converse, and fragmentary cries of village boys selling cakes and luncheons: *"Kwashi yoros—!" "Sushi yoros—!" "Bentō yoros—!"* Five minutes, and the geta clatter, and the banging of carriage doors, and the shrilling of the boys stopped, as a whistle blew and the train jolted and moved. It rumbled out, puffed away slowly northward, and the little station emptied itself. The policeman on duty at the wicket banged it to, and began to walk up and down the sanded platform, surveying the silent rice-fields.

Autumn had come,—the Period of Great Light. The sun glow had suddenly become whiter, and shadows sharper, and all outlines clear as edges of splintered glass. The mosses, long parched out of visibility by the summer heat, had revived in wonderful patches and bands of bright soft green over all shaded bare spaces of the black volcanic soil; from every group of pine-trees vibrated the shrill wheeze of the tsuku-tsuku-bōshi; and above all the little ditches and canals was a silent flickering of tiny lightnings,—zigzag soundless flashings of emerald and rose and azure-of-steel,—the shooting of dragon-flies.

Now, it may have been due to the extraordinary clearness of the morning air that the policeman was able to perceive, far up the track, looking north, something which caused him to start, to shade his eyes with his hand, and then to look at the clock. But, as a rule, the black eye of a Japanese policeman, like the eye of a poised kite, seldom fails to perceive the least unusual happening within the whole limit of its vision. I remember that once, in far-away Oki, wishing, without being myself observed, to watch a mask-dance in the street before my inn, I poked a small hole through a paper window of the second story, and peered at the performance. Down the street stalked a policeman, in snowy uniform and havelock; for it was midsummer. He did not appear even to see the dancers or the crowd through which he walked without so much as turning his head to either side. Then he suddenly halted, and fixed his gaze exactly on the hole in my shōji; for at that hole he had seen an eye which he had instantly decided, by reason of its shape, to be a foreign eye. Then he entered the inn, and asked questions about my passport, which had already been examined.

What the policeman at the village station observed, and afterwards reported, was that, more than half a mile north of the station, two persons had reached the railroad track by crossing the rice-fields, apparently after leaving a farmhouse considerably to the northwest of the village. One of them, a woman, he judged by the color of her robe and girdle to be very young. The early express train from Tōkyō was then due in a few minutes, and its advancing smoke could be perceived from the station platform. The two persons began to run quickly along the track upon which the train was coming. They ran on out of sight round a curve.

Those two persons were Tarō and O-Yoshi. They ran quickly, partly to escape the observation of that very policeman, and partly so as to meet the Tōkyō express as far from the station as possible. After passing the curve, however, they stopped running, and walked, for they could see the smoke coming. As soon as they could see the train itself, they stepped off the track, so as not to alarm the engineer, and waited, hand in hand. Another minute, and the low roar rushed to their ears, and they knew it was time. They stepped back to the track again, turned, wound their arms about each other, and lay down cheek to cheek, very softly and quickly, straight across the inside rail, already ringing like an anvil to the vibration of the hurrying pressure.

The boy smiled. The girl, tightening her arms about his neck, spoke in his ear:—

"For the time of two lives, and of three, I am your wife; you are my husband, Tarō Sama."

Tarō said nothing, because almost at the same instant, notwithstanding frantic attempts to halt a fast train without airbrakes in a distance of little more than a hundred yards, the wheels passed through both,—cutting evenly, like enormous shears.

IX

The village people now put bamboo cups full of flowers upon the single grave-stone of the united pair, and burn incense-sticks, and repeat prayers. This is not orthodox at all, because Buddhism forbids jōshi, and the cemetery is a Buddhist one; but there is religion in it,—a religion worthy of profound respect.

You ask why and how the people pray to those dead. Well, all do not pray *to* them, but lovers do, especially unhappy ones. Other folk only decorate the tomb and repeat pious texts. But lovers pray there for supernatural sympathy and help. I was myself obliged to ask why, and I was answered simply, "*Because those dead suffered so much.*"

So that the idea which prompts such prayers would seem to be at once more ancient and more modern than Buddhism,—the Idea of the eternal Religion of Suffering.

70

MRS. HUGH FRASER, *LETTERS FROM JAPAN* (NEW EDITION. NEW YORK: MACMILLAN CO., 1904), PP. 43–45, 326–328, 331

As we descended into the plain, the cottages were scattered more thickly along the road, and we passed through village streets where every house was full of cocoon piles, making the effect of snowdrifts swept back from the road into the houses. We were making for Iizuka, a station a little farther up the line than Takaski, from which we could do an hour or so of railway-travelling in the direction of Karuizawa before taking to chairs and jinrikshas again. We had found some fir-strate chair-coolies in Ikao, and they carried me down the hilly roads at a swinging trot, and with none of the misery which had attended the upward journey. But the heat was intense as soon as we reached the plain, and no words can describe how grateful and refreshing was the hospitality of the pretty tea-house at Iizuka, where we had an hour's rest before our train could pass. The little upper rooms, cool, matted, open on every side to the air under the wide verandah roof, seemed luxuriously spacious and quiet; from the eaves hung fern-wreaths grown in quaint shapes on wistaria roots, each one having a small glass bell fastened to it, and a bit of paper with a word or two of poetry dangling from the bell. The lightest puff of breeze sets the paper moving, and then the bell speaks in a little musical tinkle like the sound of running water. Our hostess brought up a fairy meal of strawberries and scraped ice and lemonade; and O'Matsu brought a fan, and kept the air cool while we tasted it. By the time the train steamed up, we had forgotten the heat and weariness of the morning, and started out refreshed for the second part of our journey. This stage brought us as far as Yokukawa, a town nestling close in at the foot of the Usui Pass, which leads up into the great dividing range, the central Alps of Japan.

Yokukawa is demoralised by the railway and tram traffic, and has very little that is picturesque about it. The railway stops here, and the traveller is carried on into the hills by a crazy tram service, composed of tiny carriages drawn by broken-down horses, up a road which is washed away by rain or whelmed in landslips at least once a week. When the cars are not thrown off the line, they jump about so alarmingly that the unfortunate passengers are black and blue by the time they reach Karuizawa; altogether, the journey was considered too sensational for me, and the Ikao coolies had been brought on to carry me up the pass. Some of the party were in jinrikshas, which can follow the tramway line; but for me there was the delightful luxury of a long chair ride through shady paths up wooded steeps, where the tendrils of the creepers brushed my face, and the delicate woodsy smell of fern and pine, wistaria and hydrangea, came in waves out of the solemn greennesses of the forest. Now and then we stopped, that the men might rest at one of those tiny brown dwellings scattered like empty chestnut burrs along the path; always planted near a stream or a trickling waterfall, with perhaps the virgin rock for a background, they consist of one tiny room open to the woods, with a bench for the pilgrim to rest on, a low-burning fire to make his tea over, and a few scrupulously clean blue cups and bowls to serve it in. And how refreshing the Japanese tea is! One of our party had followed me on foot, and was glad enough of the pale gold-coloured liquid steaming in its tiny cups. It quenches thirst far better than any of our luxurious iced drinks, and gives just the amount of nerve stimulant needed during long walks in the heat. The perfume is faint and fine, and has become so connected with our roamings in Japan that, no matter how many years had passed, it would instantly bring back to me the house in the forest or by the roadside, the kind brown faces, the balmy air, the luminous whiteness of the Eastern day.

November, 1891.

ON October 28th, early in the morning, we were roused by the most terrifying shock of earthquake that I have yet experienced. The disturbance took the dangerous form of violent vertical movement, accompanied by fearful rumblings and the crashing of stones. We were all asleep; but even in sleep that apprehension never leaves one, and before I was awake I had reached the door, and was trying to get out into the gallery. Sometimes the door gets jammed during an earthquake, and in any case it is not easy to open it when the floor is tossing like a ship at sea, and the roar and crash are so awful that you cannot hear the voice of a person standing at your elbow! As a rule the shock has a duration of from thirty to sixty seconds, and that feels like hours in the horror of dismay that it inspires; this first one of October 28th went on for seven minutes, and was followed by lesser ones for many hours. For all its terrors, it did only minor damage here; but in the south it has practically wiped out a large and thriving district, one which had always been considered exceptionally free from such visitations, and as yet the loss of life and property cannot even be estimated.

It had another most unusual quality of earthquake shocks: it had been predicted. On what grounds precisely it is impossible to say, but with confident certainty, at any rate. The last really severe earthquake (I am not speaking, of course, of volcanic eruptions, which are generally accompanied by shocks of more or less violence) took place in 1854; and it was prophesied that there would be another in thirty-seven years—a prophecy which has just been fulfilled. As, for twelve hundred years, there is no record of precisely that interval between one earthquake and another, it sounds like an arbitrary prediction. Thirty-seven is one of the Japanese mystic numbers; when that period after a death has elapsed, the survivors perform certain rites for the benefit of the dead—ornament their shrines and make offerings to them. And doubtless many of those who perished in that earthquake are being so remembered now. But this catastrophe has, I think, surpassed in horror all those remembered by living people. The centre of the disturbance was at Gifu and Nagoya. At this last place seven hundred shocks of earthquake were registered between October 28th and November 3rd. Professor Milne's beautiful seismographs were quite incompetent to register the strength of the shocks, which far surpassed anything that had been contemplated when the machines were invented. The description of the visitation at its centre is awful past belief. Two towns and many villages are completely destroyed; railway lines are twisted like wire; huge bridges tossed into the air and snapped like matchwood, the stone pillars on which they stood being sliced smoothly through their whole diameter. Mountains have slipped from their foundations; a new lake has been formed; three hundred and fifty miles of river dykes injured—one half of this totally destroyed; a grove of bamboos was taken up and flung sixty feet from where it stood; the earth has opened in frightful fissures, and in some cases closed again over the houses and bodies it had swallowed. The lowest estimation puts the houses totally destroyed at 42,345, those partially ruined at 18,106. As for loss of life, that will never be known, I fear; every turn of the spade brings dead and dying to light, and many of the wounded were so frightfully hurt that it was impossible to save them. As all the telegraph communication and railway traffic was interrupted, it was not easy to bring assistance immediately to the sufferers, and the first doctors and nurses who got to them were on their feet for days and nights, and did more than seemed humanly possible to help the poor creatures. At Ogaki Hospital, two surgeons dressed the wounds of six hundred patients in forty-eight hours.

The misery and destruction were as usual enormously increased by the fires which at once broke out. . . . Of course every kind of assistance is being given by the Emperor and the Empress, by the Government, by public subscriptions, and private individuals; nurses and doctors have flocked to the afflicted districts, and relief camps have been started, where allowances of food are dealt out; but with all that, the suffering is awful, the want all but impossible to satisfy. Here we do nothing but collect money and clothes, bandages and blankets; and the railway companies carry it all free of charge down to the scene of the trouble. I am glad to say the English trained nurse from St. Hilda's was sent down at once, with two Japanese nurses and a doctor, at the mission's expense, and have been doing good work among the sufferers, who are, every one says, perfectly patient and resigned. There has been no murmuring even at the misfortunes, and their patience and gentleness make it easy to organise and carry out the plans for their help. The excellent organisation of the Red Cross Society has shown itself now; and the indefatigable efforts of doctors and nurses have certainly allayed much suffering and saved many lives.

71

MARIE C. STOPES, *A JOURNAL FROM JAPAN. A DAILY RECORD OF LIFE AS SEEN BY A SCIENTIST* (LONDON: BLACKIE, 1910), PP. 46, 105–106

October 12.—The hour for rising gets earlier every day. This morning it was 5 o'clock, with the prospect of 12–14 hours in a wretched slow train. I am writing in the train now, at the stoppings, which are never less than five minutes, and often ten or fifteen minutes long, at every station. The whole distance in all these hours of travel will be less than 200 miles. The people in the train are, of course, a little interesting, but far more saddening. Where the train with its Western atmosphere has penetrated, the beautiful and dignified robes, the silken skirts and kimonos of both men and women, though principally of the men, are giving place to a hybrid mixture of all the vulgar and hideous garments of "civilisation." Only a few of the most cultured Japanese know how to dress in good taste in our things, the others are unspeakable.

Just now the train is skirting a part of the coast of the famous "Inland Sea," and small islands lie thickly scattered in it, with their pines clinging by great twisting roots on to their rocks. The persimmon trees, with their great golden fruits, look very beautiful beside the pines, and are richly laden with their delicious fruit, so that they are noticeable from quite a distance.

February 22.—I had been really bullied into playing Hockey to represent the world against Japanese-born British. They were, of course, far stronger than we, as nearly all live together in Yokohama and practice twice a week, while none of us had played together before. We got 2 goals to their 4, however, and patted ourselves on the back.

Returning by train (Yokohama to Tokio, of course, is *the* chief line of rail in the country, so that the incident should not be compared with doings in some far-off highland place in Scotland), the train suddenly drew up with a jerk, far from one station and about the same distance from the next. The passengers were surprised, some slightly alarmed, and the train calmly waited for some time and then started racing back to the station from which we had come. We all resigned ourselves to a broken bridge, overturned carriages on the track, or something of the sort, and finally drew up at the station we had just left—much commotion on the platform, and we learned that from the luggage van some parcels had not been delivered!

They were delivered over to the proper person and the train started off once more, to reach Tokio not a little late.

February 24.—There have been signs of the coming Dolls' Festival, to take place on the 3rd day of the 3rd month. I have mentioned them already (see p. 74). The shops are now full of them, and most fascinating they are, but too expensive to indulge in as I should like. The figures are all in little boxes, and sit solemnly, with their stiff robes spread out, as though they were really the nobles that they represent, and every one is interested in buying them, or at least gazing at them in their temporary homes. Several shops have sprung up this week filled with these boxes of dolls, and selling nothing else.

72

BARONESS ALBERT D'ANETHAN (ELEANORA MARY ANETHAN), *FOURTEEN YEARS OF A DIPLOMATIC LIFE IN JAPAN* (LONDON: S. PAUL & CO., 1912), PP. 358–359

February 11, 1904.—The lunch at the Palace went off successfully, and I am told A. spoke his speech remarkably well. I believe that both the Emperor's speech and A.'s have been telegraphed home to the *Times*.

The Japanese are very jubilant over their victories. The Port Arthur battle was entirely successful, and they succeeded in injuring two more battleships.

One of the chief incidents of this eventful week is the departure this evening of all the members of the Russian Legation and of the Russian Consulate from Japan. They left at 9 o'clock p.m., and the whole Corps Diplomatique, and many too of the Japanese, mustered to see them off. It was extremely painful, as all seemed to feel it much, though both Baroness Rosen and Princess Koudacheff kept themselves under control. A. gave his arm to Baroness Rosen to convey her down the immensely long station to the railway-carriage. Their reserved carriage was quite at the end of the train, and as they passed, from some of the third-class carriages came a few *hurlements*, which however were promptly suppressed. There was a regular army of mounted police outside the station, and rows and rows of them inside. The Russians mustered eighteen or twenty from Tokyo, and about forty altogether were passengers on board the *Yarra*, the French mail. As we drove to the station we were witnesses of the illuminations at the Ministry of Marine, and of the processions of lanterns in the streets, in honour of the Japanese victories. These manifestations of joy must have been extremely painful for the poor Russians to behold just at the moment of their departure.

February 12, 1904.—A. went down to Yokohama by the early train to bid adieu to the Rosens and to the Koudacheffs. Their boat sailed at 9 a.m. He saw all but Prince Koudacheff, who was still in bed.

We dined at the British Legation. There were rumours that Hakodate was being bombarded by four Russian men-of-war, but it appears this was a *canard*.

February 14, 1904.—We put off our official dinner for the 19th, as we found that all the Japanese were dropping out, and not only I but four of the servants were down with influenza.

My war song, entitled "Alas!" appeared in a prominent place in the *Japan Times*. I did not sign it.

73

FRANK E. YOUNGHUSBAND, *THE HEART OF A CONTINENT* (NEW YORK: SCRIBNER'S SONS, 1896), PP. 50–52

At Shan-hai-kuan we found several modern forts constructed and armed with Krupp guns—a curious contrast to the antiquated wall of defence by which they lay. An instructor to the Chinese in the use of these guns, a German non-commissioned officer, was stationed here. He spoke very disparagingly about the interest the Chinese took in their duties. It was impossible, he said, to get them to look after their guns properly. They could not be made to see the necessity of it, and costly, highly finished guns were going to ruin for want of proper care. This defect is seen everywhere in Chinese naval and military officers.

From here we went to Kaiping. On the way we passed cart after cart laden with coffins, and with a cock in a cage at the top of each. A Chinaman dislikes being buried outside the Great Wall, and as soon as his relatives can afford it, they bring him home inside it again. These were the bodies of colonists who had died in Manchuria, and were being brought back to their homes again. The cock was intended, by his crowing, to keep the spirit awake while passing through the Great Wall; otherwise, it was feared, the spirit might go wandering off somewhere and forget the body, and the body might be brought in and the spirit left behind.

As we neared Kaiping we were surprised to see two British navvies walking along the road, and there was not the slightest mistake who they were, for as we passed, one said to the other, "I wonder who the—— that is, Bill?" They were miners employed in the colliery at this place. The Kaiping coal-mine was in the charge of Mr. Kinder, who very kindly gave us a room for the night, and the next day showed us round the mine. At the time of our visit it was nine hundred feet deep, and could turn out five hundred tons of coal a day. Now, however, it can turn out its thousand or one thousand five hundred tons without difficulty. Mr. Kinder, who is still in charge, is a man of surprising energy and enterprise. Employed by a Chinese company, over whom, however, I fancy, he has a considerable influence, he first of all got this coal-mine into working order. Then he ran a small tramway down the coast, for the purpose of carrying the coals to a port. The waggons on this were at first drawn by ponies, but after a time Mr. Kinder made up a little engine, which he called the "Rocket," to do the work.

This engine he showed us with great pride. It was entirely constructed by himself on the spot, and the only parts which had been imported were the wheels, which had been brought from Hong-kong—the remnants of an old tramway service. The Chinese had been afraid of a whole engine being imported by a "foreign devil," but a machine made on the spot aroused no fears. In the course of time another more powerful engine was made and the tramway enlarged. Then, as the Chinese grew accustomed to seeing steam-engines, Mr. Kinder was able to introduce the idea of having engines from abroad instead of making inferior ones on the spot. The ice had been broken. The first prejudice had been overcome, and railways in China had been started. Engines, rolling-stock, and rails were now imported, and a railway towards Tientsin was commenced. This, Mr. Kinder, with only one European assistant to supervise the mine, was now constructing. A year or two afterwards it reached Tientsin, and has now been extended eastward to Shan-hai-kuan. Its extension to Manchuria will be the next move, and then the whole of that magnificently rich country will be opened up. If any one deserves the credit of having introduced railways into China, I think Mr. Kinder must be the man.

Mr. Kinder had many stories of his intercourse with Chinese which amused us. He was called at one time before some very high Manchu prince who had never seen a European. The prince eyed the Englishman suspiciously for a time, and then began stroking him down, at the same time saying that the gentleman was quite tame, and did not apparently bite nor kick. He had been made to believe that Europeans really were, as they are always called by the Chinese, devils, and he had expected to find a sort of wild animal brought before him. This is one of the prejudices a European, dealing with the Chinese, has to overcome.

Another sort of prejudice which often stood very much in Mr. Kinder's way, was that of "Feng-shui." This is a prejudice connected with the spirit world. The living, the Chinese consider, must conform to certain rules, or the evil spirits will enter the house, and harm will come to all connected with it. A stranger in China is surprised to notice a wall, ten, twenty, or fifty yards long, according to the size of the house, placed a few yards off straight in front of the gateway. This wall stands out by itself, and fulfils no apparent object. It is really intended to prevent evil spirits entering the houses. Evil spirits, according to the Chinese, can only go straight ahead; they cannot turn a corner. So if a wall is built straight in front of the gateway, the spirits run up against that and are unable to enter the house. This is only one instance of the superstition of Feng-shui. It has many similar prejudices with which the construction of a railway through the country was likely to interfere. For instance, it was objected by the Chinese, that if the railway were raised the spirits might go along the top of the carriages and look down into their houses. "But then," said Mr. Kinder, "just look at the embankment and think how many devils that will keep out, running for miles and miles as it does, right in front of your doorways." Much of this sort of diplomacy was needed to overcome prejudice after prejudice, but Mr. Kinder was as good at diplomacy as he was at engineering, and railways in China are now an accomplished fact.

From Kaiping we proceeded to Tientsin, passing over a dead level plain, and reaching that place on New Year's Day, 1887. The Peiho river had just been frozen over, and steamer communication with the south was blocked till the spring.

74

JOHN FOSTER FRASER, *THE REAL SIBERIA* (LONDON: CASSELL, 1902), PP. 220–230

A Manchurian "boom" town

IRON rails do not make the best bedding, and a coil of telegraph wire is not to be recommended as a pillow. Further, sleeping in the open on the top of a railway truck is more uncomfortable than adventurous.

So, when rain threatened on the second afternoon out of Vladivostok, I made ardent friendship with a Cossack officer. He discovered that in the goods van in which he was travelling with brother soldiers room might be found for a wandering Britisher.

It was a dingy place, half filled with boxes of iron bolts and bags of American flour, but almost luxurious compared with an open platform. Everybody was unshaven and rather grimy.

We were eight in that van, cramped and huddled. Yet from the pleasantries that prevailed you might have thought we were on a picnic instead of going through a disturbed country and open to attack at any hour. Provisions were shared in common—bread, tea, tinned meats, cigarettes. There was sparsity of knives, forks, plates, and cups. But no time was wasted in having these articles washed. A wipe with a bit of newspaper was all they got.

The whole country-side swarmed with pheasants. A Chinese boy coming along with a bunch swung at either end of a pole, somebody bought ten for a rouble (two shillings), and soon the soldiers had them plucked, cleansed, and in a stewpot.

For five hours we were at a standstill. The sky was low and sullen, and as soon as night set in down went the thermometer. For exercise I took a few sharp turns the length of the train, and felt sorry for the poor moujiks and Chinese closely crouching on the platforms to get the warmth of one another's bodies.

The Cossack soldiers do not mind the cold. They had large felt cloaks swathing them, and big bundles of hay to lie upon. Much of their time was spent in singing—and who that has heard a Slav song, crooning, pathetic, weird, sung by a Cossack at night in the middle of a plain silent as death, can forget it? From the chinks in the doorways of the covered vans came rapier thrusts of light and the low mumble of talk. When the night was at its blackest rain fell, and the drops rattled on the vans like shot.

Once more we went on, jerking and jolting, and often we lurched and banged as though we had run into a wall.

Suddenly there was a shaking and a clatter. We were almost knocked to pieces. Then quietness.

Our van had jumped the rails. I was the only one who seemed surprised. Everyone else took it as a matter of course, turned over, and went to sleep again. There was a good deal of shouting and lamp-flashing, but in an hour the van was back in its place. Once more we went on.

Just at dawn, as we were running past a siding, the points did not work. This time it was the engine that jumped the rails. Again, nobody minded. We might be stopped a couple of hours or a couple of days.

But Nitchevo—most blessed of Russian words in the hour of possible vexation!

Indeed, there was a general evidence of gladness. So long as the train was moving there was no opportunity of a fire, and hot water and tea. A breakdown, however, meant great fires, with people roaming round for wood and water, and consequent tea drinking by the gallon. This break turned everybody out: Russian officials, officers, soldiers, engineers, telegraph workers, traders, moudjiks, Chinese, Manchus, Koreans, and one British journalist.

It was like a camp. There was the roasting of fowls, boiling of rice, frying of fish.

A way back from the line was a Cossack post, a long, low-roofed, white-washed house, like a Scotch clay biggin', with a rude stockade, and the hardy little ponies tethered at long wooden troughs in the open. On one side was a high scaffold-like tower, and on the top was a Cossack on duty, letting his eye roam over the country on the watch for the coming of the Hung-hos, marauding bands of Manchus, who raid native villages and Russian settlements indiscriminately.

Along the whole stretch of the railway across Manchuria are Cossack posts, planted, as it were, in the midst of a wilderness.

They are not Hyde Park-looking warriors, these Cossacks. They are semi-savages, black-eyed, fierce-browed, the finest horsemen in the world, caring little for your life, little for their own, absolutely fearless, of the dashing, reckless, break-neck sort of bravery, ever impetuous. For a charge there are no troops that could equal them. But Russian officers told me that for modern operations they are not much good, that they have not the patience to seek the shelter of sand banks, nor make strategic moves, nor remain quiet for hours in the hollow of a hill ready for a particular manœuvre at a particular moment.

The Cossack soldier, in return for the land the government gives him, provides his own horse and equipment. A Cossack, therefore, with all the independence of his wild race, thinks himself more than the equal of a Russian officer. There is no servility about him. It is difficult to make him obey orders. When there is fighting he must get amongst it at once with his bare sword.

From Russia's point of view these Cossacks are the best possible guards to place along the Manchurian line.

First and foremost, the object of that line is to carry troops to the shores of the Pacific, and the phenomenal haste with which the building of it was being pushed on was—as I gathered from many Russian sources—a fear that Japan intended to precipitate a conflict for the possession of Korea. From this very line between Grodikoff and Harbin, a branch is made to the Korean frontier. Its purpose is obvious.

Russia wants no mishaps to the Manchurian railway in time of war. So it runs through a more or less desolate region, north-west, over the Hingan mountains, across a corner of the Mongolian desert, until it joins the Siberian line at Katiska Rasiez, near Chita, in trans-Baikalia.

All the towns on the route are new and Russian. Where there are Chinese towns they are contiguous to the Russian towns, which are also military centres. For twenty miles on each side the line the Chinese and Manchus have been driven back. I heard gruesome stories of what has taken place when there has been any show of resistance—the men slaughtered, the women violated, and then their throats cut.

There were some hundreds of thousands of Chinese coolies engaged on the railway, and near Harbin, and Hingan, and Hilar were also Chinese settlements. But I did not see any Chinese women. They had all been sent away for fear of the Cossacks.

Naturally I saw much of the Cossacks. Their attire, the sheepskin hats struggling over their eyes, made them forbidding. But it did not take long to find a good deal of bluff animal kindness about them. They were rough and rude; they knew nothing of town life; their tastes were simple and very primitive. They made fires for us, lent us their pans, and gave us bread, and none of us dared insult them by offering money in payment.

A couple of Cossack patrols came along, swung themselves from the saddles, and throwing their carbines aside, lay on the ground by the fire, and were served with cups of hot tea by their own mates.

It was a damp, moansome day. The Cossacks on the train got a piece of canvas sheeting, and rigged themselves a tent on their open truck.

But in the dark the wind came shrieking and snapped the cords. We heard the engine snort and shriek. It was a sign all was well again. So we curled up and went to sleep, while all night the train cumbrously jogged on. We were running through scant forest.

There were no leaves, and the trees were skeleton, save when there was a brush of fir.

We stopped and we jerked, and then stopped again. It was dreary. The mists hung round the trees and blanketed the landscape from view. It was impossible to wander more than fifty yards away, for that would have provoked fate to send the train on without you.

First we stopped seventeen hours; then we crawled for two hours; next we stopped for five hours. That makes twenty-four hours, and tells how we spent Sunday, October 13th. We probably travelled ten miles.

On the Sunday we pulled up at a struggling hamlet of new houses.

"What is the name of this place?" I asked.

THE IRON ROAD MEETS THE SILK ROAD

"It has not got a name yet," I got as a reply.

Besides Russians there were many Chinamen about. The policeman, porcine and pompous, with a willow-plate kind of design on his chest and back, and carrying a red-painted stick, was a Chinaman. He looked important. But standing near were grey-cloaked Cossacks with fixed bayonets.

Next we ran through a plain of sodden wilderness. It began to snow, followed by sleet and snow again.

Thus we reached the town of Harbin; not to be found on most maps except under the name of Hulan. It is a great junction. It came into prominence in 1900 because the Boxers destroyed the line here, and besieged the town for several weeks. The station itself is a paltry place, but there are eight tracks of rails. Huge stacks of stores for troops are guarded by soldiers.

Seven years ago there was not a single Russian in Harbin. Now there are nearly nine thousand. Old Harbin, or Hulan, where the Chinese live, is a distance away, and there are some ten thousand Celestials, a weak and puling lot of men.

But New Harbin, where the Russians are, is for all the world like a "boom" American town. It has sprung into existence in a few years. Big stores and hotels are being pushed up, and everywhere building is to be seen. Fortunes are made by men who have got patches of land centrally situated.

Theoretically this is Chinese territory, and therefore goods coming in from the sea at Dalny—Talienwan on our English maps—pay no duty.

But you do not buy them cheaper at Harbin because of that. Indeed, everything costs about double what it does at Vladivostok. Two hundred per cent. is the profit a trader must make, or he thinks he is doing bad business.

Harbin is now the principal town in Manchuria. It is a magnet to all the adventurers in Russia. There are two or three murders every week. Respectable folks who go out at night do so in bands, the men armed, and with a Cossack guard.

Russian officers, and the army of engineers engaged on the railway—they are all excellently paid to stimulate them to hurry the line to completion—make for Harbin when they get a few days' leave. A Russian's idea of good-fellowship, when in his cups, is to squander, to pour champagne on the floor, just to show he doesn't mind expense, to light his cigarette with a three-rouble note, and generally splash money round.

There is a *café chantant* at Harbin, which has the laxity of *café chantants* in other parts of the world. The night before I was at Harbin, an engineer arrived, his pockets bulging with roubles, and he showed his dea of money by making all the girls sit in a row while he poured champagne on hundred-rouble notes, and then stuck these notes (£10) on the foreheads of each of the eight girls. That is the Harbin idea of having a good time.

Now, though Harbin is in the "temporary occupation" of Russia, the Chinese have the administration of the country round. Chinese robbers, the Hung-hos for instance, are tried by Chinese authority, and the beheading that takes place is by Chinese law, and not by Russians. All these robbers when caught are executed. They are made maudlin drunk on *samshu*, and are then pulled to their knees by a

394

tug at the queue, and a swish of a sword takes off the head. These heads are stuck on poles, and planted on the wayside as a warning to evil-doers. I saw several.

Harbin and the country round provided the strongest possible evidence that, whatever diplomatic language may be used, Russia is in possession of Manchuria, and intends to stay. It is a very large plum drawn out of the Chinese pie.

Roughly, Manchuria has a population of some seventeen millions, comprises about one-tenth of China's entire area, is six times as large as England and Wales, and possesses a climate resembling that of Canada; its mountains are said to ooze gold, and its harbour, Port Arthur, is splendid, free from ice all the year round.

Though the railway does not run through a fertile region, the land is full of possibilities. And there is this thing to be said in favour of the Russian occupation: before the Russians came it was little more than a sterile waste; now money is being poured into the country, and another ten years will probably reveal wonders.

It is not, of course, so wealthy as the great western Chinese province of Sztcheum, contiguous to our Indian territory, and which the French are doing their best to slice off for themselves by running a railway to it from Tonquin, by way of Yunnan, but gold mines have already been worked, though only in a primitive way. Petroleum, copper, and tin have been found. Coal beds lie close to iron beds, and that means much. All that is wanted is machinery and enterprise.

Remember it is only five years since (1897) that a party of Cossack military surveyors, accompanied by Russian engineers, made a journey across Manchuria to spy the land for a railway. There were a couple of chains of mountains to be crossed, and on the plains the soil was unstable. The report of these surveyors was unfavourable. But political reasons pressed the importance. In 1898 the Czar said, "Let the line be laid!"

And there it is, 1,200 miles long, from Nikolsk to Katiska Rasiez, and 890 miles of it through Chinese territory. It is the seal to Russia's power in the Far East.

Nominally China conceded the right to build this railway to an anonymous company. Everybody, except people who frequent Downing Street, knows the line belongs to the Russian government. Shareholders must be either Russians or Chinese. But bonds can only be issued with the consent of Mr. De Witte, the Russian Minister of Finance. The president of the Eastern Chinese Company, as it is called, is a Chinaman. Mr. De Witte, however, appointed the vice-president, all the engineers and officials, and gives sanction to any improvements or modifications. Colloquially the Chinese president is in Mr. De Witte's pocket.

I spent part of my afternoon at Harbin shopping, buying another sheepskin, a big German sausage as hard as wood, and half a dozen tins of Singapore pineapples, exported by some patriotic Britisher, for they were of the "Jubilee Brand," had a picture of Queen Victoria, decorations of Royal Standards and Union Jacks, and displayed views of soldiers and battleships.

But nobody seemed to know when a train was to go northwards to Hingan and Hilar.

It would be easy enough to get down to Mukden and Port Arthur, and it took me an hour to make it clear I did not want to go either to Mukden or Port Arthur.

THE IRON ROAD MEETS THE SILK ROAD

Then I was informed that three miles away, on the other side of the river Sungari, it was possible I might find some goods waggons going north to-day, to-morrow, or next week. That was what I wanted.

It took me hours, however, to extract the simple fact that there was a bridge over the Sungari, and trains on the other side.

The station-master provided a trolley, and I piled my belongings on it. This was pushed along by four Russian workmen. Then I borrowed a couple of Cossack soldiers to act as guard, and I set off to walk.

The sleety tempest of the day had waned, and the late afternoon, with a watery sunlight playing over the country, was not without beauty. The railway bank was strong and well built; it had a double track, and led to a great eight-span iron bridge over the Sungari. This bridge had only been finished four days, and no train had yet passed over it. It was protected by Cossacks, but a word by my guard opened a way. So I walked over.

The Sungari here is about twice the width of the Thames at London Bridge, and as I was high perched I could see the waters of this mighty stream for far, flowing northwards until they join the mighty stream of the Amur. On one bank was the native town, a long, bedraggled street with the Chinese slithering in the mire. On the river were hundreds of pug-nosed, hump-backed Chinese junks with long venetian-blind kind of sails, dropping down stream, the men singing as they dipped the large oars, while in and out among them dodged noisy and perky little Russian government steam launches. The clouds broke, and a flush of crimson spread along the distant hills.

It was dark evening when I reached the station, a white-washed hut with a dirty oil lamp by the door. The station-master was friendly. As far as he knew a train would be going on some time in the night. So with a lantern we went exploring and found an empty goods car. That was excellent.

75

R. LOGAN JACK, *THE BACK BLOCKS OF CHINA* (LONDON: E. ARNOLD, 1904), PP. 89–93

Farewell to Chengtu

DURING our stay in Chengtu, while preparations for the next journey were being carried on, we learned first of the murder of three Germans in Shantung, and of the supposed murder of twenty officials of the Tientsin Railway, and next that Chengtu itself had been placarded with notices intimating that 'the foreigners must quit.' On the night before our projected departure for Maha, Mr. Bush telegraphed from Chung King the news of the destruction of the railway from Tientsin to Pekin, the murder of the Belgian engineers, troubles in the neighbourhood of Chung King, and the interruption of the telegraph-line to Yünnan, and asked me to consider if travelling was safe under the circumstances. I resolved to wait for further details, and requested that the British Consul at Chung King should be asked for his advice. No further news reached us, however, and we left for the South on the morning of June 19, our business being, in my judgment, urgent. We had added to our company Mr. Herbert W. L. Way, representing the Upper Yangtse Syndicate.

In consideration of the disturbed state of the country, the Viceroy directed that we should be accompanied by a party of soldiers from Chengtu as well as by local guards, each of which was to be charged with the duty of taking us across its own military district, and bringing back a receipt for us from the guard of the next district. These escorts varied greatly in numbers as well as in armament and ornament. Some carried Winchester rifles, others merely fans, pipes, and umbrellas, while others had gas-pipe matchlocks. The 'cut-and-thrust' equipment varied from bayonets to swords, spears, pikes, halbards, Lochaber axes, and tridents. Most of the companies carried also brilliantly coloured flags as well as long brass trumpets of the pattern which, according to medieval artists, is in use among the angels in bliss.

We were also accompanied as far as Shaa Ba by a Wai-Yuan named Chü Hung Chi, who held the rank of Hsien, or District Magistrate, and whose red umbrella and green chair had a most imposing effect at the head of our straggling procession, and no doubt procured for us an amount of consideration which we should have missed had we travelled in a private capacity, Chü was a very capable man, who had held magisterial office as a Hsien. He carried with him, as part of his equipment and as a souvenir, the sword with which two malefactors had been decapitated under his orders. On the journey he acted, when necessity arose, in a magisterial capacity, giving judgment in all small disputes which might arise. In one instance one of our chair coolies was jostled or kicked off the road by a mule and injured. The owner of the mule was brought before the Wai-Yuan, and evidence was led, the Writer acting as assessor or *amicus curiæ*. It seemed that nobody was to blame, as the badness of the road and the 'cussedness' of mules were sufficient to account for the disaster. At the suggestion of the assessor, the accused having done no wrong, was dismissed with a caution, and warned not to do it again. He seemed inordinately grateful for this leniency, and made the tour of the room on his knees, knocking his head on the floor in front of the judge and the other members of the party one after another. One of the 'boys,' it may be mentioned, was forced to walk, and the wounded man was carried in his chair, his fellows grumbling loudly at the indignity of having to carry a mere coolie, a man of no more importance than themselves.

At Pei-Chung Cheng (eighty-three miles) there is a handsome stone bridge with five pointed or Gothic arches, a level, well-flagged deck, and steps at both ends. Here we found, on the walls of the inn, a relic of Széchenyi's expedition in the form of a pencilled signature of the late Lieutenant Kreitner, his accomplished topographer, with the date October 16, 1879. It may be said here that we found Széchenyi's maps, so far as we travelled by them, wonderfully accurate and a never-failing comfort. Fortunately, we had had them enlarged, before leaving Shanghai, to the scale of eight miles to an inch, so far as they referred to the province of Szechuan. We had not then foreseen that his maps of Yünnan would have been of at least equal value, and later on it was a matter for constant regret that we had left them behind.

On our arrival at the prefectural city of Ya-Chow, on June 24, we met Dr. Corliss and Mrs. Upcraft, Mr. Upcraft being on a journey. They belong to an American mission, the southmost outpost of Protestantism in Szechuan. We have since learned that this party joined in the retreat from Chung King to Shanghai.

A telegraph-line had been erected by Viceroy Liu Chuan Liu from Chengtu, viâ Ya-Chow, to Ta-Chien Lu, and we had anticipated that the telegraph-station at Ya-Chow, which could be reached by a messenger from Maha in six days, would form a convenient base of communication. Our disappointment was great when we found that the line was in disrepair, and that dispatches, when received, were forwarded by runners in the time-honoured Chinese fashion. Our communication between Maha and the world was, therefore, always through Chengtu, a journey of ten or twelve days for an express runner.

Ya-Chow is situated on the right bank of the Ya Ho, a considerable river which falls into the Min at Kia Ting. We learned afterwards that Captain Ryder's party arrived at Ya-Chow from Ta-Chien Lu on the day we left (June 27), and that, on hearing of the condition of the country, he dropped down the river by boat to Kia Ting and Chung King.

While we were travelling on the following day, we were overtaken by a telegram informing me of the capture of the Taku Forts and the march of the allies on Pekin. We resumed our journey, puzzling over the question of who was at war with whom.

76

RICHARDSON L. WRIGHT AND BASSETT DIGBY, *THROUGH SIBERIA: AN EMPIRE IN THE MAKING* (NEW YORK: MCBRIDE, NAST & COMPANY, 1913), PP. 203–208

The pageant of Tsitsitcar

LEAVING the Moscow-Vladivostok railroad at Angangki, after sixteen hours' journey into Manchuria, I turned my traps over to a couple of Chinese and followed them across the sandy plain to the *Kitaiski vogsaal*, the Chinese station for the light railway up to Tsitsitcar. And in that brief half mile walk I passed as distinctly out of Russia into China as though a magic carpet had borne me in a moment of time from the Nevski Prospekt to the Inner Palace of Pekin. Russia was gone!

The little Chinese station was run by the Chinese for the Chinese. The porters were Chinese. The buildings were Chinese. A Chinaman served out tickets, and I waited five Chinese hours—which is eight—in a Chinese tea-den near by, where I fed upon Chinese viands and drank of Chinese drinks and proved quite the popular ethnological exhibit with the inhabitants of the neighboring mud hovels.

Jack's dog ticket, by the way, was so imposing an affair—a strip of paper eighteen inches by four, and full of odd Chinese chat—that on my return journey I wished to preserve some as trophies.

There was a hitch about those extra dog tickets. I had offered the money for four and counted out four on my fingers. Perhaps the presence of four dogs in a single compartment of the toyshop light-railed train would not be tolerated, I thought. Perhaps it was merely to gratify his idle curiosity by seeing what manner of man was this who traveled around Manchuria with a perambulating kennel, that the ticket agent came out of his retreat. He spied Jack and delivered an excited harangue. It then struck me that he wanted to see the other three dogs. This, of course, was unfortunate, because *non erant*—they were not!

At length, by dint of violent gesticulations doorward indicative of strong canine reserves tethered without, I prevailed. The Celestial dipped his brush in a saucer of ink, took a stack of rice paper streamers, and proceeded to paint tickets. Reappearing, he took my four dog fares, and, with a bland smile, handed me a single strip.

I explained matters to a grave bystander of superior mien and said that I had paid for four tickets and received but one.

"*Kalasho! Cheteeli*," he said, pointing to a sprawling character that looked like the tracks of a hobble-skirted spider. It was all in order, he said; the man had made out a pass for four dogs! And it took about ten minutes of very plain speaking to get rid of the puzzled but persevering Chinese conductor in the pale blue skirt who came around on the train and wanted to know what had happened to my other three dogs.

But to return to Angangki.

After eight hours, in clattered the toyshop train. Out of one of the single first class compartments tumbled a stern old Manchu trader who packed on to a wooden bullock cart much baggage—a baby with lips and cheeks rouged a bright and hideous pink, his pretty little wife in blue and pink clothing spangled with snakes and iridescent flowers; and a big blue gramophone horn.

The one miniature German engine that represents the entire locomotive stock of the Tsitsitcar Railway System had arrived dead-beat after its thirty mile journey. It had to be side-tracked and fed with water and willow logs and coal dust, and then petted and coaxed with oil cans and monkey wrenches for another hour.

Aboard the train we carried three armed guards, in addition to the gentleman in the blue skirt who collected tickets. For the authorities, ever ready to overlook youth's exuberant excesses within reason, have recently become annoyed at the number of holdups on that thirty mile line, and are beginning to take elementary steps to discourage the nuisance. So the three armed guards, big loose-limbed Chinese, with unbraided flowing locks falling around their necks, sat on the alert, swinging their feet over the edge of the platform, each with a glittering, business-like automatic rifle across his knees and two full leather cartridge cases buckled to the front of his belt.

It was an odd run up to Tsitsitcar. One might have been in lower Jersey. Green meadows showed, and pretty villages nestling in their groves of trees, a welcome sight after the eternal bare white birch and gnarled pine left behind in Siberia. Brick and neat clay-walled villages, instead of the logs and timber. Here and there a naked sandhill. Many broad, brackish pools, shallow and rimmed with salt. Duck flurrying up from the sedge beds and willow-scrub, a heron lazily flapping away to the horizon.

The Russian residents, a handful, had fled from Tsitsitcar. The Russo-Asiatic Bank stood shuttered up and deserted. Pneumonic plague; and Governor-General Jow Shoo Mo had not yet given the assurance that it had left town, which was to bring the bank staff back from headquarters in Kharbin.

If you ever happen to find yourself in Tsitsitcar, you can do worse than put up at the native hostelry of Ta Sin Shan. There is no Russian hotel or lodging in the town. Through an archway tunnel in the thick mud wall, you enter a big courtyard, flanked on every side by a row of one story fragile buildings, their fronts merely paper-covered wooden lattice work. Pull open a door, and you find yourself in a little hall with a wash basin and a chest. To the left and to the right open doors into rooms about ten feet by fifteen. One of these is your room. Rooms do not communicate. You and your fellow guest across the passage have your own front door in the common hall. Servants drop in now and again from the kitchen on the other side of the courtyard.

Your room is lit by two small oblong panes of glass let into the paper lattice facing the courtyard. It has no shelves or closets, but three clothes hooks are on the wall. Walls and ceiling are distempered white. A tarnished mirror and an atrocious ornamental (*sic*) clock of the kind that Germany makes to sell to the heathen, hang on one wall. On the table stand a big pair of china vases and another horrible clock. There is a third clock over on a stand by the window. None of them goes. Turning your back on the window, you face a platform covered with a thick felt rug, that occupies the far third of the room.

It was rather an uncanny sensation at first, strolling about the streets of Tsitsitcar among thousands of Chinese with never a European in sight. There are no modern institutions. The dusty streets, the thronged bazaars, the mud-walled houses, the odd ways of doing things, removed the place so utterly from the Occident. One seemed to be in a new world, not merely in a new country.

I attracted a lot of notice. Children ran screaming from my path, just as our apprehensive babies at home clear out from the path of a real live pigtailed Chinaman—but a "foreign devil" must be much more of an infant menace than a mere yellowish man with an amiable expression and a queue!

I did not like the looks of the people to begin with. The first morning I met 4,002 men who looked as though they would have cut my throat on the spot for the sum of ten cents, and then refunded to my executors eight cents in stamps as conscience money for an excess charge.

That is the fault of the western nations in associating the Chinese chiefly with romantic crime. Wherever, on Mott Street, New York, in Limehouse, London, or in the sundry back streets on the hill of Montmartre, two or three good inoffensive Chinese households gather together and pass their hard-won evening's leisure with a game of cards, a chat or a smoke, we thumbmark that spot as an opium den, a haunt of infamy, a gambling joint, a congregation of thugs and murderers, or a rendezvous of dauntless kidnapers. A virtuous Chinese to the respectable American with a New England conscience is a contradiction in terms.

The Chinese are a chattering, bright, vivacious people, laughing and smiling, breaking into song, joking and petting children and dogs, and taking their bird cages out to the park on holidays. They carve and sculpture and paint their signposts and town gates and roof gables. They make their places of worship spots of rare beauty. They'll have none of your little corrugated iron Bethels behind rows of iron spikes. Their temples are pitched in lovely groves, spots redolent with the scent of flowers, the music of birds, cool breezes and the gentle shimmer of checkered sunbeams slanting down through gaps in billowy avenues of foilage to ancient gray stone pathways.

I watched some mischievous boys clamber up the steep stone steps before a temple doorway, and, while the old priest slumbered in his chair, tug at the bell rope. In a Christian country, the infuriated incumbent would have promptly risen up in his wrath, cuffed the nearest lad, and, that evening, called upon the parents of all and sundry with stern accusations and demands for prompt punishment. But this being only a Buddhist temple grove in faraway heathen China, the old priest woke up with a start and smiled and shook his finger roguishly at the giggling knot of little fellows scuttling down the broad weather-worn stone steps. A moment later he had them all up by his side exploiting with glee the contents of a cabinet of queer temple accessories.

Two sounds used to wake me early each morning; the cries of hucksters and the expiring shriek of pigs. The streets were full of hucksters, men with a couple of baskets of grain or vegetables slung up at either end of a long pole balanced on the shoulder. The *genius loci* of Tsitsitcar is the wail of the dying pig. The town seems to kill pigs incessantly day and night.

Leaving the gates of Ta Sin Shan's hostelry one morning, I cannoned into a barber, twanging a big tuning fork and crying out attractive quotations for shaving and hair-braiding. The barbers have an elaborate outfit—a stool for the customer, a stove, a brass bowl and quantities of combs and odd triangular razors and loose, homemade scissors. They work in the open street. You buttonhole a passing barber, and down goes his stool. You seat yourself while he stirs up the charcoal stove, mixes some powders and gives the brass bowl the barber's courtesy whisk with a cloth. Whereupon you are shampooed on the spot.

77

SIR ALEXANDER HOSIE, *ON THE TRAIL OF THE OPIUM POPPY*, 2 VOLS. (LONDON: G. PHILIP & SON, 1914), I, PP. 3–4, 165–167, 169–172, II, PP. 82–84

On arrival in China I proceeded to Peking where I made the necessary preparations for my first journey, and on the 4th May, 1910, I left the metropolis by rail bound for T'ai-yüan Fu, the capital of the province of Shansi. Early on the afternoon of the same day the train, after running south for 150 miles through the province of Chihli, steamed into the station of Shih-chia-chuang, where, next morning, I joined the train which goes westward to T'ai-yüan Fu, a distance of 151 miles, over the metre gauge line known as the Chêng-T'ai railway. The approach from Chihli to Shansi by rail did not create a favourable impression on my mind. The line passes up through the well-known *loess* formation, then arid to a degree owing to lack of rain. The low hills, many of them inhabited by cave-dwellers, are terraced, and the terraces faced with stone to prevent denudation by rain or that detrition which is steadily going on throughout the whole loess formation, owing to its friable vertical cleavage, a detrition which must in time change the whole aspect of the provinces it overlies; but I shall refer to this subject later. It is only when T'ai-yüan Fu is neared that the country opens out and reveals a plain, 3000 feet above the level of the sea, resembling in many respects the seemingly boundless plains of Honan and stretching away to the south and south-west. Some miles to the north-west and north, the plain is hemmed in by hill ranges giving birth to streams which, uniting to the north of the provincial capital, join the Fen Ho, flowing from the north-west, whose waters and tributaries irrigate the south of Shansi and ultimately enter the Huang Ho or Yellow River before the latter, sweeping south and dividing the province from Shensi, resumes its eastern and north-eastern course through Honan, Chihli and Shantung to the Gulf of Pechihli.

Comparatively few trees dot the loess hills bounding the track of the railway; but willow, poplar, fir, date (*Zizyphus vulgaris*), *Cedrela sinensis* and *Ailanthus glandulosa* ("Tree of Heaven") find an occasional foothold. Coal, however, both anthracite and bituminous, underlies the loess, and the whole province of Shansi is known to be one of the largest and richest coal-fields in the world.

The railway station at T'ai-yüan Fu lies outside the south wall of the city, and on arrival there on the afternoon of the 5th May, I found the Principal of the

Imperial University and his wife—old friends—awaiting me, as well as the carriage of His Excellency Ting Pao-ch'üan, Governor of the province, who was good enough to place it at my disposal during my stay in the provincial capital. His Excellency was well aware of the object of my visit and at two interviews which I had with him on the 6th and 7th May, he assured me that the cultivation of the poppy had entirely ceased within his province in 1909, and that an attempt to revive cultivation in 1910 within the district of Wen-shui Hsien, a two days' journey to the south of the provincial capital, had been suppressed by a military force which, on resistance being offered, opened fire on the threatening crowd, resulting in over forty casualties in dead and wounded, and uprooted the young poppy plants.

As soon as we had reached the summit rain began to fall, and we hurried on south along a ridge separating two deep, green valleys with very little traces of cultivation. All in vain: thunder pealed and crashed all round us, accompanied by high wind and torrents of rain, which soon converted deep ruts into flowing streams, and the road itself into a slippery, slimy puddle. It was bad going; but down we went south with no greater mishap than a thorough drenching, and ultimately slid down to the north gate of the northern suburb of the district city of Yung-shou Hsien lying on the northern slope of a hill and facing a valley running east and west. The characters "Yung-shou" mean "Everlasting Old Age," and the suburb on a wet day at any rate left the impression that the city was even beyond the stage of senile decay. The official rest-house outside the south gate of the city gave us shelter after a short stage of 23 miles. There was little poppy cultivation to note during the day: when nearing the uplands after leaving Pin Chou I saw a man carrying a bundle of poppy-stalks, with capsules, down hill and near the village of Ti-yao-kou, ten miles from Yung-shou Hsien, but still within the department of Pin Chou, I observed one field of poppy-stems with capsules from which the opium had been collected.

Between Pin Chou and Yung-shou Hsien the cart traffic was the heaviest I had seen since leaving Lan-chou. From what I have already said it will be seen how impossible it is for a single cart, heavily laden, unless provided with an unlimited supply of animals, to travel by this road. It is eighteen stages from Lan-chou to Hsi-an Fu, and no heavily laden cart, that is, a cart carrying over 2000 catties (2667 lb.) can accomplish the journey in less than 23 or 24 days. And carts travel late and early, resting in summer, however, several hours during the hottest part of the day. My escorting officers were now provided with three carts, and one of the carters was a Tientsin man whom the introduction of the railway from Tientsin to Peking drove to seek a living elsewhere, and he was trying his luck between Lan-chou and Hsi-an Fu.

It was very doubtful whether we should be able to start from Yung-shou Hsien on the morning of the 25th July. It rained over night, was still raining at four-thirty o'clock, and there was every appearance that the rain would continue. But in the midst of my indecision came the jingling of the mule bells, and we were off at five o'clock to tackle a stage of 30 miles. Muleteers are not so particular in regard to weather as chair-bearers, who certainly would not have started in the rain. My experience of the latter is that they will not face rain in the morning, but if overtaken by rain during the day they will go on to the end of the stage without a murmur. Under ordinary circumstances the road between Yung-shou Hsien and Ch'ien Chou is good, and once beyond the area of the previous day's storm all was well.

To accomplish the stage of 36 miles from Ch'ien Chou to the district city of Hsien-yang Hsien, we had to make an early start. We were off at 4.45 a.m. and entered the north-west gate of the latter city at 6 p.m. We spent over thirteen hours on the road and they were long hours. We had travelled thirteen days without resting: my pony was lame, so was my cook who had fallen from his pony and hurt his foot. I had, perforce, to spend a great part of the day in the mule litter, the cook shared the cart with my Shansi escorting officer, and the two mounted soldiers led their ponies, as they had done all the way from Lan-chou. These ponies were the private property of the soldiers and were most carefully and considerately treated by them. One of the soldiers told me that when he wanted to enlist some three years before he was told to produce a horse, the bigger the animal the better.

Our course was south-east, and the road passes through four districts—Ch'ien Chou, Li-ch'üan Hsien, Hsing-p'ing Hsien and Hsien-yang Hsien. It winds about among cultivated fields, and there are so many cross-roads that it was at times difficult to distinguish the main road. Once, indeed, we followed one road too far, and had to retrace our steps. Mules are very clever at picking up the high road, probably owing to the greater number of tracks, and I have noticed them go ahead when the muleteers themselves were in doubt.

It is not uncommon for mules to make a dash at an inn gate, be it in village or city, when they think they have had enough work for the day. This frequently happened on the long stage from Ch'ien Chou to Hsien-yang Hsien, and they resented having to pass village after village without rest or refreshment; but when they ultimately saw the walls of Hsien-yang Hsien, they seemed to recognise that the city was their destination, and, without wasting more breath in braying their disapproval, hurried along at full speed. A thunderstorm burst over the city as we passed along the streets to the official rest-house; but we were fortunate enough to escape the heavy downpour of rain which followed.

The city of Yünnan Fu, at an altitude of 6420 feet above the level of the sea, lies at the northern end of a large lake—variously called the T'ien Chih and K'un-yang Hai—with which it is connected by a short canal. Junks ply on the lake, which drains into the Yangtsze from a point on its western shore, and fishing is an important industry. I visited the provincial capital in 1882 and 1883, and now, as then, I was considerably disappointed. It is a small city, and its wall, an irregular square with six gates, contains, with its southern, western, and eastern suburbs, a population of about 72,000. It is insignificant when compared with provincial capitals like Chengtu and Hsi-an Fu; but it is now the rail-head of the railway from Haiphong in Tonquin, and can be reached by steamer and rail from Hongkong in five days. This line, of metre gauge, is exceedingly well built; but the section of 280 miles within Chinese territory—from Lao-kai to Yünnan Fu—cost many thousands of lives, especially in the malarious Nam-ti valley, and 160,000,000 francs in money. Within this section there are 154 tunnels of varying lengths, and its construction presented the very greatest difficulties. It was completed in 1910, and, after a year's running, it was paying more than working expenses; but at the time of my visit freights were too high to encourage a trade by the nearest route to the most populous districts of Yünnan. Its great stand-by, however, is the carriage to Haiphong of tin from the Ko-chiu mines to the west of the port of Meng-tzu which the railway passes some eight miles to the east. The completion of the line to Yünnan Fu has reduced Meng-tzu to the south to insignificance, and a branch office of the Maritime Customs has been established at the provincial capital in the vicinity of the rail-head which is situated outside the south-east corner of the city wall. That the railway was having its influence, however, could be gathered from the fact that building on an extensive scale was proceeding inside and outside the city walls. At the time of my visit there was one daily through train both ways between Yünnan Fu and Haiphong, and three passenger trains between the capital and places at no great distance, the latter for the benefit of growers of market-produce. In the company of His Majesty's Consul-General, I took a short run by rail from Yünnan Fu to the district city of I-liang Hsien, some 40 miles east by south, for on leaving the rail-head the line, before turning south, pursues an easterly course in order to circumvent the main and other lakes that lie to the south of the capital. During this short run I counted as many as fifteen tunnels. The Yünnan table-land has a sunny, cool, summer climate, and the easy access to it by rail was attracting foreign visitors from Tonquin and from the south of China.

78

C. E. BECHHOFER, *A WANDERER'S LOG* (LONDON: MILLS & BOON, 1922), PP. 91–93

In China and Japan

I HAVE been in a certain number of Chinese cities, though never for very long; the most interesting of them that I know is Canton. The usual means of communication between Hong-Kong and Canton, away up the river, is by steamer—with the risk of pirates. A new alternative is provided by the railway which was built not long ago between the two cities. One day at Hong-Kong I decided to go to Canton by rail and to return by boat, railway travelling being as entertaining in the East as it is dull in the West. The attitudes and bewilderment of the passengers were a delight in themselves. And looking out of the carriage window, I saw a charming sight. An urchin was walking along the road beside the railway, in charge of a score or more of geese. He held out in front of him a long, slender bamboo pole from the end of which there dangled a tuft of appetising green-stuff; the geese were bustling along and jumping up at the bait. By this means the boy got them all together in front of him and was able to drive them on quickly and easily.

Arrived at length at Canton, I hired a sedan-chair and was carried off into the town. It is an incredible city, full of incredible sights, incredible sounds and incredible smells. So narrow are most of the streets that two chairs can only just scrape past one another. Often indeed, when two chairs approach, one of them has to turn rapidly down a side alley to give the other room for passage. One realises the great advantage in Canton of the chair over all other vehicles when suddenly a main street is broken by a short flight of stone steps, after ascending which it goes on as before.

Such a maze is Canton, such a medley of colour and movement, such a welter of people, houses, shops, temples, flags, animals, dirt and smells that, after the established confusion of India or the bijou rectitude of Japan, it makes the traveller feel that at last he is in an utterly strange world. Banners wave from every shop; coolies push their way through the crowd with the name of their Guild written in huge white letters on the back of their coats; a dejected criminal is led along by armed jailors; officials are borne past in smart palankeens; vendors of food and sweetmeats add their cries to the Babel of noise. In the midst of all this, your chair suddenly comes out upon a well-paved courtyard, in front of a temple.

If it is a temple where foreigners are allowed, you will be able to enter and, if you wish, the priests will discharge a salvo of crackers and other fireworks in honour of the gods. At every few yards you pass a cook-shop. Outside hang rows of things to eat; chickens especially are displayed in this way, resplendent in a thick coat of varnish that will keep them for a long time in good condition. Of Chinese cookery it is unnecessary to speak here. America has taken it, or at least a form of it, to her heart, and Chinese restaurants are fast making their way in England also. But it would be difficult to get up an appetite in Canton. The crowds, the lack of space, the fetid air—all conspire against health. And the smells! The smells of Canton!